ISBN 978-0-483-22957-0
PIBN 10192748

TWENTY SERMONS

PREACHED BEFORE

THE UNIVERSITY OF CAMBRIDGE,

IN THE YEAR M.DCCC.XXI.

AT

THE LECTURE

FOUNDED BY

THE LATE REV. JOHN HULSE,

OF ST. JOHN'S COLLEGE.

HULSEAN LECTURES for 1821.

ON THE

EVIDENCES OF CHRISTIANITY,

AS THEY WERE

STATED AND ENFORCED

IN THE

DISCOURSES OF OUR LORD:

—o—

COMPRISING A CONNECTED VIEW

OF THE CLAIMS WHICH JESUS ADVANCED,

OF THE

ARGUMENTS BY WHICH HE SUPPORTED THEM,

AND OF

HIS STATEMENTS RESPECTING THE
CAUSES, PROGRESS, AND CONSEQUENCES OF INFIDELITY.

—————————

BY JAMES CLARKE FRANKS, M. A.

CHAPLAIN OF TRINITY COLLEGE.

CAMBRIDGE:

Printed by J. Smith, Printer to the University;

AND SOLD BY MESSRS. RIVINGTON, AND J. HATCHARD, LONDON;
DEIGHTON & SONS, NICHOLSON & SON, AND THE
OTHER BOOKSELLERS IN CAMBRIDGE;
AND PARKER, OXFORD.

1821

TO THE REVEREND

CHRISTOPHER WORDSWORTH, D.D.

MASTER OF TRINITY COLLEGE,

AND LATE VICE-CHANCELLOR OF THE UNIVERSITY;

TO THE

VERY REV. JAMES WOOD, D.D.

MASTER OF ST. JOHN'S COLLEGE, AND DEAN OF ELY;

AND TO THE

REV. JAMES HENRY MONK, B.D.

PROFESSOR OF GREEK,

AND FELLOW AND TUTOR OF TRINITY COLLEGE;

Surviving Trustees

OF THE

LECTURE FOUNDED BY THE REV. JOHN HULSE,

THE FOLLOWING LECTURES

PREACHED BY THEIR APPOINTMENT

ARE

GRATEFULLY AND RESPECTFULLY INSCRIBED

BY THE AUTHOR.

"CLAUSES from the WILL of the Rev. JOHN HULSE,
"late of Elworth, in the county of Chester, clerk,
"deceased, dated the twenty-first day of July, in the
"year of our Lord one thousand seven hundred and
"seventy-seven, expressed in the words of the Tes-
"tator, as he, in order to prevent mistakes, thought
"proper to draw and write the same himself, and
"directed that such clauses should every year be
"printed, to the intent that the several persons, whom
"it might concern and be of service to, might know
"that there were such special donations or endow-
"ments left for the encouragement of Piety and
"Learning, in an age so unfortunately addicted to
"Infidelity and Luxury, and that others might be
"invited to the like charitable, and, as he humbly
"hoped, seasonable and useful Benefactions."

CLAUSE I.

"And from and after the end, expiration, or other determination of the said term of ninety-nine years, determinable as aforesaid, I give and devise the same premises to and to the use of the University of Cambridge for ever, for the purposes herein after expressed, that is to say, I will and direct that the clear rents, issues, and profits of the same premises in Newton and Middlewich shall be divided into six equal parts, of which four such

b

'sixth parts shall be paid or given to the person, being a member of the said University, to be from time to time, under the directions of this my Will, adjudged to the author of the best Dissertation on the subjects hereinafter for that purpose appointed. One other such sixth part shall be given or paid every year, as an augmentation of his salary, and for his own use, to the person, being also a member of the said University, to be from time to time appointed to the Lectureship herein after founded, and who is to preach annually twenty Sermons agreeably to this my Will."

CLAUSE II.

" And I do direct and declare that the said term of one hundred years is so vested in them the said Ralph Leeke, John Smith, and Thomas Vawdrey, upon further trust, that they, or the survivors, or survivor of them, or the executors, administrators, or assigns of such survivor, do, and shall, by and out of the rents and profits of the premises in Clive, which shall arise previous to the determination of the said term of one hundred years, and no longer, annually pay the sum of sixty pounds, (exclusive of such augmentation as herein before and herein after is mentioned,) on Saint John the Evangelist's day following the preaching of the twenty Lectures or Sermons herein after mentioned, to such learned and ingenious Clergyman in the said University of Cambridge, of the degree of Master of Arts, and under the age of forty years, as shall be duly chosen or elected at the time, and by the persons herein after mentioned and appointed for that purpose, as a salary for preaching the beforementioned Sermons or Lectures, on the days, and upon the subjects herein after more particularly mentioned and prescribed, on the determination of the said term of one hundred years."

CLAUSE III.

" And upon further trust that they the said Ralph
Leeke, John Smith, and Thomas Vawdrey, or the survivors, or survivor of them, his executors, administrators,
or assigns, do, and shall pay and apply the residue of the
rents, and profits of the premises in Clive, which shall
arise previous to the determination of the said term of one
hundred years, and no longer, and which are herein (or by
a grant or rentcharge of ten pounds per annum, dated
the fourth day of November, one thousand seven
hundred and seventy three, by me made and enrolled in
the High Court of Chancery, for certain perpetual charitable uses in the aforesaid townships of Middlewich,
and Sandbach) otherwise disposed of, to and for the use
of the person and persons, who shall from time to time
preach the before named twenty Lectures, in augmentation of the salary herein before appointed for such
Lecturer."

CLAUSE IV.

" And from and after the end, or other determination
of the said term of one hundred years, determinable as
aforesaid, I give and devise all and every my said mes-
suages, lands, tythes, and hereditaments in Clive aforesaid,
to the said University of Cambridge for ever, for the
purposes herein after mentioned and contained, that is to
say, I will and direct that the annual rents, tythes, and
profits thereof shall be divided into six equal parts or
shares, and disposed of in manner following."

" And first, it was always my humble and earnest
desire and intention, that the following donation and devise should be founded, as much as possible, on the plan
of that profoundly learned and successful inquirer into
Nature, and most religious adorer of Nature's God,
I mean the truly great and good (as well as honourable)

Robert Boyle, Esquire; who has added so much lustre, and done equal service, both by his learning and his life, to his native country, and to human nature, and to the cause of Christianity and truth."

"To the promoting in some degree a design so worthy of every reasonable creature, I direct that four parts out of six of the last mentioned rents, tythes, and profits, to arise from the premises (exclusive of such augmentations as herein before and herein after are mentioned) shall be paid, on Saint John the Evangelist's Day following the preaching of the Lectures or Sermons after-mentioned, annually to such learned and ingenious clergyman in the said University, of the degree of Master of Arts, and under the age of forty years, as shall be duly chosen or elected on Christmas-day, or within seven days after, by the Vice-Chancellor there for the time being[a], and by the Master or Head of Trinity College, and the Master of Saint John's College, or by any two of them, in order to preach twenty Sermons in the whole year: that is to say, ten Sermons in the following spring, in Saint Mary's great Church in Cambridge, namely, one Sermon either on the Friday morning, or else on Sunday afternoon in every week, during the months of April, and May, and the two first weeks of June; and likewise ten Sermons in the same Church, in the following autumn, either on the Friday morning, or else on Sunday afternoon in every week, during the months of September, and October, and during the two first weeks in November."

---

[a] It is provided, in another clause of the Will, that if either the Master of Trinity, or the Master of St. John's be Vice-Chancellor, the Greek Professor shall be the third Trustee.— The clauses here printed are carefully specified for that purpose by Mr. Hulse, as well the preamble and conclusion of the extract, which is to be made by the Lecturer in conformity to his directions.

" The subject of which discourses shall be as followeth ; that is to say, the subject of five Sermons in the
spring, and likewise of five Sermons in the autumn, shall
be to shew the Evidence for Revealed Religion ; and to
demonstrate, in the most convincing and persuasive manner, the truth and excellence of Christianity, so as to
include not only the Prophecies and Miracles, general and
particular, but also any other proper or useful arguments,
whether the same be direct or collateral proofs of the
Christian religion, which he may think fittest to discourse
upon, either in general or particular, especially the collateral arguments, or else any particular article or branch
thereof; and chiefly against notorious Infidels, whether
Atheists, or Deists, not descending to any particular
sects or controversies (so much to be lamented) amongst
Christians themselves ; except some new and dangerous
error, either of superstition, or enthusiasm, as of Popery
or Methodism, or the like, either in opinion or practice,
shall prevail ; in which case only it may be necessary for
that time to write and preach against the same."

" Nevertheless, the Preacher of the ten Sermons, last
mentioned, to shew the truth and excellence of revealed
religion, and the evidence of Christianity, may, at his own
discretion, preach either more or fewer than ten Sermons
on this great argument; only provided he shall, in consequence thereof, lessen or encrease the number of the
other ten remaining Sermons, which are herein after directed to be on the more obscure parts of the Holy
Scripture, in a due proportion, so as that he shall, every
year, preach twenty Sermons on these subjects in the
whole."

' And as to the ten Sermons that remain, of which
five are to be preached in the spring, and five in the
autumn, as before mentioned, the Lecturer or Preacher
shall take for his subject some of the more difficult texts
or obscure parts of the Holy Scriptures ; such, I mean,

as may appear to be more generally useful, or necessary to be explained, and which may best admit of such a comment or explanation, without seeming to pry too far into the profound secrets, or awful mysteries of the Almighty. And in all the said twenty Sermons, such practical observations shall be made, and such useful conclusions added, as may best instruct and edify mankind."

" The said twenty Sermons to be every year printed, and a new preacher to be every year elected, (except in the case of the extraordinary merit of the Preacher, when it may sometimes be thought proper to continue the same person for five or, at the most, for six years together, but for no longer term) nor shall he ever afterwards be again elected to the same duty. And I do direct, that the expence of printing the said Sermons shall be defrayed out of the said temporary stipend or salary of sixty pounds, with the augmentations first mentioned, or from the further provision hereby made, of the rents, tythes, and profits afterwards mentioned, for the said Lectures; and the remainder of the same given to him."

"And may the Divine blessing for ever go along with all my Benefactions! And may the greatest and the best of Beings, by his all-wise Providence, and gracious influence, make the same effectual to his own glory, and the good of my fellow-creatures!"

"An ABSTRACT of the heads or material parts" of the WILL of the Rev. JOHN HULSE, relative to the *two Scholarships*, founded by him in St. John's College, and by him directed to be added to the conclusion of the foregoing clauses, " so that such Clergyman, or persons, whom the same may concern, may know that there are such endowments, of which they may claim and take the benefit, under the regulations, and with the qualifications, therein mentioned."

The Scholars are to be " Undergraduates of St. John's College, who shall be born in the county Palatine of Chester." " Such Scholar is to be elected by the Master and a majority of the senior Fellows of the said College on Christmas-day, or in the first seven days after," and candidates are to have the preference, in the order, and with the limitations specified in the following extracts.

1.—" The son of any Clergyman, who shall at any time officiate as Curate to the Vicar of Sandbach; or next to him the son of any Vicar or Curate, who shall then live and officiate in the parish of Middlewich, as the proper Minister or Curate of Middlewich; or lastly of any Minister or Curate of the Chapel of Witton, or who shall reside and live in the town of Northwich or Witton, or the adjacent townships of Castle Northwich and Winnington, and shall do the duty of the said Chapel as the proper Minister of Witton (all of them in the said county of Chester)."

2. " And in default of such persons, then the son of any other Clergyman, who (that is which son) shall be born in either of the said parishes of Sandbach or Middlewich, or in the said Chapelry of Middlewich, shall have the preference. And if none shall be admitted, then the son of any other Clergyman shall be preferred, who (that is which son) shall be born in the said county of Chester, and next in any of the four following counties of Stafford, Salop, Derby, or Lancaster; or lastly, elsewhere in any other county or part of England, provided that it shall appear that the Clergyman who is father to such Scholar is not, if living, or, if dead, was not at the time of his death possessed of any spiritual preferment of more than one hundred and forty pounds a year, clear income; or whose income in every respect shall not exceed the clear yearly value of two hundred pounds in the whole."

"But if no son of any Clergyman, so entitled as aforesaid, shall be elected into such Scholarship, the same shall be given to the son of some lay person, whose clear yearly income does not, if living, and, if dead, did not at the time of his death amount to more than two hundred pounds; and such son being born in the counties of Chester, Stafford, Salop, Derby, and Lancaster, the counties in that order having a preference; or lastly, elsewhere in England."

"And such Scholar, whether the son of a Clergyman, or Layman, to be elected in manner aforesaid, shall continue to enjoy this my benefaction until he shall take, or be of standing to take his first degree of Bachelor of Arts, unless some other person, being the son of some of the officiating ministers at some of the Churches or Chapels before mentioned, and otherwise qualified as aforesaid, and which qualification, had he been a member of the said College at the time the party in possession of the Scholarship had been elected, would have been entitled to the preference, shall be admitted a member of the said College; in which case the Scholar, who shall then be in possession, shall only hold the same for that year; and the other, with a prior right, shall be elected to the same the year following. And I do appoint the Master and senior Fellows of St. John's College Trustees for the said Scholarships."

One third part of the moiety of Mr. Hulse's estate in Sandbach and Bradwell is appropriated to each Scholar, *after the death of certain annuitants.* One only of the Scholarships is at present established.

———◆———

POSTSCRIPT.

Perhaps it may not be amiss that the extracts from the Will should *once* be printed according to Mr. Hulse's *first* intentions. Future Lecturers may avail themselves of the liberty given them in a clause near the conclusion of his long and intricate Will, in which he permits the Lecturer to select and abridge the more material parts of the clauses printed above; though he still requires the insertion of those relating to the Hulsean Scholarships. The former extracts were ready to be struck off when the Author discovered the clause just mentioned.

PREFACE.

THE *object* of this work is so fully explained in the second Lecture, and the series of subjects and texts, which form the table of Contents, will so clearly point out the Author's *plan*, that it will be unnecessary to detain the reader by any further remarks on those topics. He deems it, however, not inexpedient, to give some account of the origin of the present publication, both as it regards the form, in which it has been brought before the world, and the manner, in which it was first suggested to his own mind.

The following Lectures were composed and delivered by the Author, in the capacity of *Deputy* to the Hulsean Lecturer, who was prevented, by indisposition, from proceeding to the discharge of his official duties, which commenced on the first day of April in the present year.—A notice being issued by the Trustees of the Lecture, dated

March 13, 1821, inviting persons to offer their services to fulfil the provisions of Mr. Hulse's Will, after such consideration as the interval between the 13th and 26th of March allowed, though with some hesitation, the Author finally announced his willingness to undertake the task. He has now to express his gratitude to those who entrusted to him, under such circumstances, the duties of the Hulsean Lectureship, which are certainly more arduous than those of *any similar institution;* yet he has endeavoured to discharge them in the best manner he could. But he must now from the press repeat the request, which he made from the pulpit in his first Lecture, that he may obtain such indulgence, as may be thought justly due to a work of this nature, composed and printed in less than nine months. It was undertaken amidst numerous ordinary engagements, and it has been pursued amidst various unavoidable, but unexpected interruptions, with a detail of which it is not necessary to trouble the reader, but which have caused the work to appear without that careful revision of so hasty a composition, which would have been exceedingly desirable. He could not, however, defer the *publication* of the work, and can therefore only say,

"Emendaturus, si licuisset, erat."

The *hesitation* of the Author, with respect to the undertaking, was occasioned by the difficulty which he felt as to the method and arrangement in which so extensive a subject should be treated. Yet he was exceedingly desirous to avail himself of such an opportunity to bring it forward, since it had been so highly satisfactory to himself, and, as he thought, was likely to be generally useful.— It was first suggested to his own mind, about two years ago, by reading to a sick parishioner the fifth chapter of St. John's Gospel; a complete analysis of which is included in the following pages. The Author was at that time much astonished, and somewhat perplexed, to find that it contained a distinct enumeration and summary of the principal arguments in favour of Christianity. In his subsequent reading of the Gospels, he was even more surprised to observe that they contained, in other parts, so much on the same subject; and he at length formed the opinion that *a complete system of evidence* might be formed in the *very words* of our Lord, and of the Sermons and Epistles of the New Testament[a]. In consequence of this, when preaching before the University in December 1820, he stated his conviction that a work might be constructed upon the principle explained in the second of the following Lectures, so as to place the subject of evidence in a point of view more intelligible, and more generally edifying, than the *separate* and abstract form, which it generally assumes. But, although he had even then formed the design to bring the subject forward, when he had fully digested and arranged it, he had not the slightest conception that he should have done it within a year from that time. And when the opportunity, of which he has been able to avail himself,

---

[a] It was not until the Author had delivered several of the Lectures, that he met with Dr. Gerard's Dissertations on subjects relating to the genius and the evidences of Christianity. He was gratified to find that so sensible a writer had taken a view of the subject so nearly resembling that here given. Many other works have also touched upon it, but none, that the Author has seen, have *completely* and *systematically* exhibited it.

occurred, it found him still more sensible than
ever of the extent, as well as of the importance
of the subject, in consequence of another perusal
of the four Gospels with a special view to the
consideration of it. He has done what he could
to elucidate it, as far as they are concerned; and
all censure which this work may deserve must
be directed against himself. He will contentedly
submit, even to incur the charge of presumption
for having ventured to undertake the following
work, rather than that the *subject* should suffer
in consequence of his unskilful management of it.
If he has treated it with any tolerable degree of
success, he thinks that it will appear that the
subject of evidence is a topic of scriptural instruction, and that it may be treated, if occasion
require, in our parochial ministrations, in a way
which is at once explanatory of Scripture, satisfactory to the believer, and applicable to practice.

The Author has only further to request that
the reader, whether, or not, he is satisfied with
the statements and representations contained in
this Volume, will at least borrow the *hint* which

is given in it, and study *for himself* the discourses of our Lord, and the narrative which accompanies and illustrates those discourses. Those divine records will thereby receive a fresh light and importance, and he, who so reads them, cannot fail to receive both delight and satisfaction from the heavenly and comprehensive instructions and reasonings of our Lord himself.

TRINITY COLLEGE,
Dec. 21, 1821.

CONTENTS.

INTRODUCTORY LECTURE I.

Human Frailty and Mortality the special Objects of God's promised Mercy.—Suitable provisions of the Gospel, more especially as they are noticed in the opening Statements of the Evangelist St. John.

JOHN I. 12—14. *As many as received him, to them gave he power to become the Sons of God, even to them that believe on his name: which were born, not of blood, nor of the will of the flesh, nor of the will of man, but of God. And the Word was made flesh, and dwelt among us, (and we beheld his glory, the glory as of the only begotten of the Father,) full of grace and truth* .... p. 1

INTRODUCTORY LECTURE II.

The Evangelic Records designed, according to St. Luke and St. John, to assure us of the *certainty* of the Gospel, by laying before us its *evidence.*—Their sufficiency for that end.—Nature and advantages of the view which they suggest; and the plan of the following Lectures in illustration of it.

LUKE I. 1—4. *Forasmuch as many have taken in hand to set forth in order a declaration of those things which are most surely believed among us, even as they delivered them unto us, which from the beginning were eye-witnesses, and ministers of the word; it seemed good to me also, having had perfect understanding of all things from the very first, to write unto thee in order, most excellent Theophilus, that thou mightest know the certainty of those things, wherein thou hast been instructed* .... p. 27

PART I.

LECTURES III—V.

STATEMENTS OF JESUS, RESPECTING HIS PRETENSIONS AND THE
OBJECT OF HIS MISSION, WHICH PRECEDED HIS ACTUAL APPEAL
TO THE EVIDENCES IN CONFIRMATION OF THEM.

LECTURE III.

Our Lord's Conference with Nicodemus.

JOHN III. 1—3. *There was a man of the Pharisees, named
Nicodemus, a ruler of the Jews; the same came to Jesus by
night, and said unto him, Rabbi, we know that thou art a teacher
come from God; for no man can do these miracles that thou
doest, except God be with him. Jesus answered and said unto
him, Verily, verily I say unto thee, Except a man be born again,
he cannot see the kingdom of God.* .... p. 53

LECTURE IV.

Our Lord's teaching in Samaria and Galilee.—At what
period, and for what reason, he began to argue in
defence of his Mission.

MATT. IV. 23. *And Jesus went about all Galilee, teaching in
their synagogues, and preaching the Gospel of the kingdom, and
healing all manner of sickness and all manner of disease among
the people.* .... p. 82

LECTURE V.

The Occasion of the Discourse recorded in St. John's
fifth Chapter, and the Persons to whom it was addressed.—Illustration and Analysis of the first portion
of it.

JOHN V. 17—20. *Jesus answered them, My Father worketh
hitherto, and I work. Therefore the Jews sought the more to
kill him, because he not only had broken the sabbath, but said
also that God was his Father, making himself equal with God.
Then*

Then answered Jesus, and said unto them, Verily, verily, I say unto you, The Son can do nothing of himself, but what he seeth the Father do: for what things soever he doeth, these also doeth the Son likewise. For the Father loveth the Son, and sheweth him all things that himself doeth. . . . . p. 104

—o—

PART II.

LECTURES VI—XVII.

THE REASONINGS OF OUR LORD RESPECTING THE EVIDENCES TO WHICH HE APPEALED IN CONFIRMATION OF HIS CLAIMS.

LECTURE VI.

Our Lord's recapitulation of his Claims connected with a reference to the presumption in their favour from his not seeking his own Will.

JOHN v. 30, 31. *I can of mine own self do nothing; as I hear, I judge; and my judgement is just; because I seek not mine own will, but the will of the Father which hath sent me. If I bear witness of myself, my witness is not true* . . . . p. 129

LECTURE VII.

Our Lord's reasonings, on the Evidence arising from the witness of John, addressed to the Rulers, to the Multitudes, to John's Disciples, and to his own.

JOHN v. 31—35. *If I bear witness of myself, my witness is not true. There is another that beareth witness of me; and I know that the witness which he witnesseth of me is true. Ye sent unto John, and he bare witness unto the truth. But I receive not testimony from man; but these things I say, that ye might be saved. He was a burning and a shining light; and ye were willing for a season to rejoice in his light* . . . . p. 152

LECTURE VIII.

Our Lord's Appeal to his Miracles as attesting *his Divine Mission.*

JOHN v. 36. *But I have greater witness than that of John; for the works which the Father hath given me to finish, the same works that I do, bear witness of me, that the Father hath sent me* . . . . p. 179

LECTURE IX.

Our Lord's Appeal to his Miracles in proof of *his Messiahship.*

MATT. XI. 2—6. *Now when John had heard in the prison the works of Christ, he sent two of his disciples, and said unto him, Art thou he that should come, or do we look for another? Jesus answered and said unto them, Go and shew John again those things which ye do hear and see; The blind receive their sight, and the lame walk; the lepers are cleansed, and the deaf hear; the dead are raised up, and the poor have the Gospel preached to them. And blessed is he, whosoever shall not be offended in me* . . . . p. 203

LECTURE X.

Our Lord's Answer to the Cavil which imputed his dispossession of Demons to Satanic agency. He appeals to that class of his Miracles as indicating the establishment of *the Kingdom of God.*

LUKE XI. 20. *But if I with the finger of God cast out devils, no doubt the kingdom of God is come upon you* . . . . p. 227

LECTURE XI.

Our Lord's Appeal to the Witness of the Father, by which he was the *subject,* as well as the worker, *of Miracles.*

JOHN V. 37, 38. *And the Father himself which hath sent me, hath borne witness of me. Ye have neither heard his voice at any time, nor seen his shape. And ye have not his word abiding in you; for whom he hath sent, him ye believe not* ..... p. 257

LECTURE XII.

Our Lord's Appeal to the Scriptures of the Old Testament, as peculiarly designed to testify of Him.

JOHN v. 39, 40. *Search the Scriptures; for in them ye think ye have eternal life; and they are they which testify of me. And ye will not come to me, that ye might have life.* .... p. 286

LECTURE XIII.

A Review of the particular Instances in which our Lord, during his life, actually cites or alludes to the Prophecies and Types of the ancient Scriptures.

MATT. XI. 12—14. *From the days of John the Baptist until now the kingdom of heaven suffereth violence, and the violent take it by force. For all the prophets and the law prophesied until John. And, if ye will receive it, this is Elias which was for to come* .... p. 311

LECTURE XIV.

Our Lord's *Debates* with the Jews. — That recorded in St. John's eighth Chapter considered—in the course of which our Lord specifies the period at which the Evidence of his Messiahship would be complete; appeals to the Purity of his Life, and of his Doctrine; hints at the Fulfilment in him of the Promise to Abraham; and asserts his pre-existence.

JOHN VIII. 28, 29, 45—47. *Then said Jesus unto them, When ye have lifted up the Son of man, then shall ye know that I am he, and that I do nothing of myself; but as my Father hath taught*

taught me, I speak these things. And he that sent me is with me : the Father hath not left me alone; for I do always those things that please him.

And because I tell you the truth, ye believe me not. Which of you convinceth me of sin? And if I say the truth, why do ye not believe me? He that is of God, heareth God's words ; ye therefore hear them not, because ye are not of God .... p. 336

LECTURE XV.

Our Lord's Statement that the Fulfilment of his own Predictions would evince his Messiahship. The manner in which he displayed and noticed his unlimited knowledge of men and things.

JOHN XIII. 18, 19. *I know whom I have chosen : but that the Scripture may be fulfilled, He that eateth bread with me, hath lifted up his heel against me. Now I tell you before it come, that, when it is come to pass, ye may believe that I am He.* .... p. 362

LECTURE XVI.

The remarkable Sayings of our Lord, at the time of his Apprehension, on his Trial, and on the Cross, considered.—His Institution of the Sacrament in Commemoration of his Death.

JOHN XVIII. 36, 37. *Jesus answered, My kingdom is not of this world; if my kingdom were of this world, then would my servants fight, that I should not be delivered to the Jews : but now is my kingdom not from hence. Pilate therefore said unto him, Art thou a king then? Jesus answered, Thou sayest that I am a king. To this end was I born, and for this cause came I into the world, that I might bear witness unto the truth. Every one that is of the truth heareth my voice* .... p. 387

LECTURE XVII.

The Method in which our Lord evidenced the Reality of his Resurrection, and his reasonings on Prophecy after
that

that event. — The distinguishing peculiarities of the Christian Faith.

LUKE xxiv. 44—48. *And he said unto them, These are the words which I spake unto you, while I was yet with you, that all things must be fulfilled, which were written in the law of Moses, and in the Prophets, and in the Psalms concerning me. Then opened he their understandings, that they might understand the Scriptures, and said unto them, Thus it is written, and thus it behoved Christ to suffer, and to rise from the dead the third day, and that repentance and remission of sins should be preached in his name among all nations, beginning at Jerusalem. And ye are witnesses of these things* . . . . p. 417

—0—

PART III.

LECTURES XVIII—XX.

OUR LORD'S NOTICE OF THE REJECTION OF HIS CLAIMS BY THE JEWS;
AND OF THE CAUSES, PROGRESS, AND CONSEQUENCES OF
INFIDELITY.

LECTURE XVIII.

Our Lord's Notice of the Rejection of his Claims by the Jews. — He specifies some of the moral Causes of Infidelity.

JOHN v. 40—46. *Ye will not come to me that ye might have life. I receive not honour from men. But I know you, that you have not the love of God in you. I am come in my Father's name, and ye receive me not ; if another shall come in his own name, him ye will receive. How can ye believe, which receive honour one of another, and seek not the honour that cometh from God only ? Do not think that I will accuse you to the Father: there is one that accuseth you, even Moses, in whom ye trust. For had ye believed Moses, ye would have believed me ; for he wrote of me. But if ye believe not his writings, how shall ye believe my words?* . . . . p. 449

LECTURE XIX.

The Infidelity of the Jews in its more *advanced* stage noticed by our Lord with allusion to a passage of Isaiah.—The occasion and purport of his Remarks; and a similar application of the same passage by the Evangelist St. John.—Other Cautions and Directions given by our Lord respecting the *Temper* and *Method* proper for Religious Inquiry.

MATT. XIII. 14—16. *And in them is fulfilled the prophecy of Esaias, which saith, By hearing ye shall hear, and shall not understand; and seeing ye shall see, and shall not perceive.— For this people's heart is waxed gross, and their ears are dull of hearing, and their eyes they have closed; lest at any time they should see with their eyes, and hear with their ears, and should understand with their heart, and should be converted, and I should heal them* . . . . p. 475

LECTURE XX.

Our Lord's Notice of Infidelity in its *last* and *confirmed* stage.—The Blasphemy against the Son of Man, and that against the Holy Ghost.—The demand of additional Evidence, when that which is offered has been rejected. —Sanctions with which the Gospel is accompanied.— Conclusion.

LUKE XII. 8—10. *Also I say unto you, Whosoever shall confess me before men, him shall the Son of man also confess before the angels of God: but he that denieth me before men, shall be denied before the angels of God. And whosoever shall speak a word against the Son of man, it shall be forgiven him; but unto him that blasphemeth against the Holy Ghost, it shall not be forgiven* . . . . p. 500

HULSEAN LECTURES

FOR 1821.

—————————————

INTRODUCTORY LECTURE I.

—o—

HUMAN FRAILTY AND MORTALITY
THE SPECIAL OBJECTS OF GOD'S PROMISED MERCY.

SUITABLE PROVISIONS OF THE GOSPEL,
MORE ESPECIALLY AS THEY ARE NOTICED IN THE OPENING
STATEMENTS OF THE EVANGELIST ST. JOHN.

A

LECTURE I.

———◆———

St. John I. 12—14.

As many as received him, to them gave he power to become the Sons of God, even to them that believe on his name: which were born, not of blood, nor of the will of the flesh, nor of the will of man, but of God. And the Word was made flesh, and dwelt among us, (and we beheld his glory, the glory as of the only begotten of the Father,) full of grace and truth.

HE, who "giveth to all life, and breath, and all things, hath made from one progenitor, and of one blood, all nations of men for to dwell on the face of the earth; and will have all men to be saved, and to come to the knowledge of the truth[a]." Yet, although all men have sprung from the same original, partake of one common nature, and are indifferently the objects of their Creator's regard, they are variously distinguished from each other. The diversities of form and countenance, station and condition, ability and pursuits, are as numerous as the individuals of

---

[a] Acts xvii. 25, 26. 1 Tim. ii. 4.

whom the race is composed. These, however, are distinctions of time only, and of this world; "at the hour of death, and in the day of judgment," they will have ceased for ever. But distinctions co-exist with these, which in some respects are already manifested; which will hereafter be more fully developed, and more completely fixed; which time cannot efface, and death cannot destroy; which will determine our destiny at the last decisive day, and continue with us through eternity. These important distinctions are such as respect our inner man; our moral and religious character; the state of our affections, and soul, and spirit, with reference to God, and his favour, and the things unseen.

To those "who believe on the name of the only begotten Son of God," belong privileges and expectations, than which none more ennobling and animating can be enjoyed by man. They derive them from the mercy, and receive them through the power of God; and the bliss and dignity which are hereby communicated to them in this world, are but a foretaste and pledge of more perfect blessedness in another. The same beloved Apostle who, in the words of our text, mentions these privileges, and also the wondrous method in which they were procured and revealed, in another part of his writings exclaims; "Behold, what manner of love the Father hath bestowed upon us, that we should be called the Sons of God." "Beloved," he adds, "now are we the Sons of God, and it doth not yet appear what we shall be."[a] It is, however, already revealed, that "redemption through the blood of Christ has procured for us the forgiveness of sins." We know that we were thus "redeemed, that we might receive the adoption of sons;" and the adoption will one day be perfected, by "the redemption of our body" from the power of the grave. And therefore "the earnest expectation of the creature waiteth for the manifestation of the Sons of God; when it shall be delivered from the bondage of corruption, into that glorious liberty" of which the children of God will partake, by being "the children of the resurrection."[b]

"The hope thus set before us" is one to which we may "flee for refuge" amidst all the fears, and adversities, and uncertainties of life. And if we are convinced that "grace and truth" have indeed "come by Jesus Christ;" and that he, as "the only begotten Son of God, the Word incarnate, hath declared to us the Father;" then "though now we see him not, yet believing, we may rejoice in him with joy unspeakable and full of glory."

---

[a] 1 John iii. 1, 2.
[b] Eph. i. 7. Gal. iv. 5. Rom. viii. 15—23. Luke xx. 35, 36.

We purpose, in these Lectures, to call your attention to the striking and satisfactory manner in which the certainty, design, and importance of the Gospel were *originally* exhibited to mankind. We shall shew you, in our next Lecture, that the Evangelists, St. Luke and St. John, themselves have directed us to such a view of the subject. St. John has also prefaced his narrative with a comprehensive statement respecting the divine and eternal glory of the Word, who "was made flesh, and dwelt among us full of grace and truth;" and the retrospective, present, and prospective, benefits of this incarnation of the Son of God. If, therefore, we devote this introductory discourse to a summary review of those important truths, into the certainty of which we are to inquire, we shall, by such a procedure, still follow the guidance of the Evangelists, and conduct our inquiries upon the plan which they suggest to us.

The Gospel announces to us an appropriate and adequate provision for our necessities, as sinful and, therefore, as dying, creatures. "For since man was a partaker of flesh and blood, the deliverer of men likewise took part of the same; that through death, he might destroy him that had the power of death, that is, the devil; and deliver them, who through fear of death, were all their lifetime subject to bondage."[a] And rightly to have meditated upon that guilt and frailty of man, which infuses bitterness into the cup of life, and sharpens the sting of death, will best teach us that humility and gratitude, with which we ought to contemplate "the exceeding riches of God's grace, in his kindness toward us through Christ Jesus."[b]

That we are frail and dying creatures is proved by universal and unvarying experience. We are carried down the stream of time; and, like every other bubble that floats upon its surface, we also, in our turn, must disappear. Not only the fleeting portion of time during which we ourselves exist, but even the generation to which we belong, quickly passes away. The tolling bell, and the opened grave, ever and anon remind us of the unwelcome truth. Man, our brother, neighbour, and friend, "goeth to his long home;" "the dust returns to the earth as it was, and the spirit to God who gave it." And, when we remember the judgment that comes after death, conscience reminds us of our transgressions, and suggests distressing, but not groundless, fears. For, by all that we can discover of the "eternal power and Godhead" of our Creator, by all that we have been taught, or can comprehend, respecting his character, we know that he is "glorious in holi-

---

a Heb. ii. 14, 15.   b Ephes. ii. 7.

ness," and the "hater of iniquity ;" "abundant in
goodness and truth," and yet of inflexible justice ;
that he "searcheth the hearts and trieth the reins,"
and will "bring every work into judgment, with
every secret thing, whether it be good, or whether
it be evil." If we dwell exclusively on the contrast exhibited to us between his perfections and
our imperfections, between his glory and our
degradation, we could scarcely do otherwise than
despair. But in order that humility may be combined with hope, we must consider these truths
in connexion, as in Scripture we are taught to do.
There all that is weak and frail in man is put in
immediate connexion with all that is mighty and
glorious in his God. Man's sinfulness and God's
mercy are noticed together, both in the general
declarations of his readiness to forgive, and also
in the more explicit statements respecting the
wondrous and consolatory provisions, which by
the incarnation and humiliation of the Son of
God, are made for our redemption and salvation.
Hence we may indeed learn the salutary lesson of
humility and self-abhorrence ; but hence also may
we be raised from the debasing depths of despair,
and taught to lift up the down cast eye, to "behold what manner of love the Father hath bestowed
upon us." We are taught "worthily to lament
our sins, and to acknowledge our wretchedness,"
in order that the remedy provided for both may be

worthily esteemed, and earnestly sought; that so we may obtain of "the God of all mercy, perfect remission and forgiveness, through Jesus Christ our Lord."[a] Yes, Christians, as "we have none in heaven but God," so "if on earth we desire none in comparison of him;" then although our "heart and flesh" may and must "fail, God will be the strength of our heart, and our portion for ever."[b] Let the Psalmist, in another place, give us the assurance and the reason of such a hope: "Like as a father pitieth his children, so the Lord pitieth them that fear him. For he knoweth our frame; he remembereth that we are dust. As for man, his days are as grass; as a flower of the field, so he flourisheth. For the wind passeth over it, and it is gone, and the place thereof shall know it no more. But the mercy of the Lord is from everlasting to everlasting upon them that fear him; and his righteousness unto children's children; to such as keep his covenant, and to those that remember his commandments to do them."[c] We are taught to take the same extensive and consolatory view by St. Peter: "We are born again, not of corruptible seed, but of incorruptible, by the word of God, which liveth and abideth for ever. For all flesh is grass, and all the glory of

---

[a] Collect for Ash-Wednesday.   [b] Psalm lxxiii. 25, 26.
[c] Psalm ciii. 13—18.

man as the flower of grass. The grass withereth, and the flower thereof falleth away; but the word of the Lord endureth for ever. And this is the word which by the Gospel is preached unto you."[a] Here the Apostle cites and explains the words, which Isaiah ascribes to the voice crying in the wilderness; when, rapt into Gospel times, he already seemed to hear it uttering the proclamation, "Prepare ye the way of the Lord; that the glory of the Lord may be revealed, and all flesh may see it together."[b] Here then we are approaching to a full discovery of the wondrous means, by which "God's people are comforted, their warfare is accomplished, and their iniquity pardoned." Turn we then once more for information respecting this interesting matter to the declarations of the Apostles of Jesus Christ. What says St. Paul? "The law of the Spirit of life in Christ Jesus hath made me free from the law of sin and death. For what the law could not do, in that it was weak through the flesh, God, sending his own Son in the likeness of sinful flesh, and for sin, condemned sin in the flesh; that the righteousness of the law might be fulfilled in us, who walk not

---

[a] 1 Pet. i. 23—25.

[b] Isai. xl. 1—8. Throughout the remainder of the chapter the prophet gives a magnificent description of the divine attributes, and applies them for the consolation of man.

after the flesh, but after the Spirit. And if Christ
be in you, the body is dead, because of sin; but
the Spirit is life, because of righteousness. But if
the Spirit of him that raised up Jesus from the
dead dwell in you, he that raised up Christ from
the dead shall also quicken your mortal bodies by
his Spirit that dwelleth in you."[c] We have in these
words a clear and consolatory description of the
blessed fulfilment of that original promise, which
accompanied the sentence of death pronounced
upon our first parents; and which shewed, that,
even then, "mercy rejoiced against judgment."
The deliverance then promised was that " wisdom
of God in a mystery, which God ordained before
the world unto our glory;" the purposes of which
were accomplished by the incarnation, and ministry,
and sufferings, of the Son of God. This hidden
wisdom "God revealed unto the Apostles by his
Spirit, that they might know the things which are
freely given us of God; which things also they
spoke, not in the words which man's wisdom
teacheth, but which the Holy Ghost teacheth."[d]
And so instructed respecting that " Lord of Glory
whom the princes of this world crucified," the
Evangelist declared, in the words of our text,
"The Word was made flesh, and dwelt among
us, (and we beheld his glory, the glory as of the

---

[c] Rom. viii. 2—4; 10, 11.   [d] 1 Cor. ii. 7—13.

only begotten of the Father) full of grace and
truth."

This passage stands in the middle of St. John's
introduction to his Gospel; and it is connected,
by the two first clauses, with the preceding verses
of that introduction, in which he speaks of the
preexistence and dignity of "the Word who was
made flesh," and of his reception in the world.
The latter clauses of the verse introduce the statement which he then subjoins respecting the exhibition of his glory, and the effects and purposes
of his manifestation in the flesh. The Evangelist
first states the original cause, and then proceeds
to state the effect; which undoubtedly corresponds
to the order of the divine intentions and dispensations. But our limited conceptions will best
enable us, first to consider the effect, and then
to ascend to its cause; first to observe the method
and consequences of the Gospel revelation, and
afterwards to advert to the origin and dignity of
him who was thus manifested in the flesh, which
afford the fullest, and indeed the only adequate,
assurance that he is "mighty to save."

"The Word was made flesh, and dwelt among
us full of grace and truth." The phraseology
both of this verse, and of the preceding ones,
can only be reconciled with the supposition that
the Evangelist speaks not here of any abstract
quality, or of the *doctrine* of the Gospel; but of

a *person*; and certainly, therefore, of him who was
"the author and finisher of our faith." And
whether or not he had existed previously to his
appearance in the world; and whatever were the
dignity which appertained to him in such a prior
state; yet that being "made of a woman," he par-
took of flesh and blood; that he "dwelt among
us" in the likeness of men, and shared in all the
affections, and infirmities, and casualties of our
common nature, was an obvious and undeniable
fact; upon the certainty of which every other
assertion respecting him avowedly proceeds. Yet
he spoke and acted as one who had authority;
he dwelt among us full of grace and truth, but in
an official character. He professed to be sent
of God; yet he had not come armed with vengeance; but as one commissioned to offer forgiveness, "to seek and to save that which was
lost:" He was meek and lowly of heart, affable and
benignant in demeanour. With lips full of grace
he invited the weary and heavy laden to seek of
him rest for their souls. By admonition and by
promise he succoured the tempted. He encouraged the suppliant to perseverance in prayer.
He animated the penitent with the assurance of
pardon. He imparted his instructions on subjects
of high and holy import with a condescension,
which shewed his unlimited benevolence; with
a readiness and calm confidence, which shewed

that he spake of heavenly things as one familiar
with them, and of earthly things as one who
"knew what was in man." "He spake as never
man spake;" as one "in whom were hid all the
treasures of wisdom and knowledge;" and to
whose view "the abundance of the heart" of man
was open. His words flashed conviction on the
soul, for they met both the avowed objections,
and the secret surmises, of the gainsayer; they
were calculated to alarm the careless; they were
adapted to the fears and wants and dangers of
the humble inquirer. Thus did he dispel those
mists of ignorance and error, which before ob-
scured the knowledge of him, "whom truly to
know is everlasting life."

"He dwelt among us, full of grace and truth;
and we," says the Evangelist, "beheld his glory,
the glory as of the only begotten of the Father."
He came not indeed in the artificial pomp of
human glory and dignity; but in mercy and tenderness, majesty and omniscience, wisdom and
power; in the bright effulgence of those perfections which we attribute to the Father, and which
constitute his glory. Those who were with Jesus
most, saw more, not of his infirmity, but of his
glory. At his baptism, by his miracles, at his
transfiguration, resurrection, and ascension "he
manifested his glory" as "the only begotten of the
Father."

To the Apostles was also vouchsafed a fuller assurance and evidence of the same truth; for they were to "bear witness, and to shew unto the world that eternal life, which was with the Father, and was manifested unto them." "Of his fulness," says the Evangelist, "have all we received, and grace for grace. For the law was given by Moses, but grace and truth came by Jesus Christ." The same grace which he exhibited in his life, was in a more especial manner exercised towards his Apostles after his ascension; that it might be evidenced to the world by the illumination of their minds, by the importance, and suitableness, and efficacy of the doctrines they taught, and by the mighty works which they wrought through the name of Jesus, that they were sanctioned, and taught, and supported from above. His was the fulness of grace and truth; and "of that fulness they received grace" abundant in degree, increasing in extent, and "instead of" that of the Old Testament, which "though it was glorious, yet had no glory by reason of that which so far excelled it." "The law given by Moses" was holy and divine, but it was "the ministration of condemnation;" and had only "the shadow of good things to come." "The grace" which it left imperfect, and "the truth" of all that it promised and prefigured, "came by Jesus Christ;" who was "the end of the law for righteousness to every one that believeth." "To know the only true God and Jesus Christ whom he hath sent," is now declared to be "life eternal."

With a similar statement the Evangelist concludes his introduction. "No man hath seen God at any time; the only begotten Son, which is in the bosom of the Father, he hath declared him." By him are fully announced to us the perfect and harmonious attributes of the Father; the relations in which we stand to him; and the way in which he will shew mercy, and can be "just, while he justifies those that believe in Jesus." The Evangelist particularly specifies that he who hath "shewed us plainly of the Father," was "the only begotten Son which is in the bosom of the Father;" intending, by such a statement, more deeply to impress us with a conviction of the grace, and truth, and authority, of the incarnate Word. He declares to us thereby his antecedent personal dignity, "the glory that he had with the Father before the world was;" and that "between him and the Father was the counsel of peace," which in due time was testified by the preaching of the Gospel. The incarnation of the Son of God did indeed cause him to submit to a state of humiliation; and it was succeeded by his "glorification as the Son of man," as "the one Mediator between God and man," as "the head over all things to his Church." But his being "crowned with glory and honour, because of the suffering of death," and his high exaltation to the throne of his mediatorial kingdom, did not confer upon him a new *personal* dignity, but only one of an *official* nature. It is true that as our Saviour, and as the Christ, he received "a name which is above every name; that every tongue should confess that Jesus Christ is Lord, to the glory of God the Father[a]." But it was *because* he was "the only begotten Son of God, which is in the bosom of the Father," that he *became* our Saviour and intercessor. In him, while he tabernacled among men, "dwelt all the fulness of the Godhead bodily;" for he, of whom these things are spoken, was "God manifest in the flesh." The whole Gospel of St. John teaches these great and essential doctrines; it opposes heresy, not by the refutation of error, but by the establishment of truth. And as, in the latter part of the introduction to his Gospel, the Evangelist notices the incarnation, glory, and success of the Son of God; so, in the former part of it, he instructs us in what *sense* we are to believe that Jesus is the Son of God. He states, in the text, that it was the "Word who became flesh;" and in the preceding verses he manifestly speaks of the Word as a *person*, one also who "came from God, as

---

[a] Phil. i. 9—11.

he afterwards went to God." Which of us will
venture to say, that he spoke not these things
by the inspiration of that "Spirit, which searcheth
all things, yea, even the deep things of God?"
We might acquiesce, therefore, in this his testimony, even if the words and works of Jesus,
and all the testimony of Scripture, did not teach
us the same.

"In the beginning was the Word, and the
Word was with God, and the Word was God."
And having thus declared his pre-existence, his
existence in the bosom of the Father even at the
creation of all things, and his divinity; he adds
the statement, that "the same was in the beginning with God;" lest while we do "not confound
the persons," we should "divide the substance."
And again; "All things were made by him, and
without him was not any thing made that has
been made." By him, by whose agency, as the
Word of Jehovah, the heavens and the earth were
made, and by whom Jehovah revealed himself to
the Patriarchs, and to their chosen posterity, by
the same has the world been redeemed. "In him
was life, and the life was the light of men." That
"light ever shined in the darkness" of the heathen
world, "but the darkness comprehended it not."
One "came for a witness, to bear witness of the
light," even of "the true light which, coming into
the world, enlighteneth every man." He was

"a man sent from God; His name John." It is
not said of him that "he was with God, and was
God;" for he was but a *man*, though sent of God.
"He was not that light, but was sent to bear
witness of that light, that all men through him
might believe." He "went before the face of the
Lord to prepare his ways; to give knowledge of
salvation unto his people, by the remission of
their sins through the tender mercy of our God,
whereby the day-spring from on high hath visited
us[a]." Yet as he, who "was in the world, and by
whom the world was made, was not known" by
the Gentile world; so also, when "he came to
his own home, even his own household," the
Jews, "received him not." For this their infidelity we can fully account; but let us not "fall
after the same example of unbelief." We may
safely confide in the truth of that record, which
announces to us, "that God hath given to us
eternal life, and that this life is in his Son."
And great are the privileges, and consequent
blessedness, which he is empowered to bestow.
For, "as many as received him, to them gave
he power to become the Sons of God, even to
them that believe on his name." Of the nature,
and future consequences, of this adoption of Sons,
which we receive through the Son of God, we

---

[a] Luke i. 76—78.

have already spoken. And "if the Son thus make us free, we shall be free indeed;" delivered here from the dominion of sin, and hereafter from "the bondage of corruption;" for he who is "the first begotten from the dead, will "change the body of our humiliation, that it may be made conformal to the body of his glory; according to the mighty working, whereby he is able to subdue all things unto himself," and to "swallow up death in victory." We are thus begotten again unto a lively hope; "but not of blood," says the Evangelist; for it is not a blessing descending by natural inheritance; nor is it confined to any one favoured race, or family, or nation. Nor does it come "of the will of the flesh;" for "that which is born of the flesh is flesh," but this is a spiritual generation to the inheritance of spiritual blessings. Nor is it "of the will of man;" his reason could not have discovered, his power could not have procured, his works of righteousness could not have deserved it. It is "of God;" "who according to his own mercy hath saved us, by the washing of regeneration, and the renewing of the Holy Ghost, which he hath shed upon us abundantly through Jesus Christ our Saviour; that being justified by his grace, we should be made heirs according to the hope of eternal life[a]."

---

[a] Titus iii. 5—7.

If, then, "God hath in these last days spoken unto us by his Son," we have received through that merciful dispensation a consolation for our fears, and a remedy for our disorders; thence we learn that sin can be forgiven, and how our weakness may be strengthened. Hope succeeds to despair when we contemplate such a provision for our frailty; when we find that God has by "the Gospel of his grace," confirmed all the assurances of mercy which he had before given, supplied all that yet was lacking, confirmed all that was promised, and brought in "an everlasting righteousness." These are unspeakably important truths; but short may be the time which remains to ourselves, for securing the blessings which they make known to us. The awful hour of death is one in which we shall fully learn the value of the righteous man's hope. It is a season which will so surely come, and which may be so near, that the contemplation of it ought to quicken us in the pursuit of those blessings, which are designed to deliver us now from the fear of it, and hereafter from its power. We seek to impress upon you the certainty of death, that you may consider its consequences; that you may make the inquiries which it suggests; that you may realize the unseen verities which lie beyond the grave, and which are eternal. We proclaim to you, with reference to eternity, the doctrines of God's word, with all their evidence, their obligations, and their consequences; you hear them for eternity. The decision to which you come respecting them is a decision for. eternity. Let then our inquiries ever be pursued with a corresponding seriousness; let the illusions of time be dissipated, and the fascinations of sense lose their power over our souls, that we may learn to walk by the *faith* of things unseen, though by the sight of them we cannot; that we may have our conversation in heaven even while we remain upon earth.

We have more than once touched upon the old and trite subject of death. But often are the most important truths obvious and familiar; and therefore are they so, because they are important. It is not, however, certain that, because they are familiar to us, we have duly profited by them. Let us then, in conclusion, once more renew the recollection of our mortality; and advert to the striking remark of Solomon, "One generation passeth away, and another generation cometh; but the earth abideth for ever[a]."

Contrast the continued succession of the generations of men, with the permanency of the earth upon which they live. Compared with their fleeting existence, it may be said to "abide for ever." After how short a period. do we find

---

[a] Eccl. i. 4.

nearly all those, amongst whom we used to dwell,
and with whom we were formerly connected, dis-
placed and gone; and succeeded by others who
have started into existence since ourselves! Nay,
how soon are all the actors on this busy scene
completely changed; for "there is none abiding."
Soon the place that knoweth us now, shall know
us no more; and others will occupy the estates
which were ours, and the dwellings we have
inhabited. Our bodies are "houses of clay, whose
foundation is in the dust;" and all that we can
call *ourselves* dwells in these frail tenements. The
works of man often long outlive him. What purpose do the magnificent ruins of the cities of the
wilderness, and the massy piles that adorn the
banks of the Nile, now serve, but to make us
wonder at the skill and diligence of those long-
forgotten people, of whose manners, history, and
language, we have now scarcely any record; and
to cause us profitably to muse on the shortness of
human life, and the instability of human grandeur!
But we need not visit these distant wonders to
have a sensible proof of the same truth; and one
which may perhaps be at once more familiar and
impressive. We are here surrounded by some of
those edifices, which are the ornament of our
country, and which excite and gratify the curiosity of the inquiring stranger. They have
served the purposes of many generations that

are past; they serve ours now; and will probably continue to invite, receive, and instruct, generations yet unborn. And in this place, assuredly,
we may most strikingly see how quickly one
generation passeth away, and another cometh!
A period of four or five years here almost
changes the scene. Those, who remove from
hence, do indeed for the most part go to form a
portion of the permanent population of some other
place. But what occasions the demand for their
services in this place or in that, but the removal
of some of our race by death? This perpetual
change, and constant transition, are caused by
the openings which death has somewhere made.
The fluctuations and varying features of social
life as certainly result from this cause, as motion
in the natural world from a vacuum. Survey the
permanent population of this or of any other
place, and it will appear, that many of those,
who, on setting out in life have little success
and employment, in a few years become pros-
perous, and, with their families, are established in
life. Why? Because many of their former rivals
have been removed, and they have succeeded to
their abodes, connexions, and emoluments. Thus
is our prosperity, nay even our very means of
subsistence, derived from the mortality of our
predecessors and ancestors : and that of our suc-
cessors and of posterity will depend equally upon

ours. Death is the debt of nature; it meets us in every time, place, and concern of life ; so true is it, that "in the midst of life we are in death," and that " one generation passeth away, and another cometh."

When we look round on the great congregation assembled in God's house, and recollect that, considering it *collectively,* we can assign the period within which all of us will have undergone the pangs of death ; we might sit down, and, like the Persian monarch, weep at the melancholy reflection, did we not remember again, that another generation will ere that have gradually arisen, upon whom the sun will shine as brightly ; for whom the earth will bring forth as plentifully ; whose will be all the joys and cares, the comforts and disappointments that we have experienced ; and who will share the same bounty and protection of the same God. All will be well ordered with respect to the fortunes and changes of the world in general. But will it be well with us as individuals ? We know the limit *beyond* which we cannot survive, but we know not within how small a span of time we have yet to move. We know also, that whenever " the body shall return to the earth as it was, the spirit shall return to God who gave it;" to render its account before him then, and at the appointed day before the general assemblage of all generations. And let

it be remembered by us, that we cannot have any
certainty that our eternal state will differ from
that which would be assigned to us this day,
if on this day the decision were to be made. We
may live long; but we may "wax worse and
worse, deceiving and being deceived," and may
thus be treasuring up wrath against the day of
wrath. We *may* live long, and see many days;
but our strength *may* be brought down in the
midst of our journey, and our days be shortened.
And who that *now* has not his loins girt, and his
lamp burning, can think that he will be ready,
if his Lord comes in an unexpected hour? How
then should we even now strive, and watch, and
pray, that the spirit may be saved in the day of
the Lord Jesus! For by every thought, word,
and deed, we sow that seed, of which the harvest
will then be reaped; and as we have sown to the
flesh or to the spirit, we then shall reap either
corruption or life everlasting.

HULSEAN LECTURES

for 1821.

―――――――――――

INTRODUCTORY LECTURE II.

―――0―――

THE EVANGELIC RECORDS DESIGNED, ACCORDING TO ST. LUKE AND
ST. JOHN, TO ASSURE US OF THE *CERTAINTY* OF THE GOSPEL, BY
LAYING BEFORE US ITS *EVIDENCE.*――THEIR SUFFICIENCY FOR
THAT END.――NATURE AND ADVANTAGES OF THE VIEW WHICH
THEY SUGGEST; AND THE PLAN OF THE FOLLOWING LECTURES
IN ILLUSTRATION OF IT.

LECTURE II.

———

LUKE I. 1—4.

Forasmuch as many have taken in hand to set forth in order a declaration of those things which are most surely believed among us, even as they delivered them unto us, which from the beginning were eyewitnesses, and ministers of the word; it seemed good to me also, having had perfect understanding of all things from the very first, to write unto thee in order, most excellent Theophilus, that thou mightest know the certainty of those things, wherein thou hast been instructed.

WE, as Christians, have been instructed in momentous truths; even in all that was taught, promised, and effected, by a divine, incarnate, suffering, crucified, and exalted, Messiah. We have been baptized into the name of Jesus Christ. Having been begotten again by him to a lively hope, we have been taught the articles of our faith, the commands of our Master, the vows which are upon us, the obligations which accompany all that a Christian ought to know and believe to his soul's health. We have, by our own mouths, ratified the promises and vows which were made on our behalf. We have received those holy mysteries,

in the participation of which we are "fed with the
spiritual food of the precious body and blood of
our Saviour Jesus Christ." We have thus become
" very members incorporate of the mystical body of
the Son of God ;" we thus "shew forth the Lord's
death until his coming again;" professing that we
are " heirs through hope of his everlasting kingdom;" and praying unto our God to "grant that, by
the merits and death of his Son our Saviour Jesus
Christ, and through faith in his blood, we and all
his whole Church may obtain remission of our
sins, and all other benefits of his passion [a]." We
have been instructed in all these great and consolatory truths; and we have professed to believe
them. If we have herein " witnessed a good confession," and are not " losing the things which we
have wrought," then " believing with the heart
unto righteousness, confession will be made by
the mouth unto salvation." Of this salvation we
may entertain a good hope through the promised
mercy of a gracious God. For we have also been
instructed, in the midst of the fears and infirmities
of our nature, and under the afflictions of this life,
to " commit the keeping of our souls to God in
well doing, as unto a faithful Creator." We have
been instructed, even in the hour of death, to
" commend our Spirits into the hands of that God

---

[a] Communion Service.

of truth who has redeemed them," " in hope of eternal life, which he, who cannot lie has promised;" and in the cheering and assured confidence, that " he, in whom we have believed, is able to keep that which we have committed to him until that day."

" So we preach, and so ye have believed." When we appear before you in this sacred place, and on this holy day, we claim not " to have dominion over your faith ;" but fain would we be fellow-helpers of your joy," by endeavouring to convince you of the value and importance of "those things in which you have been instructed;" by faithfully discharging " the ministry of reconciliation ;" and by "testifying, both to small and great, repentance towards God, and faith in our Lord Jesus Christ." And while we discharge the ministry committed unto us, you also, by your attendance here, seem to say unto us, what Cornelius expressed in words ; " Now therefore are we all here present before God, to hear all things that are commanded thee of God."—We have already alluded to some of those things, which are commanded us of God, and in which you have been instructed ; and we purpose so to address you, that you may not be wholly at a loss how to ascertain " the *certainty* of those things in which you have been instructed." It is desirable that we should always " be put in remembrance of

these things, even though we know them, and
are established in the present truth;" that we
should be instructed in their several uses and
applications, and be reminded of their certainty.
It is desirable for ourselves, that we may not " let
them slip," but " take the more earnest heed to
them," and not " neglect so great a salvation."
It is desirable for the continual benefit of all that
have yet to learn these things, that they also may
see on how solid a foundation the hope of a
Christian is built.

The topic, which is to form one prominent
feature in the discourses of the Hulsean Lecturer,
has been so often and so largely discussed, that
he cannot, perhaps, select any department of the
evidences for the truth of Christianity, abundant
and various as they are, in which he has not, in
some measure, been anticipated. But it is because
these subjects are important, rather than because
they are novel, that they demand our attentive
investigation. It is from the circumstance, that
many will *listen* to the discussion of such topics,
who might not have either opportunity or inclination to *read* much respecting them, that the
utility of preaching is to be estimated, both as to
this, and other, subjects of Christian instruction.
The preacher may not advance any thing substantially new. But the subjects themselves, of
which he treats, may have hitherto obtained only

an imperfect attention from some of those whom
he addresses; and the renewed consideration of
the same extensive and interesting subjects may
not be without its use with respect to others;
especially if the preacher's plan, or his method of
illustration, present them in some point of view
in which they have been less generally contemplated. He will probably select some line of
argument, which has already afforded satisfaction
to his own mind; which he conceives calculated
to elucidate the difficulties, and obviate the doubts,
which may suggest themselves to the mind of the
serious inquirer. And such a view will, therefore, at least have the recommendation, that it is
exhibited by one, who has inquired for himself into
the grounds of his belief; who is prepared to
avow his own conviction of the futility and falsehood of all the theories and objections of the
infidel; and who is at the same time ready to
give to every one, who stands in the posture of
a candid inquirer, " a reason of the hope that is in
him." With " meekness and with fear" would
we do this; with that meek and lowly heart to
which alone God will " teach his way;" and with
that " meekness towards all men," which re-
strains the bitter word, and the judgment of uncharitableness. We are desirous also to maintain
that " fear of God, which is the beginning of
wisdom;" and which alone consists with that

C

" good understanding," which can enable us to judge rightly of what professes to come from him. Nor must we omit to cherish a fear respecting ourselves. Even when we seem to have attained the fullest conviction, we should still bear in mind, that " he, that thinketh he standeth, must take heed lest he fall;" and we must also " fear, lest, a promise being left us by God of entering into his rest, any of us should seem to come short of it."

In such a temper of mind let us pursue our inquiries respecting "the certainty of those things in which we have been instructed." For the present let it suffice, to specify and explain the *method* which we propose to adopt. Perhaps it may be considered in some respects a new one; not certainly new in its principle, nor in the arguments and topics which we shall discuss; but yet perhaps new in the extent to which we shall apply that principle, and in the form and aspect which arguments, already familiar, may assume, when they are so arranged and discussed. We shall proceed, however, upon a principle, which, though not generally adopted, is as little novel as Christianity itself; which the Apostles themselves have taught us, at the same time that they also furnish the materials to which it is to be applied. We propose to consider the New Testament, not only as a directory in matters of Christian faith and practice, which, if Christianity be from God, demands our implicit obedience; but as being also *a repository of the several arguments in proof of the divine original of the Gospel.* We contend that Jesus and his Apostles have themselves appealed to the several evidences of the truth and divine authority of the religion which they taught; and that, since they have so stated them, and reasoned upon them, the Christian, who *understands* the authorized records of his own religion, can be as little at a loss with respect to the reasons for his belief in the Gospel, as confessedly he ought to be, with respect to the doctrines which it requires him to receive, and the precepts which it commands him to obey.

The principle which I have now briefly stated, and which will hereafter be more fully illustrated, will indeed apply to a considerable portion of the Acts of the Apostles, and of the Epistolary writings of the New Testament. But the materials furnished by the Evangelists are so abundant, that we must content ourselves with the endeavour to embody and elucidate the arguments and reasonings advanced in the *discourses of Jesus himself.* But lest we should appear to be proceeding upon unsafe or unwarrantable grounds, we will now explain in what manner the principle may be deduced; at what period in the Christian argument we may have recourse to it; and the advantages which it offers to the inquirer.

I. In the important passage, which we read to
you as our text, and which forms the preface to
the Gospel by St. Luke, the Evangelist distinctly
asserts, that certain facts had occurred in his
time, of which those, who were eye-witnesses of
them, had widely promulgated the knowledge by
oral instruction; that others had committed that
information to writing; and that he also had
deemed it expedient himself to undertake a similar
narrative for the benefit of Theophilus; with the
design, that inasmuch as he had already been
informed respecting these things by word of
mouth, he might now, by means of an authentic
written narrative, further be assured of the certainty of those oral instructions, and of the safety
with which he might rely upon the accuracy of
those accounts which he had heard[a]. The matters
which the Evangelist relates are a series of facts,
and also a series of discourses which were delivered upon the several occasions he has specified.
Upon such facts and discourses, those who had
been eye and ear-witnesses grounded the whole
system of Christian doctrine. And the Evangelist
evidently conceived that Theophilus would both
better understand those instructions, and more
easily discover their truth, if furnished with that
assistance, which a comprehensive and orderly

---

[a] "Ἵνα ἐπιγνῷς περὶ ὧν κατηχήθης λόγων τὴν ᾿ΑΣΦΑΛΕΙΑΝ.
v. 4.

narrative of such matters would afford. History, of whatever kind, is chiefly valuable because of the inferences which may be drawn from the events and experience of past ages, for our own practical direction. But never did such consequences so immediately and obviously result from any facts, as the doctrines and discoveries of the Christian religion from the transactions and proceedings by which it was established. The religion itself, in all its leading peculiarities, principally consists in a statement of the design of those facts, and in the application of this knowledge as the occasion and motive of repentance, faith, and obedience. If then we can be satisfied that the *narrative* of the facts is correct, we may employ it for the purpose which the historians designed it to serve; and see whether it justifies the inferences drawn from those facts by the founder and his followers.

The Gospel of St. John contains fewer facts than the other Gospels, but a more copious record of the discourses of Jesus. He seldom, indeed, notices any fact, except for the purpose of explaining the occasion of our Lord's discourses and reasonings, and of the debates which his hearers held among themselves. And, near the conclusion of his Gospel, he tells us the design with which he wrote, and points out the inferences which he conceives to follow from what he has recorded:

" Many other signs truly did Jesus in the presence
of his disciples, which are not written in this book;
but these are written, that ye might believe that
Jesus is the Christ, the Son of God; and that
believing ye might have life through his name[a]."

If then an author has thus stated to us the
object of his work; if he declares his conviction
that what he has written directs us to a certain
conclusion; we have only to consider the premises
upon which he builds it, in order to ascertain its
correctness and certainty. The materials upon
which to reason are fully given; but the argument
is not drawn out in form by the Evangelists themselves; for they have only narrated certain facts,
and recorded certain discourses. But those discourses contain such arguments, and are connected
with such facts, that if we have reason to believe
that they were delivered by him to whom they are
ascribed, and that the facts to which they refer,
and which are related so circumstantially, are
correctly related, then no considerate person can
reasonably doubt that the Religion which we
profess is from God; for the Gospel is found to
be its own witness, defender, and apologist, in the
very contents of its acknowledged records. We
do not say of the Gospel history, as the Mahometan
says of the Koran, that it is itself a miracle, and

---

[a] John xx. 30, 31.

that it proves in that way its divine original; but we do say, that the Gospels supply us with materials, .upon which we can reason for ourselves; and that the result of every line of argument suggested by their contents is uniformly conclusive in favour of the divinity of the Religion which they teach. Not only do the style and method, the temper and completeness, of the Gospel narratives offer to an observing reader many internal indications of the genuineness and credibility of the records; but, also, in the very contents of those records, we find assistance in examining the question with respect to the external evidence of the Religion proposed to us therein. For, as will hereafter appear, the discourses of Jesus alone bring before us so many of the leading arguments in favour of the divinity of his mission, as to be almost sufficient of themselves, if rightly understood, and duly weighed, to establish the inquirer in the belief of Christianity.

II. Probably it will be here observed, that our proposed inquiry proceeds upon the assumption, that the writings which we employ are genuine and authentic. It certainly does; and yet we do not propose to enter on that discussion. For we suppose, that both the genuineness and authenticity of the Gospel history have been so often investigated, and so fully proved, by evidence more complete and diversified than can be brought forward in corroboration of any other history whatever, that no one, who has at all qualified himself to form an opinion, would venture to deny that the question is set at rest for ever. In fact, there is less danger that we should doubt the authenticity and credibility of these documents, than that we should neglect to use them as such; much danger lest we should consider them less seriously, that we should embrace the consequences which follow from their truth, less resolutely, and less unreservedly, than in all sober reason we are bound to do. We might, if it were indispensably necessary for your satisfaction, immediately begin to ask you, how you could account for the establishment and propagation, nay even for the first publication, of Christianity, unless upon the supposition, that *some* such facts occurred. We might demand of you an answer to Leslie's celebrated argument, from the continual observance of the Christian ordinances; from their avowed object, and the institution of them in the very age, and at the time, of the events which they commemorate. But we should do this with the conviction, that you would succeed no better than the acute Middleton, even though you also attempted it for twenty years[a]. We

---

[a] See Jones's Preface to Leslie's Short and Easy Method with the Deists, in the edition published by the Society for Promoting Christian Knowledge.

might challenge you to shew how you can account
for the reception of these writings, at the time
when the verbal instructions of the declared
writers were fresh in the recollection of those who
heard them, nay even while they were yet alive,
unless they had been their genuine productions.
We might remind you of the opportunities of
accurate information which these writers had enjoyed; of the improbability that the narrative
which they committed to writing would differ
from that, which they constantly published by
word of mouth, which they began to declare
immediately after the events had happened, in the
very place where they occurred, in the hearing,
and in defiance, of those, who were interested and
disposed to contradict their statement. Such a
contradiction was impossible. For when they
stated, that "Jesus was a man approved of God by
miracles, and wonders, and signs, which God did
by him in the midst of them," the Apostles of Jesus
could add, "as ye yourselves also know." They
"could not but testify the things which they had
seen and heard;" and their testimony was incon-
trovertible, and uncontradicted, except with regard
to the consequences which they deduced from the
facts, and the system which they promulgated
in the world, by the command, and according to
the instructions, of their Master himself. There
have been those, indeed, who have denied that

there is any difference between history and fable; and who therefore contend, that we can place no reliance upon the testimony which evinces the reasonableness of our faith, and that nothing is certain but Metaphysical truth[a]. That which they would substitute for Christianity is uncertain indeed; but their very statement sufficiently betrays a conviction, that nothing, except that which subverts the credit of all history whatever, can undermine the foundation upon which we ground the authenticity of the Scriptures; and that he who has, in whatever method, retained or regained a conviction of that nature, has already entered on the path, which, if pursued, will assuredly conduct him to a belief of the divinity of the Gospel. For, having been so far disposed to allow the credibility of the Christian story, as to be willing, with candour and attention, to peruse its records, he will perceive that "Christianity was founded on argument" both by Jesus and his Apostles. The acknowledged reality and character of certain facts, and the prior existence of certain prophecies, form the basis of their reasonings. And the more we consider these reasonings, in connexion with the occasions

---

[a] See the citations from a French writer, in the Appendix to Bishop Van Mildert's Boyle's Lectures, Vol. II. p. 516, 517. His Lordship justly remarks, that the resolution, "*je m'abstiendrai toujours d'entrer dans la discussion des faits*," "involves *an implied concession* of no small importance."

upon which they were advanced, and with reference to the circumstances to which they allude,
the more decided will be our conviction even of
the credibility of those facts themselves; and the
more readily also shall we acquiesce in the conclusion, that the nature of those facts, the whole
design which is displayed in them, and the
manner of its accomplishment, bespeak not merely
the divine permission, but the special intention
and interposition of God, that he might "give
witness of his Son."

III. You will already have perceived, that we
are not about to discuss such questions connected
with the evidences of our religion, as might lead
us to any depths of abstract reasoning. Yet we
mean not to undervalue such. In their place, for
the refutation of objections which proceed upon
such grounds, and for the satisfaction of those,
whose minds are harassed with difficulties of that
nature, such abstruse inquiries have their use
and value. But the belief of Christianity does not
result from these only, or chiefly. There is a
path which humbler minds may pursue, and which
leads to the same end by a less intricate and
circuitous route; nor need the wisest and most
discerning be ashamed to walk therein. Take
the Bible itself into your hands, and inquire how
the religion of Jesus was first offered to the acceptance of mankind; upon what grounds, and

with what arguments it was then defended and
enforced. And if you are unable to shew that the
faith of those, who in that age embraced it, was
irrational, you will feel obliged to allow the sufficiency of its evidence, and that we can have no
plea for rejecting it. Examine, indeed, as accurately as you please, every objection, whether
of an historical or metaphysical nature; but still
remember the abundance, the strength, and the
consistency of the direct arguments in its favour;
and beware how you suffer objections and theories,
which in fact do not interfere with that positive
evidence, to weaken its impression on your mind.

I am desirous to set before you, as faithfully
and distinctly as I can, the evidences of Christianity as they are presented in the discourses of
our Lord, and in the accompanying narrative of
the Evangelists. We are apt either wholly to
neglect, or imperfectly to attend to, this view of
the subject. Yet I know not any writings, in
which the state of the question is so fully, strikingly, and satisfactorily exhibited. It is, perhaps,
not too much to assert, that the vindication of
his mission by Jesus himself is such as ought
to silence, if not to reclaim, the unbeliever; but
it is undoubtedly such, as affords an ever present
and effectual means for confirming the faith of
the believer. Almost every chapter of the Evangelic records instructs us, not only in Christian

doctrine, and duty, but in those arguments and considerations, which persuasively teach " the certainty of those things in which we have been instructed ;" and which may, in an hour of doubt and temptation, recall the conviction to our minds.

A disposition too generally exists, to consider the question of evidence, as something apart from the Bible ; as something which we ought to study before we venture to make ourselves acquainted with the Bible. But a knowledge, a full and accurate knowledge, of its contents, is necessary, that we may judge of the force and application of *any* of the arguments in favour of Christianity ; and that we may also ascertain whether there is ground for the several objections, which some have thought proper to advance. I believe that he, who has carefully read the Scriptures, particularly in the original, will find his faith very little harassed by objections and cavils ; for he will have seen that they have seldom any foundation, but in the objector's ignorance of the Bible, or in his misinterpretation of it, or sometimes, we fear, in wilful perversion. So that the objector is generally combating the phantom of his own brain ; and those things, which the Scriptures really narrate, reveal, and require, still rest on the same evidence, and authority. We even contend, that the Scriptures actually *include* a statement of the evidences for the religion which they teach. We refer to our Lord's discourses in corroboration of this remark. We would say to the inquirer, examine their connexion; analyze the reasonings advanced in them; compare all that you know of your own heart and life, and all that you have observed of human nature, with the appeals which are made by our Lord to the conscience. And we confidently believe that he, who has done this, will be previously fortified against the reasonings of the infidel; and will have attained a conviction of the divinity, wisdom, and value, of the Gospel, of which it will not be easy to deprive him. Without such a knowledge as that we have been describing, he is not in fact qualified to judge aright. He may refuse to believe, but he has never yet had sufficient reason to disbelieve; he may hesitate and waver, but he has never yet taken the method which can lead him to a solid and considerate decision.

We are also apt to consider the question of evidence in such a way, that the affections are not warmed, and the heart remains unmoved, even when with the understanding we assent to truths and realities so unspeakably important. We are apt to lose sight of the nature, extent, and obligations, of that into which we are inquiring; and we lay aside the inquiry, perhaps, with as little religious emotion, as if we had satisfactorily settled some question of science, taste, or criticism. But this

is not a question of mere judgment, curiosity, or
temporary interest. It inquires into the truth of
a scheme, which embraces the concerns of time
and eternity, and professes to provide for both;
but whose threatenings are as alarming to the
ungodly, as its promises are consolatory to the
faithful. The Scripture continually puts us into
a practical posture, summoning the whole man
to give judgment on this awfully important subject.
When it has advanced what may justly convince
the understanding, it then addresses the conscience; probes and dissects the heart, and lays
open all that hardens, deludes, and defiles it;
shews to us what drags down the affections, and
what darkens the understanding. These moral
causes of unbelief, which leave some undecided
and inconsistent as Christians, and which confirm
others in infidelity, are abundantly specified in
Scripture. The view, which we propose to take
of the evidences, is thus invested with a practical
character. Not that the strict accuracy of our investigation, and the hardihood with which we ought
to embrace and abide by the consequences of
it, need at all be diminished by an attention to
such considerations. Yet at the same time, also,
that we resolve carefully to scrutinize the arguments in defence of Christianity, we are bound,
both by the nature of the case, by reason, and
by interest, to remember that eternal life is too

important a stake to be ventured either upon a mere 'cavil, or even a plausible objection; much less to be sacrificed to any of those unholy and temporizing motives, which so often give both existence and permanence to our doubts respecting religious truth.

In endeavouring to illustrate the remarks, which have now been offered, it will be impracticable to review *all* our Lord's discourses, and the facts to which they refer, in chronological order. This would, indeed, make us more completely familiar with the way in which the evidences of Christianity were at first proposed, with the effects successively produced, and with the progress of the demonstration; but it would lead to frequent repetition, as well as to a less condensed, and less comprehensive, view of the subject. It would perhaps, therefore, be expedient to consider only a few of our Lord's discourses; or even, if such there be, some single one, which brings the several heads of evidence together. Now such a summary we find in the discourse recorded in the fifth Chapter of St. John's Gospel; which contains, I believe, more orderly, distinctly, and fully, than any other, the leading arguments in behalf of our Lord's mission and character. That discourse consists of *three* distinct portions. The *first* of these contains a full and awakening statement of the

pretensions which Jesus advanced, in answer to
the objections of the Jews, and in arrest of the
hasty decision, and murderous intentions, which
their rulers had adopted, because he had cured the
impotent man on the sabbath day. The *second* division contains an appeal to five important heads
of evidence in support of those pretensions. In
the *third*, our Lord states the fact of the infidelity
of the great body of the Jews; and notices, in
a striking and forcible manner, several of the
principles and errors, which were tending to, and
ultimately produced, that result; and which, being
for the most part common to all mankind, under
the form and modifications which their respective
circumstances produce, ever have been, and still
are amongst ourselves, the leading causes of
avowed, suppressed, and practical unbelief.

We shall bring forward what we have to offer to
your consideration, in the order suggested by that
discourse; not only entering upon a complete
analysis of it, but also employing it as a directory
for the convenient arrangement of many other
detached observations, and of the facts and prophecies to which those observations refer. The
first portion of our Lectures will be occupied in
considering the several statements which Jesus
made of his pretensions up to the period when
he delivered the discourse in question.—We shall
then consider the appeals which from that time

D

he began to make to the evidences in support of his mission and character; collecting under each of the five heads of evidence specified on that occasion, what our Lord elsewhere advanced on the same topics ; and afterwards considering such as are omitted in that discourse, so as to complete that department of our subject.--And lastly, we shall conclude with considering the infidelity of the Jews; the principles and dispositions to which our Lord attributes a rejection of the Gospel ; and the awful sanctions both of promise and of threatening with which it is offered to our acceptance.—But it may be expedient further to observe, that it will often be necessary to enter upon a detailed explanation of the *occasion,* upon which the several arguments were advanced; in order that we may place ourselves, as nearly as possible, in the circumstances of those to whom they were addressed. And we may also observe, that our Lord's reasonings upon evidence are *scarcely ever* separated from the statement of his pretensions, and a practical appeal to the conscience ; and that the two latter topics are generally found in connexion with each other, even when unaccompanied by the first.

We have been now endeavouring to shew you, that a full acquaintance with the contents of the Gospel history is as sufficient, as it is necessary, to furnish just views of "the *certainty* of those things

in which we have been instructed." But a full
acquaintance with all that Scripture teaches is
requisite, in order that we may rightly understand
the *nature* of "those things in which we have
been instructed," and in which many of us are
called to instruct others. "Let, then the word of
Christ dwell in us richly in all wisdom." The
more we contemplate for ourselves, and exhibit to
others, the genuine doctrines of Scripture, in the
manner in which Scripture itself reveals them, the
better will our teaching be *understood*, and the
more will it *edify*. The more shall we be "joined
together in unity of spirit, by the doctrine of the
Apostles and Prophets;" the less will heresy or
infidelity disturb, and ignorance and immorality
darken, our Zion; and the more shall we "grow
into a holy temple in the Lord."—Revealed religion is not a metaphysical theory. Many such
have been made, and substituted for religion; but
they have been as unsatisfactory, and as baseless,
as any in philosophy. Thousands more might be
created, as fast as the canvas receives form and
colour from the painter's hand. They *may* speak
the same things as "the law and the testimony;"
if they do not, "it is because there is no light in
them." But a knowledge of the real nature of
Revelation, of its connexion, and extent, and circumstances, would banish all strange doctrines
and devices of men, and would prevent the recur-

rence of the theoretical propensity; just as the Newtonian philosophy subverts our belief of the old philosophical theories, and supplies us with one of real knowledge, because grounded on certain facts. Thus the mind is disciplined to reason, and brought into a habit of calm investigation; is emancipated from the power of imagination; and is taught to prefer plain and sober, though it be yet imperfect truth, to the brightest and most complete vision that fancy ever conjured up. And as theories are not to be adopted as our Religion, so neither are they a legitimate *objection* to it; and for the same reasons. The Gospel comes with higher claims; with facts which challenge our belief; with observations the truth of which all experience has proved, and still does prove; with "the witness of God which he has given us of his Son." Let us not then "make him a liar," by rejecting it; let us not be "moved away from the hope of the Gospel which we have heard;" but rather let us gladly meditate on its declarations, rely upon its promises, desire its consolations, live in obedience to its precepts, and, anticipating the prospects which it holds out to us, "rejoice in hope of the glory of God."

HULSEAN LECTURES

FOR 1821.

<hr>

PART I.

LECTURES III—V.

—0—

STATEMENTS OF JESUS, RESPECTING HIS PRETENSIONS AND THE
OBJECT OF HIS MISSION, WHICH PRECEDED HIS ACTUAL APPEAL
TO THE EVIDENCES IN CONFIRMATION OF THEM.

LECTURE III.

St. John III. 1—3.

There was a man of the Pharisees, named Nicodemus, a ruler of the Jews; the same came to Jesus by night, and said unto him, Rabbi, we know that thou art a teacher come from God; for no man can do these miracles that thou doest, except God be with him. Jesus answered and said unto him, Verily, verily I say unto thee, Except a man be born again, he cannot see the kingdom of God.

To peruse the works of the mighty masters of reason, eloquence, and pathos, with that sensibility to their beauties, which attention and reflection alone can awaken, affords a pleasure, at once pure in its kind, diversified in its form, and salutary in its influence. Those, however, who have accurately studied the discourses of our Lord; who have made themselves familiar with his manner of instruction; who can judge of the propriety of his remarks from a knowledge of that which occasioned them; and still more those, who feel that interest in the subjects on which he treats, which

their importance is so fitted to excite;—all such
will be disposed to assent to the declaration;
"Never man spake like this man." "His word
is with power;" for "he knew what was in
man." He appeals to the conscience in a brief,
yet impressive, manner. He displays the attribute of Omniscience, "which understands long
before the thoughts" of the heart; manifests an
acquaintance with the intentions of his hearers;
and answers the doubt, objection, and cavil, when
"scarce struggling into birth," or, at least, not yet
clothed in words. The questions upon which he
decides, without hesitation, embarrassment, or
ambiguity, are such as calm the fears, remove the
doubts, and answer the inquiries, which have in
all ages exercised the sagacity of our fellow men.
He opens to us the door of hope, points out the
objects of faith, and describes the pathway of
obedience. He speaks as befits one who "has
the words of eternal life;" with that solemnity,
which challenges our attention; with that authority,
which evidences not the presumptuous confidence
of the conceited sciolist, but the deep and abiding
conviction of him, who "speaks of what he has
known, and who testifies what he had seen."
And as he declares to us the awful alternative of
either believing in him, or of dying in our sins;
so he also directs our attention to those several
facts, considerations, and inquiries, by which we

may be assured that he "came forth from God;" and that " no one cometh to the Father, but by him, as the appointed way, the truth, and the life."

We proposed to consider our Lord's discourses with more especial reference to the last mentioned topic; having previously noticed such as inform us respecting the claims which he advanced.— Now the *earliest* statements of our Lord respecting his mission and character and office, are both important in themselves, and also furnish a key for the right understanding of his subsequent discourses. To several of these, therefore, we shall direct your attention; all of them such as were delivered previously to any of those reasonings respecting the *evidences* of his mission, upon which he entered at a more advanced period of his ministry. Such is the conference with Nicodemus; and that with the Samaritan woman, and some of her countrymen. Such also is the account given by the first three Evangelists of the general tenor of our Lord's teaching in Galilee; and, more especially, the account given by St. Luke of his discourse in the synagogue of Nazareth. Such also is the opening portion of the discourse recorded in St. John's fifth chapter, which may, in some measure, be considered a continuation of the discourse with Nicodemus. A cursory review of these several discourses of our Lord, will form the first general division of

our Lectures; and will introduce us to the consideration of the second portion of the last mentioned discourse, which contains our Lord's first
appeal to the evidences in confirmation of his
claims.

The remainder of our time on this day will be
occupied by the consideration of our Lord's conference with Nicodemus, which took place at an
early period of his ministry. And it will be expedient, in order to the better illustration of our
Lord's remarks on that occasion, first to take
some notice of the circumstances recorded by
St. John in his two first chapters, and of the
particular observations with which he introduces
his narrative of this conference.

Very shortly after his first miracle at Cana in
Galilee, Jesus went up to the passover at Jerusalem. He then, for the first time, shewed his
zeal against the profanation of his Father's house,
by the removal of the traders, and their mer-
chandize, from the outer court of the temple.
For the full proof of his "authority to do these
things," he referred to the future sign of his
resurrection from the dead: declaring, figuratively
indeed, but in a manner which the event proved
to be distinctly and accurately prophetic, that
when they should "destroy the temple of his
body, he would raise it up in three days." Even
his disciples, who had already believed on him,

did not understand this " till after he was risen
from the dead." But in consequence of the testimony of John the Baptist, of the more than
human knowledge displayed by Jesus, and of the
manifestation of his glory by the miracle at Cana,
they had already received sensible, intelligible,
and sufficient evidence, to justify a belief in his
prophetic character; even though they did not at
first understand the purport of all that he said,
and the reason of all that he did. And, at this
passover, Jesus exhibited, and, as it should seem,
very publicly, similar proofs of his divine commission. Although we are not told the particulars respecting them, we are fully apprized of their
effects upon those who were present. " When he
was in Jerusalem, at the passover, in the feast-
day, many believed on his name, when they saw
the miracles which he did." And afterwards,
" when he was come into Galilee, the Galileans
received him, having seen all the things that he
did at Jerusalem at the feast[a]." But Jesus,
" knowing all men, and not needing that any
should testify of man, because he knew what was
in man[b]," was well aware beforehand, as the
event has fully shewn to us, that much fuller
evidence would be necessary so to convince them
of his heavenly mission, as to dispose them finally

---

[a] John ii. 23. iv. 45.   [b] John ii. 24, 25.

to receive him in all his offices, and not to be
offended in him, because of what he came to do,
and to teach.. To such he "did not, commit,"
or trust, "himself," by a premature declaration
of his office and purposes. But this general rule
was not without exception; as the case of Nicodemus, and of the Samaritans, will shew. To
them he made a more explicit declaration of
himself than for some time he did to others, even
than he made to the twelve disciples. And the
reason of this certainly was, that the rule, which
prudence, guided by a divine knowledge, led him
generally to adopt, did not apply to them. He acted,
in each of these cases, according to his accurate
knowledge of what was proper and expedient.
This observation, premised in fact by the Evangelist himself before he relates these incidents,
should be attentively borne in mind in the consideration of both of them; and we trust that the
distinction between these two cases, compared
with each other, and also with the general conduct
of our Lord during his ministry, will appear from
what we offer in this, and a subsequent, discourse.
This observation of the Evangelist, is indeed one
of great importance; for it explains the principle
upon which Jesus acted *throughout* his ministry.
And. as an important rule for the interpretation
of the Gospels is suggested by it, we must not
lose sight of it while we endeavour to ascertain,

from some of our Lord's earliest discourses, the several views in which he places his character, and office.

We are informed, by the Evangelist, immediately afterwards, that "there was a man of the Pharisees, named Nicodemus, a ruler of the Jews, who came to Jesus by night," and made the following profession of his own belief, and probably that of some others; together with the reasons upon which it was founded. "Rabbi, we know that thou art a teacher come from God; for no man can do these miracles that thou doest, except God be with him." This was a declaration, which implied his full conviction of the reality of those miracles; and which shews that he drew from them that inference, in the propriety of which the records of the Old Testament would abundantly instruct him; which must ever be drawn by every unprejudiced inquirer from an evident and well-attested miracle; and which, indeed, cannot consistently be set aside, except by subverting all reliance on human senses and human testimony, or by proving that there is no God to reveal his will to man. It was not upon such grounds that the rulers and people of the Jews ever hesitated to admit the authority of Jesus; but because their prejudices, and fondly cherished expectations, were painfully counteracted and disappointed. The miracles, and some parts of our

Lord's teaching, frequently operated to produce a conviction in his favour, and that apparently deep, decided, and vehement in its character. But the current was always arrested in its course, and ultimately seemed to be wholly diverted in another direction, by his faithful and precise annunciation at such times of the mysterious and unwelcome truths, which must be received by all that would be his disciples. "Some even of the rulers believed on him;" but the temporal penalties which the power and unbelief of their brethren would draw down upon them, deterred them even from advancing so far as Nicodemus. In *him* our Lord had a candid judge, and a willing disciple; one impeded, as much as his fellow countrymen, by the peculiar prejudices of a Jew and a Pharisee; but who, amidst all the doubts and difficulties which perplexed his mind, and amidst all the weakness and fear which, in some measure, kept him back from an open acknowledgement of his faith, still retained that hardihood of a candid and reasonable mind, which resolves, and which sooner or later acts upon the resolution, to abide by truth, however unwelcome, which is evidenced to be such by undeniable and sufficient proofs. He comes to our Lord with a conviction, and in a temper, which he seems to have ever retained. He comes with all his prejudices strong, and with his mind imperfectly

apprehending the office of him, whom he respected as "a teacher come from God." But
believing him to be such, he is willing to learn
from him "the way of God more perfectly."
Jesus, therefore, knowing both his imperfect knowledge, and his desire of instruction; and that he
would never employ it to further the hasty and
malignant opposition of his brother Pharisees,
gives to such a one an early, and comprehensive,
though at that period to him a difficult, statement
respecting "the mysteries of the kingdom of
heaven." But Nicodemus adopted, in all its
bearings, the principle which he afterwards recommended to the Jewish council, and which it
becomes us also to adopt, as claiming the assent
of every impartial judge in this matter. "Doth
our law judge any man, before it hear him, and
know what he doeth[a]?" *He* observed the works
and conduct of Jesus, and attentively considered
his instructions. By proceeding in the same way,
we can judge upon grounds as reasonable as he
did; and shall doubtless, come to the same conclusion respecting "Jesus, who is called Christ."

The instructions, which our Lord gave in
answer to the profession of Nicodemus, connect
themselves immediately with the previous decla-

---

[a] See John vii. 51.

rations of the Baptist respecting the near approach of the kingdom of heaven, the baptism with water unto repentance, and the predicted baptism of the Spirit. And we may be well assured, that one who was a member of that council, which sent an official deputation to John to inquire who he was, and why he baptized, was well aware of the tenor and purport of the Baptist's instructions. We cannot, indeed, at all doubt it, when we consider the publicity of his labours, and the inquiring temper of Nicodemus. And we may, with great probability, suppose, that the authoritative act of Jesus in the temple, connected with his miracles, disposed this ruler to suppose, that he was the mightier one of whom John spoke; and either that he was the Christ, or that Prophet whom they expected. If he had also been informed that John had borne witness personally to Jesus, he might have already come to the conclusion, which others afterwards expressed; "John did no miracle, but all things that John spake of this man were true[a]." In some such frame of mind, however, he came to Jesus, and Jesus meets his implied desire of instruction from a divine teacher, by unfolding to him more fully and definitely than John had taught it:

---

[a] John x. 41.

1. The necessity of baptismal and spiritual regeneration, in order to *see* and *enter* into the kingdom of God; either to understand its nature and provisions, or to enter upon the possession of its privileges.

2. The certainty of the mysteries of the kingdom of heaven, as taught by the Son of man, who came down from heaven.

3. The great and crowning event, which would lead to the setting up of that kingdom, with a statement of its origin and design; and the necessity of faith in the Son of God in order to partake of the blessings thereby procured.

4. The condemnation of those, who disbelieve, and its justice evinced by the motives which give rise to such a rejection.

I. The answer which Jesus gives to the declaration with which Nicodemus accosted him, appears, at first sight, abrupt; and it is, in fact, an answer to something implied, rather than expressed, in the words of Nicodemus. But if we bear in mind the observation which the Evangelist has premised, that Jesus "needed not that any should testify of man, because he knew what was in man;" and if we remember also, that Nicodemus declared his confidence in Jesus as a divine teacher, at a time when the Jews were expecting the establishment of the kingdom of God, and after the approach of that kingdom had already

E

been announced by the Baptist; it seems probable that he supposed that the mission of Jesus, sanctioned by miracles, and superior, therefore, to that of the Baptist, had reference to the kingdom which John had proclaimed. And such indeed was the subject, in which Jesus was prepared to instruct those, who allowed him to be "a teacher come from God." He therefore immediately entered upon it with Nicodemus; thereby confirming his suspicions, and meeting his wishes; although he began by a statement which was designed to rectify his erroneous conceptions. "Verily, verily, I say unto thee, Except a man be born again, he cannot see the kingdom of God."

A *Gentile,* when converted to Judaism, abandoned his former principles, and began, as it were, a new life; and they themselves inculcated upon him such a thorough revolution of sentiment, and acknowledged the necessity of it. But a change of the same nature was also requisite for the *Jew,* as the very door and entrance into the kingdom of God. The many incorrect notions, which they had adopted, would be an insuperable obstacle, until they were abandoned, and replaced by others of a wholly different aspect. This Jesus announced in general terms at first; and in words which appear to refer only to obstacles of such a nature as we have just mentioned, whether, in fact, they be Jewish or Gentile prejudices. "Verily, verily, I say unto thee, Except a man be born again, he cannot see the kingdom of God." The verb ($\gamma\epsilon\nu\nu\eta\theta\widehat{\eta}$) being in the past tense, both in this verse, and in a subsequent one, it would, perhaps, be more accurately rendered, "Unless any one has been born (or rather *begotten*) anew, he cannot see the kingdom of God." He does not yet speak of *water* and the *Spirit;* nor does he yet use the expression, "*enter* into the kingdom of God." There seems reason to believe, that this difference of expression is not merely casual; and that in this proposition he does not advance so far as in the subsequent one; but that he speaks only of the disposition to which we have already alluded, viz., a readiness to abandon all those preconceived opinions, which, as long as we resolutely abide by them, oppose the admission of revealed truth; and to embrace those which bear the impress of divine authority, though they may have been unexpected, and are at variance both with our prejudices, and inclinations. This, in fact, seems to parallel another of our Lord's declarations, in which he speaks of the necessity of being "taught of God[a];" and also that of St. Paul, in which he declares, that "no man, speaking by the Spirit

---

[a] John vi. 45.

of God, calleth Jesus accursed; and that no man can say that Jesus is the Lord, but by the Holy Ghost[a]." The same Apostle also laments that the Jews, "being ignorant of God's righteousness, and going about to establish their own righteousness, have not submitted themselves to the righteousness of God; for Christ is the end of the law for righteousness to every one that believeth[b]." "Christ crucified was to the Jews a stumbling-block, and unto the Greeks foolishness;" but he, who had been begotten anew to more correct views of the kingdom of God, would see that "Christ was the power of God, and the wisdom of God;" and thus seeing and believing, would desire to be "baptized in the name of Jesus Christ for the remission of sins, that he might receive the gift of the Holy Ghost[c]."

This further step in the way of salvation by the Gospel, our Lord proceeded to explain to Nicodemus, who misunderstood the former statement, by supposing it to speak of a literal birth. "Jesus answered and said, Except a man be born of water and of the Spirit, he cannot enter into the kingdom of God." The full import of these words Nicodemus certainly could not comprehend; but their general tenor he might have

---

[a] 1 Cor. xii. 3. [b] Rom. x. 3, 4.
[c] 1 Cor. i. 23, 24. Acts ii. 38.

apprehended, from the passages, in which Moses speaks of the *circumcision of the heart,* and in which David prays for the *renewal of a right spirit,* and his *establishment by the free Spirit of God,* in order that, "having been shapen in iniquity, and conceived in sin, he might be made to know wisdom[d]." The same also might he learn from many passages, in which the prophets connect the promise of the Spirit with an allusion to the *pouring out and sprinkling with water,* in order that God might "write his laws upon their hearts in the latter days[e]." And more especially, might he have learnt the meaning of these things, if not, as "the Teacher of Israel," yet as the disciple of the Baptist, who had accompanied the preaching of the kingdom with the administration of baptism; at the same time exhorting to a repentance issuing in reformation, and predicting the baptism of the Spirit. We, at least, comparing the baptismal doctrine of John with these words of our Lord, with the remainder of his teaching, with his last commission to the Apostles, and with their practice and declarations in consequence of it, can surely be at no loss to understand the meaning of our Lord. And we

---

[d] Deut. x. 16; xxx. 6. Psalm li. 5—13.
[e] Isai. xliv. 3—5; lv. 1. Jer. xxxi. 31—34. Ezek. xxxvi. 25—27. See also Numb. xix. 20.

shall not surely doubt, that, although "to be baptized with water and the Holy Ghost, to be
received into Christ's holy Church, and to be
made lively members of the same," is assuredly
"that thing, which by nature we cannot have ;"
yet that "a means by which we receive the same,
and a pledge to assure us thereof," is instituted in
Christ's Church[a]. We, as Christians, have already been instructed to believe, that, "after that
the kindness and love of God our Saviour towards
man appeared, not by works of righteousness
which we have done, but according to his mercy
God hath saved us, by the *washing of regeneration,*
and the *renewing of the Holy Ghost;* which he
hath shed upon us abundantly through Jesus
Christ our Saviour; that, being justified by his
grace, we should be made heirs, according to the
hope of eternal life[b]." This is certainly the instituted, covenanted, and ordinary way, in which we
are brought to "*enter* into the kingdom of God ;"
by which we are enabled to walk therein as the
sons of God, and to grow in grace and holiness,
till we are made meet, by means of God's word,
and the various ordinances of his house, to be "partakers of the inheritance of the saints in light."

The end for which these doctrines are revealed,

---

[a] Baptismal Service, and Catechism.

[b] Titus iii. 4—7.

and these assistances provided, is undoubtedly
this, "that we may be sanctified wholly; and that
our whole spirit, and soul, and body, may be preserved blameless unto the coming of our Lord
Jesus Christ[c]." Our Lord obviously refers to this
subject, when he says to Nicodemus, "That which
is born of the flesh, is flesh; and that which is
born of the Spirit, is spirit." And it must occur
to every one who is acquainted with the language
of the New Testament, that a like phraseology is
employed in many other passages; perhaps in
almost all that treat of the nature, and operation,
of human depravity; and of that "renovation in
the spirit of our mind," by which we are "created
anew in knowledge, righteousness, and true holiness, after the image of him that first created
us[d]." By our natural birth, we also, as well as
Adam, are made "living souls;" but by our
descent from him, we also partake of that "fault
and corruption of the nature of every man, that
naturally is engendered of the offspring of Adam;
whereby man is very far gone from original righteousness, and is of his own nature inclined to evil,
so that the flesh lusteth always contrary to the

---

[c] 1 Thess. v. 23.

[d] See more particularly from Rom. vii. 14. to the 17th verse
of the following chapter. 1 Cor. ii. 9—16. and iii. 1—4. xv.
42—54. Gal. v. 13. to the end, and vi. 1—8.

Spirit[a]." The *spirit* of man, the intellectual and more exalted part of his nature, is, in consequence of the fall, so impaired and disordered, as to have lost its ascendancy over the *body* and *soul*, the inferior and merely animal part of his frame; which in another passage is called the *flesh*, with its *affections and lusts*[b]." "In our flesh dwelleth no good thing;" for "we see a law in our members warring against the law of our mind, and bringing us into captivity to the law of sin which is in our members;" so that "they that are in the flesh cannot please God." "But," adds the Apostle, "ye are not in the flesh, but in the spirit, if so be that the Spirit of God dwell in you[c]." For, as our Lord observes, "that which is born of the flesh, is flesh; and that which is born of the Spirit, is spirit." And we must derive this spiritual life from "the second Adam, who was made a quickening spirit[d];" for he "baptizeth with the Holy Ghost[e]," and has instituted the external and visible sign of water in baptism, as a symbol of the inward and spiritual grace of regeneration by the

---

[a] Article IX. On Original or Birth Sin. — A reference to the remainder of that Article will further shew, how closely our Reformers adhered to the *scriptural* representation of the constitution of our nature, and of the disorder which the fall has occasioned.

[b] Gal. v. 24. [c] Rom. vii. 18, 23; viii. 8, 9.

[d] 1 Cor. xv. 45. [e] John i. 33.

Holy Ghost; to be "a means whereby we receive the same, and a pledge to assure us thereof."

He who has observed, and duly considered, this Scriptural view of the constitution of man, as consisting of "body, soul, and spirit[f]," will find that many passages have appeared obscure, principally in consequence of inattention to the uniformity and consistency which characterises the language of Scripture on this subject. He will see how the word of God "pierces even to the dividing asunder of soul and spirit[g]," in its accurate descriptions of the state of human nature; and how wondrously the blessings which it announces are adapted to the spiritual necessities of man. A summary of the design of the Gospel, as "the ministration of the Spirit[h]," and of its necessity in order to the regeneration and salvation of mankind, is given by our Lord to Nicodemus; the whole of which we will now cite, in the hope that the preceding remarks may have tended to elucidate them. "Verily, verily, I say unto thee, Except a man be born of water and of the Spirit, he cannot enter into the kingdom of God. That which is born of the flesh, is flesh; and that

---

[f] The original words are σῶμα, ψυχή, and πνεῦμα; and σάρξ is frequently used, and contrasted with πνεῦμα, as including the two first.

[g] Heb. iv. 12.　　　　[h] 2 Cor. iii. 8.

which is born of the Spirit, is spirit. Marvel not
that I sàid unto thee, Ye must be born again.
The wind bloweth where it listeth, and thou hearest
the sound thereof, but canst not tell whence it
cometh, and whither it goeth; so is every one
that is born of the Spirit."

By the comparison employed in the conclusion
of these words, our Lord teaches us, that although
he, "who is born of the Spirit," cannot discover
the cause, or comprehend the mode, of the operations of the Spirit, this does not disprove their
necessity, or their reality; for he can perceive their
effects. To adopt the language of an Apostle on
this subject, such an one knows that the "natural
man (ψυχικός ἄνθρωπος) receiveth not the things of
the Spirit of God, neither can he know them,
because they are spiritually discerned[a]." He
knows that there is a "spirit in man; and that the
inspiration of the Almighty giveth them understanding[b];" so that "he that is spiritual judgeth all
things." He knows that "if he lives after the flesh,
he shall die; but if through the spirit, he mortifies
the deeds of the body, he shall live;"—that "if
he have not the Spirit of Christ, he is none of his;
and if Christ be in him, the body is dead, because
of sin, but the spirit is life, because of righteousness[c];" that "they that are Christ's, have crucified

---

[a] 1 Cor. ii. 14, 15.   [b] Job xxxii. 8.
[c] Rom. viii. 13, 9, 10.

the flesh, with the affections and lusts;"—that
"if he walks in the spirit, he shall not fulfil the
lusts of the flesh[d];"—that "as many as are led by
the Spirit of God, they are the Sons of God;"
—that "the Spirit itself beareth witness with their
spirit, that they are the children of God; and if
children, then heirs; heirs of God, and joint-heirs
with Christ[e]."

Thus comprehensive and important is this first
and most difficult portion of the discourse of our
Lord to Nicodemus. We shall now do little more
than refer to the remaining parts of it; especially
as some of the views, which they contain, will
hereafter come under our notice, particularly in
the discourse delivered after the cure of the
impotent man; which is a continuation and
enlargement of some of the statements made to
Nicodemus.

II. Surprised and perplexed by what he had
just heard, Nicodemus asked, "How can these
things be? Jesus answered and said unto him,
Art thou a master of Israel, and knowest not
these things? Verily, verily, I say unto thee, We
speak that we do know, and testify that we have
seen, and ye receive not our witness. If I have
told you earthly things and ye believe not, how
shall ye believe, if I tell you of heavenly things?

---

[d] Gal. v. 24, 16.   [e] Rom. viii. 14—17.

And no man hath ascended up to heaven, but he that came down from heaven, even the Son of man, which is in heaven." As if he had said, " I have spoken of things, respecting which the oracles of God, committed to you, are by no means silent. I have described them in phraseology which you yourselves have also employed upon a similar subject. I declare them from my own knowledge and observation. And yet you do not seem disposed to receive my witness respecting them, though you have had evidence that I am a divine teacher; and though that evidence has induced you to think me such. Yet I am sent to reveal truths still more sublime. But if ye believe not what I tell you respecting "earthly things," which relate personally to yourselves, which are attested by your own experience, and which can be illustrated by allusion to terrestrial and familiar objects; "how will ye believe, if I tell you of heavenly things," which are so remote from your apprehensions; which none ever yet knew, which none could ever communicate, but the Son of man. For no other man hath ascended into heaven, but he came down from heaven; for heaven is his native and peculiar abode.

III. Having thus adopted, for the first time, the title of the Son of man, in a manner which clearly implied that he applied it to himself, and the prophetic usage of which Nicodemus would probably recollect[a], Jesus proceeded further to instruct Nicodemus respecting the method in which the Son of man would accomplish his mission, and alluded, prophetically, to the closing scene of his life. He compared with it the last miracle of the life of Moses, which bore a typical resemblance to it; thereby again stating respecting the kingdom of the Son of man, what would by no means be conformable to the expectations of a Jew. "As Moses lifted up the serpent in the wilderness, even so must the Son of man be lifted up, that whosoever believeth in him should not perish, but have everlasting life." Asserting, once and again, the necessity of faith in the Son of man, in order to a reception of the benefits of his mission, Jesus yet more distinctly announced to his disciple the universal extent of the intended mercy, the spiritual nature of the blessings which it conferred, the pure source from whence they flowed, and the divine original of the Son of man, who was sent to reveal, and to communicate them. "God so loved the world, that he gave his only begotten Son, that whosoever believeth in him, should not perish, but have everlasting life. For God sent not his Son into the world, to condemn the world, but that the world through him might be saved."

---

[a] Dan. vii. 13, 14.

The truths conveyed in these words are, indeed, familiar to our ears, and memories, and understandings. They are truths in which we have been again and again instructed. We have need, however, to see to it, that, while we do in words, and even in our judgment, acknowledge their certainty, we do not "frustrate the grace of God, and receive it in vain." We have need frequently to call to mind, that as the comforts and prospects which they offer to us, are great and eternal, so the end of them "that obey not the truth in the love of it," and who are not through it "transformed by the renewing of their minds," is a fearful and a hopeless one. I know not what words can more forcibly represent these things to us, more fully represent to us the justice of our condemnation, and more powerfully call upon us to inquire into the real cause of our unbelief, negligence, and disobedience, than the concluding words of our Lord's discourse.

IV. "He that believeth on him is not condemned; but he that believeth not is condemned already, because he hath not believed in the name of the only begotten Son of God. And this is the condemnation, that light is come into the world, and men loved darkness rather than light, because their deeds are evil. For every one that doeth evil, hateth the light, neither cometh to the light, lest his deeds should be reproved. But he that

doeth truth cometh to the light, that his deeds may
be made manifest, that they are wrought in God."
Men would fain attribute their unbelief to other
causes rather than this. And there are, undoubtedly, "sinful desires of the mind," as well as "of the
flesh." There is a perversity of understanding,
which can offer plausible apologies for error, both
doctrinal, and practical. But we fear that the
cause specified in the text is of more general influence than meets the ken of mortal eye. Even
when we endeavour to analyze our own principles,
we may overlook the love of sin as a primary,
though concealed, cause, whether of infidelity, or
of perversion of the truth. We must, then,
earnestly "examine ourselves whether we be in
the faith." We must see "that the light that is
in us be not darkness; for if it be, how great is
that darkness!" how impenetrable! how dismal!
and how fatal! And the great danger of such
a situation is, not only that we *are* in darkness,
when we walk in the paths of sin, but that we
"*love* darkness rather than light!" For "light is
that which makes manifest," and the lamp of God's
word shews us the appalling view of our guilt, and
condemnation, and danger. We cannot bear such
a light, and we therefore hate it. We will not
come to it, lest our deeds should be reproved. We
become, at length, so habituated to our state, and
so reluctant to change it, that as soon might we

suppose that one who has been brought up in the depths of a mine, or been immured for years in the darksome dungeon, can bear to emerge at once into the light of the midday sun, as that the man, whose principles and conduct are inconsistent with the dictates of religion, will readily subject them to the text of that word of God, which is "a discerner of the thoughts and intents of the heart." Yet the works of darkness are "unfruitful works;" and "the end of them is death;" but, on the contrary, "reproofs of instruction are the way of life." Let us then resolve, to "walk in the light of the Lord;" and to "prove what is the good, and acceptable, and perfect will of God." Let us not defer this resolution; lest our heart become more "hardened through the deceitfulness of sin;" and we at the same time become so familiar with those truths, which ought to undeceive, reform, and sanctify us, as to disqualify *them* from giving, and *ourselves* from receiving, the necessary instruction and conviction. But if we receive the word in an honest and good heart, and press on towards perfection, we shall derive abundantly more satisfaction in the conviction, "that our deeds are wrought in God," than ever the ways of sin could afford. And our security will be as great as our happiness. But those on the contrary, who hate the light of truth, destitute alike of knowledge to direct the steps, and of comfort to rejoice the heart, will walk on still in darkness; until "their feet stumble upon the dark mountains; and while they look for light, the Lord their God turn it into the shadow of death, and make it gross darkness[a]."

[a] Jer. xiii. 16.

LECTURE IV.

MATTHEW IV. 23.

*And Jesus went about all Galilee, teaching in their
synagogues, and preaching the Gospel of the kingdom,
and healing all manner of sickness, and all manner of
disease among the people.*

WE know that " Jesus of Nazareth went about
doing good ;" that he imparted health to the
diseased, consolation to the distressed, and instruction to the ignorant. As in reading the history of the benevolent Howard, so also in perusing
that of Jesus, our admiration is mingled with
a feeling of thankful satisfaction that such an one
has appeared among mortals, gifted with the disposition and the ability to alleviate " the miseries
of this sinful world."—But it is not merely as
a Philanthropist that we must contemplate the
character of Jesus. For at the moment that we
are sympathizing in the joy of those who are
rejoicing because he has dried up their tears, we
find a claim presented to ourselves for somewhat
more than admiration. We find that he has

somewhat to declare to *us,* as well as to the immediate objects of his more than human beneficence. He has excited indeed a deep interest in our minds; but we perceive that his design is not accomplished, unless he can prevail upon us to recognize in himself the features of a messenger of God, and, with unabated interest, and also with implicit obedience, to listen to his heavenly doctrine. And if, after such a discovery, we manifest a disposition to stifle the feelings of admiration, to withdraw our confidence, and to retire from his presence, he suffers us not to depart, till he has changed his tone of invitation into that of solemn, but affectionate, warning, as to the ingratitude, inconsistency, and danger, of disregarding his instructions. We find that we must still follow him, not only for the gratification of our benevolent feelings; not only because we can " eat of the loaves and be filled;" nay, not only because we can " see some miracle done by him," and learn thereby that " God is with him;" but that we may " labour for, and be nourished by, the meat which endureth unto everlasting life, which he, as the Son of man, shall give unto us; for him hath God the Father sealed." And if we ask, " What shall we do, that we may work the works of God?" we hear him declaring, " This is the work of God, that ye believe on him whom he hath sent." We naturally inquire *in what cha-*

racter he is sent; and *what evidence* we have to
assure us that he is, for purposes so important,
" sealed, sanctified, and sent into the world."—
Upon this principle we proposed to conduct our
inquiries; and taking occasion from the brief
statement given in our text, let us now so far
consider the detail of his earlier ministrations, subsequently to the discourse with Nicodemus, as to
learn from his own lips what he says of himself,
and also " what signs he shews that we may see
and believe him."

Subsequently to the solemnities of the Passover
at Jerusalem, and to the conference with Nicodemus, Jesus went from the city into Judea; and,
because John had then retired into Galilee, tar-
ried there for the space of probably six or seven
months, and baptized. But knowing that the
Pharisees were aware, that he had made and baptized even more disciples than John; and probably
apprehending that the Pharisees, being jealous of
his success, might follow the example of Herod,
who had imprisoned John in Galilee; he left
Judea, and journeyed towards Galilee, that he
might labour in the footsteps of his forerunner.
" And he must needs go through Samaria."—
Thither let us accompany him, and behold him,
wearied with his journey, sitting at the well of
Jacob, near the city Sychar. For there shall we
hear his heavenly doctrine, and an explicit avowal

of the character in which he delivered it, at the well-known and interesting interview with a Samaritan woman[a].

As Jesus sat by the well, the woman came to draw water; and Jesus asked for a draught of the water. The request was received with an expression of wonder which almost implied a refusal; because the mutual enmity of the Jews and Samaritans had long prevented all intercourse of a friendly nature. But our Lord, who came to remove the enmity between Jew and Gentile, and to reconcile them to each other, so as to bring them into one body by his cross, checked rather than encouraged her indulgence of this national animosity; and, borrowing, as his custom was, an illustration from the objects immediately before him, in a gradual and familiar manner he led her to the consideration and apprehension of the great truths in which he designed to instruct her.

" If, says he, thou hadst known the gift of God, and who it is that says to thee, Give me to drink, thou wouldest have asked of him, and he would have given thee living water." Her attention and curiosity were excited by the latter expression, which seemed to allude to present and sensible things; but the first clause which pointed out the

---

[a] John iv. 5—42.

divine origin and source of that, concerning which he spoke, seems not to have made so strong an impression. She answers *first* to the last clause of our Lord's remark, " Sir, thou hast nothing to draw with, and the well is deep, from whence then hast thou that living water?" Being also unable to understand the meaning of Jesus in the preceding clause, in which he seemed to her to state that he was a greater one than she supposed, she added; " Art thou greater than our father Jacob, which gave us the well, and drank thereof himself, and his children, and his cattle?" Our Lord did not stay to refute her probably unauthorized claim to be a descendant of Jacob, but proceeded to the more important endeavour to lead her thoughts to that gift of God, of which she yet knew so little, but of which it was his desire to apprize her. " Whosoever drinketh of this water shall thirst again; but whosoever drinketh of the water that I shall give him, shall never thirst; but the water that I shall give him shall be in him a well of water springing up into everlasting life." She evidently did not yet perceive the drift of our Lord's remark; and therefore with a mingled feeling of embarrassment, astonishment, and incredulity, she added, " Sir, give me this water, that I thirst not, neither come hither to draw."—Jesus next proceeded to deal with her in a different manner; but we stay, for a moment, to inquire what was the living water of which he spake.

We know that the prophets described, under this significant image, the future spiritual blessings of the Gospel; and that one passage specifies the particular blessings which were thereby intended. "I will pour water upon him that is thirsty, and floods upon the dry ground; I will pour out *my spirit* upon thy seed, and *my blessing* upon thine offspring[a]." Our Lord afterwards used the same figure on the last and great day of the feast of tabernacles, when they drew from the pool of Siloam, and solemnly offered and poured out water; thus, by an observance apparently sanctioned only by tradition, commemorating the miraculous supply of water in the wilderness from the smitten rock. An Apostle has said, that "they drank of that spiritual rock which followed them, and that rock was Christ[b]." Accordingly Jesus here speaks of himself as having the power to bestow this gift of God; and in the last day of the feast of tabernacles, resuming the subject, he cried, "If any man thirst, let him come unto me and drink. He that believeth on me, as the Scripture hath said, out of his belly shall flow rivers of living water." The Evangelist

---

[a] Isai. xliv. 3—5. lv. 1. Ezek. xxxvi. 26. Hosea xiv. 5.

[b] 1 Cor. x. 1—4.

adds a comment upon this beautiful and persuasive declaration. "This spake he of the Spirit, which they that believe on him should receive; for the Holy Spirit was not yet given, because Jesus was not yet glorified." He adds, that "many of the people, when they heard this saying, said, Of a truth this is the Prophet; others said, This is the Christ[a]." *They* knew the writings of the prophets, and hence they drew their inference. But the Samaritans probably received only the five books of Moses; and yet our Lord proceeded to shew the Samaritan woman, in a manner suited to her circumstances, both that he was " a prophet," and also that he was " the Christ." And we may here remark, that only on the day of that interview, and the two which immediately followed it, did he labour among the Samaritans. Yet they believed in him. And when the Apostles, in obedience to our Lord's order, became " witnesses to him in Samaria," and preached him among them as the Christ, they then also " gave heed with one accord to the things preached to them" by Philip the deacon. And " when the Apostles heard that Samaria had received the word of God, they sent Peter and John," who communicated to them the gifts of that Holy Spirit, of which Jesus had so long before spoken amongst them[b].

---

[a] John vii. 37—43.   [b] Acts viii. 5—17.

But to proceed with our more immediate subject. Jesus desired the woman " to call her
husband," and come to him again. Her simple
declaration that " she had no husband," with the
suppression of the disgraceful circumstances which
made her declaration true, gave occasion to Jesus,
to shew her, that he was fully aware of those very
circumstances, of the whole course of her past life,
and of her impure and illicit connection at that
time. Astonished and confounded, like Nathanael,
to whom our Lord displayed a knowledge of his
more commendable private history, she confessed
her conviction, at length, that she had not hitherto
appreciated his character. " Sir, I perceive that
thou art a prophet." But not immediately avail-
ing herself of this opportunity to ask the full
import of what that prophet had just declared to
her, she proposed for his decision the controverted
question, so long debated between themselves and
the Jews, whether Gerizim or Jerusalem was
" the place in which men ought to worship."
Our Lord decided this in favour of the Jews;
instructed her further in the true *nature* of
worship, as always more important than the *place*
where it was performed; and assured her that
shortly the very ground and occasion of their
debate would be removed, by the introduction of
a spiritual and more extensive dispensation.
" Woman, believe me, the hour cometh, when

ye shall neither in this mountain, nor yet at
Jerusalem, worship the Father. Ye worship ye
know not what; we know what we worship; for
salvation is of the Jews. But the hour cometh,
and now is, when the true worshippers shall worship the Father in spirit and in truth; for the
Father seeketh such to worship him. God is a
spirit; and they that worship him must worship
him in spirit and in truth." In this intimation of
the near approach of a season, respecting which
it had been predicted that " in every place incense,
and a pure offering should be offered unto the
name of the Lord of hosts^a," the woman appears
to have acquiesced; for Jesus therein spoke as
a prophet, and she had been convinced that he
could justly claim that character. But Jesus had
yet to announce to her that he was " more than
a prophet;" that bis was that title and character,
which authorized him, by her own confession, to
claim her ready and unreserved assent to his decision of the question. " The woman saith unto
him, I know that Messias is coming; when he is
come, he will tell us all things.—Jesus saith unto
her, I that speak unto thee am he."

We have here a declaration, which, in one
word, communicates to us a knowledge of the
office and character, to which Jesus laid claim;

---

^a Mal. i. 11.

but which he had never before stated in those
precise terms, nor afterwards did, until his last
arraignment before the High Priest. On that
occasion he replied in the affirmative to the
solemn "adjuration by the most High God, that
he should tell them whether he were the Christ,
or not." If we ask the reason of his openness
on this occasion, and of his reserve upon others,
we answer, that at this time only, during his
personal ministry, did he instruct the Samaritans,
at all other times, he laboured amongst Jews.
In Samaria "the fields were already white unto
the harvest;" and accordingly, when "the fulness
of the blessing of the Gospel of peace" was
preached unto them by the companions of the
Apostles, then also they "gladly received the
word." Yet as our Lord never visited them
again as a teacher, and also directed the twelve
not to enter into any city of the Samaritans;
so neither does it appear that John had preached
among them as our Lord's forerunner. He
laboured among the Jews only; because among
them it was necessary that "every valley should
be filled, every mountain and hill be made low,
the crooked made straight, and the rough places
plain; before all flesh could see the salvation of
God." They had so joined the notion of
Messiah's office as a prophet and a priest, with
his kingly prerogative, as to make the latter
supersede, or at least neutralize, the former.

They were therefore dealt with in a manner, which these partial and carnal prejudices rendered necessary; in order that, whether or not they ultimately recognized the real office of the Messiah, and received Jesus as that Messiah, they might, at least, not frustrate the end, for which he was manifested. Had he in so many words declared to *them* that he was the Messiah, they were at that time prepared to understand the term as first and principally denoting not only a descendant of David, but the heir of his temporal kingdom. The mass of the Jewish people wanted only an avowal on his part that he was the Messiah, to induce them resolutely "to take him by force, and make him a king;" and to raise such a tumult as would effectually have prevented the designs of the "prince of peace," if it had been successful; and, if it had been otherwise, would have prematurely terminated his own ministry, and perhaps the existence of the Jews as a nation. Though he was indeed a king, yet was his kingdom "not of this world; and therefore, when his hour was come, his servants did not fight that he should not be delivered to the Jews. To this end he was born, and for this cause he came into the world, that he might bear witness to the truth [a]." Conformable to this end was his teaching and

---

[a] John xviii. 37.

conduct, both among the Samaritans, and among
the Jews; and among both, "every one, that
was of the truth, heard his voice."

Among the Samaritans, as we have seen, he
explicitly declared himself to be the Messiah.
We cannot suppose it probable, that the opinion
which the woman expressed respecting the
Messiah, antecedently to the declaration of Jesus,
was peculiar to herself, or derived from any other
source than the common traditional notions of
her fellow-countrymen. In fact she so states it,
as to imply that it was the settled and prevalent
opinion. "I know that Messiah is coming,—he
will tell us all things." She conceived of Messiah
as a divine teacher; and expected that the time
of his appearance was not far distant. Her fellow-
countrymen, who "believed in him not only
because of her word, but because they heard
him themselves," at the same time that they
expressed their firm conviction that he was the
Christ, explained their notion of his office as such,
by the declaration, "we know that this is indeed
the Christ, *the Saviour of the world.*" Bishop
Horsley has shewn at large, that the five books
of Moses, which alone they admitted as canonical
Scripture, afforded sufficient ground for this their
expectation. But from their use of the term
Messiah, which they could not derive from the
Pentateuch, we may suppose that they were not

unacquainted with the later prophecies; indeed it would be difficult to conceive otherwise, when we consider that the Samaritans lived in the very midst of the Jews, and that there was so great a similarity in the religious system of the two nations; although we allow that they did not receive the prophetic books as *canonical* Scripture. Be that, however, as it may, they had not abandoned the principle, which the Pentateuch ought to have taught to the Jews, as well as to them, that he that was to come would be "a prophet," and "a blessing to all nations." And received in such a character, Jesus declared to the woman that he was the Messiah; and other Samaritans, to whom she communicated the intelligence, heard him themselves. He doubtless enlarged, in their hearing, also upon the same truths which he had declared to her, respecting the living water, the worship of God, and the blessings about to be revealed; and probably contributed to the maturity and definiteness of their expectations respecting the salvation of the world, by some such declarations as he had lately made to Nicodemus; who like the Samaritans, had attained to a conviction, that he was "a teacher come from God."

Comparatively few of those, whom our Lord had to instruct unto the kingdom of heaven, had either the correct views, or the candid

dispositions, of the Samaritans and of Nicodemus.
When, therefore, we follow Jesus into Galilee,
where, until the next passover, "he taught in
their synagogues, and proclaimed the glad tidings
of the kingdom," we do not find that he was
so explicit in his declarations. Yet it is obvious,
that what he taught was the same in substance,
and preparatory, "as they were able to bear it,"
to that final avowal of his Messiahship, without
which he did not leave even the Jews, who were
so ill-prepared to understand it aright. Each of
the two first Evangelists has given us a summary
of the topics, which for a time formed the subject
of his discourses ; and St. Luke has handed down
to us a notice of some leading particulars in the
remarkable discourse, which, after some time,
he delivered in the synagogue of his own city
Nazareth. We at least, after having been
acquainted with his previous statements, cannot
be at a loss with respect to his meaning and
design in those annunciations and exhortations,
which we shall now very briefly notice.

St. Mark relates, that Jesus coming into
Galilee, "preached the Gospel of the kingdom
of God, saying, The time is fulfilled, and the
kingdom of God is at hand; repent ye, and
believe the Gospel[a]." It will doubtless occur

---

[a] Mark i. 14, 15. See also Matt. iv. 17. Luke iv. 15.
John iv. 45.

to every one, who hears these words, how *similar*
they are to the tenor of John's preaching in
Judea, and probably, therefore, to his more recent
preaching in Galilee. Yet it is never said, by
any Evangelist, that "the glad tidings of the
kingdom" were preached by the Baptist; for
the proclamation of the Gospel itself was peculiar
to that office, to which Jesus was anointed; as
he himself expressly stated shortly afterwards in
the synagogue at Nazareth. Both Jesus and
his forerunner announced the approaching establishment of the kingdom of heaven; and urged
it as a motive to repentance. But Jesus advanced
still further, when he said, "The time is fulfilled, and the kingdom of God is at hand."
We may suppose that he enlarged upon those
"signs of the times," which, when compared
with the intimations given by the prophets,
shewed that the season marked out by them for
the advent of him whom they predicted had
fully come. The kingdom of God was therefore not only near at hand; but the glad tidings
of it, which explained its nature and object, as
well as its approach, were then to be proclaimed.
Jesus himself was the anointed herald, of whom
John had already said to his disciples, that he
"spoke the words of God, and testified that
which he had seen and heard, and that God had
given all things into his hand." Jesus, therefore,

did not only continue to urge the call to repentance, but also demanded a ready belief of the
glad tidings which he proclaimed. But, because
his hearers had erroneous views of the nature
of the Messiah's *kingdom,* he did not on that
account adopt another term; for the term itself
was perfectly proper. It was his principal aim to
lead them to affix right ideas to it, and to attend
also to the other characteristics by which the
future dispensation, and its author, had been
described.

Probably the discourse at Nazareth is only
a specimen of the method which he adopted in
other places. But we know that there, at least,
he taught his hearers to expect and seek after
spiritual blessings; and to consider him as appointed to proclaim the offer, and to accomplish
the bestowment, of them. Having, on the sabbath-day, stood up to read in the synagogue of
his native city, he found the place of the prophet
Isaiah, where it is written, "The Spirit of the
Lord is upon me; because he hath anointed me
to preach the Gospel to the poor; he hath sent
me to heal the broken-hearted, to preach deliverance to the captives, and recovering of sight to
the blind, to set at liberty them that are bruised,
to preach the acceptable year of the Lord[a]."

---

[a] Luke iv. 16—22. Isai. lxi. 1—3.

G

Well might Jesus begin to say, when he had closed the book, "This day is this Scripture fulfilled in your ears." For never did circumstances more accurately correspond to prophetic description, than the condescension, doctrine, and beneficent works of Jesus to these anticipations of Isaiah. I say, anticipations; for surely Isaiah "spoke not these things of himself, but of some other" and greater man; even of him, who was the fruitful and animating theme both of himself and all the other prophets. From this Scripture, therefore, may we begin and preach Jesus as the Christ; that is, as the word signifies, as the Anointed; as him " upon whom is the Spirit of Jehovah, because Jehovah hath anointed him to preach the Gospel to the poor, and the acceptable year of the Lord" to those whom he, as the Son, can make free, and translate them into the glorious liberty of the children of God.

If, then, we listen to the statements, which our Lord and Master, advanced respecting himself, principally by applying to himself the predictions of the prophets, we cannot be ignorant that he claimed a divine commission, as "anointed with the Holy Ghost and with power," to give liberty, light, and salvation, to all that feel, and lament, and acknowledge, the slavery, darkness, and peril of sin;—that he came in that fulness of the season which God had foreseen, appointed, and

prepared, and which the prophets had circumstantially described;—and that he was no other
than the promised Messiah, the desire of all
nations, the Saviour of the world. Of the certainty of these momentous and consolatory truths
God hath, "by many infallible proofs," "given
assurance unto all men;" and it will shortly be
our endeavour to point out to you, and to elucidate,
several passages of our Lord's discourses, in which
he appeals to, and enforces, the evidences of his
divine authority.

But allow me, before I conclude this Lecture,
to call your attention to one remarkable circumstance, with regard to these appeals and reasonings
of our Lord. They were not advanced in the
earliest part of his ministry; nor at all, until the
opposition and objections of the Jews was excited
against him; and scarcely ever publicly but upon
such occasions. And those particulars, the public
notice of which was not called forth in this manner,
were pointed out to his disciples in private, more
especially towards the close of his ministry. But
both at the beginning, and during the whole
course, of his ministry, the *evidences* themselves
were furnished in great abundance. For while
he proclaimed in their synagogues " the glad
tidings of the kingdom," he also " healed all
manner of sickness, and all manner of disease
among the people." But he left these mighty

works, and the other divine attestations to his
mission, to speak for themselves; until either a
denial of his claims rendered it necessary to appeal to them, or cavils against the reality and
conclusiveness of those evidences led him to refute
the objectors. He did not, like the Arabian impostor, boldly claim a divine mission for which no
sufficient proof appeared; nor did he vauntingly
magnify and set off some seeming evidence, which,
without such a special notice, might never have
been observed. He was too well aware of the
justice of his pretensions, of the publicity and
splendour of his miracles, of the notoriety of
the prophecies, and of their manifest fulfilment in
himself, to think any such laboured and suspicious
proceeding necessary. He was ready to allow
that sufficient evidence might justly be expected;
and, accordingly, one of his earliest remarks on
this subject, was that which he made previously to
his cure of the nobleman's son at Capernaum;
"Except ye see signs and wonders, ye will not
believe[a]." Signs and wonders he did therefore
perform; but I find not that he expressly connected his miracles with his doctrine, so as to
argue with those who saw the miracles, until he
wrought the cure of the paralytic[b]; for the purpose
of proving his right to say to him, "Son, thy sins

---

be forgiven thee." But it was not until the succeeding passover, that he again thought it necessary to argue with those who saw and heard him ;
and then it was, that, being brought before the
ruling powers for a supposed breach of the sabbath, he delivered that eloquent and comprehensive
defence of his mission, the whole of which will be
reviewed in our future Lectures, and the first portion of which will form the next subject of our
consideration.

The subjects which have been brought before
your notice this day are fruitful in topics of practical instruction. I might take occasion to caution
you against the prejudices and hardness of heart,
which may lead you to be offended in Jesus, by
setting before you the unbelief of the people of
Nazareth, and that murderous attempt, from which
a miracle only preserved our Lord. I might enlarge upon the warnings which he at that time
gave them, lest, by a just retribution for the non-
improvement of religious privileges, they should
lose them, and others only be benefited by them.
I might recommend to you the candour, the earnestness, and the faith of the Samaritans ; and
shew what encouragement may be derived from
observing the condescension which our Lord manifested to their infirmities, and the readiness with
which he staid with them, and instructed them.
I might exhort you to "ask of him, who will

freely give you to drink of that water of life," by which the thirst after sin and worldly gratifications is quenched, and the thirst after righteousness satisfied. I might entreat you to listen to him, who preaches "to all nations the glad tidings of great joy, that unto them is born a Saviour, Christ the Lord." And I might, in fine, recommend to your serious consideration that exhortation with which Jesus accompanied his proclamation; "Repent ye, and believe the Gospel;" reminding you also of the necessity, the nature, and the genuine effects of such a "repentance towards God, and of such a faith in our Lord Jesus Christ." But time only permits me to express an earnest desire, that none of these considerations may be forgotten in your private meditation, and that they may be made the subjects of earnest prayer. For scriptural knowledge will little profit us, unless we are thereby made "wise unto salvation;" unless the things which "happened unto others for ensamples, and which are written for our admonition," are suffered to operate for our warning, and encouragement, and guidance; unless we know, and also are established in the love and belief of those truths, which, in the sacred pages, have been so clearly revealed. It will little avail you to receive the best instructions, and in your judgment to be convinced of the certainty of them, unless "with the heart you believe unto righteousness, make confession with the mouth unto salvation," and "in all things adorn the doctrine of God your Saviour." "Wherefore, give diligence to make your calling and election sure; for if ye do these things, if ye add to your faith, virtue; and to virtue, knowledge; and to knowledge, temperance; and to temperance, patience; and to patience, godliness; and to godliness, brotherly kindness; and to brotherly kindness, charity; if these things be in you, and abound, they shall make you that ye shall neither be barren nor unfruitful in the knowledge of our Lord Jesus Christ; and so ye shall never fall; but an entrance be ministered to you abundantly into his everlasting kingdom[a]." And soon will he accomplish that prayer which we offer, when we assemble round the opened grave. Soon will he "accomplish the number of his elect, and hasten his kingdom." Soon will the time of his second coming be fulfilled. Soon will each of us be consigned to that grave, in which we must await the summons of that day. "The kingdom of God," with which our final redemption shall draw nigh, "is near at hand.. Repent ye therefore, and believe the Gospel."

---

[a] 2 Pet. i. 5—11.

LECTURE V.

———

THE OCCASION OF THE DISCOURSE RECORDED IN ST. JOHN'S FIFTH CHAPTER, AND THE PERSONS TO WHOM IT WAS ADDRESSED.——ILLUSTRATION AND ANALYSIS OF THE FIRST PORTION OF IT.

———

St. John V. 17—20.

Jesus answered them, My Father worketh hitherto, and I work. Therefore the Jews sought the more to kill him, because he not only had broken the sabbath, but said also that God was his Father, making himself equal with God. Then answered Jesus, and said unto them, Verily, verily, I say unto you, The Son can do nothing of himself, but what he seeth the Father do: for what things soever he doeth, these also doeth the Son likewise. For the Father loveth the Son, and sheweth him all things that himself doeth.

IN the concluding words of our text our Lord commences that important discourse, which first suggested to the Lecturer's own mind the subject to which he has solicited your attention; which guided him in the formation of his plan; and the successive portions of which, in their order, will come under review in this, and in many subsequent Lectures. Our first endeavour will therefore be, to explain the circumstances which called

forth this enlarged statement of the claims of our
Lord ; especially as our attention will thereby also
be directed to some other declarations, which he
made on occasions of a like nature. For these
several statements mutually illustrate each other ;
and also suggest some reflections, which are, perhaps, peculiarly appropriate to the day on which
we are assembled[a].

The discourse in question was delivered very
shortly after the cure, which our Lord had miraculously wrought at the pool of Bethesda, upon one
who, for a period of thirty-eight years, had been
afflicted with an infirmity, and was then waiting
beside the pool, that, upon the troubling of the
waters, he might step in, and be healed. Jesus
not only healed him immediately, but also directed
him to take up the bed on which he lay, and to
carry it thence to his own house. This procedure
afforded a full and public demonstration of the
reality of the cure ; nor did the man hesitate to
comply with the injunction. And when he was
told, that, as " it was the sabbath-day, it was not
lawful for him to carry his bed," because the Jews
refused, even with superstitious scrupulosity, to
carry any burthen on the sabbath, the man deemed
it a sufficient defence to answer ; " He that made
me whole, the same said unto me, Take up thy

---

[a] This Lecture was delivered on Easter-Day.

bed, and walk." Yet, until he was afterwards accosted by Jesus in the temple, he had not known that it was Jesus who had made him whole; because Jesus had, at the time, suddenly " conveyed himself away, a multitude being in that place." When however he thus became acquainted with the person of his benefactor, " he departed, and told *the Jews*, that it was Jesus, which had made him whole."

The Evangelist then adds, that " *the Jews* did, therefore, persecute Jesus, and sought to slay him, because he had done these things on the sabbath-day." It is very obvious, that this is not to be understood of the attempts of isolated individuals, much less of any ebullition of popular indignation; but of a legal procedure commenced against Jesus, by persons in authority; with whom, of course, it rested, to enforce that provision of the Mosaic law, which assigned capital punishment to a breach of the sabbath. A prosecution was doubtless commenced against him by the Sanhedrim, upon the information of the man who had been cured; as the original word, used in this place by the Evangelist, distinctly informs us[a]. And though it is observed, that " *the Jews* persecuted Jesus, and sought to kill him," yet the same phrase is used in many other passages of the

---

[a] Καὶ διὰ τοῦτο ʾΕΔΙΩΚΟΝ τὸν Ἰησοῦν οἱ Ἰουδαῖοι. v. 16.

Gospels, where we cannot properly understand it of any others, than of the men in authority among the Jews. Thus we are told, that "the Jews sent priests and Levites from Jerusalem to John, to ask him, who art thou?" It belonged to the Sanhedrim, officially, to make such an enquiry.—We are told that "Jesus would not walk in Jewry, because *the Jews* sought to kill him;" and that though there was at that time "much murmuring among the people concerning him, no man spake openly of him, for *fear of the Jews.*" And the reason of this sufficiently appears, when we read, that afterwards "*the chief priests and Pharisees* had given a commandment, that if any man knew where he were, he should shew it, that they might take him;" and that, even at an earlier period, "*the Jews* had agreed already, that if any man did confess that he was the Christ, he should be put out of the synagogue."—Again we are told, that "Caiaphas was he which gave counsel to *the Jews,* that it was expedient that one man should die for the people." Caiaphas was the *high priest* that same year; and we know that the advice specified was given at "a council gathered by the chief priests and Pharisees" after the raising of Lazarus, in order to consider what must be done to prevent the national danger, which they thought likely to result from the growing popularity of Jesus[b].

---

[b] John i. 19. vii. 1, 13. ix. 22. xi. 47—57.

There can, therefore, be no reasonable doubt, that this discourse of our Lord was *a defence of his conduct delivered before the ruling authorities at Jerusalem.*

Behold, Jesus, then, having done a miracle, at which, as he afterwards observed, "they all marvelled[a]," summoned before the rulers of the Jews to answer for his life, "because he had done these things on the sabbath-day." Afterwards, when "he was oppressed and afflicted," and brought before the same assembly, he avowed himself to be the Christ; and having referred to the prophecy of Daniel, respecting the future glory of the Son of man, he assented to their inference from thence, that he thereby claimed to be the Son of God. At this time he did not, in so many words, declare that he was the Christ; for "his hour was not yet come." But he declared, and that fully and openly, his claim to those attributes, which their Scriptures ascribed to the Lord's anointed; nay, he largely unfolded and reasoned upon them; for this was yet "the day, in which Jerusalem might have learnt the things which made for her peace, before they were hid from her eyes."—"My Father worketh hitherto, and I work," was all that he at first answered to those things, which they witnessed

---

[a] John vii. 21.

against him; and he left the mysterious and unhesitating assertion to work such effect as it might. They conceived that he had now, "not only broken the sabbath," but spoken blasphemy. And, assuredly, we can put no obvious and consistent sense upon the words, but that which they put upon them, viz. that " he called God his own proper Father, making himself equal with God ᵇ." For he thereby explicitly declared, that his own performance of miraculous works of mercy was to be placed in the same rank, and was defensible upon the same grounds, as the daily exercise of the bountiful Providence of the Father of the Universe, to whom every day is, in this respect, alike. If he were not " equal with the Father, as touching his Godhead," and, even as the Son of man, acting in perfect unison with him, then, according to the injunctions of their law, they now *justly* "sought the more to kill him," on account of the words which he had spoken. But if it were otherwise, then he who was the Son of the Father, in a sense in which no other being is, could justly appeal to the example of his Father; and he who was, equally with him, Lord of the sabbath, might, if need were, dispense with its observance. Then was he proved to be authorized

---

ᵇ " πατέρα ἴδιον ἔλεγε τὸν Θεὸν, ἴσον ἑαυτὸν ποιῶν τῷ Θεῷ." v. 18.

to give such a command to the impotent man, in order to shew his power over the sabbath, though it appeared to them a violation of it. "If they did not believe him, they might have believed the works;" and both this miracle, and all that he had before wrought, proved that "the Father was in him, and he in the Father." To these works, and to the various other evidences of his authority, he appealed in his discourse on this occasion; and they could justify no other conclusion, than that the Father had sent him. The rulers, whom he addressed, were thereby so far silenced, and convinced, as not to venture to put him to death as a blasphemer; either because they had not yet fully steeled their hearts against all evidence; or because they feared the people, and shrunk, for a time, from the unhallowed attempt to put him to death, and thus fill up the measure of their fathers' crimes.

At the succeeding feast of tabernacles, when Jesus referred to this wish to compass his death, some of the people seem to have been aware that their rulers entertained such a design; though others professed, at least, to be ignorant of it, and answered, " Thou hast a devil; who goeth about to kill thee?" Jesus took occasion to remind them of this miracle, which he wrought at the preceding passover, and of his arraignment in consequence of it; and, then also, he defended his conduct with regard to the supposed breach of the sabbath, though upon grounds somewhat different. "Jesus answered and said unto them, I have done one work, and ye all marvel. Moses therefore gave unto you circumcision, (not because it is of Moses, but of the fathers,) and ye on the sabbath-day circumcise a man. If a man on the sabbath-day receive circumcision, that the law of Moses should not be broken ; are ye angry at me, because I have made a man every whit whole on the sabbath-day ? Judge not according to appearance, but judge righteous judgment[a]."—The incident here referred to seems to have been the first instance of the disregard of the sabbath imputed to our Lord. But it is remarkable, how many of our Lord's most signal miracles were wrought on the sabbath-day. And we know how frequently he thereby gave umbrage to the Jews, and occasioned both many of the objections, which were expressed to him when present, and also the insinuations, which were circulated among the people to his disadvantage. But we should ever bear in mind the sanction which his conduct in this respect received from the miracles themselves. On one occasion, when "the Scribes and Pharisees watched him, whether he would heal on the sabbath-day, that they might find an accusation against him," he

---

[a] John vii. 21—24.

wrought a miracle, under circumstances of peculiar force and significancy. He commanded the
man with the withered hand, publicly to stand
forth in the midst of the synagogue; he then
entered upon the disclosure of principles specially
directed against their secret reasonings, opinions,
and intentions; and lastly, by causing the stretch-
ing out of the withered hand to be attended by
the complete restoration of its muscular power,
he did, indeed, prove to them that he, the Son of
man, whom they had summoned to their bar, was
" Lord even of the sabbath-day[a]." As such, he
has, indeed, connected with the *sabbath* a portion
of " that liberty wherewith he maketh us free."
But while we refuse to be " entangled again in the
yoke of bondage," let us not break through all
restraint. Let us remember, that, by establishing
the exceptions, he has proved the rule with respect
to sabbatical observances; that we have no
countenance from him to venture beyond the
limits which he has marked out; and that he has
marked them so definitely, that " he that runs may
read." If any one here present has had doubts respecting the moral obligation, and the preceptive
detail, of sabbatical observances; if any one's
conscience suggests that he may be guilty as concerning this thing; let him peruse, compare, and

---

[a] Luke vi. 1—11.

study, all that our Lord did and taught respecting it, the very copious records of which form so prominent a feature in the Gospel history; and I doubt not that he will derive the fullest satisfaction, and the clearest light and direction, on a subject most essentially connected with the prosperity of personal, family, and national religion. Our Lord has summed up the whole doctrine respecting it in two short but expressive apothegms. Each of these rescues the subject from Pharisaical superstition, but each also enforces the proper observance of the great and original precept, which was coeval with the creation of mankind; and the latter will well prepare us to enter on the consideration of our Lord's discourse before the Sanhedrim.

" The sabbath was made for man, not man for the sabbath." It is a day, the observance of which, whatever be its use, cannot be supposed necessary to the absolute and indefectible glory either of our Creator, or of our Redeemer. Man, therefore, was not created merely that he might observe the sabbath; for it was instituted after the time of man's creation, and because he existed; and its design and utility result from the relation between him, and his God. By considering, therefore, both the present circumstances and the future destination of man, let the command be interpreted. It is designed for the full benefit of

H

a creature, living in this world as a partaker of flesh and blood; surrounded by the present claims of time and sense, and of social and terrestrial connections; but who also is destined for a better world, for spiritual blessedness, for an eternal portion, for communion with " the general assembly and Church of the first-born which are written in heaven, with God the Judge of all, with the spirits of just men made perfect, and with Jesus, the Mediator of the new covenant." Conformable to both these considerations must be our observance of the sabbath. Go and learn what this means, " I will have mercy, and not sacrifice," and you will see that, while God requires works of piety, he no longer demands them in the particular form of public prayer and praise, if his providence has either placed us in circumstances where the exercise of them is clearly impracticable, or has presented to us urgent claims for the performance of acts of laborious and persevering benevolence to others. But still must we be " fervent in spirit, serving the Lord ;" though " he that loveth God, must love his brother also," and " provide for him things that are needful for the body."—For go and learn also, that " the sabbath is made for man ;" that God hath blessed it, and sanctified it, and required that it be observed, and that its holy design be remembered. And we shall then see, that we must esteem it "a delight, the holy of the Lord, honourable."—We shall then be convinced, that on this day we must "honour him, not doing our own ways, nor speaking our own words, but delighting ourselves in the Lord." Then, "for the mouth of the Lord hath spoken it," we shall be "blessed in our deed."

Let the mind of a conscientious man be impressed and directed by such views, and he will be no unskilful casuist in this matter. This is, indeed, a day of rest; it is a day on which we are to rest from our worldly employments. But it is so, principally, in order that we may rest from worldly cares, and sinful desires; that we may repose in God, and diligently and earnestly prepare for an eternal sabbath of perfect holiness and bliss. It is true also that our Lord has conveyed to us those views of this important subject, which are usually and rightly summed up in the observation, that works of piety, necessity, and charity, are lawful on the sabbath, and not a breach of its rest. But it were earnestly to be wished, that Christians, while they condemn, as justly they may, a Judaical observance of the sabbath, had not often run into the opposite extreme, and used their Christian liberty in a manner, which their Lord and Master would have condemned, even more severely than that merely ceremonial observance, which the erroneous traditions of the Jews had recommended and sanctioned.

But the most important principle yet remains to
be noticed; for it declares to us what we have so
much need to call to mind, the sanction of the
commandment.—" The Son of man is Lord, even
of the sabbath-day." I doubt not that you have
already referred this declaration to the precepts
and decisions which we have been reviewing;
and to the miracles, with which they were accompanied, and by which their authority was established. I doubt not that you have already anticipated the remark, that, as on this day, the Son of
man rose from the dead; and also, that on that
same day, which we, in imitation of the Apostles,
call " the Lord's day," our Lord did, generally, at
least, shew himself to his disciples after his resurrection; that on that day he poured out the seven-
fold gifts of his Spirit; and, to his beloved disciple,
" being in the Spirit on the Lord's day," shewed
the things which should be hereafter. Therefore
do we, ' in imitation of the first followers of
Christ, assemble for public worship on the day on
which our Saviour rose,' that we may thereon
" continue stedfastly in the Apostles' doctrine, and
in breaking of bread, and in prayers." But this
authoritative claim of our Master and only
Saviour, has a much more ancient original, and
includes a much more extensive obligation. Why
was the sabbath instituted? " Because that on
the seventh day God rested from all his work
which he created and màde; and, therefore, blessed

that day, and sanctified it." And who *rested* from
his work, but he that *made* the worlds? And by
whom, and for whom, were "all things created,
that are in heaven, and that are in earth, whether
visible or invisible; and by whom do "all things
consist, but by him who is the image of the invisible God, the first-born of every creature;" who
is before all things, and, therefore, heir of all
things? And who is he but the Son of God; the
same that is also styled the Son of man; who
"was made flesh, and dwelt among us, and declared to us the Father, whom no man hath seen
or can see;" and received of his Father the promise of the Holy Spirit: to whom, as the Son of
man, is given, according to prophecy, dominion,
and glory, and a kingdom; and who will one day
come in the clouds of heaven, with power and great
glory? The Son of man is, therefore, Lord of
the sabbath, as the Creator and upholder of the
universe; as the angel of the covenant to his people
in the wilderness; as the Mediator of the new
covenant; as the first-begotten from the dead; as
the head over all things to his Church; as the
judge of quick and dead. *His* is the commandment; *he* has imposed, and ratified, and declared,
our obligations to this reasonable service; and to
him we must give account.

Thus sacred is "this day, which the Lord hath
made." Thus are we bound to "rejoice and be

glad in it." Thus intimately is it connected with
all that God has done for man, and with all that
he has revealed of himself to man; sanctioned
and recommended, as it is, by all that is great in
the Creator, merciful in the Redeemer, and consolatory in the Sanctifier. Thus does the observance of it rest, not merely on the narrow and
slippery basis of human recommendation, and general expediency, but on the extensive, solid, and
immoveable, foundation of divine and explicit
authority.

We have not in this lengthened discussion been
wandering from the principal subject of this day's
Lecture. For it has been stated to you, that the
sublime discourse, to the consideration of which
we must now proceed, was a defence made by our
Lord, against the accusation that he had violated
that sabbath. We shall now, I trust, be prepared
more fully to understand, and more duly to appreciate, the exalted claims which he therein advances
as the Son of the Father, acting in his mediatorial
capacity as the Son of man; and which we have.
in fact, already deduced in a great measure from
other parts of his instructions on this subject,
compared with the general tenor of Scripture.
The views which have in this manner come before
us, will probably be thought to illustrate the words
with which our Lord commenced his answer to the
objections of the Jews. " My Father worketh

hitherto, and I work." That remark clearly shewed them what was the nature of the claim which he advanced. And he was so far from rectifying their interpretation, (or misinterpretation, as some would fain have it,) that he proceeded more fully to unfold his claim; and to state all its bearings, circumstances, and consequences, even until the consummation of all things.

" Then answered Jesus, and said unto them, Verily, verily, I say unto you, The Son can do nothing of himself, but what he seeth the Father do; for what things soever he doeth, these also doeth the Son likewise. For the Father loveth the Son, and sheweth him all things that himself doeth; and he will shew him greater works than these, that ye may marvel. For as the Father raiseth up the dead, and quickeneth them, even so the Son quickeneth whom he will. For the Father judgeth no man, but hath committed all judgment unto the Son; that all men should honour the Son, even as they honour the Father. He that honoureth not the Son, honoureth not the Father, which hath sent him."

These words remind us of the statement which our Lord made to Nicodemus, that " he spoke that which he knew, and testified that which he had seen; for that he, who alone had ascended into heaven, even the Son of man, which is in heaven, could testify of heavenly things." He now fully unfolds to those, who conceived that his recent declaration was presumptuously spoken, the origin, object, and extent of his commission as the Son of man; of which his authority over the sabbath was but a part. He announces his perfect acquaintance with all the counsels and proceedings of the Father, in consequence of the love of the Father to him. And though he was now acting in *subordination* to the Father, as *sent* by him to execute a divine commission; and though he "did nothing of himself, but what he saw the Father do;" yet his knowledge was not more extensive than the authority committed to him. For as " the Father sheweth him all things that himself doeth," so also " what things soever the Father doeth, these also doeth the Son likewise." Hence, if such were his authority and power, it was no presumptuous statement which he had advanced, when he said, " My Father worketh hitherto, and I work." Nay, " the Father would shew him greater works than those," at which they had already marvelled, that " they might marvel" the more. For though the miraculous works which he had already done, furnished such evidence of his official character and authority, as ought to exempt him from the charge of unjustly asserting a claim to a parity of operation in conjunction with the Father; yet they would see him " raise the dead and quicken them;"

not, as the prophets of the Old Testament, by
external and visible applications, through the instrumentality of which his Father then raised
them, but evidently by his own power, and at his
own will.

But our Lord is not here principally intending
to speak of his eternal generation, of his pre-existence, and of his glory with the Father. Those
doctrines are in other places distinctly revealed,
and they alone are *consistent* with the statements
here made. But Jesus is immediately describing
the authority and work of the Son of man, as
appearing among men in the form of a servant, to
finish the work which the Father gave him to do; as
acting therefore in a subordinate capacity, though
in unison with the Father; as sent to ratify and
promulgate the new covenant, of which he was the
visible Mediator, with the same authority, which
belonged to those dispensations of the Old Testament, which were conducted more expressly in
the name of the Father. Even then, indeed, the
Father was employing the agency of the Son,
though it was not, as yet, so openly announced.
But now, as our Lord stated, and as was evinced
both by his past miracles, and by the " greater
works" of which he spoke, " the Father, who
himself judgeth no man, had committed all judicial
authority to the Son." And as he now " spoke
by his Son," therefore was the Son to be obeyed

with equal readiness, and to be received with
equal honour. For the very end and design of
this revelation was, " that all men might honour
the Son, even as they honour the Father;" a
statement, which, although it applies to Jesus
appearing in the likeness of man, yet would not
consistently be applicable to any other, than to
one who is also the Son of God, in a sense in
which no other son of man is so. In fact, Jesus
announced all that we have yet noticed, before he
spoke of himself under any other character than
the Son of the Father; although he afterwards
states, that " authority is given to him to execute
judgment also, because he is the Son of man."
In fact, it was in consequence of his becoming
incarnate, and therefore visible to us, and a partaker of our nature, that he proclaimed and procured to us the blessings of salvation. And therefore Jesus, speaking in his own person, adds the
words; " Verily, verily, I say unto you, He that
heareth my word, and believeth on him that sent
me, hath everlasting life, and shall not come into
condemnation, but is passed from death unto life."
This is a declaration which Jesus had already
made to Nicodemus; and which apprizes those,
who admit the authority of Jesus, of the nature of
the salvation which he offers, and of the means by
which it is to be obtained.

Our Lord proceeds, in the same solemn manner,

to make a further annunciation. " Verily, verily, I say unto you, The hour is coming, and now is, when the dead shall hear the voice of the Son of God, and they that hear shall live. For as the Father hath life in himself, so hath he given to the Son to have life in himself; and hath given him authority to execute judgment also, because he is the Son of man." The *concluding* words of this passage immediately introduce a reference to the general resurrection. In the *former* part of it he refers, either to those who were raised from the dead in the subsequent part of his ministry ; or to those saints " which arose, and appeared to many, after his resurrection ;" or, as is more closely connected with the last verse, and more fully illustrated by the prophecies of the Old Testament, to the raising of the world from a state of *spiritual* death to *spiritual* life ; or, it may be, to all these, for in all these is it fully verified.

But I am aware that there is another and an awakening interpretation of these words, which considers them as parallel to several difficult and mysterious passages in the prophetic writings, in other discourses of our Lord, in the Epistles, and in the book of Revelation. I allude, of course, to the literal interpretation of the expression, " the presence of the Lord Jesus[a] ;" and to that event,

---

[a] Matt. xxiv. 3. 1 Cor. xv. 23. 1 Thess. ii. 19. 2 Thess. i. 9.

or course of events, which St. John predicts, by
stating, that the righteous " shall live and reign
with Christ a thousand years, though the rest of
the dead shall not live again until the thousand
years are finished." " This," adds he, " is the first
resurrection[a]." If any such interpretation, whether literal or figurative, be correct; if there is
any consistency in the language of prophecy, by
which we can as yet attain to its true interpretation; the event predicted is probably near, even
at the doors, to us who live in these latter days.
Time only can determine this. But, assuredly,
whatever be our views of this matter, " blessed
and holy is he that hath part in the first resurrection ; on such the second death has no power[b]."
For we cannot doubt, whether any one, who does
not now " rise and walk in newness of life," can
have any part or lot in such blessings. None but
those, " who do God's commandments," can have
any " right to the tree of life[c];" none else can
look forward, with hope or complacency, to that
awful and final transaction, of which our Lord
next speaks, in words, respecting the interpretation of which we can entertain no doubt.

" Marvel not at this, for the hour is coming, in
the which all that are in the graves shall hear the
voice of the Son of man, and shall come forth ;

---

[a] Rev. xx. 4—6.   [b] Ibid. xx. 6.   [c] Ibid. xxii. 14.

they that have done good, unto the resurrection of
life; and they that have done evil, unto the resurrection of damnation." These are, indeed, decisive words, and they speak of a decisive day; and
we know that " God hath appointed a day, in
which he will judge the world in righteousness, by
that man, whom he hath ordained; whereof he hath
given assurance unto all men, in that he hath
raised him from the dead." That event, which
gives us so certain and so awakening an assurance,
we are, this day more especially, commemorating.
On this day we are placed, as it were, on another
Pisgah, from whence we can both look back on
scenes that are past, and on scenes yet to come,
both of which alike display the wonderful works
of God, both in mercy and in judgment, such as
may attract the attention of the dullest eye, and
arouse the feelings of the most sluggish heart.
On this day we celebrate that event, which declared the acceptance of the ransom paid for our
redemption, which shewed the triumph of the
Saviour over sin and death, the curse and the
grave; which has laid the sure foundation for our
fondest hopes, and has made us rejoice in the
clear promise and earnest of our future inheritance
of " the purchased possession." " Thanks, therefore, be unto God for his unspeakable gift;" for
" he giveth us the victory, through our Lord
Jesus Christ." The sabbath is ever a joyful,

though a sacred, day; on which we may call to mind all that is consolatory, as well as all that is awful, in Revelation. For we celebrate it in commemoration of our Saviour's resurrection, by which he was " declared to be the Son of God, with power." And every argument which evinces to us the certainty of the event, also demonstrates to us the certainty of that declaration, that " he that believeth on the Son of God, hath everlasting life ;" but also, on the contrary, that " he that believeth not, is condemned already, because he hath not believed in the name of the only-begotten Son of God." Though, therefore, I wish not to check the feelings of gratitude and " triumph in Christ," but to encourage and excite them ; yet, referring to those last cited words of our Lord, in which he speaks of his coming to judgment, I would say in the language of our excellent Lightfoot, " I shall leave it to him, who hears and reads them, to make the most feeling and dread commentary upon them that he can, towards the awing of his heart to a preparedness against that dreadful time when it shall come[a]."

---

[a] Lightfoot's Harmony, in loco.

HULSEAN LECTURES

FOR 1821.

PART II.

LECTURES VI — XVII.

—o—

THE REASONINGS OF OUR LORD RESPECTING THE EVIDENCES TO
WHICH HE APPEALED IN CONFIRMATION OF HIS CLAIMS.

LECTURE VI.

—◆—

OUR LORD'S RECAPITULATION OF HIS CLAIMS CON-
NECTED WITH A REFERENCE TO THE PRESUMPTION
IN THEIR FAVOUR FROM HIS NOT SEEKING HIS OWN
WILL.

—◆—

St. John V. 30, 31.

*I can of mine own self do nothing; as I hear, I judge;
and my judgment is just; because I seek not mine own
will, but the will of the Father which hath sent me.
If I bear witness of myself, my witness is not true.*

In these words our Lord recapitulates the declarations made in the opening of his discourse; and,
while he in some measure enlarges them, he also
passes on to notice those considerations, which
evinced the justice of his claims, by first stating
the presumption in their favour, which his whole
life, conduct, and doctrine, suggested; and then
the principle upon which plain and positive proofs
were provided for their complete establishment.
The principle, to which we here allude, is laid
down in the conclusion of our text. On a different
occasion, our Lord stated another, which is, in
expression, the reverse of this; which, therefore,
it will be expedient to compare with it, in

order that the force and application of each may be ascertained.

It being our object to consider the question of our Lord's divine mission in the precise point of view, in which his own discourses present it, we shall proceed on this occasion, first, to prepare the way for our future inquiries by the examination of the two *principles* which we have noticed; secondly, to consider the *statements* repeated, and enlarged, in our text; and, thirdly, the *presumption* therein also noticed in favour of the truth of those statements.

I. The principle laid down in the text is thus expressed; "If I bear witness of myself, my witness is not true." This is briefly and generally expressed, without noticing the limitation, which it obviously admits and requires. We do not, universally, conclude, that every testimony so circumstanced is necessarily false; for we are continually acting on the contrary supposition. But we are satisfied in so acting, only when we are concerned with a person of known veracity, when we have no reason to suppose him influenced by undue motives, and when he is fully qualified, in point of information, to deliver a true testimony in the particular instance in question. But our unhappy experience of the deceit and falsehood of our fellow men, frequently disposes us to receive such unsupported testimony with caution, even in the ordinary affairs of private life; and, in solemn and judicial proceedings, it is considered wholly insufficient. In such cases we at least suspend our judgment, unless we have independent corroborating testimony. And, therefore, our Lord, having granted the equity of such a maxim, proceeds, after having stated his record respecting himself, to specify some separate and independent testimonies in support of it. But if none of them had existed, it would not therefore follow, that his record was absolutely and necessarily untrue. On the contrary, in this, as well as in many other cases, we must learn from the person himself the claims which he advances, and then, having ascertained the nature and circumstances of the matter in question, we proceed to investigate and consider that which is offered in confirmation of it. Hence the maxim is to be interpreted as applicable, not to the *absolute* truth of the matter in debate, but to the grounds upon which we can properly *judge* of its truth, and to the degree of our conviction. Our Lord grants, that if he bear record of himself, and can offer *nothing more* than his unsupported assertion, his testimony is not true; that the maxim, in compliance with which they usually rejected such a record, is just, proper, and expedient; and, therefore, he appealed and referred them to the positive confir-

mation, which God had vouchsafed to supply for
the satisfaction, even of the most scrupulous
inquirer. But, at another time, when they cited
this obvious, and to them familiar, maxim, and
wished to urge it beyond its proper application,
he then stated that the contrary maxim is, in some
circumstances, really admissible, and that it was
so with respect to himself. Teaching in the
temple, he declared himself to be "the light of
the world," and stated the consequences of such
a doctrine. "The Pharisees, therefore, said unto
him, Thou bearest record of thyself, thy record
is not true. Jesus answered and said unto them,
Though I bear record of myself, yet my record
is true : for I know whence I came, and whither
I go ; but ye cannot tell whence I came, nor
whither I go. Ye judge after the flesh ; I judge
no man. And yet if I judge, my judgment is
true: for I am not alone, but I and the Father
that sent me. It is also written in your law,
that the testimony of two men is true. I am
one that bear witness of myself, and the Father
that sent me beareth witness of me[a]." Our Lord
here advances some assertions similar to those in
our text; and briefly alludes to one of those independent testimonies, which, in the subsequent
part of the discourse more immediately before

---

[a] John viii. 12—19.

us, he states more fully and distinctly. In the
former part of it, as we have already seen, he
is occupied in stating those claims, of the correctness of which he, who thus advanced them,
had the fullest knowledge, inasmuch as he could
not but "know whence he came;" and, therefore, if we find his words established by the
mouth of two or three other witnesses, how can
we, upon any principles of right judgment, refuse
our assent to them? Nay, further, are we not
often even independently of collateral testimony,
and before we have at all proceeded to examine
it, disposed to feel a strong and justifiable
conviction that we may safely rely upon a single
testimony; a conviction which is rather strengthened and matured, than newly produced, by any
additional confirmation? Do not the general
character, conduct, and aims, of an individual,
and also the matter and manner of his statements,
frequently induce us to confess, that there is
a strong previous presumption in his favour,
which recommends him to our favourable regard,
patient attention, and unbiassed judgment? Such
a presumption in favour of our Lord's divine
mission and authority will be suggested to every
candid and serious inquirer, who takes even a
general view of his character, proceedings, and
instructions; and he, who has most fully considered these, will most decidedly entertain such a

presumption. Our Lord himself frequently noticed the considerations by which it is suggested;
and, in our text, he adverts to it, in its natural and
immediate connexion with what he had previously
stated respecting his commission. In the two
remaining divisions of this discourse, it will be our
aim to illustrate each of these topics in the order
in which they lie; principally by citing, or alluding to, other passages in our Lord's instruction
and history, which are parallel with them.

II. We were to consider, *secondly*, the statements which are repeated, and somewhat enlarged,
in our text.—It will be remembered, that, upon
being arraigned for a supposed violation of the
sabbath, our Lord took occasion, in his defence,
to lay before the Jews the whole extent of his
commission; within which that particular right, of
acting as he had done on the sabbath, though important and extensive in its connexion, was in fact
included. He spoke of himself as the Son of God,
as if God were his own proper Father; but with
reference, not so much to his prior and divine
glory, as to his commission and authority as the
incarnate Mediator, and as invested with all judicial
authority, "because he is the Son of man." Having proceeded to state that he was commissioned
to exercise that authority in all its bearings, even
until its last and final exertion, when it would
really and truly be the *judgment* of all mankind

at the general resurrection, he again addresses himself to the establishment of his authority, in answer to their disbelief of his being invested with it. And, in the outset, while he spoke of it as derived from, and exercised in, the name of the Father, he yet spoke of it as unlimited in extent. "Verily, verily, I say unto you, The Son can do nothing of himself, but what he seeth the Father do; for what things soever he doeth, the same doeth the Son likewise. For the Father loveth the Son, and sheweth him all things that himself doeth." After having branched out this his commission into all its bearings, with reference to the performance of greater works than he had yet done, and having spoken of its final exercise in the day when he shall appear no longer as a Saviour, but as a *judge*, he then, in our text, restates the source whence he derived his authority to execute judgment, and the original and character of that judgment itself: "I can of mine own self do nothing; as I hear, I judge; and my judgment is just; because I seek not mine own will, but the will of the Father which hath sent me."—The words are few, but weighty, and important. In other parts of our Lord's instructions we find statements, the knowledge of which is necessary to the full understanding of this passage, and which fully elucidate the several particulars contained in it.

As "the Son can do nothing of himself," so he states that what he heard of the Father was his rule of judgment, and that the judgment administered according to such a rule is just. Hear the following similar statements: "My doctrine is not mine, but his that sent me. If any man will do his will, he shall know of the doctrine whether it be of God, or whether I speak of myself. He that speaketh of himself, seeketh his own glory; but he that seeketh his glory that sent him, the same is true, and no unrighteousness is in him[a]." Our Lord declared to his disciples upon another occasion; "I have called you friends; for all things that I have heard of my Father, I have made known unto you. If I had not come and spoken unto them, they had not had sin, but now have they no cloke for their sin. He that hateth me, hateth my Father also[b]." In his concluding prayer, our Lord declares of his disciples, "They have kept thy word. They have known that all things whatsoever thou hast given me are of thee. For I have given unto them the words which thou gavest me; and they have received them, and they have believed that

---

[a] John vii. 16—18. It was after these words that our Lord referred to the miracle, which occasioned the discourse now under consideration.

[b] John xv. 15—21.

thou didst send me[c]." In connection with the
last·clause, and in illustration of the connection
of the words which Christ had heard of the Father,
with the judgment of the last day, we may now
cite another passage : "He that believeth on me,
believeth not on me, but on him that sent me.
And he that seeth me, seeth him that sent me.
I am come a light into the world, that whosoever
believeth on me should not abide in darkness.
And if any man hear my words, and believe not,
I judge him not; for I came not to judge the
world, but to save the world. He that rejecteth
me, and·receiveth not my words, hath one that
judgeth him; the word that I have spoken, the
same shall judge him in the last day. For I have
not spoken of myself, but the Father which sent
me, he gave me a commandment what I should
say, and what I should speak. And I know that
his commandment is life everlasting : whatsoever
I speak, therefore, even as the Father said unto
me, so I speak[d]." We know that our Lord declared, even·before Pilate, that "to this end he
was born, and that for this cause he came into
the world, that he might bear witness to the
truth." We know also that he declared, that
"the Son of man came not to be ministered unto,

---

[c] John xvii. 6—8. 　　[d] John xii. 44—50.

but to minister, and to give his life a ransom for many." And as "the Father loveth the Son," so did the Son declare, "Therefore doth my Father love me, because I lay down my life, that I might take it again. No man taketh it from me, but I lay it down of myself. I have power to lay it down, and I have power to take it again. This commandment have I received from my Father[a]."—We may now perceive the purport of our Lord when he said, "My meat is to do the will of him that sent me, and to finish his work." Those words were spoken when our Lord was at Samaria, and when he foresaw, and was deeply interested in, the successful result of his approaching interview with the people of that place. And I would fain hope and believe, that, however little you may be convinced by any reasonings I may have to offer, yet that, as I have recited to you the words of our Lord more largely than is perhaps usual, you may be able to say with those Samaritans, "Now we believe, not because of thy saying; for we have heard him ourselves, and know that this is indeed the Christ, the Saviour of the world." I know not, indeed, how I could illustrate the words of our text more clearly than in the manner I have adopted, or how I may be likely more strikingly to exhibit to

---

[a] John x. 17, 18.

you, the claims, which he, "whom we preach,"
has upon your reverence, faith, and obedience.
And, before I proceed to reason upon the argument which our text suggests to us, I would cite
one other passage, which at once includes the
same statement, in almost the same words, and
which declares to us what is that will of God
concerning us, which is revealed, accomplished,
and proposed for our compliance, in the Gospel.
"All that the Father giveth me," said our Lord,
"shall come to me; and him that cometh to me
I will in no wise cast out. For I came down
from heaven, not to do mine own will, but the
will of him that sent me. And this is the Father's
will which hath sent me, that of all which he hath
given me, I should lose nothing, but should raise
it up again at the last day. And this is the will
of him that sent me, that every one that seeth
the Son, and believeth on him, may have everlasting life, and I will raise him up at the last day [a]."
And may we not truly remark, that "blessed also
are they, that have not seen, and yet have believed;" who so receive, understand, and obey,
those things which are written, that they believe,
as indeed they have highest moral demonstration
to induce them to believe, " that Jesus is the
Christ, the Son of God, in order that, believing,
they may have life through his name."

[b] John vi. 37—40.

III. That, as far as the subject before us this
day gives occasion, we may convince the gainsayer,
and assist the believer to build himself more se-
curely on his most holy faith, let us now in the
third place, proceed to consider that presumption
in favour of the claims of Jesus, which he notices
in the text, and in many other parts of his discourses : " I seek not my own will, but the will of
the Father, which hath sent me."

Was he not sent by the Father ? Then must
he, that thinks so, believe, either that he knowingly
palmed an imposture upon the world, and taught
a cunningly devised fable ; or even that he was
more weak than wicked, and published, under the
influence of delusion and enthusiasm, the infatuated reveries of a heated fancy. Yet, if the
latter and more charitable supposition be adopted,
why do we find so much that is sublime and undeniable in theology; pure, holy, and enlightened,
in morality? Could an *enthusiast* surpass all the
ancient schools of philosophy? Could such a
teacher promulgate principles, which led even
those who opposed the Christian system to reform
their own; which the wisest of men still allow to
be consonant with the most improved dictates of
human reason ; which have left speculation little
exercise in religious and moral inquiries, except
in demonstrating and arranging anew the important truths, which have been revealed, or in the

barren research of useless curiosities ; and which
have in such a manner both advanced and
extended the knowledge of religious truth, that
a large proportion of the poor and unlettered
inhabitants of Christian countries, attain to a
more extensive, more certain, and more efficacious
acquaintance with God and their duty, than the
wisest Greeks and Romans ? If, with the Prus-
sian monarch, we deny the great and more mysterious peculiarities of Christianity, and reject all
as a divine revelation, we cannot do less than
value and admire, as he is said to have done, its
morality. We cannot but admit the truth of its
statements respecting morality, the unity and
spirituality of the Deity, and a future life. But
how can we *separate* these portions from others,
when inquiring whether the Gospel is a divine
revelation? And do not even the more mysterious
parts of the Gospel doctrine provide us with a
satisfactory elucidation of matters of anxious inquiry to sinful, ignorant, weak, dying mortals;
with the only information respecting them, on
which we can place any reliance? All surely is
delivered as claiming the same authority; how
then can we select some as excellent, and condemn the other as the dictates of enthusiasm ?

But in what manner can the charge of enthusiasm be suggested, except by our own *reluctance* to admit these instructions as true? And

how did the delusion of a Jew take an aspect and direction so entirely different from all established opinions and prejudices? And, if that were the case, how are we to account for the absence of all the characteristics of enthusiasm? We find no vehemence, pride, conceit, or uncharitableness, in Jesus. He had none of the impetuosity, forwardness, or haste, that we should expect to have found in an enthusiast. His whole doctrine, though unfolded by degrees, is harmonious and connected; and contains no visions or rhapsodies. Neither would enthusiasm have at all enabled him to verify ancient predictions, or to deliver others respecting himself and his Church, which equally have been verified. He could not have long persevered in attempting miracles, much less could he have made others believe that he wrought them, unless they were realities. We must then adopt some probable solution. And the supposition that he was sent from God, and performed *his will,* satisfactorily explains the whole mystery.

If he were an *impostor,* and knowingly deceived others, then he "sought *his own will,"* and was influenced by some sinister inclination, from which no one, engaged in such a cause, could be free, but one who had been sent from God, and sought the will, and spoke the words, of him that sent him. But such an imputation is so much at variance with the character and the

doctrines of Jesus; with all that he did, and all
that he omitted to do; that it is in every point
of view improbable. His object could not be
covetousness; for he continued in a state of
poverty, and made no attempts to rise above it.
He was so far from courting the favour of the
rich and powerful, that he checked their disposition towards *himself;* though he would fain
have persuaded them to embrace the truths which
he taught. He required of the rich young man
to sell what he had, and to give the price, not
to himself, but to the poor. We learn, inci-
dentally, that Jesus also gave to the poor, even
from his own scanty stock, which he committed
to the care of his only faithless disciple, and that
knowing his character. And trifling indeed were
the opportunities which Judas had for dishonest
gain, since he covenanted to betray his Master
for thirty pieces of silver. Though some
"ministered to Jesus of their substance," yet
it was never sufficient to provide him, even the
ordinary comforts, much less the elegancies, of
life. And as he threw no temptations in the
way of the rich to draw them to him during his
life, so neither did he hold out any inducement
of a gratifying nature. For he repeatedly declared, and the nature of what he taught and
required abundantly tended to shew the propriety
of the declaration, that "they that trust in worldly

riches," and therefore, too generally, those who possess them, would with difficulty enter his kingdom. Did we say that he spoke of a kingdom? We may ask, then, with Pilate, was he a King; and did he advance and forward such a claim? Yes, but his was not a kingdom like those of this world, or that displayed "the glory of them." "If my kingdom were of this world, then would my servants fight, that I should not be delivered to the Jews; but now is my kingdom not from hence." Neither did he himself fight, or attempt any political innovation, authority, or disturbance; nor did he direct, or authorize, his servants to do so. He endured, with a patience, and a submission which he proposed as the model to all his followers, contempt, violence, and persecution. Ambition had no share in influencing his mind, or directing his actions. He predicted the establishment, not of an earthly, but of a spiritual, kingdom; and occupied most of his time, labours, and instructions, in teaching its nature, while he gave evidence of its authority. He did not profess to attain it by triumphs in the field, in which he should merely expose his life, but only by his actual death. That death he predicted distinctly, though figuratively, to the Jews; but to his own disciples openly, literally, and repeatedly. And in the way in which he predicted and expected, and for which he prepared, was his kingdom set up. Yet it never offered any allurement to worldly ambition, but included, in its nature, all that was opposed to the desires, and, in its accompaniments and transactions, much that was at variance with the comforts, and hopes, and attempts of the ambitious, and even with human feelings. And Jesus himself never spoke of his attainment of earthly, but of heavenly, glory. Had he been an impostor, we may judge, with certainty, what would have been the nature of his aims; and we know also, that the time at which he lived, the expectations of the Jews at that time, the situation of his country, and the known feelings of his countrymen towards the Romans, and their hopes and disposition towards himself, would have abundantly favoured any such interested intentions. But he did not act consistently with the adoption and furtherance of *any* selfish design. Opportunities offered for the gratification of such, beyond what his fondest wishes could have anticipated; but he never availed himself of them. He courted not popularity for its own sake; he retired and hid himself when it was tending to actions in his favour; he repelled it, and cooled its fervour, when of a more quiet, though, as he taught his followers, mistaken character. He did not shew himself to the world, as one that sought to be known openly, in any way which human wishes or corruptions

K

could have suggested. He declared that he expected misrepresentation and obloquy; nor did
he act as one desirous to avoid it for its own sake.
He did not court it, yet neither did he shrink from
it. He did not seek his own glory, but taught, and
exemplified, meekness and lowliness of heart.

Thus, both in the *nature* of his pretensions,
and in the *means* by which he promoted and
advanced them, was there an obvious and unequivocal indication that "he sought not his own
will." His were not the artifices and measures,
which alone an impostor would have employed.
He proceeded in a manner wholly different; and
adopted, in great abundance and variety, with
all publicity and evidence, such means as no
impostor *could* employ. Such were his miracles, his acquaintance with the thoughts and dispositions of his hearers, the accurate adaptation
of the events of his life and of his death and of all
that he taught, professed, and accomplished, to
the prophecies, promises, types, and spirit, of all
the writings of the ancient Scriptures, and of the
religious dispensations which they record. To
pursue this train of argument further, would lead
us insensibly to anticipate some subsequent topics.
What we have just hinted may suffice to shew,
how high this general presumption rises; and
how fully it applies to the most extensive review
of the whole scheme described in Scripture,

though we can only touch upon some of the principal features even of a more confined view. But as we have endeavoured to shew, negatively, that Jesus did not seek *his own will,* let us now, though we have little space left for it, shew that we have a positive and sufficient presumption, that he " sought *the will of the Father, which sent him.*"

What can we answer to his own appeals on this subject? " Me the world hateth, because I testify of it, that the works thereof are evil. Because I tell you the truth, ye believe me not. Which of you convinceth me of sin? And if I say the truth, why do ye not believe me? He that is of God heareth God's words; ye therefore hear them not, because ye are not of God. I honour my Father, and ye do dishonour me; and I seek not my own glory; there is one that seeketh and judgeth. If I honour myself, my honour is nothing; it is my Father that honoureth me, of whom ye say that he is your God; but ye have not known him; but I know him; and if I should say I know him not, I should be a liar like unto you; but I know him, and keep his saying [a]."—Is it not true, that the works of the world are evil; that depravity has formed a resisting medium through which even the rays

---

[a] John vii. 7. viii. 45—55.

of divine truth have too often in vain endeavoured
to penetrate ; and yet that the mists of error and
sin have been dispersed, and the world enlightened, by the Gospel only ? In what other way
has Jesus seen of the travail of his soul, except
by bringing many to righteousness ? Has not his
doctrine most eminently promoted the knowledge
and glory of God? Has it not been received, and
valued, principally by the friends and lovers of
whatsoever is holy, and just, and good ? And have
we not, therefore, the most abundant reason to
acquiesce in the argument urged by our Lord
on another occasion, and which we cited in a
former part of this Lecture. " My doctrine is
not mine, but his that sent me. If any man will
do his will, he shall know of the doctrine, whether
it be of God, or whether I speak of myself.
He that speaketh of himself seeketh his own
glory ; but he that seeketh his glory that sent him,
the same is true, and no unrighteousness is in
him[a]."—We may indeed confidently deny that
there was any unrighteousness in Jesus. For
he did himself illustrate the purity of his doctrine
by giving an exhibition of embodied virtue, by
doing all things which pleased the Father? How
constant his devotion, how lively his faith in God,
how great his zeal for the honour of his temple,

---

[a] John vii. 16—18.

how strict his care to "fulfil all righteousness,"
by the observance both of moral and positive
precepts! How little did he consult his own ease,
when he endured fatiguing journeys by day, and a
houseless rest by night on the mountain or on the
sea, that he might go about doing good! How
little can we suppose that he was engaged in
a pious fraud, when we consider that he referred
to the approach, manner, and consequences of his
death, as the proof and completion of his design.
Yet he could neither foresee nor control these,
except he were divine; and that we should have
had no confidence or hope in him, if his predictions
had failed. How could we still further expatiate
on the complacency, with which he looked forward
to such a death, on his patience and submission to
the will of his Father, when the bitter cup was
put into his hand, and when the approach of the
betrayer 'gave dismal note of preparation' for
that trial, scourging, and crucifixion. Meditate
on his silence, meditate on his sayings, during
these solemn scenes; and say, to what other conclusion can you come, than that he "gave himself
for our sins, that he might deliver us from this
present evil world, according to the will of God,
and our Father[b]!" Say, whether this was not he,
"whom the Father sanctified and sent into the

---

[b] Gal. i. 4.

world[a]!" Say, whether it was not "for the sake
of his disciples, and of those that should believe
on him through their word, that he sanctified
himself, that they also might be sanctified through
the truth[b]!" Say, in short, whether this was not
he of whom David spake, for David said it not of
himself: "Sacrifice and offering thou didst not
desire; mine ears hast thou opened; burnt-offering.
and sin-offering hast thou not required. Then
said I, Lo, I come; in the volume of the book
it is written of me; I delight to do thy will, O my
God; yea, thy law is within my heart. I have
not hid thy righteousness within my heart; I have
declared thy faithfulness and thy salvation. I have
not concealed thy loving-kindness and truth
from the great congregation[c]." Assuredly Jesus
"sought the will of his Father that sent him."
"By that will we are sanctified, through the
offering of his body once for all[d]." And God
"willeth also, that all men should be saved, and
come to the knowledge of the truth;" saved
through the "one mediator between God and
man, who gave himself a ransom for all, to be
testified in due time[e]." Let us receive the testimony thus given of the Son of God. Him let us
preach, and not refrain our lips from declaring,

---

[a] John x. 36.   [b] John xvii. 19, 20.   [c] Ps. xl. 6—10.
[d] Heb. x. 10.   [e] 1 Tim. ii. 4—6.

to the great congregation, faith in his name for
the remission of sins.   In him let us believe, and
him let us obey.   Let us follow the example he
has left us, and "prove what is the good, and
acceptable, and perfect will of God."   And " may
the Lord direct our hearts into the love of God,
and into the patient waiting for Christ'."

' 2 Thess. iii. 5.

LECTURE VII.

—◆—

—◆—

St. John V. 31—35.

*If I bear witness of myself, my witness is not true. There
is another that beareth witness of me; and I know
that the witness which he witnesseth of me is true. Ye
sent unto John, and he bare witness unto the truth.
But I receive not testimony from man; but these things
I say, that ye might be saved. He was a burning and
a shining light; and ye were willing for a season to
rejoice in his light.*

THESE are the words of him, whom we revere as
"the faithful and true witness;" who needed not
that any should testify to him either concerning
man, or concerning himself; who knew full well
man's original disposition, and necessities; who
knew also whence he himself came, all things that
should in this world come upon him, and whither
he went; and whose record, even when he bare
witness of himself, was true. Yet as he came

to purchase for us, and to offer to us, salvation, he condescended to exhibit to us his heavenly credentials; and, in appealing to our understandings, he lowers himself to our capacities, by reasoning with us upon our own principles. This he did, not for his own sake, but for ours, "that we might be saved;" that we might be enabled to recognize his divine commission, and become acquainted with his benevolent designs, and "be saved from wrath through him."

That particular department of the Christian argument, upon which our Lord reasons in our text, was one peculiarly adapted for the conviction of his contemporaries. For they had attended personally on John's ministry, and had heard his testimony so soon afterwards confirmed by the proceedings, character, and doctrine, of our Saviour, and by the great events of the Gospel history. To us, also, it is both intelligible and important. For we have in the Gospels a record of the principal facts and statements of John's ministry, which, although concise, is yet sufficiently copious to supply us with the materials upon which we may reason, so as to come to a satisfactory decision. And whether it be our object to ascertain the doctrines of the Gospel, the nature and design of the sacrament of baptism, the method in which the Gospel was promulgated, or the evidences of its divine original, it will be found advantageous in all these cases to attend particularly, and, if we follow the plan of the New Testament, primarily, to the ministry of John. By omitting to do so, we shall have neglected to employ an important portion of the materials provided for us; I had almost said, a portion, without a due attention to which, we shall probably entertain imperfect, if not erroneous, views. We propose not only to consider, in this Lecture, the words of our Lord in the text, but also to take occasion from them, to embody and arrange all the discourses, in which our Lord refers to the witness of John, principally with the view of leading his hearers to attend to the evidence which it afforded in proof of his divine mission and Messiahship[a]. We shall notice,

1. Those addressed to the persons in authority among the Jews, of which our text is one.

---

[a] The author has not included in this course a particular review of the baptismal doctrines and predictions of John, and of the connection between the missions and ministrations of John and Jesus, because, only a few months before the delivery of these Lectures, he had discussed the subject at large, as select Preacher for December 1820. He has therefore, in this Lecture, confined himself to the view more immediately suggested by the text.—The message of the Baptist to Jesus is more largely considered in Lecture IX; and Lecture XI, also takes some notice of the evidence arising from the miraculous, and other, circumstances attendant on the births of John and Jesus.

2. His conferences on the same subject with the multitudes, with the disciples of John, and with his own disciples.

I. We have already observed, that the discourse, the heads of which we are examining in detail, was delivered before the Jewish Sanhedrim. In the former and concluding clauses of our text, our Lord refers them, *generally,* to the testimony of John, as corroborating that which he advanced respecting himself. Some of them, at least, had probably acquainted themselves with the general tenor of John's instructions, by a personal attendance as his hearers. At any rate, they had certainly heard it from others, who had done so; and, in fact, they were so fully aware, from what they had thus heard, of his remarkable appearance, teaching, and proceedings, and of the attention which he had excited among the people, who believed him to be a prophet, that they had conceived it necessary to send priests and Levites from Jerusalem, to ask him, who he was, and in what character he adopted such a line of conduct[b]? It was, indeed, the acknowledged duty and prerogative of the Sanhedrim to enquire into the justice of the pretensions of those, who assumed the prophetic character; and to this exercise of their public duty, our Lord *specially* refers in the third

---

[b] John i. 19—27.

verse of our text; and therefore, he addressed those, who had every qualification, which adequate information could give, to judge of his own pretensions, as far as the witness of John was concerned in supporting them.

Having defended himself against the charge which they had now brought against him, by claiming a divine commission, which, if admitted, would fully justify his supposed violation of the sabbath, and also prepare them to judge aright respecting all his other proceedings, he wishes them to consider the *proofs* of such a commission. Adopting a judicial principle, in arguing before an official body, he ceased to bear further witness concerning himself; as they would not receive this as true, unless, in his defence, he could support his own assertions by other, and independent, testimony. Now there was another, who had appeared as his witness; and who, both in public and private, had delivered a decided, consistent, and persevering testimony in his favour. Jesus himself was fully aware, that the witness which John bore was true; both because he was fully acquainted with his own original and commission, and also because he had been present at, and immediately concerned in, that visible communication of the Spirit, and that audible attestation from heaven, which was the crowning evidence to convince John himself, that Jesus was the person, of whose approach and office he had testified. Upon that evidence, John had afterwards enlarged to such as had considered his previous instructions. But as our Lord was addressing those, who had themselves taken the pains to obtain, officially, a statement from John's own mouth; he therefore more especially referred them to the answer which John had given. "Ye sent unto John; and he bare witness to the truth." For, " he confessed, and denied not; but confessed, that he was not the Christ;" " neither Elias," at least in person, and for the purposes which they expected Elias to fulfil; "neither that prophet," nor a prophet at all in the sense in which they looked for a prophet to appear among them, by rising from the dead. When a definite answer was demanded from him, he referred them to that prophecy of Esaias, of which their own interpretation, was in the main, correct; and explicitly declared, that his was the voice of him, that was to cry in the wilderness, "Prepare ye the way of the Lord." In this he manifestly implied, that his office only authorized him to bear testimony to another; that he was, therefore, to be compared to " a sound, which, as soon as it has expressed the thought of which it is the sign, dies into air, and is heard no more[a]."

---

[a] Fenelon, cited by Bishop Horne in his Considerations on the Life and Death of John the Baptist.

Whether, therefore, they considered the prophecy, and its usual interpretation; or the express testimony of John; they could not have rightly considered, nor could they finally decide upon, his witness, unless they looked out for another, whose way he prepared, and whose forerunner he was. Of such a one, greater than himself in office, power, and dignity, he expressly spoke to them; of one, who when John testified this, had already taken his station among them, but whom they had then not known; one, who was to come after him, but who existed before him, and who was to be preferred to him; one whose office was more extensive than his own, which merely authorized him to baptize with water[a].—We may consider Jesus as demanding of them, in the words of our text, whether these things had been duly considered? They had known, or might have known, or might easily ascertain, that John had pointed out Jesus, personally and expressly, as him of whom he had spoken. If he were so, the question assumed an important aspect, and was of extensive connexion. Here was a declaration of the approach of the kingdom of heaven; a claim to the office of its herald, and precursor; and a specification of the person, whose approach was to be thus preceded and prepared. They had, therefore, to

---

[a] John i. 26, 27.

meet this great question, to consider these extensive claims. If they neglected to do this, they would incapacitate themselves for judging in a comprehensive and sufficient manner; and would, probably, in consequence of their narrow and partial views, again object, as they were now doing, against some supposed breach of the law, or apparently hasty statement, while they were wholly inattentive to the miracles wrought previously, and at the time; and though they had never fully comprehended, or duly considered, the extent and purport of his claims. Hence they would be likely, both to blaspheme against the Son of man, who was now personally preaching the Gospel of the kingdom amongst them, and also against the Holy Ghost, of which John spake, and who, though not yet given, was hereafter to be given. Now our Lord never required of any, that they should have made advancements beyond the information and evidence which had been communicated to them. He was satisfied with, and commended, those, who were *not far* from the kingdom; who were willing to judge impartially of what had come before them; and who, although some doubts and difficulties remained, were willing to suspend their judgment, and not hastily to exaggerate such doubts, so as to dismiss all further inquiry. All would in due season be set before them; so much already had

been exhibited, that it ought to arrest their attention, and to claim their serious investigation. It
remained with themselves to make a proper and
successful use of what had been advanced, and
of what was yet in reserve. John had long ago
borne witness to the truth, and Jesus was now
himself declaring his office and authority. Not
that he himself received the testimony from man,
but he had "received from his Father a commandment, what he should speak," and perform. They
might derive this assurance, not from his words
only, but from other sources. And these things
he declared to them, "that they might be saved."
If they refused to hear and consider them, theirs
was the danger, and the responsibility rested with
themselves.

But our Lord went on further to remind
them, that, if they finally rejected the testimony of
John, they were in a measure self-condemned.
He was the burning and the shining light of that
age and country; the excellence of his instructions,
and their success and beneficial tendency, they
could not deny; even they themselves, "for a
season, were willing even exceedingly to rejoice
in his light." Thus had they themselves, both
felt and virtually confessed, his prophetic character. Some of them might even have been of the
number of those Pharisees and Sadducees, who
came to his baptism. But they were by him

warned, reproved, and convicted. They found
that he proclaimed not that which they wished
and expected; they saw that he would not be
subservient to their carnal and temporizing policy ; they saw their influence, authority, and interests, at stake; they felt their prejudices attacked
and exposed; they were offended and alarmed;
and therefore their joyful hailing of him who proclaimed the approach of the kingdom of heaven,
their reverence for his character, and their admiration of his instructions, were succeeded by a
sullen neglect, enmity, and contempt. The fact
is several times explicitly and publicly stated by
our Lord[a]; and, in one passage, which we have
yet to notice, to persons in authority, at a time,
and in consequence of an incident in our Lord's
ministry, of leading importance. You will readily
suppose, that we allude to the question proposed to our Lord, after he had entered Jerusalem
in the lowly triumph described by Zechariah,
and had a second time purged the Gentiles' court
of the temple. "By what authority doest thou
these things; and who gave thee this authority[b]?"
The conversation which followed this question,
places the connexion between John's testimony,
and our Lord's mission, in a very clear point of

---

[a] Matt. xi. 16—19; xvii. 9—13. Luke vii. 29, 30; xvi. 14—17.
[b] Matt. xxi. 23.   Mark xi. 28.   Luke xx. 1, 2.

view ; though it is not always rightly represented by the commentators.

The question was proposed by the " chief priests, and the scribes, and the elders of the people," under whose cognizance our Lord's pro-, ceedings certainly fell. He answered by proposing another question. " I will also ask you one thing, which if you tell me, I in likewise will tell you by what authority I do these things. The baptism of John, whence was it? of heaven, or of men ?" that is, was it of *divine,* or of *human* authority? Now their answer was, that "they could not tell;" and Jesus, therefore, refused to tell them " by what authority he did these things." They had declined to answer his question, or rather they had openly declared their inability to answer it. Now this implied, either that they still allowed that John's baptism possibly might be of divine appointment; or that they had not come to an official decision; or that they did not think themselves concerned to do so. The fact was, as we are fully informed in other places, that they rejected John's baptism, and refused to allow its *divine* authority. But they reasoned with themselves, that if they should say thus publicly that it was *of men,* the people, who were fully persuaded that John was truly a prophet, would raise a tumult, and stone them. Their personal safety, therefore, prevented an avowal of their disbelief. Nor could they make

a declaration, which would coincide with the prepossessions of the people, without a virtual re-
cantation of the opinions, which in their conduct,
at least, they had hitherto avowed; without a violation of consistency, as it regarded the past, an
imprudent committal of themselves for the future,
and a liability to be subjected to the unanswerable
reproof of Jesus, " Why then did ye not believe
him ?"

Yet this was not an evasive question, proposed
in order to *bring* them into this dilemma; though
it is too generally so represented, or is left imperfectly explained. It was the most proper answer
which could have been made, as a few brief remarks will shew. It reminded them of the words
of our text, judicially spoken before them; which,
had they been duly considered, might have led
them to a right knowledge of the source and
nature of the authority of Jesus. And it also
reproved them, because they neither admitted the
authority of John, nor, because of their unworthy
fear of the people, did they disabuse them of what
they conceived an erroneous opinion; though, as
the guardians of religion, and the judges of prophetic claims, they ought, officially, to have done
one or the other. By declining to give any definite answer to our Lord's inquiry, they left him
no opportunity of entering on such a line of
argument, as would have evinced his authority

to do these things; yet he clearly taught them
that the question, to which he required an answer, was a *previous* question, the decision of
which would lead to an easy solution of their own.
—You will perhaps ask, why did not our Lord
take some *other* line of argument? I might answer, and the answer would be sufficient, that our
Lord knew what was in man; and we might,
with satisfaction, acquiesce in the conviction, that
in this, as well as in other instances, he did all
things well. But we can answer more fully, and
state, that his question related to the very point of
evidence which it was in this instance proper to
consider. He had entered Jerusalem in pro-
cession, as the meek and lowly King of Zion,
amidst the repeated acclamation, " Hosannah to
the Son of David! Blessed be the King of Israel,
that cometh in the name of the Lord!" This was
a visible accomplishment of the prediction of
Zechariah. Was, then, the authority, which Jesus
claimed in the *temple,* conformable to the divine
purposes, and to the intimations of prophecy?
Assuredly it was. It was designed, as to its object, to effect the removal of the desecrating traffic,
that was carried on in the house of his Father.
It was designed to espouse the cause of the Gentiles, that the outer court might be restored to
them, and that, according to prophecy, the house
of God might be made " a house of prayer for all

nations[a]." That the Messiah should thus actually come in suddenness, and to the confusion of transgressors, to vindicate the honour of the house of God, as "the Lord of the temple," and "greater than the temple," was an especial subject of prophecy; and it was foretold in immediate connexion with the prediction of that *Messenger*, whom John declared himself to be. For although, when questioned by the priests and Levites, he cited the words of Isaiah; yet a passage of Malachi, in which he is also mentioned, specifies the same reason for his mission, and also connects it with the appearance of the Lord, whom the Jews expected, in the temple. "Behold, I send my messenger, and he shall prepare the way before me; and the Lord, whom ye seek, shall suddenly come to his temple, even the messenger of the covenant, whom ye delight in.—And he shall purify the sons of Levi, and shall purge them as gold and silver, that they may offer unto the Lord an offering in righteousness. Then shall the offering of Judah and Jerusalem be pleasant unto the Lord, as in the days of old.—And all nations shall call you blessed; and ye shall be a delightsome land, saith the Lord of

---

[a] Isai. lvi. 6, 7. Mede observes, in his sermon on this subject, that "the place alleged (by our Lord) to avow the fact, speaks of Gentile-worshippers, not in the words τοῖς ἔθνεσι only, but in the whole body of the context." Works, p. 46.

hosts[a]."—By attending to the various and connected transactions thus predicted respecting John
and Jesus, we at once discover the propriety of
our Lord's conduct on this occasion, and the evidence in vindication of his authority, which, under
such circumstances, he pointed out as forcibly by
declining any further statement, as if he had entered on a detail of the argument. If the authority
of the precursor were admitted, it involved the
admission of his own; if they had really so little
considered the former question, as to be yet undecided, they then avoided, or hastily passed over,
the proper and sufficient evidence which was yet
open to their consideration.

But, though they were afraid to encounter our
Lord's arguments, and sought to avoid them, he
left them not unreproved and unwarned. In three
parables,—that of the obedient and disobedient
sons, who were requested to work in their father's
vineyard,—that of the wicked husbandmen,—and
that of the wedding garment,—he exposed the
guilt, impotency, and danger of their unbelief,
and also predicted their approaching murderous
rejection of himself, their forfeiture of the blessings of the kingdom, and the transfer of them to
the Gentiles, whose cause he had been espousing,
and who would bring forth the proper fruits.

---

[a] Mal. ii. 1, 3, 4, 12.

They saw the purport of the parables; they writhed under their severe correction; they could not refrain from deprecating the accomplishment of his predictions; yet they proceeded, even with increased eagerness, in the furtherance of their bloody designs.

Of the first parable he made an express application, which it will be expedient to notice with reference to our subject. He obtained from them a confession, that the son who first refused, but " afterwards repented and went" into the vineyard, "did the will of his father." And he then answered, " Verily, I say unto you, that the publicans and the harlots go into the kingdom of God before you. For John came unto you in the way of righteousness, and ye believed him not; but the publicans and the harlots believed him. And ye, when ye had seen it, repented not afterwards, that ye might believe him[a]." Our Lord here notices the excellence of John's character, and the efficacy of his instructions. Such a consideration they ought not to have neglected. They had been reminded of it in our text, and themselves must have felt it, when they beheld the salutary effects produced by John's labours, upon those whom they themselves had yet been unable to reform, even if they had indeed attempted to

---

[a] Matt. xxi. 31, 32.

do it. Yet this had not induced them to retrace their steps, but had, perhaps, operated to strengthen their prejudices.—The same principle applied, and still applies, to our. Lord's instructions, as well as to those of the Baptist. They are intelligible to those, who have neither leisure nor capacity for philosophical research, or systematic morality. The same Gospel, which is preached to the rich and learned, is preached also to the poor and illiterate. By one and the same Gospel must both be instructed, edified, and saved. Let us, then, value the wisdom and sublimity of its design and contents; let us also admire its universal adaptation and utility; and let neither the pride of station, nor the prejudices of learning, nor the vulgarity of a poor man's religious observances, his uncouth phraseology, and his imperfect, and often mistaken, opinions, prevent the serious examination, and cordial acceptation, of the same truths, which reform, edify, and comfort him. For they were not intended to remedy the disadvantages of station, and the defects of education, excepting only so far as holiness here, and happiness hereafter, may thereby be affected.

Such were our Lord's reasonings and statements, in connexion with the witness of John, as delivered to the ruling authorities of the Jews. We have now only to notice the more remarkable addresses of our Lord on the same subject to the disciples of John, the multitudes, and his own disciples.

II. The earliest of these was on occasion of the memorable message sent to Jesus by John. The *disciples of John* had given him early information respecting the popularity and success of him, " to whom he had borne witness beyond Jordan." The Baptist had then, in the last of his discourses which is recorded, endeavoured to divest them of any jealousy respecting his own honour, by directing them to the remembrance of his former statements; by re-assuring them of the divine and superior dignity of Jesus; and by exhorting them to a reception of his doctrine. Being informed by them, at a later period, of the still growing fame of Jesus, of his repeated miracles, and especially of the raising of the widow's son at Nain, John actually sent them to confer with Jesus, and to obtain, from his own mouth, an answer to the question, " whether he was he that should come, or whether they were to look for another?" They, probably, as well as the rest of the people, were in some degree of suspense, because Jesus had not, in so many words, declared himself the Messiah. Our Lord retained them with him, until he had wrought several additional miracles; and then, in a brief manner, led them to infer his Messiahship, from the miracles which he performed; for they were such as the prophets ascribed to the Messiah, He reminded them, also, that the Gospel was by him preached to the poor, according to another prophecy of Isaiah; and then cautioned them against suffering the faith, produced by such considerations, to be impaired and subverted by any inconsistency which presented itself to their minds between his humble appearance and their expectations. Thus our Lord at once shewed the correctness with which John had described him as one "mightier than himself," and as a teacher who "spoke the words of God;" pointed out the agreement of John's testimony, with the prophecies respecting the Messiah, and the miracles which he was to perform; and intimated the probability and danger of that rejection of his testimony, of which also the prophets had spoken.

The discourse which our Lord addressed to the *multitudes,* after the departure of John's disciples, also very fully discusses the character and office of the Baptist[a]. Of these his own disciples entertained such an opinion, as made their views end in him, and, therefore, for a time, prevented the proper object of his mission. But there was no such danger with the multitude; but rather one of a contrary character. They were in danger of losing the impressions, which

---

[a] Matt. xi. 7—19.

the appearance and preaching of· the Baptist had
produced. And yet they did not abate this respect
for him, in order to transfer it ·to the Messiah ;
but were disposed to err, both with respect to
him and his precursor. Our Lord, therefore,
adapted his discourse to the character of the persons addressed ; endeavouring to recall their former
feelings, in order that he might direct them to
a proper end and object. ·He reminded them
of the earnest attention, which had been excited
among them, by the solemn and unvarying testimony of that holy and self-denying man. He had
appeared, not as the· herald or attendant of an
earthly monarch, though he proclaimed the setting
up of a kingdom. They allowed him to be a prophet; but he was more. For, citing the words of
Malachi, our Lord applied them to him ; and
declared that he was " the Messenger who was to
prepare the way of the Lord." Thus he at once
directed their thoughts to the kingdom of the
Messiah, and pointed out what might prepare
them to discern its real nature. He spoke distinctly of the introduction of a new religious
dispensation; of the superiority of the least prophet of that dispensation, even to John ; as more
honoured, and more enlightened, and more successful. They as yet had been under the guidance
of the law, and of the prophets. But each of
these had prophesied of more glorious times.

Those times had begun with the appearance of John. Now the kingdom of heaven had commenced; not guarded, like Mount Sinai, in order to repel and alarm; but permitting, and even inviting, all to approach and enter. They expected Elias to come. Though no Elias, such as they looked for, would come; yet he who was to come, he whom Malachi had predicted under that title, had already come; for this was no other than John the Baptist. This was important information; a statement to be attentively heard, and earnestly examined. And our Lord therefore added; "he that hath ears to hear, let him, therefore, hear."

Thus did our Lord declare the proper view, in which they were now to examine the mission of John; thus did he assist them in that examination, and direct them rightly to employ the means which already existed, for forming a correct decision, and which the progress of his ministry rendered continually more abundant. Yet he well knew, both from the past conduct, and present disposition, of that generation, and from his foreknowledge of their future proceedings, that the connected mission of John and himself, and the different conduct and demeanour which suited their respective functions, would not meet the prejudices, or engage the impartial consideration, of all. They had their favourite and obstinate prejudices, which operated against each of these messengers. Two consecutive, but distinct, methods had been employed for the introduction of the kingdom of heaven. "John came neither eating nor drinking;" to him they objected, because he came in a severe and repulsive character; of him they said, "He hath a devil." "The Son of man came eating and drinking;" not declining to join in social and familiar intercourse with the world, and yet, however inconsistently, they found in this also a motive to reject and calumniate him. "Behold, said they, a gluttonous man, and a wine-bibber, a friend of publicans and sinners." They appeared therefore not disposed to be satisfied with any thing, however expressly calculated to obviate and remove their prejudices. They therefore acted as perverse a part, as those "children," whom "when assembled in the market-place" for their pastime, no variety of proposal, suggested by a spirit of compliance and accommodation on the part of their companions, could persuade to join in the amusements of the hour. But however they might thus "reject the counsel of God against themselves," "the children of wisdom," all of candid and reflecting minds, would perceive and acknowledge that both these methods were adopted by divine wisdom, and that they might justly be applauded and admired.

As too many among the Jews were offended,

both by the austere demeanour of John, and the
social one of Jesus, so the *disciples of John* were
backward to approve of the latter, and exclusively
admired the former. They therefore demanded
of Jesus, why they, and the disciples of the Pharisees, fasted often, but his, like himself, did not
fast, but ate and drank like others, without any
such abstemiousness. Here also Jesus endeavoured to satisfy the well disposed inquirers; and,
in several parabolical illustrations, shewed the
propriety of this part of his conduct. These you
will readily call to mind; and we have only time
to observe, that he adopted, in one instance, the
same figure in which John had instructed them
respecting himself. For John had spoken of Jesus
as the bridegroom, and of himself as the attendant
of the bridegroom. And Jesus now observed,
that his chosen disciples, as well as John, were
attendants of him the bridegroom, but that he
called them not to any premature austerities;
because these comparatively were the days of
their festivity. But after he had trained them
up for their future work, "the bridegroom would
be taken from them; and then they would
fast in those days[a]." For the event to which he
alluded, and for its consequences, he was gradually

---

[a] Mark ii. 18—22. Luke v. 33—39. The inquiry seems to
have been proposed, not only by the disciples of John, but also by
the Scribes and Pharisees.

preparing them; but if he adopted the procedure to which they alluded, so harsh a discipline, employed in the first instance, would too much discourage them.

The *disciples of our Lord* do not appear to have entertained any objection to the proceedings and appearance, either of John or Jesus. The fact, "that the bridegroom should be taken from them," was thàt, at the mention of which they were confounded, in whatever manner it was couched. They also expected, as other Jews did, and as the Scribes taught, that "Elias would first come, and restore all things;" and, probably, at the transfiguration, they conceived that their expectations were about to be fulfilled. But their joy and eagerness was soon checked by the injunction to "tell the vision to no man, until the Son of man was risen from the dead." This recalled to their minds the parallel declarations made by their Master a short time before; and they could not either understand "what the rising from the dead should mean," as applied to their Master, or how it could be reconciled with their past expectations, and present suppositions, respecting Elias. They proposed the difficulty to their Master, and received, in answer, a statement, calculated to remove their doubts, if not immediately, yet soon afterwards. With the citation of that answer, and of another remark of our Lord to his disciples, we may conclude this review of his reasonings respecting John.

.   "His disciples asked him, saying, Why then say the Scribes that Elias must first come? And Jesus answered, and said unto them, Elias truly shall first come, and restore all things.   But I say unto you, that Elias is come already, and they knew him not, but have done unto him whatsoever they listed; likewise also shall the Son of man suffer of them.   Then the disciples understood that he spake unto them of John the Baptist[a]."   And when the Son of man had "suffered many things," and had "risen from the dead," then did our Lord again direct their thoughts to that particular prediction of the Baptist, which he had himself also delivered, and which was then about to be accomplished; thus, in another instance, pointing out to them the difference of their respective functions, and the tendency which their consecutive ministrations had to accomplish the purposes of God in the establishment of his kingdom.   "Wait, said he, in Jerusalem, for the promise of the Father, which ye have heard of me.   For John truly baptized with water; but ye shall be baptized with the Holy Ghost, not many days hence[b]."

We may, I think, derive from the whole series

---

[a] Matt. xvii. 10—13. Mark ix. 11—13.   [b] Acts i. 4, 5.

of our Lord's reasonings on this subject, and from
a comparison of his remarks with the instructions,
predictions, and transactions, to which they refer,
a conviction of the completeness and force, even of
this single head of evidence. It shews to us the
divine authority of the witness of John; and how
clear a light is from thence reflected on the authority of Jesus. And may we, therefore, be " children of wisdom," and justify its proceedings. We
are men of like passions with those, who rejected
the instructions both of Jesus and of John. We
may be under the influence of prejudices equally
powerful; we may, in like manner, be inattentive
and obdurate. But, though John were " a burning and a shining light," he was not " that light,
which, coming into the world, enlighteneth every
man;" he was sent only " to bear witness of
that light;" to exhibit to the world, as it were,
the dawn of the rising " Sun of Righteousness."
But "the day-spring from on high has now
visited us." " The true light now shineth."
Let us "be willing," not "for a season" only,
but continually and perseveringly, " to rejoice in
the light of him, who declared himself to be " the
light of the world." Let the convictions, which
from time to time we feel, be encouraged, and
not stifled. Let the resolutions, to which they
give rise, not be "like the morning dew," and
refresh us only for a time; but be so cherished

M

and renewed, as to abide the scorching sun of temptation and persecution. Let such a stedfastness be maintained, that hope may arise, and gather strength and maturity, within us. Yet a genuine and well-grounded hope cannot even exist in the soul of him, who does not know and obey the promises and precepts of the Gospel. But if hope has respect to the blessings which Jesus has purchased, and be founded on a scriptural faith, and attended by that "charity, which never faileth," it will then be "an anchor of the soul, both sure and stedfast, which entereth within the vail, whither our forerunner is for us entered, even Jesus." He, as the Baptist declared, is "the Lamb of God, which taketh away the sin of the world." And John also bare witness, "that he is the Son of God;" and solemnly said to his disciples, "He that believeth on the Son hath everlasting life; and he that believeth not the Son, shall not see life; but the wrath of God abideth on him [a]."

---

[a] John i. 29, 34; iii. 36.

LECTURE VIII.

OUR LORD'S APPEAL TO HIS MIRACLES AS ATTESTING
HIS DIVINE MISSION.

—◆—

St. John V. 36.

*But I have greater witness than that of John; for the
works which the Father hath given me to finish, the
same works that I do, bear witness of me, that the
Father hath sent me.*

In whatever point of view the serious inquirer
contemplates the facts and circumstances of the
Christian story, or any portion of them, he cannot fail to be impressed with a conviction, that
he therein discerns the arm of the Almighty not
obscurely revealed, but employed for great and
holy purposes. The evidence arising from miracles doubtless affords to us one of the most obvious
and intelligible indications of this truth ; and one
which has been observed and acknowledged even
by those, who have taken a less detailed and
complete survey of the whole, and who have,
therefore, perhaps, not attended much to the

M 2

evidence arising from the proceedings, character, and witness, of John. The Gospel records, however, present to us the latter of these as the earliest subject for our examination ; and no one, who has given to it the attention which it deserves, will be disposed to deny, that it affords a most satisfactory evidence of the truth of Christianity. In our last Lecture we took the particular view of this extensive argument, which was suggested by the words immediately preceding our text. In our text our Lord states, that the miracles which he wrought are "a greater witness than that of John." Not that the one was of divine appointment and interference, and the other not ; but because miracles are the visible tokens of divine interposition, from which the inference is more immediate, and of which the evidence is more sensible. And, indeed, the witness of John, considered merely as the testimony of a zealous and holy person, and even as that of a prophet, is not complete without the evidence of miracles; for these were necessary in order to prove Jesus to be the mightier one of whom he spoke. John's ministry wonderfully prepared the way for that of our Lord, that he might, with more advantage, appear as the worker of miracles, and as the authoritative teacher of a more enlarged scheme. But the miracles themselves were the greater, more definite, and more unequivocal demonstration of his authority, and of the divinity of his doctrine.

The words of our text might, indeed, be considered as referring, not merely to the mighty works which he performed in order to our conviction, but also to "the whole work which the Father gave him to do." And, undoubtedly, from the great design itself, and its accomplishment, an argument arises which includes all others, and which sets them before us with the greatest advantage; because we then not only discern the force of each, separately considered, but of all as connected with each other, and as manifesting, both the unity and consistency of the design, and the completeness of its accomplishment. But that the words of our text have a more *limited* reference, appears from the phraseology which our Lord employs on other occasions. And in the first passage which we shall cite, there seems decidedly to be such an allusion to the very words of our text, as clearly to shew, that our Lord intended therein to refer to his *miracles.*

Shortly after the cure of the man born blind, some of the Jews, who, as the context shews, probably were persons in authority, "said unto him, How long dost thou make us to doubt? If thou be the Christ, tell us plainly. Jesus answered them, I told you, and ye believed not; the works that I do in my Father's name, they

bear witness of me[a]." In a subsequent part of the
same conference, he again alluded to the "good
works which he had shewed them from his
Father;" and added, "If I do not the works of
my Father, believe me not. But if I do, though
ye believe not me, believe the works ; that ye may
know and believe, that the Father is in me, and
I in him." To his disciples he delivered similar
statements ; which, being more enlarged, point
out to us more fully the connexion of these miracles
with the doctrines, in proof of which he wrought
them; and the criminality of not attending to that
proof:—"Believest thou not," said he to Philip,
"that I am in the Father, and the Father in me?
The words that I speak unto you, I speak not
of myself; but the Father that dwelleth in me,
he doeth the works. Believe me that I am in
the Father, and the Father in me, or else believe
me for the very works' sake. Verily, verily,
I say unto you, He that believeth on me, the
works that I do, shall he do also ; and greater
works than these shall he do, because I go unto
my Father. And whatsoever ye shall ask in my
name, that will I do, that the Father may be
glorified in the Son[b]." Shortly afterwards, when
speaking to his disciples of their future sufferings
in his cause, he observed, "These things will

---

[a] John x. 24, 25.   [b] John xiv. 10—13.

they do unto you for my name's sake, because they know not him that sent me. If I had not come and spoken unto them, they had not had sin; but now have they no cloke for their sin. He that hateth me, hateth my Father also. If I had not done among them the works which none other man did, they had not had sin; but now have they both seen and hated both me and my Father[c]."

The works referred to in these passages, of which our Lord spoke as already past, had been publicly exhibited in the presence of those whom he addressed. And the miracles wrought by the Apostles, in the name of Jesus, and through the prayer of faith, of which our Lord spoke as yet future, were afterwards exhibited with equal publicity. The Jewish people could not deny, and did not in fact doubt, that they were really miraculous works, impossible to the unaided powers of a human being; although they conceived, that the authority of their traditions, and their received interpretations of the Old Testament, justified them in refusing their assent to the doctrines and dispensation, of which these were the sanction and demonstration. That dispensation and its doctrines are as important to us, as they were to them. But we are circumstanced with respect

---

[c] John xv. 21, 24. Some of the passages here quoted will, in future Lectures, be more *particularly* considered.

to the miracles, which prove its divine authority, in a manner somewhat different. We cannot *see* them; and to resolve, except we *see* signs and wonders, not to believe, would be to require that which would make them cease to be miracles. Ours, therefore, cannot be that sensible and striking impression of their reality and evidence, which would be felt by the subjects and spectators of miracles. Yet what we lose in this respect is abundantly supplied by the more enlarged knowledge which we have of the connection of miracles with other branches of evidence, then not so fully exhibited, and with the complete system of truth, of which they proved the divine revelation. Yet we do not lose much by the absence of such an overpowering evidence; for a sufficient conviction of their *reality* alone is necessary to establish the conclusion; and of that we have abundant evidence. It is, indeed, derived from the testimony of others; but a reliance upon well authenticated, and well circumstanced, testimony, is as much a law of our moral nature, as the belief of the ordinary laws by which the universe is governed is of our understanding. We ordinarily act with as little hesitation upon a sufficient moral certainty, as upon the clearest philosophical analogy, or mathematical demonstration. We cannot in either case make our own personal experience the test of all possible facts; and to

believe nothing, but that which we have ourselves
seen, is as unreasonable, as it would be em-
harrassing. Whenever, therefore, distance of time
or place prevents us from being spectators of any
transaction, we can become acquainted with it
only by testimony; nor have we any just ground
to reject such testimony, if it be attended with the
proper marks of credibility. The case is very little
different, if the facts in question be of that character which we call miraculous. They differ from
other facts principally with reference to the cause
which produced them. It is essentially requisite
that they should be subject to the apprehension
and examination of the senses of mankind; but
their miraculous nature is merely an inference
from their reality as facts, and from a conviction
that neither the ordinary procedure of nature, nor
the agency of man, could have produced them.
In our inquiries respecting them, we may justly
scrutinize, with all possible accuracy, the testimony
which reports that they occurred; we may with
equal care weigh and compare the circumstances
of the facts in detail, with a view of discovering
whether there were any imposture or delusion.
But if, after such an examination, the inference
that they resulted from a miraculous agency,
is the only tenable one; the nature of the conclusion at which we have arrived is by no means
to be applied as an objection to its truth and

correctness. That the *ordinary* laws of nature are
wise, useful, and constant, and that they are
designed for the benefit of all creatures that live,
affords no sufficient presumption that their progress
may not be counteracted or superseded, to provide for objects so important, as the spiritual and
eternal interests of man. And if such a design
appear evident, as in the case of the Christian
miracles, the end is confessedly desirable and
necessary. The means by which we receive an
assurance that the end is attained, though they
involved a partial and temporary suspension, or
counteraction, of the laws of the universe, did not
at all supersede, or even interrupt, their *general*
beneficial operations. Yet they conferred valuable
personal benefits upon the individuals, who were
the subjects of them, at the same time that they
permanently provided for the continued consolations, and lively hopes, of all future generations.

The facts, to which our text refers, are those
upon which our religion is founded; and, without
allowing the truth of them, we cannot account for
its success. For the pretence to miraculous
powers, of such a kind, and under such circumstances, would, if they had not been real, have
ruined the cause which it did so effectually promote. Now the Gospel records of these facts
being so circumstantial, full, and perspicuous, we
are thereby enabled to place ourselves, as it were,

in the midst of the scenes so described, and become
qualified to judge, perhaps, as accurately as those
who actually witnessed them, of their reality as
exertions of divine power. We are therein furnished with the testimony of eye-witnesses; with
the written narrative of those things, which they,
day by day, and from year to year, proclaimed by
word of mouth, " both to small and great," both
to Jew and Gentile; in the midst of persecution
and opposition, but without contradiction from
those, who, if there were a possibility of denying
them, were both interested and disposed to do so,
but who endeavoured to suppress the propagation
of Christianity, in defiance of these extraordinary
facts, rather than venturing to deny their truth.
Upon the *practical* proof, which these witnesses
gave, of the correctness and fidelity of what they
attested, this is not the place to enlarge; they evidently themselves believed these things to have
been as they related them. For no other motive,
than the love of truth, can be assigned for their
diligence and earnestness in promulgating the
Gospel; or for their stedfastness and patience
under the trials to which their testimony exposed
them. The written narrative which they have
left us, is not composed in the adorned style of
other histories, but in a manner peculiar to themselves. The miraculous facts are related in the
same brief, circumstantial, and inartificial manner,

as the ordinary ones. An impression is left on the mind by a perusal of these narratives, that the authors did not write under the influence of imagination, but of the vivid recollection of obvious, though astonishing, facts.; and that they had felt a conviction of the reality of what they saw, which nothing could impair or destroy. In very many instances they mention such particulars, as render it impossible to conceive but that the facts, which they so particularly and graphically describe, took place just in the manner in which they relate them. And each Evangelist, in other instances, makes such omissions of many particulars, and such transitions from one incident to another, as would be wholly inexplicable, except upon the supposition that the writer's mind was more occupied with the remembrance of circumstances which he had actually observed, than with the construction and arrangement of a fictitious narrative.

Another circumstance tends to shew, that the Evangelists did not invent the miracles which they record. They are not mere acts of power, exhibited with pomp and ostentation, so as merely to dazzle and astonish the multitude; nor are they characterized by moroseness, superstition, or revenge. Yet such have those been, which have either been put in competition with the Gospel miracles, or which some have attempted to add to

them. Why have men of far superior education
succeeded so ill in comparison with the Evangelists,
but that the former related what were either
fictions or impostures, the latter real facts? Nor
are the miracles of Jesus isolated facts, referred to
no good or declared end, but expressly wrought
for the promotion of the greatest of purposes;
connected with important incidents and discourses,
so as to add force, and dignity, and authority, to
the instructions, at the same time that they also
serve to illustrate them. Even when they are
most public, there is no appearance of ostentation,
but every feature of sobriety, dignity, and de-
corum; and often were they accompanied by
a remarkable humility and concealment of himself.
They were works of compassion and benevolence;
beneficial in their immediate effect, as well as
with reference to their ultimate purpose.

Such was the general character of the works
which Jesus did; and a more particular notice of
their nature and circumstances shews them to be
so decisively *miraculous*, as to present a very
strong case even to those, who argue for the antecedent improbability or impossibility of miracles.
As it is undeniable that some such works were
done, we ask of the sceptic only a candid investigation of the facts of the case; because we believe
that this will be of itself sufficient to induce him
to assent to the words of Jesus; " the same works

that I do, bear witness of me, that the Father hath sent me." Jesus addressed those, who were familiar with the facts in question; and *we* must, in like manner, make ourselves acquainted with them, before we can come to any just decision respecting their competency to assure us of the truth of the Gospel. The facts *may* be so circumstanced, as to be wholly inexplicable on any other supposition, than that the Author of nature is the Author of these extraordinary phenomena. It is ours to ascertain how far that is the case; and our Lord proceeded during his ministry in a manner which offers to our consideration a great variety of facts. Even before the imprisonment of John, at which time he may properly be said to have commenced his preaching, he began his miraculous works; thus exhibiting his credentials before he delivered his message. And this procedure may be observed, not only in the general plan of his ministry, but in the particular portions of it. He generally taught *after* the exhibition of his mighty works. Some of his more important discourses were immediately preceded and occasioned by them. And the most full and particular statements, which he delivered, were at the close of his life, when he may be said to have at length suspended the exercise of his power. In every point of view, therefore, it is necessary to ascertain the real state of the question with respect to the *nature* of the facts, that we may decide whether they are, or are not, *miraculous*. And if we find ourselves obliged to admit that they are so, it is an admission of a fact in the history of the world, which may justly make us conclude, that all reasonings in denial of the possibility of miracles, are futile and erroneous; and if they are so, surely we may also admit the obvious inference, that God has spoken by Jesus; and we should receive, with humble and adoring faith, the testimony which he has given us respecting that " eternal life, which is in his Son."

Consider then, still more particularly, the *obvious* nature of these facts. They were of such a nature, as to be subject both to the senses and understandings of all. If they were so, those, who were the subjects and spectators of the miracles, had complete evidence of their reality; and the only evidence which could apply. The greater number of these miracles consisted in the cure of the diseased; the blind, the lame, and the maimed. Their previous infirmity was notorious; in many instances it had been of long duration, and had baffled the skill of physicians. Their recovery was equally ascertainable, and was found, in all cases alike, to be complete and lasting. The change from the one state to the other was, in most instances, effected, or, at least, preceded, by

a word, by the touch, by some external application,
whose very nature shewed that it was not the
powerful agent which of itself produced the
change. That it could be neither the result of
imposture, nor the effect of imagination, the number of the instances is sufficient to prove. If
imagination could be supposed to cure diseases of
every kind, under every circumstance, and of
every duration, it could not raise the dead. Much
less could any such causes suspend the operation
of gravity upon the body of Jesus, and that of
St. Peter, and cause " the winds and the sea to
obey him." That no ordinary physical cause
could have produced any of these effects, is obvious to common sense, and not deniable by
philosophy. There are only two tenable suppositions ; and, as far as the argument is concerned,
it is indifferent which we select. Either it was
a suspension, modification, or counteraction, of
the ordinary laws of nature, by the *immediate*
operation of divine power ; or it was a deviation,
for which the Creator had *provided,* in the *original*
formation and arrangement of the world ; which
took place exactly in that age, and at that moment,
when one, claiming to be a divine messenger,
accompanied these, even on this hypothesis,
extraordinary occurrences, by such visible signs,
as to connect them with his own teaching, and
with the other proofs which he gave of his divine

commission[a]. On either of these suppositions the proof of divine attestation is equally cogent.

The proof itself, and the sufficiency of its premises, are also rendered more evident by the *greatness, number,* and *variety,* of these miracles. Impostors seldom venture on many attempts to perform such wonders, as excite astonishment, and provoke inquiry. But in this case the inveteracy of the disorder, and the reality of death, were not more certain, than the speedy, and even instantaneous recovery of health and of life. To what, then, but to a supernatural power, can we ascribe that perfect and permanent efficacy of apparently inadequate means, which neither the strictest scrutiny, nor the lapse of time, could ever disprove? Yet the number of such miracles is very considerable. Upwards of fifty distinct instances are related in detail; besides many references of the Evangelists to others, of which they have given only a general notice. Now a *number* of the same kind certainly adds to the probability of each; but much more a number of *various* kinds. One or two might be the effect of chance; but, as the number and variety of regular phenomena prove the existence of one designing cause, so do the number and variety of our Lord's mira-

---

[a] See the latter hypothesis ably supported by M. Bonnet, Recherches de Christianisme, Chap. vi.

cles tend still more and more to shew the certainty of the position, which they were wrought
to prove, that he spoke the words of God. And
the variety of *manner* in which he performed
them, tends still more strongly to establish the
same conclusion. For we find that even the
same diseases are sometimes cured by one external
application, and sometimes by another; sometimes
only by a word, sometimes even when the sufferer
is in a distant place; as if to shew us that it was
not by any charm, any more than by chance, but
by the power of God, that the effect was produced.

Consider further the *publicity* of the miracles.
They were not wrought, like the pretended ones
of ancient or modern times, in private, or under
circumstances which might evade scrutiny, or
render it inapplicable; but openly, in the face of
day, before assembled multitudes of friends and
foes; on the highway, in the house, in the synagogue, and in the temple; wherever an unfortunate
sufferer presented himself, or application was made
on his behalf. When the actual *performance* of
the cure was more private, its reality and permanence was equally ascertainable. It was obvious
to all who had known the previous condition of
those who had received it; and they themselves,
even when Jesus attempted to restrain them,
published abroad the miracle which had been

wrought, and that Jesus was he, who had made them whole. To this frequency and publicity of the miracles of Jesus is to be attributed that full persuasion, which all applicants evinced, of his ability to grant their request. For such confidence could result only from their knowledge of his previous miracles. To the same cause must we also ascribe the remarks made by the astonished multitude, that he had "done all things well;" and that "it was never so seen in Israel." Hence also they asked, "whether when Christ came, he would do more miracles than Jesus." Hence also their disposition, on some occasions, even forcibly to urge him to assume a temporal kingdom; and on others, their confident expectation that he would do so of his own accord. But, at all such conjunctures, Jesus shewed in another way his superhuman qualities. He was always *aware* of their designs and wishes; and displayed his knowledge of them by his words and by his actions. Nay, during the whole course of his ministry, in various ways, and on numerous occasions, he manifested this his intimate knowledge of the spiritual as well as of the material world; and, as he saw fit, employed either the one or the other to evince his divine authority.

The publicity and reality of the miracles of Jesus are *attested* even by his *enemies*. For, since they were not themselves convinced by them, they deemed it necessary to diminish, if

possible, their influence on the people. They
therefore circulated cavils against them; but of
such a nature, as implied no doubt of their reality.
Once, indeed, they ventured to scrutinize one of
the miracles of Jesus; but they were unable in
any degree to disprove it. They could only conceal their inability to deny the fact, by objecting
to the character of Jesus. "Give God the praise,"
said they to the blind man, to whom Jesus had
restored his sight; "we know that this man is a
sinner, because he keepeth not the sabbath-day."
But all their opposition and misrepresentations
were insufficient to check the prepossessions of the
people in his favour; and therefore, as they were
not disposed to abandon their own disbelief, they
found it necessary to have recourse to violence.
This resolution they made, not because Jesus had
given no proof of his mission, but because he had
proved it so abundantly. "This man, said they,
doeth many miracles; if we let him alone, all
men will believe on him."

And why should not all men believe on him?
For the method which was taken by his enemies
to arrest the progress of his doctrine, does not
invalidate, but supports and confirms, the argument, that "the works which he did bore witness
of him, that the Father had sent him." They confessed that miracles were done; and how can we
conceive them to have been done without divine

assistance? Why was Jesus divinely assisted, if
not also divinely commissioned; and if "the works
which he did, were not those, which the Father
had given him to finish?" His works were
wrought to prove the divine authority of what
he taught, and the divine appointment of what
he did and suffered. The proof is sufficient
for the conviction of mankind, if these works
were so wrought. And that they were, we
have evidence various in its kind, satisfactory
in its nature, and infallible in its consequence.
There may have been many unfounded reports
of miraculous works; many instances, in which
knavery has contrived the semblance of a miracle, and in which credulity has too readily
admitted such pretences. But an examination of
the Gospel miracles soon evinces their decided
superiority over the boasted wonders of heathen-
ism, superstition, and imposture. They were
wrought not among friends, but in the midst of
enemies; not in support of an established religion,
but as the foundation of a new one; in furtherance of a religion, not which favoured the prejudices
of mankind, but which ran entirely counter to
them. They were wrought by the author of that
religion among those to whom miracles were not
unknown; who demanded them of him in proof
of his mission; who well understood the force and
nature of the evidence which they afforded; who

were qualified to judge of their reality; and who, because of his humble and unambitious life, were not afraid to scrutinize them.

Jesus came in humility. But these his mighty works abundantly compensated for this want of the trappings of outward dignity. We recognize in him such wisdom, benevolence, and dignified condescension, as powerfully bespeak our veneration. He claimed to be the Son of God; the Christ, the Saviour of the world; and by his works we believe him so to be; for if we deny the veracity of the Messenger, we insult the authority of him who sent him. Other than sent of God, Jesus could not be. The peculiar authority with which he both spoke his doctrines, and also commanded the unclean spirits, the winds and the waves, the diseases of the living and the spirits of the dead, might, indeed, have seemed to argue a confidence little suited to one "in the likeness of man," had they not invariably obeyed him, and proved him more than man. For we see exhibited in the splendour of his miracles, all the dignity of the Messiah, all the glory of the Divinity; a dignity and a glory, in comparison of which all the splendour of earthly kingdoms is poor and fading. The one is the glory of man; the other the glory, the wisdom, and the power, of God. Yet the Jews were so prejudiced against the *doctrines* of Jesus, which exposed their depravity, and taught them a purity after which they hated to be reformed, that his *miracles* scarcely restrained them from ridding themselves of his .reproofs. But by these miracles we may see demonstrated the divinity of his doctrine. Whether it attacks our vices, abases our pride, reveals our ignorance, or calls us in repentance, humility, and self-abasement, to submit to the righteousness of God, we reject it at our peril.

"I have greater witness than that of John," said our Lord in the text, when alluding to his works. He elsewhere connected the witness of John with the witness of his own works, in a manner which presents to us a striking coincidence in the train of thought, and which may, perhaps, appeal to our *hearts* more effectually than even the most convincing reasonings.—When Jesus had concluded that address to the multitudes, in which, after the departure. of John's disciples, he instructed them respecting the character and office of John, and how "wisdom would be justified of her children," both with respect to John and himself; he then began, by a transition similar to that in the text, "to upbraid the cities in which most of his *mighty works* were done, because they repented not[a]." "Woe unto thee, Chorazin, woe unto thee, Bethsaida; for if the mighty works

---

[a] See Matt. xi. 20—30.

which were done in you, had been done in
Tyre and Sidon, they would have repented long
ago in sackcloth and ashes; Sodom would have
remained unto this day. But I say unto you,
That it shall be more tolerable for Tyre and Sidon,
and Sodom, in the day of judgment, than for you."
If so, how shall it fare with some of us in that
day; whose prejudices are less inveterate, and
yet, perhaps, also less excusable, than those of
the Jew; who with the judgment and understanding believe in Jesus, and yet have not
repented; it may be are still wedded to our sins,
and have resolved to delay repentance. "Repent,
and believe the Gospel," were the first words
which Jesus delivered in the cities of Galilee,
where his mighty works had been done, and
where they continued to be done, in confirmation
of his authority. We may know, then, that if
our's is not that "godly sorrow, which worketh
repentance unto salvation," if we do not with the
heart believe unto righteousness, then,—whether
the seed be taken out of our hearts by the father
of the lies of infidelity, or whether in time of
temptation we fall away, or whether the seed be
choked by the cares of this world, or the deceitfulness of riches,—it shall be more tolerable for
Tyre, Sidon, and Sodom, in the day of judgment,
than for us. For "God is no respecter of persons," and "his judgment is according to truth."

If such be the condemnation to which we are liable, how ought we to be stirred up to strict and serious self-examination, when we hear our Lord address the Father, who had sent him, in words like these; "I thank thee, O Father, Lord of heaven and earth, because thou hast hid these things from the wise and prudent, and hast revealed them unto babes. Even so, Father, for so it seemed good in thy sight." Now if there be sins, errors, and delusions, of the understanding; if there be "a way that seemeth right unto a man, but the end of which is death;" if we "cannot enter into the kingdom of God, except we be converted, and become as little children," in all docility, humility, innocence, and sincerity; let us then pray, that "the thoughts of our hearts may be cleansed by the operation of his holy Spirit," and that, "as new-born babes, we may desire the sincere milk of his word that we may grow thereby." If such be our desire of divine instruction, and such our fitness to receive it, then shall we duly prize, and study, and obey those holy Scriptures, which, through faith in Christ Jesus, can make us wise unto salvation. Then will our faith and hope be strengthened, and our religious inquiries be directed, by our Lord's next words: "All things are delivered unto me of my Father; and no man knoweth the Son, but the Father, neither knoweth any man the Father, save the Son, and he to whomsoever the Son will reveal him." We may partake of so divine a benefit, as to "know the only true God, and Jesus Christ whom he has sent," if we are truly disciples of Jesus. He was sent by the Father to be our teacher and our Saviour; and he is as condescending and gracious, as he is powerful and glorious.

This alarming, yet affectionate, discourse is concluded with words, which always appear to me to exemplify that consummate wisdom, that divine charm, by which our Lord's instructions delight the ear, captivate the affections, and impress the conscience; which must even penetrate and warm the heart of the unbeliever; and which 'have a beauty and pathos in them, which although the Christian feels, the commentator cannot express[a].' Compare with the words last cited those which we are about to cite; their meaning will then be obvious, and may God impress them on our hearts! "Come unto me, all ye that labour and are heavy laden, and I will give you rest. Take my yoke upon you, and learn of me, for I am meek and lowly of heart; and ye shall find rest unto your souls. For my yoke is easy, and my burden is light."

---

[a] These are the words of Bishop Horne in his Commentary on Ps. lxxiii. 25, 26. But they are as applicable to these words of our Saviour, as to those beautiful words of the Psalmist.

LECTURE IX.

——◆——

——◆——

St. Matthew XI. 2—6.

Now when John had heard in the prison the works of Christ, he sent two of his disciples, and said unto him, Art thou he that should come, or do we look for another? Jesus answered and said unto them, Go and shew John again those things which ye do hear and see; The blind receive their sight, and the lame walk; the lepers are cleansed, and the deaf hear; the dead are raised up, and the poor have the Gospel preached to them. And blessed is he, whosoever shall not be offended in me.

THIS message of the Baptist to Jesus is an incident of so remarkable a character, that probably few attentive Christians peruse the account of it, without a wish to be satisfied respecting the occasion and the object of it. A reference to the Commentators will certainly make the inquirer acquainted with several different opinions on the subject; some of which rest upon mere conjecture and gratuitous assumption; and others do not in-

clude that extended review of the ministry of the
Baptist, which is so necessary in order to the
right apprehension both of this and of many other
questions. Such opinions, however, we shall not
notice in a way of formal refutation, but only so
far as may be necessary to clear our path in that
inquiry, which will in the first instance occupy our
attention, viz. how the question respecting the
character and office of Jesus was situated, at the
time when the Baptist sent this message to him.
And as our Lord, in his answer, appeals to his
works in support of a claim to somewhat more
than merely a divine mission; it will be our endeavour in the latter part of this Lecture to shew
the nature and justice of that appeal.

I. In order to ascertain the occasion, and
intention of the Baptist's message, which we are
first to consider, we must have recourse to the
Evangelical records; which afford sufficient, and
the only legitimate, materials for our purpose.—
When the Baptist sent his disciples to Jesus, his
own public labours had for some time ceased;
for he had been shut up in prison by Herod the
tetrarch of Galilee. But, ever after that event,
Jesus had gone about the cities of Galilee, pro-
claiming the glad tidings of the kingdom, and
healing all manner of sickness and disease among
the people. After some time he selected twelve

of his disciples to be his constant attendants;
giving them the title of Apostles, with reference
to their future mission round Galilee in his life
time, and to all nations after his death. He still
continued to exercise his miraculous powers, in
healing the diseased; and, at length, he raised to
life the only son of a widow, whom she, attended
by much people of the city of Nain, was carrying
out for burial as Jesus was entering the city.
A great impression was produced by this signal
miracle. "There came a great fear on all; and
they glorified God, saying, That a great prophet
is risen up among us; and, That God hath visited
his people. And this rumour of him went forth
throughout all Judea, and throughout all the
region round about. And the disciples of John
shewed him of all these things[a]." This statement of St. Luke, that they "told him concerning
all these things," leaves us no room to doubt that
they gave him a full account of all the proceedings
of Jesus. He might with reason rely on the correctness of their report; and the subject was one
of such interest to him, that he would as little
want the disposition, as he did the time and
opportunity, to hear all that they could tell him
respecting the doctrine and miracles of Jesus.
That Jesus had not yet stated himself to be the

---

[a] Luke vii. 11—18.

Messiah, it is scarcely necessary to remark. And, therefore, as far as that fact is considered in connexion with the conduct of the Baptist, a reason appears why, when, upon hearing all these things, John sent two of his disciples to Jesus, the *question* propounded by them was, " Art thou *he that should come,* or do we look for another ?"

But again, we know that a person named Jesus had formerly come from Galilee to John, to be baptized of him. John then bore to him a remarkable testimony ; stating that he was the very person of whom he had before spoken in several predictions ; and applying to him not only the attributes which he had previously specified, but also several others still more exalted. And before he separated from Jesus, to meet him no more, he directed several of his own disciples to him. They were afterwards numbered with the twelve Apostles ; whom Jesus had selected from the body of his disciples previously to the question proposed by John. That question affords not the slightest indication that he supposed the Jesus, who was now so celebrated in Galilee, to be a person different from him whom he had baptized in Judea, and who had come from Galilee for that purpose. His own disciples could have satisfied him on that point ; for at an earlier period, after John had retired into Galilee, they came to him, and said, " Rabbi, *he that was with thee beyond Jordan, to*

whom thou barest witness, behold *the same* baptizeth, and all men come to him[a]." It was no
long time afterwards that John was imprisoned;
and Jesus, who had become so well known in
Judea, and whose miracles the *Galileans* also had
seen at the feast of the passover, himself went
into Galilee; taught in their synagogues, being
glorified of all, and increased continually in
notoriety and popularity even till the time that
John sent to him the message by his disciples.
It is also certain that no others but John and
Jesus had appeared as divine teachers, and with
a belief on the part of the people of their prophetic character; and certainly that no other than
Jesus had wrought miracles. And he, having
wrought his first miracle at Cana in Galilee,
shortly after his baptism, afterwards wrought
others in Judea; and then, upon beginning his
stated ministry in Galilee, wrought them unin-
terruptedly up to the period when he raised the
widow's son, and the incident now under consideration occurred.

So far then all is sufficiently obvious. John the
Baptist, when he sent to ask of Jesus, whether he
was " he that should come," could not but have
been assured, that he, to whom he had borne witness beyond Jordan, was the very person, the

---

[a] John iii. 26.

miraculons attestation to whose divine mission
was now so decided and notorious. In this the
supposed difficulty consists. Why, it is asked,
should he, who had so long known that Jesus was
the Messiah; now give reason to suppose that he
doubted it? Why should he who had pointed
him out as the Messiah to others, now ask to be
satisfied upon that point himself?—I am ready to
allow that John might *believe* Jesus to be the
Messiah; for so were many of the people disposed
to believe, who had not been favoured with the
divine intimations which he had received. He
expressly taught both the messengers of the Sanhedrim, and his own disciples, that he himself was
" not the Christ," but that he was " sent before
him[a]." Some of his own disciples he introduced
to Jesus, stating that he was " the Son of God,"
" the same who would baptize with the Holy
Ghost," and " the Lamb of God, that taketh away
the sin of the world." They indeed made the
inference for themselves, and it was doubtless
a just one, that they had " found the Messiah[b]."
But we are not authorized from hence to conclude
that John had *expressly taught* them this; for we
do not find it upon record that he *ever* did, nor
have we any reason to believe that he was *commissioned* to do so. It is, however, this gratuitous

---

[a] John i. 20. iii. 28.   [b] Ibid. i. 41, 45.

hypothesis, which has brought an appearance of difficulty upon the question before us, which has subjected the Baptist to the imputation of inconsistency, and which, in a great measure, has prevented a right apprehension of the real state of the case. But we confidently deny that we have any authority, from the Evangelical records, to say that John ever ascribed to Jesus the title of the Messiah. It was, in fact, as expedient that John should not made such a declaration, as that Jesus himself should avoid it. And we know that Jesus did not, among the Jews, *publicly* avow his Messiahship in express terms, except when he solemnly declared it to the Sanhedrim at the *close* of his ministry; but only to the Samaritans, for reasons explained above, and to the Apostles in private after their own confession of his Messiahship. — This circumstance should never be forgotten in the perusal of the Gospels.

Having now disposed of those visionary hypotheses, which serve only to perplex the question, it will only be needful briefly to recal to your minds some of the statements of the Evangelists, respecting the proceedings of the Baptist and of Jesus, in order that the object of John's message may be fully seen.

John proclaimed that " the kingdom of heaven was at hand ;" and stated that his was " the voice of one crying in the wilderness, Prepare ye the

O

way of the Lord." He spoke of one to "come after him;" adding, that himself "came baptizing with water, in order that *he* might be made manifest to Israel." But, as he denied that himself was either the Christ, or Elias, or that prophet, so neither did he state which of these characters belonged to his successor. Yet he specified many definite parts of his character, office, and proceedings; and one especially, which was speedily verified in Jesus, that his successor would be one "mightier than himself," for "John did no miracle." When the jealousy of his disciples was excited by the growing popularity of Jesus, as if they had wholly misunderstood his own frequent reference to one who was to surpass him, he reminded them that he had told them that "he was not the Christ, but was sent before him." And though he was not commissioned to declare to them that Jesus was *the Christ,* he very solemnly inculcated upon them the necessity of receiving his testimony; and while he stated that his joy was fulfilled by the intelligence which they brought, he also declared to them, "He must increase, but I must decrease." It would be superfluous to dilate upon the circumstances which fully accomplished this prediction; for you know how John's public ministry was entirely terminated by his imprisonment, while that of Jesus still proceeded with uninterrupted success. We observe, however, more than once, besides on the occasion of the message to Jesus, that several are distinguished both by name, and by their proceedings, as still remaining peculiarly the disciples of John. Nor did circumstances allow that he, to whom they remained so much attached, should, even then, explicitly declare to them that Jesus was the Messiah. As he himself told them, "a man can receive nothing, except it be given him from above." He knew that such a declaration would be beyond *his commission* from above. But, after the miracle at Nain, and all the others of which he had heard in the prison, he judged it expedient to send two of his disciples to put the question to Jesus himself. He thus indicated to them his own expectations ; and though he could not himself venture to declare the fact, if indeed he were yet fully acquainted with it, yet he might suppose that he,—of whom he had declared that " he came from heaven, and was above all, that to him the Spirit was given without measure, and that the Father, loving him as the Son, had given all things into his hand,"—might see fit, at that period, to give an explicit answer to the question, " Art thou he that should come, or do we look for another ?"

I have said that John might *at that period* have indulged such a supposition. That he supposed some such thing, the proposing of the question at

all sufficiently shews. But I have not said, without reason, that at that particular period he conceived such a notion. There is a peculiarity in
the phraseology of St. Matthew in our text, which
seems distinctly to inform us of this, and to confirm
all that we have already advanced with respect to
the Baptist's views and proceedings.. In the verse
preceding our text, he says, " When *Jesus* had
made an end of commanding his twelve disciples,
he departed thence, to teach and to preach in their
cities." But he does not go on to say, " When
John had heard in the prison the words of Jesus,"
but, " when John had heard in the prison the
works of *the Christ* (τοῦ Χριστοῦ), he sent two of
his disciples." Now it is very true, that in some
of the later books of the New Testament, we find
the official title *Christ*, and the proper name *Jesus*,
applied to our Lord, as perhaps convertible terms.
But if that be the case in this passage, it is the
only instance in the Gospels, and, I think I may
say, in the historical books of the New Testament,
where it is so used in the ordinary *narrative*.
There is, I believe, no other instance where it
does not occur as a title of the *office* which we
ascribe to Jesus, and not as the *proper name* of
him as an individual. And this consideration will,
I think, dispose us to think, that neither is this
passage a solitary exception; that St. Matthew
meant by using that term in our text, to say some-

thing more, than is usually understood by the
passage; more, in short, than if he had merely
stated, that "John had heard in the prison the
works of Jesus." I conceive that he meant to
say, that when John had been told of all these
things by his disciples, he perceived that he had
received intelligence of the performance of the
works of the Messiah, of those ascribed to him
by the prophets. And, therefore, after Jesus had
exhibited such indication of his Messiahship, he
might suppose the period arrived, when he could
properly send his disciples to ask of him " whether
he was he that should come." And though the
reasons, because of which Jesus had hitherto declined an explicit avowal, still existed, and therefore
he did not give a direct answer; yet, as we shall
soon see, his answer was such as would fully confirm the expectations of the Baptist. Whether his
ideas of the character of Jesus were previously so
full and definite, we have no data to determine;
but we may at least venture to conclude, that he,
who like Simeon, had waited for and announced
the consolation of Israel, did not see death, until he
both had seen, and recognized, the Lord's Christ,
respecting whom it had before been revealed to
him by the Holy Ghost, that he was "the Lamb
of God, which taketh away the sin of the world,"
and that " whosoever believeth in him, the Son
of God, hath everlasting life."

It will be expedient to notice somewhat more particularly the *question* itself, which John's disciples proposed, in compliance with their master's direction.—"Art thou *he that should come,* or do we look for *another?*" This evidently implies a supposition either that Jesus was the Messiah, or that the Messiah was to succeed him. It is well known, that in consequence of the passage of the prophet Malachi, which spoke of the Messiah's forerunner under the title of Elijah, the Jews expected Elijah to return in person, and inaugurate the Messiah. John had disavowed all claim to the character of Elijah in that respect. But we find that our Lord's disciples, after his transfiguration, proposed to him a question respecting the opinion of the Scribes, " that Elias must first come." And previously to that time, when our Lord asked of his disciples, what were the prevalent opinions respecting himself, they mentioned, that " some said that he was Elias." It is far from improbable, that, although the question of the Baptist was occasioned by the report of works characteristic of the Messiah, it was supposed by him, or at least by his disciples, that they *might* indicate Jesus to be Elijah. For the more immediate occasion of the message was the raising of the young man of Nain from the dead; and that was a work which Elijah had wrought, as recorded in the Old Testament. The state of things at that time, therefore, appeared to justify the conclusion, either that Jesus was actually the Messiah; or that he was Elijah, and that they must still expect another as the Messiah. Our Lord gave an answer obviously designed to strengthen the opinion that he was *he that should come*; but he left it to John to inform them more fully what were the works characteristic of the Messiah, and how the prophecies were fulfilled in him. He himself, after high encomiums upon the Baptist, taught the multitudes that he was " the Messenger, who was to be sent before the face of the Lord, to prepare his way;" and he also instructed them to consider him as " that *Elias which was for to come*[a]." And we know how he afterwards declared to his disciples that "Elias had already come, and that they had done to him what they listed;" so as to make them "understand that he spake to them of John the Baptist[b]." And if John were the Elias, then Jesus was the Messiah, of the Prophets.

It now remains that we notice the *answer,* which Jesus returned, to a question proposed under the circumstances, and with the views, which we have now, at some length, endeavoured to explain.

The disciples of John arrived at a time, when several opportunities offered themselves to our

---

[a] Matt. xi. 14.   [b] Matt. xvii. 10—13.

Lord for the exercise of his miraculous powers. "In that same hour he cured many of their infirmities and plagues, and of evil spirits; and unto many that were blind he gave sight[a]." They had seen and heard of his former mighty works, and they beheld him still equally ready and able to continue them. "Then Jesus answering said unto them, Go your way, and tell John what things ye have seen and heard; how that the blind see, the lame walk, the lepers are cleansed, the deaf hear, the dead are raised, to the poor the Gospel is preached; and blessed is he, whosoever shall not be offended in me."

This answer consists of three parts; first a statement respecting his *miracles*, next respecting his *teaching*, and lastly a *caution* against being *offended in him*. And the question being, "whether he was he that should come," since it was only from the prophets that they could learn that any Messiah might justly be expected to come, and by what characters he might be known when he did come, we may rightly be prepared to suppose, that an appeal is herein made to the prophecies. Yet it is not actually so stated. It appears, at first sight, to be merely a statement of present and obvious facts; and unless the reality of those facts were undeniable, no inference whatever

---

[a] Luke vii. 21.

could be drawn from it. But the language which our Lord uses is almost literally a citation of well known prophecies; and that he should be able *in such a manner* to describe what John's disciples had both aforetime, and in that very same hour, seen and heard, could not but strikingly convince them that the prophets had spoken of what was now before them, and that he who thus wrought, and thus taught, was " he that should come, and that they needed not to look for another."

The Baptist was himself described by the prophet Isaiah; and certain words in the fortieth chapter of that prophet, he had applied to himself[b]. In the same chapter, the prophet adds, " Say unto the cities of Judah, Behold your God. Behold the Lord God shall come with strong hand, and his arm shall rule for him; behold, his reward is with him, and his work before him[c]." The Baptist had seen, and had borne record that Jesus was *the Son of God;* and stated that, " coming after him, he was *mightier* than he." That attribute was now verified by his miracles. But Isaiah had been still more particular on that subject. " Behold your God shall come with vengeance, even God with a recompence; he will come and save you. Then shall the eyes of the blind be opened, and the ears of the deaf shall

---

[b] Isai. xl. 3—5. John i. 23.   [c] Isai. xl. 9, 10.

be unstopped ; then shall the lame man leap as an
hart, and the tongue of the dumb sing [a]." And
again, "He will swallow up death in victory [b]."
And again, " Thy dead men shall live, together with my dead body they shall arise [c]."
Many passages occur to the same effect. The
works to which they refer had been already performed by Jesus before the disciples of John
came to him ; others were performed in their
presence, of which we have no *particular* account;
and with unfailing power did Jesus persevere in
these divine works. We can examine for ourselves the evidence of their reality.

---

[a] Isai. xxxv. 4—6.   Also xlii. 6, 7.   [b] Isai. xxv. 8.

[c] Isai. xxvi. 19.   See also Job xix. 25.   Dan. xii. 2, 9—13.
Hos. xiii. 14.   Gen. iii. 15, 19.   It is not, in so many words,
predicted by the prophets, that Messiah would raise the dead.
For, perhaps, the passages cited above rather refer to the general
resurrection, than to the miracles of the Messiah.   Yet, as they
speak of the consequences which would result from his successful
undertaking, which was, in its original design, the redemption of
man from mortality as the penalty of sin, by obtaining the pardon,
and effecting the abolition of sin; the raising of the dead, equally,
if not more than other miracles, was a proof of his Messiahship,
which had, virtually at least, been noticed by the prophets.   And
our Saviour's statements in John v. 21—29. may be considered
as a *comment* on such passages as we have referred to.   If " the
Son quickeneth whom he will," and proved his possession of this
power, even during his ministry on earth, by causing " the dead
to hear his voice, and live," we need not marvel at this, because
"the hour is coming, when *all* that are in the graves shall hear his
voice, and shall come forth."

"The blind receive their sight." Can we forget the cure which Jesus wrought, in the presence of the multitude, upon the two blind men who sat by the way-side begging; and that *gradual* cure of the blind man near Bethsaida, by which Jesus so fully shewed that every change was by his agency, and at his will. "Since the world began it was not heard that any man opened the eyes of one *born* blind." Yet this still more signal miracle Jesus performed; and we shall do well to examine the full relation, given by the Evangelist St. John, respecting restoration of sight to the man who was blind from his birth. For this miracle was severely scrutinized by the Jewish council; but, to their confusion, the more they examined, the less were they able to deny either that the man was *born* blind, or that he now *saw*, or that *Jesus* had opened his eyes.—"The lame walked" also at the command of Jesus. Let it be sufficient to instance the cure of the impotent bed-ridden sufferer at the pool of Bethesda; and the paralytic who was let down through the roof, because of the multitude who crowded the doors, but who, at the word of Jesus, was enabled to take up his bed, and walk.—Many "lepers also were cleansed." And, that the reality of the cure might be legally ascertained and recorded, Jesus commanded them, as the law required, to "go and shew themselves to the priests, as a testimony

against themselves " if they afterwards ventured
to deny the cure.—Do we ask whether he also
made "the deaf to hear?" Let the confession of
the multitude who were eye-witnesses satisfy us.
" He hath done all things well; he maketh both
the deaf to hear, and the dumb to speak."—The
"dead also were raised up." Not only the widow's
son at Nain, who was *about* to be committed to
the *grave*, was restored to life; but the daughter
of Jairus, who had *just* expired; and Lazarus also,
who had been dead *four days*, upon whom the
mouth of the sepulchre had been closed, and the
witnesses of whose resurrection were numerous
friends of the family who had come from Jerusalem
to condole with them. Rightly, therefore, did the
people observe, "When Christ cometh, will he do
more miracles than this man doeth?" They were
the very works of the Messiah, and they needed
not to look for him in any other than Jesus.

But our Lord, having directed the inquirers to
these considerations, added another, which might
make the conclusion still more satisfactory. "To
the poor the Gospel is preached." It was not his
miraculous power alone, but the *subject of his
doctrine*, and the *persons* to whom it was preached, and for whom it was suited, that evinced him
to be " he that should come." The Baptist had
himself " seen the Spirit descending upon him,
and remaining on him," and had testified that

"God gave not the Spirit by measure unto him."
Both he and his disciples would remember of
whom it had been declared by the same prophet
Isaiah, "The Spirit of the Lord God is upon me,
because the Lord hath anointed me to preach glad
tidings to the meek[a]." If, then, such were the
ministry of *Jesus*, they had another circumstance
to corroborate that inference, which they might
draw from his miracles, in favour of his Messiahship.—But the same prophet had also uttered
other predictions, which would equally be fulfilled
in their season; though blessed were they only to
whom the darker portions of them did not apply.
"Thus saith the Lord God, Behold I lay in Zion
for a foundation stone a tried stone, a precious
corner-stone, a sure foundation; he that believeth
shall not make haste[b]," or stumble at that stone.
Again, Isaiah says in another place, "He shall
be for a sanctuary; but for a stone of stumbling,
and a rock of offence to both the houses of Israel;
for a gin and a snare to the inhabitants of Jerusalem. And many among them shall stumble, and
fall, and be broken, and be snared, and be taken[c]."

Blessed is he, said Jesus in conclusion, and
alluding to these predictions, "Blessed is he, whosoever shall not be *offended* in me." Too many
of the men of that generation were, however,

---

[a] Isai. lxi. 1. [b] Ibid. xxviii. 16. [c] Ibid. viii. 14, 15.

offended in him ; for he came not in that pomp,
and with those offers of temporal ease, and riches,
and pre-eminence, which alone were congenial to
their carnal and groveling desires. He that should
come, was "meek, lowly, and having salvation ;"
but a salvation from sin and condemnation, and
which led to pardon, and holiness, and immortality.
"They would not come to him, that they might
have life." Miracles of vengeance, therefore, overtook them, because miracles of mercy failed to
convince.

We shall hereafter have occasion to advert to
the motives and objections, which made the cross
of Christ, and his character, and doctrines, to
become, even before his crucifixion, a stumbling-
block to the Jews. But we may surely observe
at this period of our course, that the miracles
which he wrought proved that "the Father had
sent him ;" and that the correspondency of these
miracles, as well as of his doctrine, and of the
whole of his ministry, to prophetic description,
proved him to be the *Messiah*. And, before
I conclude, I would notice some other prophecies
respecting the Messiah, and compare them with
another appeal to his miracles in proof of his Messiahship, which our Lord made upon another occasion, and in a different connexion.

We quoted above, from the fortieth chapter of
Isaiah, the words in which the prophet speaks of

the "Lord God coming with a strong hand, having his reward with him, and his work before him." He thus proceeds in the following verse. "He shall feed his flock like a shepherd; he shall gather the lambs with his arm, and carry them in his bosom, and shall gently lead those that are with young." Compare with the whole of that passage another in the prophecy of Ezekiel. "Thus saith the Lord God; Behold I, even I, will both search out my sheep, and seek them out.—I will feed my flock, and I will cause them to lie down, saith the Lord God. I will seek that which was lost, and bring again that which was driven away, and will bind up that which was broken, and will strengthen that which was sick; but I will destroy the fat and the strong; and I will feed them with judgment.—And I will set up one Shepherd over them, and he shall feed them, even my servant David; he shall feed them, and be their shepherd. And I the Lord will be their God, and my servant David a prince among them; I the Lord have spoken it[a]."—Now compare, with these passages, our Lord's beautiful and well known discourse concerning himself as the good Shepherd, delivered immediately after he had wrought one of the miracles *mentioned in our text*, the healing of the man born blind. That

---

[a] Ezek. xxxiv. 11—24.

discourse, the previous instructions, and the recent miracles of Jesus, caused a division among the Jews; and they therefore came round about him in Solomon's porch, and said unto him, "How long dost thou make us to doubt? *If thou be the Christ,* tell us plainly." Jesus answered them, referring, as it should seem, to his discourse before the Sanhedrim after the miracle at Bethesda, " I told you, and ye believed not, 'the works that I do in my Father's name they bear witness of me.' But ye believe not, because ye are not of my sheep, as I said unto you[a]." He then spoke of his power to save, of his unity with the Father, and of the sanction given by his miracles to his claim of the title "Son of God," as being "he whom the Father had sanctified and sent into the world."—It would be easy to shew, from a comparison of the whole of these statements with prophecy, that he here appealed to his works in proof of his Messiahship; and also that he endeavoured to lead them to acknowledge, that his claim to *divinity,* his *doctrines,* and the professed *object* of his mission, all corresponded to the prophetic description of the *Messiah.*

The preaching of a lowly, spiritual, and crucified Messiah, ever was to the Jews a stumbling-block; and to the Greeks it appeared foolishness.

---

[a] John x. 24, &c.

The offence of the cross has not even yet ceased. Some there are, even at this day, who cavil at the evidences of the Gospel. Some are ashamed of the peculiar doctrines of the cross of Christ, in which they should rather glory. And others value not the offer of pardon, aspire not after the holiness to which they are called, and are averse from the practice of self-denial, and the cultivation of humility. But still, " blessed are they whosoever are not offended in Jesus!" And should any one of you ask, who they are that attain this blessedness, and what are the rewards promised for your encouragement, I would answer in the divine words of my Master and your's : "Blessed are the poor in spirit; for their's is the kingdom of heaven. Blessed are they that mourn ; for they shall be comforted. Blessed are the meek ; for they shall inherit the earth. Blessed are they which do hunger and thirst after righteousness ; for they shall be filled. Blessed are the merciful ; for they shall obtain mercy. Blessed are the pure in heart; for they shall see God[b]."

We have seen that Jesus, in proof of his authority, gave sight to the blind. From this miracle he also borrowed an illustration to teach us the nature of his mission, and our responsibility and danger in consequence of it. " For judg-

[b] Matt. v. 1—8.

P

ment am I come into this world, that they
which see not might see, and that they which
see might be made blind[a]." "I am come a
light into this world, that whosoever believeth
on me should not abide in darkness[b]."—Did he
also raise up the dead? He did it that we might
"believe that the Father had sent him;" that we
might know that he is "the resurrection, and the
life; that he that believeth in him, though he
were dead, yet shall live, and that whosoever liveth
and believeth in him shall not die eternally." And
He still demands of us as he did of Martha, "Believest thou this?" Blessed shall we be, if we can
concur with her in the declaration, "Yea, Lord,
I believe that thou art the Christ, the Son of God,
that should come into the world[c]." Once more
then I repeat by way of caution, "Blessed is he
whosoever shall not be offended in Jesus!"

---

[a] John ix. 39.   [b] Ibid. xii. 46.   [c] Ibid. xi. 25—27.

LECTURE X.

———◆———

OUR LORD'S ANSWER TO THE CAVIL WHICH IM-
PUTED HIS DISPOSSESSION OF DEMONS TO SA-
TANIC AGENCY. HE APPEALS TO THAT CLASS OF
HIS MIRACLES AS INDICATING THE ESTABLISH-
MENT OF *THE KINGDOM OF GOD.*

———◆———

St. Luke XI. 20.

*But if I with the finger of God cast out devils, no doubt
the kingdom of God is come upon you.*

THESE words form a portion of that discourse, in
which our Lord answers the well known cavil of
the Pharisees, who more than once ascribed to
Satanic co-operation the miracles mentioned in our
text. Of no miracles have the Evangelists made
more frequent mention, of none have they given
a more circumstantial description. They are
moreover of so remarkable a character, as to
suggest an inquiry into their nature; and as our
Lord entered into an argument with a view of
evincing the reality of *divine* co-operation in that
particular class of miracles, and, having established
his position, specified the particular inference to

be drawn from it, the consideration of this subject must not be omitted, in a course of Lectures designed to review and illustrate our Lord's reasonings respecting the evidences of his mission.

Our attention must, in the first place, be directed to the *nature* and *reality* of the miracles in question.—The Evangelists state [a], that there were brought unto Jesus such as were "possessed with devils," such as were "vexed with unclean spirits;" and that "he healed them," and "cast out the spirits with a word." To whatever decision we come as the nature and origin of the affliction described in these terms, of its reality we can entertain no doubt. In some instances the Evangelists have recorded, either in their own words, or in the words of those who requested Jesus to extend his compassion to the sufferers, many of the symptoms of the disorder with which they were affected. They were the visible and pitiable exhibitions of melancholy, furious distraction, and convulsion. That all these ceased at the will and by the word of Jesus is not less evident. "The people were amazed, insomuch that they questioned among themselves saying, What thing is this? What new doctrine is this? for with authority commandeth he the unclean spirits, and

---

[a] Matt. viii. 16. Luke vi. 18.

they do obey him [b]." " The unclean spirit came
out of one, and hurt him not [c];" "the people
found another sitting, and clothed, and in his
right mind [d];" the daughter of the Syrophenician
woman " was made whole from the hour," in
which Jesus declared to her that her petition was
granted [e]. The Pharisees never denied the reality
of the cure, though they endeavoured to account
for it in such a way as might obviate the inferences which the multitude were disposed to
make from it. And the fact itself must have been
both notorious and undeniable, which drove them
to the necessity of adopting such a procedure.

But still the question remains to be answered,
what was the *nature* of the calamity itself, to
which these unhappy sufferers had been subjected,
and from which they were delivered? We are
told by some that all these were cases either of
insanity or of epilepsy; and that they are to be
considered as ordinary disorders, resulting from
natural causes. Such an opinion makes this class
of miracles to differ little, if at all, from the
healing of the sick, the lame, and the blind.
We have, in that case, a greater variety of instances of the same description of miracle; and
undoubtedly, the reality of the miracle being

---

[b] Mark i. 27.   [c] Luke iv. 35.   [d] Luke viii. 35.
[e] Matt. xv. 28.

undeniable, the same general inference is deducible in favour of the divine mission and Messiahship of Jesus. But it cannot but occur to us,
that there is a *peculiarity* in the *inference* drawn
in the text from these miracles, which may dispose
us to hesitate, at least, in admitting such an
opinion ; and to suppose that there may also be
a peculiarity in the *miracles* themselves. But of
this we shall be better prepared to judge hereafter.

There is, however, another difficulty in admitting that opinion. If the Evangelists had
merely, as in other cases, described the *symptoms*
of these disorders, the question whether they were
at all different from ordinary disorders would never,
probably, have been agitated. Did it appear,
that those only who applied to Jesus in behalf of
their suffering friends, ascribed their disorder to
a *demoniacal* possession, and had we been told,
at the same time, that such was the general
opinion of the Jewish nation in that age, we
might at once have granted that the notion was
merely a vulgar error. But we naturally pause,
when we find that the Evangelists themselves
ascribe the disorder to the same cause, in a great
variety of form and expression, repeatedly *distinguishing* the demoniacs from other sick and
afflicted persons[a]. Even this perhaps might not

---

[a] Matt. iv. 24.   Mark i. 34.   Luke vi. 17, 18.

stagger us, or be inexplicable. But we find that
our Lord uses precisely the same language on all
occasions. When enumerating his own miracles,
and when specifying those which he empowered
his disciples to perform, he clearly distinguishes
the expulsion of demons from healing the sick,
cleansing the lepers, and every other species of
miraculous cure[b]. When we learn from the
Gospel narrative how he " cast out the spirits
with his word," we find that he spoke in a manner
which was, at least, perfectly consistent with the
opinion that those persons who were supposed to
be under demoniacal influence, were really so
influenced; and also that the conduct of these
persons themselves appears from several circumstances to corroborate the same opinion[c]. And
when our Lord reasons with the Pharisees on
this very subject in the text and context, he not
only argues with them on their own principles,
but he never hints that their notions were erroneous; and both on that occasion, and also when
the seventy returned, expressing their "joy that
even the demons were subject to them through
his name," the conclusions, and assurances which
he brings forward, so far from discountenancing

---

b Matt. x. 1, 8 ; xvii. 21. Mark iii. 15; xvi. 17. Luke ix. 1 ;
x. 17 — 20 ; xiii. 32.

c Matt. viii. 28—32. Mark i. 24, 25 ; iii. 11, 12. Luke iv.
34—41 ; viii. 28—32.

the notion of demoniacal possession, appear to
justify the opinion that the admission of its reality
is of no small importance in order to a right apprehension of the object both of his own mission,
and of that of the Apostles[a].—Those who are
familiar with the contents of the Gospels will have
already called to mind the several passages to
which we have alluded, and the citation of which
would have made it necessary to dwell much
longer on this topic.

Those Christian divines who undertake to
shew that "there never was a real demoniac in the
world," are of course prepared to explain the remarkable phraseology employed by our Lord and
the Evangelists. They observe that it was the
popular language on this subject, and that our Lord
adopted it, not with a view of countenancing the
notion in which such expressions originated, but
because the refutation of such errors in philosophy
and nosology was not one of the objects of his
mission, and because it was not either necessary
or expedient to run counter to the prevailing
opinion. Yet since they themselves strenuously
contend that this opinion has been the occasion
of much fraud and superstition, and that it is little
better than a relic of Paganism, we might have

---

[a] Matt. xii. 25 — 29.   Mark iii. 23—27.   Luke x. 17 — 24 ;
xi. 17—26.

supposed it expedient that our Lord should not
so apparently give countenance to it, even if it
were not, in other respects, more than a question
of philosophy. If the received opinion be correct,
it has an intimate connexion with the important
question relative to the power, designs, and agency
of our great spiritual " adversary, the Devil."
And if it be true that in our Christian warfare
" we do not wrestle against flesh and blood only,
but against powers, against the rulers of the
darkness of this world, against spiritual wicked-
ness in high places;" then it behoves us not only
to " take unto ourselves the whole armour of God,
that we may be able to stand against the wiles of
the devil," but also to " make ourselves acquainted
with his devices," and fully to inform ourselves
how " the Son of God was manifested to destroy
the works of the devil."

We are told indeed that the possessions in the
Gospels, are not, with the sanction of the original,
to be termed *diabolical*, but *demoniacal*, and that
wherever the plural word "devils" occurs in
Scripture, it is in the original " demons." We
allow the truth of this remark. But still the
question recurs, whether, or not, the scriptural
description of *possessing demons* supports the
received opinion. Much learning has been employed to shew, that by the word *demon* is
meant " the spirit of a dead mortal,"—that such

only were worshipped as deities by the heathen world,—that such is the use of the word in Scripture,—and that, since the popular opinion referred possession to such agents, we are to understand the possessing demons in the Gospel in the same sense, and not as at all alluding to " the devil and his angels." This is not the place to enter upon such an inquiry as this question requires[a]. Suffice it then to remark, that it is not true that even the heathen writers meant by this term only the spirits of dead men ; and the sense in which it is used in the Gospels with respect to possessions, will best be determined from the Scriptures themselves.

It is scarcely necessary to remind you that the arch-apostate, the seducer of our first parents, is called in Scripture by various titles, descriptive of his character, influence, and operations. He is called the wicked one, the tempter, Satan, or the adversary, the prince of this world, the devil[b].

---

[a] This, and most of the other questions connected with this subject, were treated very largely, and the arguments on both sides very fully detailed, in the celebrated controversy between Farmer and Worthington. A luminous and masterly treatise was written at the time by John Fell, entitled, " An Inquiry into the Heathen and Scripture doctrine of Demons ; in which the hypotheses of the Rev. Mr. Farmer, and others, on this subject, are particularly considered."

[b] 1 John iii. 12. v. 18. Matt. iv. 3. 1 Thess. iii. 5. Job ii. 6. 1 Pet. v. 8. 2 Cor. iv. 4. &c.

Now if we find some of these titles used by our
Lord on other occasions, when not speaking of
the subject of demoniacal possession, we can
scarcely be at a loss to understand of what description of beings he is *then* speaking. For instance,
he three times mentions " the prince of this
world[c]." He also speaks of " the devil and his
angels[d] ;" of " the devil as being a murderer and
liar from the beginning[e] ;" and of " Satan as desiring to sift St. Peter as wheat[f]." And the Evangelists ascribe the apostacy of Judas by the phrase
that " Satan entered into him[g]." Now if we find
that the *same terms* are connected with the subject of *demoniacal possession,* it will afford no
slight presumption that they are in fact to be
referred to the *same agents.* What inference,
then, is suggested by the following passage in the
tenth chapter of St. Luke? " The seventy returned
again with joy, saying, Lord, even the demons
are subject to us through thy name. And he said
unto them, I beheld *Satan* as lightning fall from
heaven. Behold, I give you power to tread on
serpents and scorpions, and over all the power of
the enemy[h] ; and nothing shall by any means hurt
you. Notwithstanding in this rejoice not, that

---

[c] John xii. 31. xiv. 30. xvi. 11. [d] Matt. xxv. 41.
[e] John viii. 44.   [f] Luke xxii. 31.
[g] Luke xxii. 3. John xiii. 2, 27. [h] See Matt. xiii. 39.

the spirits are subject unto you ; but rather rejoice because your names are written in heaven[a]." Hear also the following words of St. Peter, recorded in the Acts of the Apostles, where the word, upon which the antidemoniac system is founded, is not employed. " God anointed Jesus with the Holy Ghost and with power ; who went about doing good, and healing all that were oppressed of *the devil ;* for God was with him[b]." Again, when our Lord himself speaks of the woman who is described by St. Luke, as having had a spirit of infirmity eighteen years, he says, that " *Satan* had bound her[c]." We may remember also, that it was Satan who was permitted to afflict Job with his sore diseases[d]; and that the infliction of bodily disorders for the correction of the incestuous offender at Corinth, was termed by the Apostle, " the delivery of such an one unto Satan[e]."—It is sufficiently evident from the passages just cited, in whatever manner they be explained, that the limited power, which according to Scripture, is permitted in some cases over the bodies of mankind, is ascribed to no other than " that same old serpent, called the Devil and Satan, which deceiveth the whole world," " who beguiled Eve by his subtilty," and by whose

---

[a] Luke x. 17—20.   [b] Acts x. 38.   [c] Luke xiii. 16.
[d] Job i.   [e] 1 Cor. v. 5.

influence, as the tempter, our minds may also be "corrupted from the simplicity which is in Christ."

But the discourse from whence our text is taken, affords perhaps the most decisive evidence of the propriety with which we may refer demoniacal possessions to the same fallen being. The Pharisees gave no indication that they doubted the reality either of the possession, or of its removal. They were chagrined at the inference which the multitude were disposed to draw from it, and they endeavoured to suggest to them another. "The multitudes marvelled, saying, It was never so seen in Israel. Is not this the Son of David? But when the Pharisees heard it, they said, This fellow doth not cast out demons, but by Beelzebub, the prince of the demons[a]." The god of the neighbouring nation of the Philistines was called by this or a similar name, and thence probably they borrowed it. But the question to be determined is, *whom* they intended to designate by it, and what was the nature of the imputation cast upon our Lord. His answer would not have been pertinent, unless it met them on their own ground, and was conformable to their own ideas. The Evangelist, prefacing the mention of our Lord's answer by a significant declaration, states that " he, *knowing their thoughts,* said

---

b Matt. ix. 33, 34.

unto them,—If Satan be divided against himself, how shall his kingdom stand? because ye say, that I cast out demons through Beelzebub." If then the casting out demons through Beelzebub, be in fact synonymous with casting them out through Satan, and if that imply the division of Satan against himself, it must necessarily follow that those who were possessed with demons, were, in the opinion of our Lord, possessed with *Satan* or his associates.

It was observed above, that we cannot doubt the *reality* of the disorders, from which those termed " Demoniacs" were delivered, whatever opinion be adopted respecting their *nature*. We have also endeavoured to ascertain the notion which both our Lord and the Evangelists convey to us respecting the real *origin* of these possessions. Both to the believer and to the unbeliever such information is needful, in order to form a correct judgment respecting this class of our Lord's miracles, and what the sacred writers teach us concerning them. But we must advance still further, and point out some of those circumstances, which *evidence* the reality of these *as demoniacal possessions*; though upon this, and every other, department of this extended subject, we must observe that brevity which our limits require, though the difficulty and importance of the subject would seem scarcely to allow it.

You have doubtless remarked, that the demoniacs manifested a very correct apprehension of the character and office of Jesus; and that he, therefore, "charged the demons to hold their peace, and to come out;" and he "suffered them not to speak, because they knew that he was Christ[a]." They accosted him as "the Holy One of God, the Son of God, the Son of God most high, the Christ[b]." These professions, and their fear of him, as "coming to torment them before the time," though remarkable, are, notwithstanding, explicable upon supposition that these individuals were really under the influence of wicked spiritual beings. But, if these declarations were only the ravings of ordinary madness, we are at a loss to conceive how the subjects of it had derived, at that time, the *distinct* knowledge of the character of Jesus, upon which so positive a testimony must have been grounded. They made it, in several instances, at an early period of his ministry; but both then, and afterwards, the popular opinions respecting Jesus were not so decided either as to what was the character of Jesus, or as to the attributes which might be ascribed to him. The supposition, therefore, that these were merely *insane* persons, who eagerly embraced from

---

[a] Mark i. 25—34. Luke iv. 41.

[b] Matt. viii. 29. Mark i. 24; iii. 11. Luke iv. 34, 41, viii. 28.

hearsay, and pertinaciously retained, an opinion that Jesus was the Christ, is insufficient to explain their full testimony respecting him. It is much more probable that we may recognize herein an exemplification of the remark which St. James has applied to the existence and unity of God; "Even the demons believe, and tremble." In one instance, indeed, the proposed hypothesis, even if admitted, is entirely inapplicable. For one of these attestations was given by the demoniac mentioned by St. Luke; whose disorder the anti-demonists themselves rank rather under the head of *epilepsy,* than of insanity. And in narrating the cure of that sufferer, the Evangelist has also used an expression, which is scarcely consistent with the notion, that his disorder was either epilepsy, or madness, of any *ordinary* character; though it is perfectly intelligible to those who admit the reality of possession. "When the demon had thrown him in the midst, he came out of him, and *hurt him not*[a]."

But the migration of the demons, who had possessed the two Gadarenes, into the neighbouring herd of swine, and the catastrophe which followed, are circumstances, which most decisively establish the supernatural character of these afflictions, and which, perhaps, were designed for

---

[a] Luke iv. 33—35.

.that purpose. The opinion that this numerous herd .was *driven* into the sea by the two demoniacs, is inconsistent with the narrative of the Evangelists. Others, who deny that the two demoniacs were really such, ascribe the madness of the swine to the immediate infliction of God. For what end it does not sufficiently appear. If we adhere to the statement of the Evangelists, it appears that Jesus permitted the demons, *at their own public request,* to go into the swine; and as the swine could not be confederates in any fraud, the madness which ensued, and its consequence, was a full and visible proof of the reality of that demoniacal influence, from which the two men, who, from that time, remained in their right mind, had been delivered [b].

It now only remains that we notice the reasoning by which our Lord proved to the Pharisees, that it was "by the finger of God that he cast out demons;" and also the inference, which he drew from thence, that therefore "the kingdom of God was come upon them."

Either Jesus cast out demons by his own unaided powers, or by compact with the prince of demons, or by the finger of God. The first

[b] Mark v. 1—20. Luke viii. 26—39. Not only the circumstance noticed above, which is *peculiar* to this instance of possession, but almost every other very strongly corroborates the opinion that it was a case of real possession.

supposition the Pharisees ventured not to advance. The only pretext which they could find for a denial of the last position, was to contend for the second, that " by the prince of the demons he cast out demons." Jesus refuted that, and thereby established the true and only remaining supposition. And, in this refutation, he made a tacit appeal to the purity, and excellence of the doctrine, in recommendation of which he wrought his miracles. If it was impossible to suppose that an apostate, wicked, and seducing spirit would lend his aid to establish such a doctrine, then was their insinuation groundless. And, if that insinuation had any force, it could still only prove that Satan was himself, whether wittingly, or unwittingly, subverting his own power and kingdom; so that still the inference would remain, that his power was falling, and the kingdom of God about to be established. For, answered our Lord, " Every kingdom divided against itself is brought to desolation ; and every city or house divided against itself shall not stand. And if Satan cast out Satan, he is divided against himself; how then shall his kingdom stand[a] ?"

Our Lord next subjoins an argument, the precise bearing of which we cannot, perhaps, accurately determine ; though in any sense in which we take it, it is certainly conclusive against the

---

[a] Matt. xii. 25, 26.

Pharisees. "If I by Beelzebub cast out demons, by whom do your children cast them out? therefore shall they be your judges." If we suppose our Lord to refer to the miracles of the ancient prophets, we may suppose that he wished them to consider the consequences of their objection; since there was no circumstance attending his own miracles, which would not equally apply to those of the prophets, whom they believed to be divinely assisted. His were even more numerous, signal, and undeniable miracles. But, more probably, Jesus refers to the dispossessions, whether real or pretended ones of the Jewish exorcists; some of whom, as we learn both from the Gospels, and from the Acts of the Apostles, attempted to cast out demons in the name of Jesus [b]. But at any rate, the same slander would apply to them as well as to himself; for no reason appeared why their dispossessions should not be ascribed to satanic assistance, if they were correct in so ascribing his. His argument does not necessarily grant that any such miracles were really the consequence of their attempts; and indeed the surprise of the people at these instances of the power of Jesus, shews that they were as *unprecedented*, as they were signal and astonishing; for they openly avowed, that "it was never so seen in Israel." But

---

[b] Mark ix. 38.   Acts ix. 14.

Q 2

waving such a comparison, if they persevered in their cavil, their own children would accuse them of calumniating their power as exorcists, and, if appealed to as umpires in the dispute, would condemn them, and acquit him. The only tenable supposition was, that he "cast out demons by the finger of God," or, as St. Matthew expresses it, "by the Spirit of God ;" by that divine influence and power, with which he "was anointed to heal all that were brought into subjection by the devil," and by which he "proclaimed deliverance to the captive, and set at liberty them that were bruised."

"But," adds our Lord, "if I with the finger of God cast out demons, no doubt the kingdom of God is come upon you." Let it be here remarked, that he does not say, "No doubt I am *sent of God,*" nor yet, "No doubt I am *he that should come .*" He speaks not so much of the Messiah's personal office and character, as of the *dispensation* which he was to introduce. Both John and Jesus began their ministry with the proclamation, "The kingdom of heaven is at hand ;" and both the twelve, and also the seventy, disciples were sent out by Jesus, to deliver the same annunciation. And when their message was rejected by the inhabitants of a city, they were commissioned to "shake off the dust of their feet as a testimony against them," and to declare,

"Notwithstanding be ye sure of this, that the kingdom of God is come nigh unto you." Now we find it expressly mentioned that the twelve were, in the first instance, empowered to "cast out demons;" and the seventy, when they returned, joyfully declared to their Master, "Lord, even the demons are subject to us through thy name." And Jesus took occasion from the remark of the seventy to anticipate the downfal of Satan, and the future triumphs of his own servants. "He said unto them, I beheld Satan, as lightning, fall from heaven! Behold, I give unto you power to tread on serpents and scorpions, and over all the power of the enemy; and nothing shall by any means hurt you." And these several considerations, taken in connexion with our text, readily suggest to us, that this particular miracle was peculiarly *appropriate* as an evidence of the introduction of the kingdom of God. Now I know not how far this remark of our Lord may of itself justify us in asserting, that the Jews expected that the Messiah, who of course was to introduce and set up the kingdom of God, would cast out demons. For this is perhaps not definitely and expressly predicted in the prophets. But still as even the apocryphal book of Wisdom states that "through envy of the devil sin entered into the world," and as the history of the fall could not but be understood of the seduction of some spiritual

but wicked being; and as also the Jews themselves stated in commenting upon the first promise
that "a remedy would be applied to the heel of
the woman's seed in the days of king Messiah,"
we may conclude that the persons, to whom our
Lord addressed the words of the text, had before
them such *data* as would enable them to understand the tendency, and to appreciate the cogency,
of our Lord's argument. For even the multitudes
felt themselves authorized, after witnessing his
cure of a demoniac, to exclaim, "Is not this the
Son of David [a] ?" Nor is it easy to conceive how
such an inference was suggested to their minds,
except by such considerations as we have noticed.
Yet the objection, which the Pharisees circulated
in order to check the disposition to adopt that
opinion, was not at all directed against the insufficiency of the premises, if admitted, to establish
that conclusion. They knew that, if Jesus did
"cast out demons by the finger of God," they
could not disprove his claim to be the Son of
David, and the heir of his everlasting kingdom.
They ventured, therefore, to deny that these
miracles were wrought by divine assistance; but
their's was a mere assertion, not supported by any
semblance of argument; and our Lord, as we
have seen, unanswerably refuted it, by shewing
its manifold absurdity.

---

[a] Matt. xii. 23.

In the words following the text, our Lord more fully explained his argument, by means of a suitable, though familiar, illustration. He had refuted the notion that Satan had been his confederate. On the contrary, there was a trial of strength between them; and those, who watched the progress of the conflict, would see, that the power of Satan was on the decline, in spite of all his efforts, and in consequence of the onset of one superior in might. "If I, said our Lord, by the finger of God, cast out demons, no doubt the kingdom of God is come upon you.—Or else how can one enter into a strong man's house, and spoil his goods, except he first bind the strong man? and then he will spoil his house. When a strong man armed keepeth his palace, his goods are in peace; but when a stronger than he shall come upon him, and overcome him, he taketh from him all his armour wherein he trusted, and divideth his spoil [b]."

Our Lord subjoined, on this occasion, the solemn caution respecting the blasphemy of the Holy Spirit, and a statement of its unpardonable criminality. That subject will come under our notice in the last department of our Lectures. At present we shall only request your attention to the words which immediately follow those last cited;

---

[b] Matt. xii. 29. Luke xi. 21, 22. Comp. Isai. xlix. 24—26.

and which may be considered as the application and improvement of all that we have been reviewing.

" He that is not with me, is against me, and he, that gathereth not with me, scattereth abroad[a]." If there be such parties, engaged in such a warfare; — if there be a "prince of this world," a " spirit that worketh in the children of disobedience;" and also "a king, whom the God of heaven and earth would place upon his holy hill of Zion," and who dwells and reigns in the hearts of those, who are " turned from the power of Satan unto God;"—and if he, who " cometh in the name of the Lord to receive the kingdom of his father David," be "the stronger one," as well as the more holy; then, surely, it cannot be a matter of indifference, whether we rank ourselves under the standard of Satan, or of Christ. The Captain of our salvation, who went forth conquering and to conquer, and who calls upon all who value their life, to follow him, hath himself distinctly declared, and divine and undeniable is his authority, that in this warfare there can be no neutrality. He who takes part with the Devil and his angels, will undoubtedly share in their future overthrow and punishment. But whosoever also does not actually espouse the

---

[a] Matt. xii. 30.

cause of Christ, and " fight manfully under his banner," will in this life be really promoting the interests of Satan's kingdom, and at the decisive day will be dealt with as having sided with him. He will thus draw down upon himself the penalties, to which Jesus alluded when he said, " As for those mine enemies, that would not that I should reign over them, bring them hither, and slay them before me."

That such is the meaning of these words of our Lord, is evident from the connexion in which they stand. On another occasion, and in another connexion, he delivered a statement, which, at first sight, appears of a contrary tendency. Yet that also is an instructive declaration ; and before we conclude, we shall cite it in his own words. But the circumstances, under which it was spoken, are so necessary to understand it aright, so striking in themselves, and so illustrative of the subject of this Lecture, that we cannot refrain from briefly adverting to them.

We have seen that our Lord taught his hearers to consider the miracles, which he wrought on the demoniacs, as indications of the approaching establishment of the kingdom of God. The scene which was exhibited to the three favoured disciples, on the mount of transfiguration, was doubtless a signal exhibition of the glory of him, who had come to be " a Prince and a Saviour." There was much in that transaction which tended to shew the spiritual nature of his kingdom. But the splendour of it seems to have raised to the utmost the expectations of the disciples; nor were they wrong in supposing, that he was then very shortly about to enter on his glory. Yet they could not comprehend what was then told them, of " the decease which he should accomplish at Jerusalem." On descending from the mountain, retaining, to the amazement of the multitude, a portion of the glory in which he had been arrayed, he found the Scribes disputing with his disciples, who had been unable to cure a demoniac, and probably, therefore, triumphing over them because of the apparent failure of the power of Jesus[a]. Jesus, lamenting the infidelity and perverseness of that generation, by a word effected the cure. He also gently reproved his disciples, either because they had attempted the cure prematurely, and without divine suggestion, or because in attempting it, they had distrusted the readiness of God to co-operate in order to its success; yet, at the same time, he spoke of the future efficacy of that miraculous faith, which they would afterwards so signally exercise. But both they and the multitudes were deeply impressed by the miracle. " They were all amazed at the mighty power of God." Pro-

---

[a] See Matt. xvii. Mark ix. Luke ix.

bably even the people in general were more than
ever disposed to "think that the kingdom of God
should immediately appear." And the scene on
the mountain on the preceding day had very much
strengthened such expectations in the minds of
some of his disciples. But he took occasion to
rectify their apprehensions with regard to the
future transactions and real nature of that kingdom of God, the approaching establishment of
which had again been evidenced by the recent
miracle. " While they wondered every one at all
things which Jesus did, he said unto his disciples,
Let these sayings sink down into your ears; for
the Son of man shall be delivered into the hands
of men." They understood him not, and they
feared to ask an explanation. Yet so fully occupied were their minds with anticipations respecting "the dominion, and glory, and kingdom,
which were to be given to the Son of man," that
they "debated among themselves which of them
should be the greatest" in those days of approaching exaltation. When Jesus inculcated humility,
as the qualification of those who would either be
great in the kingdom of heaven, or could even
enter therein, one of those disciples, who had
desired that he and his brother should " sit on
his right hand and on his left in his kingdom," made a remarkable protestation of his zeal
in his Master's cause. " Master, said he, we saw

one *casting out devils in thy name;* and we forbad him, because he followeth not with us." This drew from our Lord many remarks, both immediately in answer to the statement of John, and also of general concern. We have time only to notice that, which is more immediately connected with our present subject, and which we proposed to compare with the observation that occurs in the discourse from whence our text is taken. " Jesus said, Forbid him not; for there is no man which shall do a miracle in my name, that can lightly speak evil of me. For *he that is not against us is on our part.* For whosoever shall give you a cup of water to drink in my name, because ye belong to Christ, verily I say unto you, He shall not lose his reward."

Our Lord's remarks, on this occasion also, are sufficiently explained by the circumstances to which they refer. When he observed, that " whosoever was not with him was against him," he was addressing those, who not only did not actually join the company of his constant followers, who not only had need that he should help their imperfect belief, but who actually disbelieved, and maliciously cavilled against that which was sufficient for their conviction. They persevered in blaspheming the Son of man; and he judged it necessary to caution them respecting the danger of blaspheming against the Holy Spirit. But he, whom John had ventured to forbid, had even such a favourable opinion of Jesus, as openly to shew a respect for him, by " casting out demons *in his name ;*" and, for ought John knew, might be a decided believer.   But such a one would at least not be disposed, even from inconsiderateness, much less in malice, to speak ·evil of the Son ·of man ; but rather would he bē inclined to believe that " the kingdom of God had ·come," and that Jesus was the Christ.   And if every kindness done even to themselves, in the ·name of their Master, and because they were *Christ's,* would not lose ·its reward, it was both unnecessary, and inexpedient, to forbid such a one to shew his confidence in the power, and his respect for the character of their Master, even though he did not follow him with them.   It would therefore become them ·to ·regulate their own *behaviour to others* by the maxim, that " he is on their part, who ·is not against them ;" and to leave it to every one's conscience to consider for himself that *individual responsibility* which was declared in the words, " He that is not with me, is against me ; and he that gathereth not with me, scattereth abroad."

" To our own Master we stand, or fall." From his omniscience neither our external conduct, nor our secret principles, can be concealed. A day will come " when God will make up his jewels, and spare them that have feared him, and that have

thought on his name; when we shall discern between the righteous and the wicked, between him
that serveth God, and him that serveth him not."
That Jesus, whose authority we have been main-
taining, the object of whose kingdom we have
been explaining by his own words and works, and
who will hereafter appear as our Judge, has himself
declared, " Many will say to me in that day, Lord,
Lord, have we not prophesied in thy name? and
in thy name have *cast out devils?* and in thy
name done many wonderful works? And then
will I profess unto them, I never knew you; depart
from me, ye that work iniquity." Now if even
a participation of the miraculous powers and gifts
of the primitive ages was not, of itself, a decisive
proof that men were truly Christ's, so as to be
" confessed by him when he shall come in the
glory of his Father," what jealousy should we, of
these latter days, exercise over ourselves! We
have seen that he came to establish the kingdom
of God upon the ruins of that of Satan. We have
seen that in this warfare none can be neuter. We
know that the kingdom of God is " righteousness,
peace, and joy in the Holy Ghost;" and that those
" are of their father the devil, who do the lusts of
their father." If then you would rightly judge of
your own situation in this matter; if you desire to
ascertain whether you have been " delivered from
the power of darkness, and translated into the

kingdom of God's dear Son," you perceive the
sufficient, and the only, test which you are to
apply. It is also fully explained in the words of
the beloved Apostle. " Little children, let no man
deceive you. He that doeth righteousness is
righteous, even as he is righteous. He that committeth sin is of the devil, for the devil sinneth
from the beginning. For this purpose was the
Son of God manifested, that he might destroy the
works of the devil.—In this the children of God
are manifest, and the children of the devil; whosoever doeth not righteousness is not of God,
neither he that loveth not his brother[a]."

But at the same time that our subject calls
upon us to warn and to direct you, it also enables
us to console and to encourage you. The kingdom
of God has been established, and it will never be
destroyed. But it was established by the Son of
man, who came " not to destroy men's lives, but
to save them." He " gave his own life a ransom
for many," " that through death he might destroy
him that had the power of death, that is, the devil,
and deliver them, who, through fear of death, are
all their lifetime subject to bondage." We may,
therefore, be assured, that God hath made us
" more than conquerors, through him that loved
us;" that Jesus has " spoiled principalities and

<hr>

[a] 1 John iii. 7—10.

powers, triumphing over them in his cross;" and that " Satan shall be bruised under our feet shortly."

It is, indeed, through the revelation of the Gospel, that the temptations, the subtilty, and the devices of the prince of darkness have been so distinctly made known to us. By the attack which he made on our Saviour at the commencement of his ministry, and by the exhibition, during our Lord's ministry, we may almost say, of his visible and sensible influence over the bodies and souls of men, we have been fully assured of his existence, and power, and malignity. Yet are we not left in despair. For he, who has given us the opportunity to learn these things, has also given us assurance of his own superiority; has conquered in our behalf; has assured us that " greater is he that is in us, than he that is in the world;" has declared to us the Father, and poured out the gifts of the Spirit; and has thus furnished us with that divine panoply, clad in which we may "withstand in every evil day, and quench all the fiery darts of the wicked one."

LECTURE XI.

———◆———

———◆———

St. John V. 37, 38.

And the Father himself which hath sent me, hath borne witness of me. Ye have neither heard his voice at any time, nor seen his shape. And ye have not his word abiding in you; for whom he hath sent, him ye believe not.

This passage is certainly involved in considerable difficulty. If we refer to the original itself, we find that although, in some respects, its purport might be more distinctly expressed, it requires the assistance of the Commentator, rather than the amendments of the Translator. For the difficulty principally consists, not in the ambiguity of particular words, but in that apparent want of connexion between the different clauses, which has probably been occasioned by the conciseness of the passage. As far, however, as these words of our Lord will be employed in suggesting topics

R

for our present consideration, we shall proceed on
the most evident and certain grounds. Nor am
I without a hope, that we shall be able to illustrate
the scope of the whole passage, by comparing the
first clause of it with those that precede and
follow it. For such a comparison shews, that we
cannot, as many have done, identify its subject
with that which is treated either in the former, or
in the subsequent verses; since by such a supposition we both neglect the most obvious meaning
of the passage, and impair the order and completeness of this very methodical discourse of our
Lord.

" The same *works*, that I do," argued our
Lord, " bear witness of me, that the Father hath
sent me." He then adds, " And the Father,
which hath sent me, *himself* hath borne witness
of me." The first of these appeals we have considered in a former Lecture; the latter is the
subject of our present Lecture. And I have
retained the exact *order* of the words of the original in reciting the latter clause; because it thus
very obviously appears, that it is not subjoined
merely as a continuation and enlargement of the
former, but as an addition and contrast to it. Our
Lord had contended, that the works, which the
Father enabled him to perform, proved that he had
been sent by the Father. He then *assumes* the
truth of that inference, and proceeds to speak of

the Father, as " the Father which had sent him."
And he stated, still further, that the Father, as
having sent him, had even given a personal,
direct, and express declaration respecting him.
This, therefore, must be something distinct from
the miracles which our Lord himself wrought.—
Some having observed this, and also the mention
in the latter part of the text, of the *word of the
Father,* have referred this to the *written word of
God* in the law and the prophets. But to adopt
this opinion, would identify the subject of this
passage with that of the *following* verses, in which
our Lord makes a distinct appeal to the Scriptures,
or *written* word of God. But here he evidently
speaks of a *personal* testimony ; nor can we have
much hesitation in concluding that he referred
therein to that personal and audible testimony,
which was borne to him by a voice from heaven,
when, having been baptized by John, he came out
of the waters of Jordan. And this reference
was, if not on this occasion necessary, yet very appropriate and convincing. For in the opening of
his discourse, as we have already seen, he spoke of
God, as " his own proper Father;" of himself, as
" the Son whom the Father loveth, and who sought
the will of the Father which had sent him." Now
when that " Father which had sent him, himself
bore witness of him," on the occasion which we

have specified, he declared, " This is my beloved
Son, in whom I am well pleased^a."

The same heavenly voice, which witnessed to
Jesus at his baptism, also witnessed, and in nearly
the same words, at his transfiguration.—I mention
this now, in order to remark, that if we require
any further proof that we have been giving
a correct representation of our Lord's meaning,
we may find it in a well-known passage of St.
Peter. For that Apostle first argues from the
testimony given to Jesus by the voice from heaven
at his transfiguration, and then from the testimony of prophecy ; exactly in the same manner
in which our Lord subjoins an appeal to prophecy
to his notice of the similar testimony given by the
Father at his baptism. "We have not," says
the Apostle, "followed cunningly-devised fables,
when we made known unto you the power and
coming of our Lord Jesus Christ, but were eye-
witnesses of his majesty. For he received from
God the Father honour and glory, when there
came such a voice to him from the excellent glory,
This is my beloved Son, in whom I am well
pleased. And this voice which came from heaven
we heard, when we were with him in the holy
mount. We have also a more sure word of
prophecy ; whereunto ye do well that ye take

---

heed, as unto a light that shineth in a dark·
place [b]." And the Apostle then enlarges upon the
right principle of the interpretation of prophecy,
and its divine original.

By thus considering, singly, the *first* clause of
our text, and also by connecting it with the preceding words, we have, I think, ascertained its true
purport. The *remaining* clauses will strengthen
us in the same opinion, and will present themselves for consideration in a subsequent part of
this Lecture.

It will be expedient, therefore, now to direct
our attention to the remarkable incident specially
referred to, and to the *two other* occasions on
which the Father, in the same way, bore witness
to Jesus. We may, I think, even extend our
view still further. For there were several other
occasions, on which Jesus was exhibited to us as
the *subject* of miracles, as well as the *worker* of
them; not, indeed, receiving a divine attestation
by means of the audible voice of the Father from
heaven, as in the three instances just specified;
yet in a manner, which is decidedly distinguishable
from his own miracles, and which, equally with the
former instances, bespeaks the interposition and
approbation of the Father. Each of these facts
tends to establish the justice of the claim which

---

[b] 2 Pet. i. 16—19.

· Jesus advanced to the dignity and knowledge, the
· power and authority, of the Son of God. And
when all are considered in connexion, they furnish
a distinct and important body of evidence.

As the instance, specially referred to in the
text, occurred at the commencement of our Lord's
public ministry, so the first occurrence of a similar character accompanied his first introduction
into the world.—The *miraculous conception* of
our Lord in the womb of a virgin, is of the
highest importance, whether we consider it with
reference to the doctrines of the Gospel, or to its
evidences. If we consider it with reference to
the divinity of our Lord, we shall find that it is no
easy task to reconcile it with any other supposition, than that he, who was thus born of a pure
virgin by an unprecedented and supernatural
generation, was our Emmanuel, "God with us;"
and that it was the divine, pre-existent, and eternal Word, who "was thus made flesh." And we
shall therefore confess the propriety and evidence
with which the Angel, after having announced to
the Virgin the approaching overshadowing of the
power of the Highest, added these words, "Therefore also that holy thing, which shall be born of
thee, shall be called (or rather, *shall be acknowledged to be*) the Son of God [a]."

---

[a] Luke i. 35.—κληθήσεται υἱός Θεοῦ.

It will appear, in the sequel of this Lecture, that Jesus, by the three declarations from heaven, received a divine attestation of his investiture with the three offices of priest, prophet, and king. And if the fact of his miraculous conception, and the attendant circumstances of his birth, be established upon sufficient evidence, we are thereby also, as we shall immediately shew, assured of a previous divine interposition. These will likewise evince, by the nature of the facts themselves, by the circumstances connected with them, and by the angelic declarations which then explained their design, that Jesus was both qualified to undertake those offices on our behalf, and that he was actually invested with them.

We find in the evangelical records, an ample and perspicuous detail of these incidents, resting upon the same authority as the rest of the narrative. Two Evangelists, indeed, have not touched upon the subject of the birth of Jesus; but St. Matthew and St. Luke, who have done so, both concur in the same general statement, though St. Luke specifies some incidents which are omitted by St. Matthew, and omits others which the latter has related [b].—But we are told by the Unitarian, for reasons as well known to us as to himself, that we are not to consider the two intro-

---

[b] Matt. i. and ii. Luke i. and ii.

ductory chapters of St. Matthew and St. Luke, as either genuine, or authentic. The writings, in which that opinion is espoused, you can compare at your leisure with the full and satisfactory answers which they have called forth. But if it occur to you, as it has done more than once to myself, to hear such opinions broached in ordinary conversation, you may answer, that such a mutilation is sanctioned by no one single manuscript or version; that the early reception of these parts of the Gospel is proved by the sentiments of the early Christian writers, and by their actual citations of them; and that the only countenance for such a curtailment of the Gospels is derived from the extravagant procedure of two heretical sects, who, not by the sanction of any rules of criticism, or historical testimony, but in consequence of their pre-conceived heretical opinions, rejected these chapters, and with them the larger portion both of the Old and New Testaments. But admitting, as by every rule of just criticism we are bound to do, the genuineness and credibility of these chapters, an examination and comparison of the events recorded in them, will shew them to be such, so numerous, and so connected with each other, that the supposition of imposture and concert, and indeed of any other principle, than that they happened by the wonderful providence, and signal interposition of God, is both untenable and unreasonable.

That the Virgin could have no doubt, either of the visit of the Angel, or of her conception according to his annunciation, if they really took place, it were absurd to suppose. If these circumstances were fictitious, they were certainly only a small portion of an imposture, which had many and strange ramifications. Then were Zacharias, and Elizabeth, and Joseph, and the Shepherds, and the Magi, and Simeon, and Anna, all concerned in it; and Herod and the Sanhedrim were incautiously brought into connexion with the scheme. But consider the parts which they respectively acted, and the number, situation, and circumstances, of all concerned; for all these effectually tend to evince the reality of the events, and to remove, at every step, the supposition of imposture. Zacharias must have begun to carry it into execution in the *sanctuary* of the temple; on the only day, perhaps during his whole life, when he burnt incense in the order of his course [a]; acting indeed in a manner which made all the congregation witnesses of his state. Coincident with this, was the preternatural conception of the *aged* Elizabeth; and then the visit of Mary to her, after an *angelic* annunciation, and *supernatural* conception. Remember that the whole imposture,

---

[a] It seldom, if ever, happened, that the burning of incense fell twice to the lot of the same priest.

if such it was, proceeded upon the perilous assumption of the *sex* of both the children; and upon the assumption also, that having come to mature age, they would *willingly*, and *successfully* appear in two distinct and remarkable characters, assumed by them indeed, and specified by the predictions of those concerned, but also corresponding to the descriptions of the ancient prophets, and expected as about that period to appear, though in a far different manner. Consider again the incidents occurring at the circumcision of the son of Zacharias, which were noised abroad among the neighbours, which excited their attention, and awakened their expectations. Consider the extraordinary coincidence of political events, by means of which Mary, usually resident in Galilee, brought forth her promised Son at Bethlehem, the only birth-place suited to the character which her Son was to assume. Consider the shepherds abiding on that night in the fields of Judea, addressed by an angel, who announced to them the glad tidings of a Saviour, Christ, born to them in Bethlehem, the city of David; and hearing a chorus of the heavenly host praising God, and saying, "Glory to God in the highest; and on earth peace, good will towards men." Consider the infant Jesus, visited in his lowly cradle, not by the Shepherds only, but by the Wise Men; who were summoned from a distant country by an extraordinary celestial luminary, and, being directed by Herod himself and the Sanhedrim to Bethlehem, as the birthplace of the expected King of the Jews, saluted the new-born Jesus with royal presents. Consider Herod, and all Jerusalem with him, troubled at the intelligence; the sanguinary attempts of the Jewish monarch to crush him in his infancy; his deliverance by a divine premonition to Joseph; and the inspired declarations of Simeon and Anna in the temple, at Jerusalem, not only to his parents, but "to all that looked for redemption in Jerusalem."—Consider, I say, all these things. Reflect on the number of those concerned, and the difference of their respective stations, residences, and views. Call to mind the visit of angels to Zacharias in the sanctuary, to the Virgin in her solitude, to Joseph in his nightly repose, to the Shepherds in their nightly watches;—the heavenly signal which directed the Magi, and the dream which warned them of danger;—the providence of God delivering Jesus from a massacre, and, by his Spirit, inspiring prophets to predict his future glory. Sum up all these things, and consider the improbability of an imposture, the success of which was so remote, as well as so uncertain; nay, rather confess its impossibility under all the circumstances; and say to what other conclusion you can come, but that these things, explicitly and satisfactorily attested as they are, are the witness of God, which he has given us of his Son, little less expressly than by his own audible declaration from heaven[a].

Many of those, who had been concerned in the transactions we have been considering, had been gathered to their fathers, and a period of thirty years had elapsed, when Jesus prepared to fulfil his high destiny, by entering on his public ministrations. He had been ushered into the world by circumstances which indicated the special interposition of the Father, and in which, therefore, he gave witness, that he had sent him for some great and holy purpose. We shall have to point out *three* distinct repetitions, during the short period of his *public life*, of " the witness of the Father." And after the *separate* consideration of each of these, we shall also re-consider in connexion with it the witness of the Father, which had been given to the same effect, by the circumstances attendant on his birth.

I. At the usual age for entering on the Aaronic priesthood, Jesus came from Galilee, where he had been brought up, into Judea, to partake of that baptism, which John had been divinely commissioned to administer in the name of him who

---

[a] He who wishes to see this most satisfactory argument fully discussed, may refer to the late Dr. Bell's Inquiry into the Divine Missions of John the Baptist and Jesus Christ; a work which deserves to be more generally, and very attentively perused.

should come after him. When Jesus had received
the rite of baptism, and was coming out of the
water, "the heavens were opened, and the Holy
Spirit, in a bodily appearance, as a dove, de-
scended upon him, and, as John testified, "abode
upon him." At the same time there came also
a voice from heaven, saying, "This is my beloved
Son, in whom I am well pleased[b]."—Thus had
the Father himself given to Jesus authority to
declare, as he did in the early part of the discourse, from whence our text is taken, "The
Father loveth the Son, and sheweth him all things
that himself doeth." For he audibly announced
that he was that "beloved Son, in whom he had
ever been well pleased[b];" and thus he testified
that he sanctioned and approved the office which
he was about to undertake. According to prophecy, he then also "put his Spirit upon his servant, whom he upheld, his elect, in whom his
soul delighted[c]." Thus was the Baptist himself
enabled to point him out to others, as that exalted
personage, to whom appertained the office of
"baptizing with the Holy Ghost;" for he had
now seen the exhibition of that signal which had
been promised for his direction. Hence he could
announce him as the Son of God, because he had

---

[b] Matt. iii. 17.—ἐν ᾧ εὐδόκησα.

[c] See Isai. xlii. 1. Also 2 Sam. vii. 14. Psal. lxxxix. 26, 27.

heard it so declared from heaven by that witness
of the Father, which was evinced both to the eye
and to the ear; and the reality of which does,
from the very nature of the fact, prove its divinity.

But the Baptist also declared, by the same
divine inspiration which had before guided his
declarations, that Jesus was "the Lamb of God,
which taketh away the sin of the world." If so,
then Jesus was he, for whom "a body was to be
prepared," that he might "come, as in the volume
of the book it was written of him, to do the will
of God, when God no longer desired sacrifice and
offering, nor required burnt-offering and sin-
offering[a]." Then was Jesus that "most Holy"
one, who was to be "anointed, to finish the
transgression, and to make an end of sins, and to
make reconciliation for iniquity, and to bring in
an everlasting righteousness, and to make the
sacrifice, and oblation to cease[b]." Then was
Jesus he, who was to be "a priest upon his
throne[c]," uniting in himself the prerogatives of
Aaron and of David: for, though "not called after
the order of Aaron, he was called to be a priest
for ever after the order of Melchizedec[d];" and
though he was David's Son, he was also "David's
Lord[e]." Jesus is indeed "the High priest of

---

[a] Isai. xl, 6, &c.   [b] Dan. ix. 24, 27.   [c] Zech. vi. 13.
[d] Heb. v. 6, &c. and chap. vii.   Ps. cx. 4.   [e] Ps. cx. 1.

our profession." By his participation of human nature, he was made acquainted with our infirmities, and thus can be "a merciful as well as a faithful high priest in things pertaining to God." But by his supernatural and immaculate conception we know that he is "such an high priest as became us, holy, harmless, undefiled, separate from sinners," because he is not "shapen in iniquity, nor conceived in sin[f]." Thereby we also know that he is the Son of God, and therefore, "because he continueth ever, hath an unchangeable priesthood[g]."—And by the witness of the Father at his baptism we know that as he was called of God to be a high priest, so was he also consecrated by God. "The word of the oath, of which David spoke in the hundred and tenth Psalm, maketh the Son a high priest, who is consecrated for evermore[h];" and the voice from heaven at his baptism declared that the Father was well pleased in the priestly functions which he was then about to discharge. He was at that time visibly inaugurated, in the sight of men, in a manner analogous to that by which the Aaronic priests were consecrated[i]. As *they* were washed with water, so was *he;* and as *they* were anointed with oil, so did

---

[f] See Heb. ii. 16—18 ; iii. 1, 2 ; vii. 24—28.

[g] Heb. vii. 24.   [h] Ps. cx. 4.   Heb. vii. 28.

[i] Exod. xxix. 4—7. Lev. viii. 6—10.

he partake of the measureless and abiding unction of that Holy Spirit which was thereby typified.

This attestation of the Father had already been given to Jesus, at the time when he spoke the words of our text. If it be connected with the witness of John, with his supernatural birth, and with the prophecies of the ancient Scriptures, it points out to us Jesus, as the Son of God, appearing as our high priest. But if considered merely as a *detached* fact, it is declaratory of his divine mission. And our Lord, in the latter part of the text, so applies it for the conviction of those whom he addressed. And since his remarks referred to that incident, we must adopt that particular exposition of the allusion, which corresponds to our opinion respecting the circumstances of that fact; for he therein specifies three of the particulars concerned, the *audible voice* of the Father, the *visible appearance,* and the *word* which was heard. If, according to the opinion entertained by some, and which seems the impression naturally produced by a perusal of the narrative, we suppose that this heavenly appearance and declaration took place in the sight and hearing of those who came to be baptized by John; and that possibly, therefore, some of those whom our Lord addressed, were themselves present, we shall of course render the first clause of the passage interrogatively, as the original will certainly allow us to do: " The

Father, who hath sent me, himself hath borne witness of me. Have ye never at any time heard his voice, nor seen his appearance? And ye have not his word (his declaration) abiding in you; for whom he hath sent, him ye believe not."— If we suppose, with others, that *only John and Jesus* were present at this scene, then we may understand our Lord as granting, that they had not themselves heard the voice, and seen the appearance, when the Father testified that "he was his beloved Son, in whom he was well pleased." Yet as John had both seen, and heard, and also had publicly testified of these things, they erred by not retaining an abiding recollection of this declaration of God; and, by not believing in him whom the Father had sent, they were neglecting and despising the express witness of God himself. —But even if we suppose that John alone was, with Jesus, the spectator and auditor of these things, yet two instances of a similar kind soon afterwards occurred, which are attested by a greater number of witnesses; so that these incidents derive support from each other, both as to the certainty of the fact, and as to the heavenly information thereby conveyed.

II. The Father himself again bore witness of Jesus at the time of his transfiguration.— Those, who were with Jesus at the time, were Peter, and James, and John. The incident is

S

related, circumstantially, by each of the three first Evangelists; and St. John also seems principally to refer to it when he says; "We have beheld his glory, as that of the only-begotten of the Father[a]." St. Peter also, in words which we have already quoted from his second Epistle, largely states its certainty, its circumstances, and the evidence which it gave to Jesus. At the time, the splendour of a scene so glorious impressed St. Peter so powerfully, that, in energetic language, "not knowing what he said," he gave vent to his feelings; in language, however, which, though unadvised, proved his full conviction of the reality of the unexpected scene. But in the words which we cited from his Epistle, written but a short time before he sealed his testimony with his blood, he speaks of it with a coolness, which indicated a sober and matured conviction of the reality of that scene, of which he and others had been eye-witnesses, of which he retained so vivid a recollection, and of the design and evidence of which he had now so distinct an apprehension. Not only was *Jesus* seen by the three disciples, arrayed in the "body of his glory," but *Moses*, the legislator and prophet of the Jews, was there; and *Elias* also, one of the most eminent later

---

[a] Matt. xvii; Mark ix; Luke ix; John i. 14.

prophets, and the restorer of the law. With them Jesus held familiar converse, the grand subject of which was his approaching death. But shortly they retired, and Jesus was left *alone;* then to receive that testimony from heaven, which was to declare his divine and unrivalled dignity. "A bright cloud overshadowed the disciples; and, behold, a voice out of the cloud, which said, This is my beloved Son, in whom I am well pleased; *hear ye him.*"

It will readily occur to any one, who considers the terms of this declaration, that it supplies us with a divine interpretation of that prediction, which was delivered by Moses to the Israelites, when they had desired that they might not again see the awful glories, and hear the appalling thunders and voices of mount Sinai. "The Lord thy God will raise up unto thee a Prophet from the midst of thee, of thy brethren, like unto me; unto him shall ye hearken[b]." Such a prophet and mediator was to be sent to the Israelites, in compliance with the request which they had made, and in condescension to human infirmity. But though man should not again "hear the voice of the Lord God, nor see that great fire," as in Horeb, on the day of the assembly; yet would God reveal his will in a manner equally authori-

---

[b] Deut. xviii. 15—19.

tative, though with milder and less tremendous glory. The Lord said to Moses, after the solemn delivery of the law, "Thus shalt thou say unto the children of Israel, Ye have seen that I have talked with you from heaven [a]." And after Jesus had been transfigured on the holy mount, the Father did again " talk with man from heaven;" declaring Jesus to be the mediator of the new covenant, as Moses had been of the old. He, to whom the Father thus gave witness, was sent to make known to us " the truth which he had heard of God." For God had declared by Moses respecting that Prophet, " I will put my words in his mouth, and he shall speak unto them all that I shall command him." When, therefore, the Father, giving testimony to Jesus, says to us, " Hear ye him," may we not be sure that " as the Father gave him commandment, so he spoke?" Although, therefore, in the dispensation of which Jesus is the prophet, " we are not come to the blackness, and darkness, and tempest, and terrible words" of mount Sinai, but to the milder glories of mount Sion ; yet " the word, which went forth from Sion," has its threatenings, as well as its grace and truth. " It shall come to pass," said the Lord again, " that whosoever will not hearken unto my words, which that prophet shall speak

---

[a] Exod. xx. 22.

in my name, I will require it of him." And very justly, therefore, does the Apostle give to us the exhortation; "See that ye refuse not him that speaketh; for if they escaped not, who refused him that spake on earth, much more shall not we escape, if we refuse him that speaketh from heaven;" even God himself, who "in these last days hath spoken unto us by his Son ᵇ."

Did we say that this heavenly Messenger was the *Son* of God?—What said the voice that came out of the cloud? "This is *my beloved Son;* hear ye him." And was not the same testimony also given, when he was about to *enter* on his ministry? And had not that declaration, which avouched Jesus to be "the beloved Son, in whom the Father was well pleased," been previously declared *before* his birth, and been also confirmed by the *manner* of his birth? Did we not recite to you the words of the angel, announcing to the Virgin her approaching conception by the "over-shadowing of the power of the Highest?" "*There-fore,*" said the heavenly herald, "that holy thing, which shall be born of thee, shall be called *the Son of God.*" Though Jesus appeared "in the likeness of sinful flesh," yet are we to believe in him upon principles, and with views, which could not be applicable to any one, who was nothing

---

ᵇ Heb. xii. 25. i. 1, 2.

more than a prophet of the human race. We have many declarations from the Father that he is the Son of God; many declarations from himself, supported and confirmed by the witness of John, of his own works, and of prophecy, that he is the Son of God. Let then the " word of the Father abide in you, that ye may believe in him whom he hath sent." Hear him with that unreserved obe‑ dience of the full assurance of faith, which he may justly claim, who "came down from heaven;" and who possessed that extensive and familiar acquaintance with the divine will, which could be attained only by him, who was from eternity "in the bosom of the Father," who "came from God, and went to God."

In this manner has it been testified to us, that to Jesus belong the commission, and the authority, of the *Prophet* promised by Moses. And hence may we see, that while "Moses was faithful in all his house, as a *servant,* for a testimony of those things *which were to be spoken after* ; yet that Jesus was so, as a *Son* over his *own* house [a]." But, by a *third* witness of the Father concerning him, he was declared to be "the *King* whom, as his only-begotten Son, God would set upon his holy hill of Zion, though the rulers of the earth took counsel against him, and against his Anointed [b]."

---

[a] Heb. iii. 5, 6.   [b] Ps. ii.

III. This third testimony was given, as it should seem, on the day on which Jesus entered Jerusalem in his lowly triumph, and on which he was saluted as "the Son of David, and the King of Israel," by the eager multitudes, whose enthusiasm he *refused* to repress. Probably it was even in the temple itself, but certainly in Jerusalem, that the Greeks, who had come up to the feast, applied to the disciples that they might be permitted to see Jesus[c]. Whether he granted their request, or not, is uncertain. But the discourse which he took occasion to deliver, and the incident which followed, especially deserve our attention. He immediately referred to that death, which he suffered only a few days afterwards, under the figure of corn, which, "except it fall into the ground and die, abideth alone; but if it die, it bringeth forth much fruit." His human nature felt all the fears and horrors which the prospect of his approaching sufferings might be expected to excite. But this public declaration of them was followed by as public a "witness of the Father" from heaven.—"Now is my soul troubled. And what shall I say? Father, save me from this hour? But for this cause came I unto this hour. Father, glorify thy name." This, whether it was the language of submission, or of prayer, equally

---

[c] See John xii. 20—36.

prepares us to attend to what followed. " Then came there a voice from heaven, saying, *I have both glorified it, and I will glorify it again.* The people, therefore, that stood there, and heard it, said, That it thundered; others said, An angel spake to him." The voice was distinctly audible to many, if not to all. The Greeks, if they were present, might not understand the language; and some of the Jews might be disposed to misunderstand and misrepresent it. But let us hear the remarks of Jesus respecting it, and we can easily judge whether they were *verified*. " This voice came not because of me, but for your sakes. Now is the judgment of this world; now shall the prince of this world be cast out. And I, if I be lifted up from the earth, will draw all men unto me. This he said, signifying what death he should die."

The Jews then present were unable to reconcile this with their late joyful hailing of Jesus as their Messiah, and with their expectations respecting the Messiah.—" The people answered him, We have heard out of the law, that Christ abideth for ever; and how sayest thou, The Son of man must be lifted up? Who is this Son of man?" Now though our Lord did not at that time add any explanation of the statement he had just made; he exhorted them to "walk while they had the light, because the light would be with them only for a little while." Soon the event, to which he alluded, was to take place. And on a former occasion he said to them, " When ye have lifted up the Son of man, then shall ye know that *I am he,* and that I do nothing of myself, but as my Father hath taught me, I speak these things." The Father had just given witness to him, and he had " done many miracles before them." They ought, therefore, both to receive those communications which they could then comprehend, and also to believe that all others would afterwards be made intelligible. But very shortly the Father did "glorify his name ;" and, "in consequence of his being lifted up," Jesus was " crowned with glory and honour," and " all men were drawn to him."

Was Jesus forsaken and disowned of the Father, because he was " given up into the hands of wicked men, and suffered death upon the cross?" The Father had spoken to him from heaven, and an angel from heaven strengthened him during his agony. But had he prayed to the Father to deliver him from the suffering of death, though he would " presently have given him more than twelve legions of angels," yet " how then could the Scriptures have been fulfilled, that thus it must be ?" Yet even in those very transactions, which were so ignominious and so pitiable, was the testimony of the Father given to Jesus.—For remember the preternatural darkness, which, at the time of the full moon, and beginning at noonday, for three hours overspread the land. And can we forget the circumstances which attested the truth of those words, so full of horror and yet so abundant in consolation,—so expressive of glory accruing to God, and of good will derived to men, —which were uttered by the lips of our dying Saviour? With a loud voice he cried, IT IS FINISHED. He bowed his head, and dismissed his Spirit.— Then was the law accomplished, then were the prophecies fulfilled, then was the salvation of man perfected. For did not God himself confirm this declaration, by the rending of the veil of the temple at the hour of incense, by the quaking of the earth, by the rending of the rocks, by the opening of the graves? The centurion, who stood near to the cross of Jesus, had before heard him exclaim, " My God, my God, why hast thou forsaken me ?" But when he saw that Jesus, uttering the declaration, " It is finished," expired under circumstances, which so manifestly declared the interposition of God, he was so impressed with the solemnity of the scene, and with the majesty of the innocent sufferer, that " he, and they also that were with him, feared greatly, saying, Truly this was the Son of God[a]."

Thus did the Father " again glorify his name," by giving testimony to his Son. Thus

---

[a] Matt. xxvii. 54.   Mark xv. 39.

did he confirm the authority, and sanction the
conduct of him, who had refused to repress the acclamations of the multitude who hailed him as "the
Son of David, and as the King of Israel that cometh
in the name of the Lord;" who himself also avowed
to the high priest, that he was ". the Christ, the
Son of the Blessed."—And had not the Father
given the same testimony by the mouth of an
angel, before he was conceived in the, womb of
the Virgin? " He shall be great, and shall be
called the Son of the Highest ; and the Lord
God shall give him the throne of his father
David, and he shall reign over the house of
Jacob for ever ; and of his kingdom there shall
be no end[b]." He was " made of the seed of
David according to the flesh;" but, by the
manner in which he was made a partaker of flesh
and blood, we also see, that he was David's Lord,
as well as David's Son ; and therefore that he, as
" the Christ, does indeed abide for ever," though
as ruling, not on earth, but in heaven. For God
himself has visited his people, by redeeming them
from spiritual slavery; and, in the house of his
servant David, hath raised up a horn of Salvation
from sin and condemnation ; by him, who was
" called Jesus, because he would save his people
from their sins."

---

[b] Luke i. 32, 33.

Though, therefore, the Jews demanded of Jesus, as the proof of his authority, " a sign from heaven," and though their demand was refused, yet we see that, in fact, several such tokens were given; not, however, exactly in the manner which they presumptuously, and in the spirit of disbelief, required of Jesus, " tempting him." For we must be content to receive the evidences of our faith in the manner in which they are *proposed* to us, and to abide by the inference to which they both severally and jointly lead us. Probably it is still true, that such as are not convinced by the numerous miracles which *Jesus* wrought, will not more readily be impressed by those, in which *the Father himself* bore witness of him. But when the demand of a sign from heaven was refused to those, who in such a temper demanded it, *the sign of the prophet Jonas* was promised to them[a]. That sign also has been given. " Three days was the Son of man in the heart of the earth," and then was he *again*, and " with power, declared to be the Son of God, by the resurrection from the dead." Then was the witness of the Father *completed;* and then also began that witness of the Spirit, the rejection of which renders men incapable either of repentance or of pardon.

Calling to mind, then, all the wondrous events,

---

[a] See Matt. xii. 35—42.

and heavenly testimony, which we have been
surveying, with what reverence, confidence, and
obedience may we listen to the words, which our
Saviour spoke, after he had predicted the sign of
Jonas the prophet. " The men of Nineveh
shall rise in judgment with this generation, and
shall condemn it; for they repented at the
preaching of Jonas, and, behold, *a greater than
Jonas* is here! The queen of the south shall
rise up in the judgment with this generation, and
shall condemn it; for she came from the uttermost parts of the earth to hear the wisdom of
Solomon, and, behold, *a greater than Solomon* is
here!" We have this day learnt that he was
" *the beloved Son of God,* in whom he is well
pleased, and whom we are commanded to hear." Let
us then " take up our cross and follow him ;" let
us " abide in his word, that we may be his disciples indeed ;" let us glory in his cross; let us
confide in his atonement; let us pray for pardon
through his blood and righteousness; let us rejoice in his intercession ; and let us pray to be
sanctified by his word, and by his Spirit. For,
very shortly after he had spoken the words just
cited, he said also, " Whosoever shall do the
will of my Father which is in heaven, the same is
my brother, and sister, and mother[a]."

---

[a] Matt. xii. 38—50.

LECTURE XII.

———◆———

OUR LORD'S APPEAL TO THE SCRIPTURES OF THE
OLD TESTAMENT, AS PECULIARLY DESIGNED TO
TESTIFY OF HIM.

———◆———

St. John V. 39, 40.

*Search the Scriptures; for in them ye think ye have
eternal life; and they are they which testify of me.
And ye will not come to me, that ye might have life.*

WE observed, in our fourth Lecture, that our
Lord either left the attestations to his divine
mission and character to convince by their own
native force and palpable evidence, or proposed
them in the most simple manner, until fuller statements and more detailed arguments were called
forth by the doubts and difficulties, the prejudices
and opposition of his contemporaries. But when
such occasions arose, he unfolded to them as much
as the imperfect accomplishment of the purposes
of his mission, and therefore the incomplete
exhibition of its evidences, would permit. Often,
however, his statements are applicable to, and anticipate the fuller developement of the evidences;
of which, indeed, the discourse in which our text

occurs is a remarkable instance. Those of his reasonings in this discourse, which we have already considered, are sufficient to establish the justice of this remark. When he noticed to them the presumption in his favour from his not seeking his own will, when he appealed to the witness of John, to the witness of his own miracles, and to the witness of the Father, he had laboured so long and so publicly among them, that enough was already before them, if not finally to convince, yet at least to arrest the attention. Enough had been already seen and heard to claim for him an impartial hearing ; enough to induce them, if not even then to believe in him, yet to pause ere they rejected his claims. And in order to come to a just and satisfactory decision, it was requisite that they should observe, in a candid frame of mind, his future conduct; and should also deliberately consider the more enlarged reasonings, upon which he would be ready to enter, whenever their difficulties called for appropriate statements, and whenever fresh facts either illustrated his former arguments, or supplied the materials for others.

The same remark is also applicable, and, in some respects, more fully, to the appeal made in the text to the written testimony, which the Scriptures of the Old Testament afforded to Jesus.— The events, in which any prophecy is accomplished, alone can finally decide, either its true *interpretation,* or the particular *object* to which it referred. It follows from hence, that the events in question must have come to pass, and their particulars must be fully known, before that interpretation can be definitely settled, and the attestation of prophecy can be rightly ascertained. Now the prophecies of the Old Testament, which relate to the Messiah, are very numerous, and refer to a great variety of particulars. Of course, therefore, when the Messiah came, before he could be completely identified, all the characteristics by which the prophets had described him must have been exhibited ; and therefore all the events, in consequence of which they were to be developed, must have taken place. We believe that, at the very time specified by the prophets, their predictions were fulfilled in Jesus of Nazareth. If in him they were not accomplished, there is certainly no other in whom they were ; no other, respecting whom the assertion can be advanced. But the great argument, deducible from a collective view of all the prophecies, could not be complete, until after those transactions which closed his ministry and life; by which so large a proportion of the prophecies were rapidly, but minutely, fulfilled. Yet even at the time when our Lord spoke the words of our text, much had already become sufficiently obvious. And since an apprehension of the entire prophetic argument could not be attained, except by discerning the correspondence of a great number of particular events to at least as many particular predictions, it would have been well if those, whom our Lord addressed, had even then commenced the inquiry. For having thus seen the fulfilment of prophecy already evinced to a certain extent, they might have been prepared to watch the progress of his ministry, and would have recognized thereby, more and more clearly, him, " of whom Moses in the law, and the prophets, did write."

Rightly to apprehend the evidence which arises from the word of prophecy, we must have recourse to that repository, in which it has been handed down to us. We must comply with the exhortation, which our Lord in the text addressed to the Jews. We must " search the Scriptures." We must investigate and study the particular predictions therein contained, and observe their order and connexion ; and, by comparing them with those events which correspond to them, as recorded either in the same Scriptures, or in other writers, we must trace their accomplishment. Such an undertaking would evidently be too extensive to be brought within the compass of our present design. There is, however, a more limited range, which falls within the path we at first marked out. For we proposed to contemplate the subject of evidence, either as it is actually *con-tained* in our Lord's discourses, or immediately *suggested* by them. Now our Lord has himself actually cited many important prophecies, to many he obviously alludes, and others afford at least a valuable elucidation of his statements. Even this more confined review exhibits, in a very satis-factory manner, the testimony of prophecy to Jesus; and also, which is even still more im-portant, it supplies us with such directions and sug-gestions as are sufficient to lead us to a proper and conclusive view of the whole argument. It will be the object of our next Lecture, to take a cursory view of these actual citations and illus-trations of prophecy by our Lord himself. In the remainder of this we shall consider the subject more *generally*, but still in immediate connexion with our text.

We have just cited the first clause of it, as containing an *exhortation* to " search the Scrip-tures." But many have preferred a translation of the verb in the indicative mood. According to this view, we must understand our Lord as grant-ing to the Jews, that they did search the Scrip-tures; a concession, which all that we know of that nation, and especially of its leading men, shews to be made according to fact. To under-stand the words in this manner is, perhaps, more consistent with the *style* and *method* of argu-

mentation throughout the whole discourse, which
in no other instance is in the hortatory form.
But still the same recommendation, which is
expressed in the other translation, perhaps more
agreeably to the *phraseology* of the original, is in
this *implied* with almost equal force. Our Lord
evidently conveys, in either case, his decided com-
mendation of their attention to Scripture; and he
assigns the powerful motive, which either did, or
ought to influence them in such a pursuit: " Ye
search the Scriptures, for in them ye think ye
have eternal life."

With respect to the Jews of that time, this
motive might have considerable difference of character and operation. Some of them seemed to
think that the *mere* searching of the Scriptures,
and "making broad the phylacteries" on which
its words were inscribed, were of themselves
meritorious acts; and that thereby " they had
eternal life." Others might think it attainable
by observance of the *ritual* law of Moses. Others,
like the scribe with whom Jesus conversed, doubtless esteemed the *moral* law as more than all
"whole burnt-offerings and sacrifice," and that the
things therein prescribed they must " do, to inherit eternal life." And, doubtless, they looked
forward to the Messiah, as their own writings
testify, as the *bestower* of eternal life on the *Jews;*
and some of those, who waited for " the consola-

tion of Israel," probably derived from the Scriptures an expectation less free from the general
prejudices of their nation ; and expected him who
was to be " the glory of his people Israel," would
also be "·a light to lighten the Gentiles."—But to
all these our Lord's argument was equally cogent.
Whatever were the modifications of their sentiments, it was believed by all, except the Sadducees,
that in them they had *eternal life ;* and therefore
did they value them, and therefore were they bound,
by their own principles, to make themselves fully
acquainted with their contents.   We also are
assured, that the Holy Scriptures are able to make
us wise unto salvation ; and that their record is,
not only that " God hath given to us eternal life,"
but also " that this life is in his Son ;" and that,
' both in the Old and New Testament, everlasting
life is offered to mankind through Jesus Christ, as
the only Mediator between God and man[a].'   Yet
the Jews in general " were not willing to come to
him that they might have life."   They had un-
traced such interpretations of the prophecies, as
could result only from attending to some, and
overlooking others.   And when these others were
pointed out, and when the event shewed the
proper sense both of these and of the former, their
prejudices in favour of their own interpretation,

---

[a] Art. VII.

and against the external humility of a suffering
Messiah, armed their perverse and depraved wills
against the decision, which would have been suggested by an unfettered judgment; and therefore
were they "unwilling to come to Jesus that they
might have life." They themselves thought that
in the Scriptures they had eternal life; and, added
our Lord, "they are they which testify of me."

In this important declaration, our Lord not
only asserts that the Scriptures would be found
to predict and testify of him, but that he was that
exalted Person, who, as Jewish writers themselves
have confessed, is the great and continual theme
of all the prophets. He lays down therein that
principle, which is, in fact, a guide to the consistent and complete elucidation of the whole prophetic scheme. Prophecy had indeed a present
and immediate use in supporting the hope, and
exercising the faith, of those to whom it was first
delivered. But even this end was attained by
speaking of good things to come; and by giving
repeated assurances that a personage, who, after
having been designated by various other titles and
characteristics, was at length called "Messiah the
Prince," would in the latter days appear to accomplish the purposes of God, and to complete
the felicity of man. To predict the advent of
Messiah—to communicate the previous knowledge
of those marks by which he might be recognized

as he that was to come—to display the necessity,
and to explain the object of his coming—and to
attest the importance of his mission, by shewing that
all the revolutions of the world, as well as of the
Jewish people, were overruled in order to prepare
for his advent, and for the establishment of his
kingdom—this was the main end and aim of "all
that was spoken by the mouth of God's holy
prophets which had been since the world began."
Thus had the matter been stated by Zacharias in
his prophetic hymn; thus was it stated by our
Lord, when, after his resurrection, "he expounded
to them in all the Scriptures the things concerning
himself, beginning at Moses and all the
prophets." Thus did the Apostles declare, that
"to him give all the prophets witness;" thus did
the angel declare also to St. John, "the testimony
of Jesus is the spirit of prophecy[a];" 'the spirit
of prophecy having no other use or end than to
bear testimony, and to do honour, to him[b].'

---

[a] Luke i. 68, &c. xxiv. 27, 44. Acts x. 43. Rev. xix; 10.
See also 1 Pet. i. 10—12. 2 Pet. i. 19—21.

[b] Bishop Hurd in Serm. II. on the Prophecies.—He who, like
the Ethiopian convert (Acts viii. 27, &c.) is ready to say, "How
can I understand what I read in the Prophets, except some man
should guide me?" may with great satisfaction and benefit peruse
Bishop Hurd's Introduction to the Study of the Prophecies, Serm.
I—VI; Bishop Sherlock's Discourses on the Use and Intent of
Prophecy; the four first Sermons of Bishop Horsley, Vol. II; and
two

Let this principle be kept in view, and it will
shew, in the clearest manner, the object, and the
connexion, of all that the prophets have spoken.
It will teach us rightly to estimate the nature and
the evidence of prophecy. It will shew that it was
not vouchsafed to gratify the curiosity of mankind,
or to serve a merely temporary purpose; but that
it was designed to demonstrate not so much the
general superintendence of divine providence, as
that particular and important exercise of it, which
was subservient to the establishment of the Gospel.
Hence it will also appear that the prophetic spirit
was generally confined to one family and nation,
not out of a peculiar favour or preference to them;
but that these oracles were committed to their
care, in order that the priority of their existence,
and their uncorrupted preservation, might be gua-
ranteed and demonstrated. For, at the arrival
of that period which was the fulness of the time,
considered with reference to the predictions themselves, and the fitness of the time, considered with
reference to the actual state of the world, "the
Gentiles were to become fellow-heirs, and of the
same body, and partakers of *the promise of God*

---

two very valuable tracts by Mr. Rotherham, published in 1753,
and 1754, entitled, " The Force of the Argument from a collective
view of Prophecy," and "a Sketch of the one great Argument,
formed from the several concurring Evidences, for the Truth of
Christianity."

in Christ by the Gospel."—The argument from prophecy is, therefore, one, which appeals alike to Jew and Gentile. To the Jew—because he, for other and independent reasons, receives, venerates, and preserves the Scriptures as the word of God; and because he, therefore, has a deep interest in the promises of the Messiah therein contained, and is bound to inquire into the reality of their accomplishment. To the Gentile—because the prior existence of such a volume of predictions, does, if they have been fulfilled, bespeak his assent also to the revelation made by that God, who "has in these last days spoken by his Son," and has employed the wonders of his providence to assure us of the wonders of his grace. In order to enable the Jews to verify the claims of the Messiah when he appeared among them, one prophecy had been added to another, beginning from the first general promise of the efforts and triumphs of the seed of the woman, proceeding to limit the line of his descent within continually narrower bounds, and then, in succession, specifying a great variety of features in his character, and of circumstances in his life and proceedings, so unprecedented, so remarkable, and apparently so inconsistent, as to defy the most ingenious *fiction* to be so constructed before the event, as to unite them in one character, with a semblance of fulfilment.—When we contemplate the ap-

pearance of Jesus, we see at once that *some* remarkable personage has been manifested, assuredly
of the house and lineage specified in *earlier* prophecy; and answering, both in the place and the
circumstances of his birth, to the predictions of
the *later* prophets. He appears as a prophet sent
from God; and having discerned, in the first
instance, the approach of some Great One, we
proceed, on a nearer view, to the discovery of one
feature after another, until we recognize in him
the personage previously described, and anxiously
expected, though not appearing at first in that
character and dignity, in which the Jews most
frequently and most fondly expected the Messiah.
But circumstance is added to circumstance, till
we find him to be the Messiah, to whom all the
prophets gave witness; and that he has accomplished, or is setting forward the accomplishment
of all that the prophets had predicted; so that not
one word has failed of all that they had spoken,
and that the Evangelists have narrated "no other
things than those, which the prophets and Moses
did say should come."

It is manifest, from what we have already observed, that the prophetic argument is one of great
extent, comprehension, and force. When we
consider its *extent*, we immediately perceive that
the materials for its developement began to be
provided from the very beginning of the world,

and that they were continually accumulating
through a series of more than four thousand years.
We shall find also, that many of the earlier predictions receive much illustration from considering
the *time* at which they were delivered, and the
circumstances of the *persons* to whom, or by
whom, they were spoken. They are, in fact,
arranged in such an order, that each succeeding
one, till, at least, the time of David, would lose
much of its force and propriety, if delivered at an
earlier period, and if the order were even disar-
ranged at all[a]. We gather from hence, that they
are means used in order to further one uniform,
momentous, and continually advancing scheme;
we see how suited they were to the immediate
purpose of inspiring, cherishing, and elevating,
the faith and hope of primeval times; and we pass
on to watch, with calm and increasing confidence,
for their full and evident accomplishment. And
whether we thus advance from the consideration
of them in their order and variety, to contemplate
the events of the age in which they were fulfilled;
or whether we begin from those events, and refer
back to the prophecies; we cannot but observe,
with wonder, that they not only furnish a distinct
evidence in themselves, but that they had speci-

---

[a] See this strikingly illustrated in Rotherham's " Argument
drawn from a collective View of Prophecy," p. 10, &c.

fied beforehand every other evidence, and that every other evidence is illustrated by them. For the prophecies are found to have their fulfilment not only in that particular series of ordinary events which occurred during the life of Jesus, but also in such facts, and instructions, and proceedings, as themselves are independent evidences of a divine mission. Almost every circumstance which has been considered in our former Lectures, was a fulfilment of prophecy; we may almost say that the very *arguments* themselves are pointed out by the prophets; but at least we have found that each of our Lord's reasonings could be very satisfactorily *illustrated* by a reference to the Old Testament predictions. This remark, which points out the *comprehensiveness* of the argument from prophecy, also very obviously suggests the great *force* which it possesses. And prophecy will still more constantly and prominently connect itself with the subjects of our future inquiry. Well therefore might our Lord observe in language so significant, "The Scriptures are *they which testify of me*[b]." As if he had said, 'They are the special, comprehensive, and sufficient testimony respecting me. My coming, my character, my proceedings, my instructions, and the object at which I aim, are all attested by them. My future sufferings and ex-

---

[b] ἐκεῖναι εἰσιν αἱ μαρτυροῦσαι περὶ ἐμοῦ. v. 39.

altation will be in conformity to their predictions. Every argument which I can offer, will be found justified by their intimations, if you will but search them, as well as by the facts which are familiar to you, and upon which I have been reasoning.'

It should also be remembered, that these prophecies were delivered, not only at a great diversity of times, ages, and countries, but in a great variety of methods. Sometimes God himself communicated the promise in words. Sometimes he revealed it in a dream or in a vision, and provided that a prophet or an angel should give an interpretation of these, which itself became a prophecy, to be explained only by the event. Sometimes he immediately inspired the prophet himself to deliver it in his own words. " Thus, at sundry times, and in divers manners, God spake in time past unto the Fathers by the Prophets." And they, who were either the recipients, interpreters, or promulgators of these diversified communications, were men of all ranks, ages, conditions, and circumstances ; severally according to their own necessities, or the situation and circumstances of others, or of their country, or of the world, receiving intimations of those things which should come to pass. The events which were to precede, and to prepare the way for the fulness of the time in which the Promised One was to appear, were those transactions and revolutions of the four great monarchies, which are the well known subjects of ancient and classical history. The predictions respecting *these* were fulfilled only in the course of many centuries. Those, which respected the personal appearance of the Messiah, were sometimes delivered conjointly with the former, sometimes were distinct from them; but were fulfilled in the course of a very few years. All together formed one connected chain. The events were such, and so numerous, as to exclude the possibility of accounting for this conformity to previous annunciation by the supposition of *casual coincidence;* nor could the mere *conjectures* of the wisest mortals have so accurately described them. Either we must say that they were delivered by the communication of him, who alone could *foresee* those *contingent* events, which are brought about by the ordinary motives and proceedings of human conduct; or that the same great Being, "who doeth according to his will among the armies of heaven, and among the inhabitants of the earth," *moulded, controlled* and *adjusted* the motives, actions, and successes of all these numerous assents, so as to *produce* an exact conformity to the predictions of the prophets. Either of these suppositions involves the *interposition* of the Deity. And in the same manner as a miracle implies and teaches the exercise of the same *Omnipotence* which created the world, and which gave to the course of nature a law unbroken, except at the will of the Creator; so does the clear previous existence of prophecy, and the certainty of its extensive fulfilment, prove that he, whose *omni-science* perceives, whose *prescience* foresees, and whose *providence* overrules all things, must in this case also have interposed. And we need surely no argument to convince us that he, who is the God of nature, is the same God, who alone " declares the end from the beginning, and from ancient times the things that are not yet done ; saying, My counsel shall stand, and I will do all my pleasure." His alone is that " wisdom, which reacheth from one end to the other mightily, and doth sweetly order all things."

We have now taken a general survey of the manner in which the Scriptures of the Old Testament give testimony to Jesus, as the Messiah promised of old. We have principally alluded to the *express predictions* of the Old Testament; and also to the history of the earlier ages of the world, as indicating a tendency of all the *arrangements of Providence* towards the fulfilment of those predictions in their season. In the mean time, those assurances of mercy thus given to the Fathers, and the holy covenant into which God entered with them, were sufficient to animate and guide them in their pilgrimage through this world to a better and a heavenly country. For by the

miracles which sometimes accompanied the delivery of these predictions, and by the partial
fulfilment of them, or of others of a similar
origin, they had such evidence of the care and
gracious intentions of that God, " who had provided
better things for us, that they without us
should not be *made perfect,*" as that even they
" died in faith ; not having received the promises
indeed, but having so seen them afar off, as to be
persuaded of them, and to embrace them."—And
in another way also did the provisions of earlier
revelation provide a testimony to the promised
Messiah. The method of worship by sacrifices,
the various ceremonies of the Mosaic ritual, and
very many of the peculiar arrangements of their
civil and political system, were all occasioned by
the design of raising up out of the Jewish nation
that Deliverer, who was predicted by their own
prophets. The consideration of the numerous
particulars to which we have alluded is highly
satisfactory ; for it tends to strengthen more and
more our conviction that the Scriptures of the
Old Testament, are *they that testify* of Jesus.
For it shews not only that their predictions
describe him, and that the events which they
relate were preparing for his advent, but also
that the civil and political injunctions were designed to shew that he was born of the promised
house and lineage, and that the religious cere-

monies, in a vast variety of methods, represented
and typified his character and understanding[a].

"Search, then, the Scriptures; for in them
ye think ye have eternal life. And they are those
which testify of Me," said Jesus, whom we believe
to have been the Christ.—Now the Scriptures,
eternal life, and Jesus Christ, are terms familiar
to us, and in some degree, at least, understood by
all of us. And it is by allowing the connexion
and mutual dependency of the ideas thereby
conveyed, that the Christian deduces those principles and motives, and cherishes those hopes
and expectations, which distinguish him from the
Jew and the Infidel.—The Infidel, indeed, either
does not at all concern himself about the hope of
eternal life; or he derives it from the boasted
arguments of natural religion, independently both
of the Scriptures, and of him, who, "through the
Gospel, has brought life and immortality to light."
—The Jew does indeed look forward to eternal
life, but he derives not that hope from the record
which God has given of his Son Christ Jesus.
For he believes not that Jesus was one whom God
had sent; and, therefore, while he admits the
divine authority of the Scriptures of the Old

. [a] Among other excellent works which would elucidate this
part of our subject, I would refer more especially to "Allix's
Reflections on the Old and New Testament." They are reprinted
in Bp. Watson's Tracts, Vol. I.

Testament referred to in the text, and allows that
they testify of a promised Messiah, he believes not
that Jesus is that Messiah. Multitudes of Jews
have, indeed, even in modern times been induced,
from the evidence of the prophecies, to admit the
Messiahship of Jesus, and have embraced the
Christian faith. Very many of these have been
learned men, and have left behind them, in their
several writings, a statement of the reasons which
influenced them[b]. But *as a nation*, they reject
the claims of Jesus. In the apostolic times also,
" great multitudes of Jews," " many even among
the chief rulers," believed on him; and " a great
company of their priests became obedient to the
faith[c]." But then also, *as a nation*, they rejected
him. The motives and grounds of that rejection,
in some respects common to unbelievers of all
ages and nations, our Lord notices in the words
following the text, which will be considered in
a future Lecture. But when our Lord delivered
this discourse, these principles had not yet come
into full operation. The question of his divine
mission and Messiahship was as yet, in a great

---

[b] See a very interesting account of the conversion and writings
of Jewish Rabbis, and of their labours among their countrymen,
at the end of Chapman's Eusebius ; who gives references to those
authorities which he says would have enabled him to enlarge his
list.

[c] John xii. 42.   Acts vi. 7 ; xxi. 20.

measure, undecided. The Jews, and more especially their rulers, were evidently prejudiced
against him, and rather disposed to oppose and
persecute him, than to admit his claims. This
prejudice and opposition had not, however, proceeded to the lengths to which it afterwards did ;
but only so far as to draw from our Lord a more
full statement respecting his claims, and the several
arguments which he was able to produce in support of them. We have heard what claims he
advanced, we have considered his reasonings, we
have surveyed and scrutinized the facts to which
he referred, and we have now considered that
testimony of Scripture to which our Lord last
directed the attention of those whom he addressed.
How then are we affected with regard to this
important question, respecting eternal life, and that
divine messenger who was sent to offer, who died
to procure, and who was exalted to bestow a boon
so unspeakably precious? Do we virtually sym-
bolize with the Jew and the infidel, either refusing,
because of the objections which are suggested to
our understanding, or neglecting, because of the
backwardness of our hearts, to " come to Christ
that we may have life?"

If we entertain doubts respecting the fulness
and conclusiveness of the Christian argument,
have we given to it that deep and serious attention, by which alone we can be advancing to a

solid and abiding conviction? I cannot persuade
myself that it can, in general, be necessary to
enter on a large and laborious investigation of
philosophical objections, and metaphysical reasonings, in order to attain a conviction sufficiently
enlightened and rational; one upon which any
thinking man will act, who remembers the shortness of life and the magnitude of the objects at
stake, who considers the obvious force of the various
reasons in favour of revealed religion, and the
anxious scrutiny, both by friends and foes, which
has not discovered the weakness, but shewn the
strength of its evidence. Let us beware lest, after
all, the truth be, that "we are not *willing* to come
to Christ that we may have life;" because we are
aware that he who will enter into life must keep
the commandments, and that the narrow way that
leadeth unto life is a way of holiness and self-denial.
The defect is more generally in the will than in the
understanding; and even when it appears to be in
the understanding, it generally proceeds from that
predominance of the will, enslaved by its affections
and lusts, which is, in fact, the essence and operation of almost all the modifications of human
depravity.

It is this unhappy slavery, this love of sin, of
the world, and of our present interest, that
operates, not only to produce infidelity, but many
other errors, which deviate from the doctrine

according to godliness. I cannot but persuade myself, however, that a remedy is proposed in the text, which, if duly adopted, would be effectual, both as to errors in doctrine, and inconsistency in practice; which can make us both wise unto salvation, and also thoroughly furnished unto all good works. " Search the Scriptures, for in them ye think ye have eternal life." 'Our ignorance, or our crude, partial, and unsanctified, knowledge of the Scriptures, is the fruitful source of error. Do we desire that it should be otherwise with us? We must imitate the example of the Bereans; and the same effects will follow in us with respect to the whole range of Christian doctrine and duty, which were produced in them with respect to that fundamental truth of our religion, the Messiahship of Jesus. " They received the word with all readiness of mind, and searched the Scriptures daily, whether those things were so; and therefore many of them believed[a]." Few comparatively, we trust, are they, who do not acknowledge them as the words of eternal life; who do not know that they testify of Jesus, as " the end of the law unto righteousness," and " as the power of God unto salvation to every one that believeth." We fear, however, that few do value and *search* them

---

[a] Acts xvii. 11, 12.

as such. Yet is there an expediency, almost amounting to a necessity, that both the preacher and the hearer of the Gospel should be well acquainted with these divine records. None doubt that " if any man *speak*, he must speak as the oracles of God;" and that from the discourses of our Lord, and the writings of his Apostles, he must learn, both the subject and the manner of Christian instruction. But a competent knowledge of the same Scriptures is also equally necessary to the Christian *hearer*. The allusions, reasonings, statements, and exhortations, of the preacher, will not otherwise be sufficiently intelligible and impressive. We fear, therefore, that the success of our ministrations is much less than it might be, if the word of God were more read in the family and in the closet. Our success would probably be far less than it is, if the reading of Holy Scripture were not so prominent a part of our public Service. For the knowledge and influence derived from that source we have, perhaps, more abundant cause to be thankful than we have yet been aware of. Yet how much greater would be our Christian edification, if the family altar, and the hour of retirement, could witness to our perusal of the Scriptures ! From how many errors would this guard us, from how many temptations would it preserve us ! How powerfully, though, perhaps, imperceptibly, would it dispose us to be not willing only, but eager, and thankful, to come unto Christ, that we may have life!—Receive, then, and search the Scriptures, " not as the word of man, but, as they are in truth, the word of God, which effectually work also in them that believe." Value and obey them, as those who know the authority which they possess, and the obligations which rest upon yourselves.   For you rightly " think that in them you have eternal life."

LECTURE XIII.

A REVIEW OF THE PARTICULAR INSTANCES IN WHICH
OUR LORD, DURING HIS LIFE, ACTUALLY CITES OR
ALLUDES TO THE PROPHECIES AND TYPES OF THE
ANCIENT SCRIPTURES.

St. MATTHEW XI. 12—14.

*From the days of John the Baptist until now the kingdom
of heaven suffereth violence, and the violent take it by
force. For all the prophets and the law prophesied
until John. And, if ye will receive it, this is Elias
which was for to come.*

THIS explicit and comprehensive declaration did
Jesus make to the assembled multitudes, after the
dismissal of John's disciples with the answer to
their master's message. He uttered these words
with all the confidence and composure of one who
" spoke that which he knew, and testified that
which he had seen;" and he subjoined in this
instance, as well as on other important occasions,
the awakening words, " He that hath ears to hear,
let him hear."

The statement, which he had just advanced,
did indeed demand attention, if they considered
him from whom it proceeded. It came from one

to whom John had just been proposing the question, " Art thou he that should come, or look we
for another?" It came from one who had been
performing in their presence such miracles, that the
simple enumeration of them served as an answer to
that question; miracles, in consequence of which
they themselves " glorified God, saying, That a
great prophet has risen up among us, and, That
God has visited his people."—The declaration also
demanded attention, if they considered the purport
of it. It announced to them the termination of
that season, during which the glories of the latter
days were made known to the sons of men only
in consolatory promises, foreshadowing types, and
prophetic anticipation. It announced the actual
presence, exhibition, and offer of the expected
blessings. It referred them to the valedictory
declaration of the last of the prophets, with which,
four hundred years before, the voice of prophecy
had ceased, and by which the volume of inspiration had been completed. " Remember ye," said
the Lord of hosts by Malachi, " the law of Moses
my servant, which I commanded him in Horeb for
all Israel, with the statutes and judgments. Behold, I will send you Elijah the prophet, before
the coming of the great and dreadful day of the
Lord[a]."—Thus were the Jews, to adopt the ex-

---

[a] Mal. iv. 4, &c.

pression of an Apostle, to be " kept under the law, shut up unto the faith which should afterwards be revealed[b]." Yet the law and the prophets were not silent respecting " good things to come." Both the one and the other " prophesied." Previously to the appearance of John the Baptist, these prophecies had not received their accomplishment. But then had that period commenced, in which " the God of heaven would set up a kingdom that should never be destroyed[c]." "From the days of John the Baptist," said our Lord, " the kingdom of heaven suffereth violence, and the violent take it by force. And if ye will receive it, this is Elias, which was for to come. He that hath ears to hear, let him hear."

Such declarations as these also claim the attention of us Gentiles. For the things of which the law and the prophets prophesied, were spoken of " the last days, in which it was to come to pass that the mountain of the Lord's house would be established in the tops of the mountains, and be exalted above the hills ; and all nations would flow into it." And already has it come to pass that many nations have said, " Come ye and let us go up to the mountain of the Lord, to the house of the God of Jacob ; and he will teach us of his ways, and we will walk in his paths ; for out of

---

[b] Gal. iii. 23.　　　[c] Dan. ii. 44.

Zion hath gone forth the law, and the word of the Lord from Jerusalem[a]." He, who was the messenger of the new and universal covenant, through whose doctrine " the idols have been utterly abolished[b]," and in whose name we trust, appealed to the law and to the prophets as giving witness to himself. He came " not to destroy, but to fulfil them." He referred to the Scriptures, as " they that testify of him," and to Moses, as " writing of him." He declared that " all things that were written by the prophets concerning the Son of man would be accomplished[c]." And as he declared that " the law and the prophets prophesied *until John,*" so did he manifestly thereby intimate, that in his time we may justly expect to find the accomplishment *begin,* and that from his time we shall be able to trace *its progress.*

In the investigation of this, as well as of the other evidences of the mission and character of Jesus, we may take his own discourses as a faithful and sufficient directory. He has not omitted either expressly to cite, or very intelligibly to refer to, the entire prophetic testimony respecting the Christ, and has required of us to inquire and judge for ourselves whether it has not received its fulfilment in himself. During his personal mi-

---

[a] Isai. ii. 2, 3.　　　　　　[b] Ibid. v. 18.
[c] Matt. v. 17. John v. 39, 46. Luke xviii. 31.

nistry, indeed, as we observed in the last Lecture, the proof from prophecy could not be fully stated and exhibited, because the most signal events to which the prophets referred had not then taken place. But the transactions of his crucifixion and resurrection having rapidly, and beyond all human calculation, evinced the fulfilment in Jesus of one large class of predictions, occasion was thereby given to appeal to them; and the way was also then prepared for the fulfilment of many others. But even during the progress of his personal ministry, a *portion* of the proof from prophecy was already developed, and was accordingly appealed to by Jesus.—And it is also worthy of remark, that during this period he made provision for the elucidation of the remainder, and also for the establishment of his own character as an original prophet, by express, literal, and enlarged predictions of *those very events*, which furnished the *clue* for unraveling the whole mystery of the prophecies, which reconciled the apparently contradictory attributes of the promised Messiah, and which displayed fully and finally the character of his office, the nature of his kingdom, and the purposes for which he was manifested. These several particulars we shall endeavour, under the guidance of the statements of Jesus, to elucidate in some future Lectures; confining our attention, during the remainder of this, to his actual citations and allusions to the law and prophets during his *personal ministry.*

One of the circumstances upon which Jesus insisted, both at the opening, and once and again during the progress, of his ministry, was the fulness of the season marked out by a particular class of predictions, which had indeed already led the Jews previously to admit and adopt an opinion, that the promised Messiah would shortly come. "The *time is fulfilled,* and the kingdom of God is at hand[a]." And again, when they demanded "a sign from heaven," he said, "Ye can discern the face of the sky and of the earth; but how is it that ye do not discern *this time*[b]?" At another time, also, he referred them to "the *signs* of the times," which would prepare them, "even of themselves, to judge what was right[c];" since they must either conclude that Jesus was "he that should come," or that another speedily would come to accomplish the predictions of the prophets.

Jesus himself appeared in the character of "a *teacher* come from God," referring to his works as a proof that he was "sent by God," and that he "spoke the words of God." He therefore taught "as one that had *authority.*" He declared that he "came to seek and to save that which was lost," to "call not the righteous, but sinners to

---

a Mark i. 15.   b Matt. xvi. 1—3.   c Luke xii. 56, 57.

repentance." He invited the "meek to learn of him ; the weary and heavy laden to come to him for the rest which he would give to their souls." In proof of this as the proper office of him, whom the prophets had announced, he referred, both in the synagogue at Nazareth, and also in the conference with John's disciples, to the passage in the sixty-first chapter of Isaiah, in which all this, with great particularity and variety of expression, was ascribed to him, upon whom would be " the Spirit of the Lord, because he was anointed to preach these glad tidings [d]."—The same was also specified in many other passages of the Old Testament [e].

Though Jesus, as well as the Baptist, taught that the kingdom of heaven was at hand, yet he adopted, as the ordinary description of his official character, the title of " the Son of man." And from the way in which, on various occasions, he connected that title with other statements, he evidently intended to direct their attention to the following words of the prophet Daniel. " I saw in the night visions, and behold, one like the Son of man came with the clouds of heaven, and came to the Ancient of days, and they brought him near before him. And there was given him dominion,

---

[d] Isai. lxi. 1—3.
[e] Ibid. xi. 1—5 ; xlii. 1—8 ; lvii. 14—18, &c.

and glory, and a kingdom, that all people, and nations, and languages should serve him; his dominion is an everlasting dominion, which shall not pass away, and his kingdom that which shall not be destroyed[a]." These words evidently describe a state of glory and exaltation; and yet he, by whom such glory was to be attained, is called " one like the Son of man."—That phrase, at least, certainly applies to Jesus, who appropriated the title to himself; for he did undoubtedly appear " in the likeness of men." But consider the remarkable manner and connexion in which he employed it as his appropriate designation. He spoke of a time when there should indeed "appear the sign of the Son of man in heaven ;" referring to that expectation of " a sign from heaven " which the Jews had derived from this prediction of Daniel, and of which they had several times required the exhibition. When calling God " his own Father," and speaking of himself in a manner consistent with such a claim, he declared that he, the Son of God, "had authority to execute *judgment* also, *because he is the Son of man.*" He spoke also of a time " when the Son of man should come in the clouds of heaven, with power and great glory; in the glory of his Father, with the holy angels." He not only spoke to Nico-

---

[a] Dan. vii. 13, 14.

demus of "the Son of man coming down from heaven, and being in heaven," but also declared that "the Son of man must be lifted up;" but he declared publicly to the Jews, "when ye have lift up the Son of man, then shall ye know that I am he." And when on another occasion he declared that "when he was lifted up from the earth, he would draw all men to him," he had just said, "the hour is come that the Son of man should be glorified." And when he had affirmed, in answer to the question of the high priest, that he was the Christ, the Son of God, he added these remarkable words, "Nevertheless I say unto you, Hereafter shall ye see the Son of man sitting on the right hand of power, and coming in the clouds of heaven." Thus both by his assumption of this title, and also by his application to *himself* of those attributes, which appertained to him whose it really was, Jesus appealed to those prophecies which described the humanity, humiliation, and subsequent exaltation of Messiah ; although he avoided the title of Messiah, which suggested to the minds of the Jews only the idea of earthly power[b].

---

[b] Matt. xxiv. 30. John v. 27. Matt. xxv. 31. John iii. 13, 14; viii. 28; xii. 23. Matt. xxvi. 64. The Jews by adopting the title of Christ or Messiah, as the usual designation of "him that should come," seem to have connected with their expectations of him only the ideas immediately suggested by the title "Messiah

the

The prophecies, upon which perhaps Jesus
dwelt most largely, were those which respected
his forerunner, and their connected mission. He
expressly cited to the multitudes the prophecy of
Malachi, which spoke of him, as "the messenger
who was to be sent to prepare the way of the
Lord;" stating that John was he of whom this
was written. He also added, with reference to the
expectation which they still entertained respecting
the *personal* appearance of Elijah, that "if they
would receive it, he was the *Elias who was to
come;*" John being described under that name
in the concluding words of Malachi[a]. And the
prediction of "the messenger of the Lord," was
immediately followed by the assurance that "the
Lord whom they sought should suddenly come to

---

the prince." (Dan. ix. 25.) Hence our Lord, and also the Baptist,
principally adopted the *other* prophetic descriptions of the promised
deliverer. We have contended in several passages of these Lectures,
as indeed even a superficial observation of the Gospel history
teaches us to do, that John did not call Jesus the Messiah, and
that Jesus did not himself publicly adopt the title. We, as
Christians, rightly conceive that this and the other scriptural
titles of our Lord are convertible terms. In the Epistles, as being
addressed to *Christians,* it is the term generally adopted. But
when we peruse or interpret those parts of the New Testament,
which record the discussions of those periods, when it was still
in debate, whether Jesus was *the Christ,* and also whether the
functions of the Christ were of a *spiritual* nature, we must bear
in mind the *errors of the age* respecting that title, as well as its
full and genuine import.

  [a] Mal. iii. 1—4; iv. 5, 6.

his temple, to purify the sons of Levi, and to purge
them as gold and silver, that they might offer unto
the Lord an offering in righteousness, and that
the offering of Judah and Jerusalem might be
pleasant unto the Lord, as in the days of old."
When, therefore, the witness of the Father and
of the Baptist had declared of Jesus that he was
the *Son of God*, he entered the temple, and
expelled the traders from thence with the words,
"Make not *my Father's* house a house of mer-
chandise[b]." And at a later period he exercised
the same authority; which indeed belonged to him,
if he was "one greater than the temple[c]." And he
then accompanied the act with the still more remarkable words; "It is written, My house shall
be called a house of prayer for all nations[d]." He
therein actually cited a prediction of Isaiah respecting the calling of the Gentiles; and also brings to
our recollection the prophecy of Haggai, that
"the Desire of all nations should come, and that
the Lord of hosts would fill that house with glory;
and that the glory of the latter house should be
greater than that of the former[e]." Let it be remarked in addition to our former remarks on these
transactions, that in the first instance the Jews
asked him "what *sign* he shewed, seeing he did

---

[b] See John ii. 13—22.   [c] Matt. xii. 6.

[d] Mark xi. 15—17. Isai. lvi. 7.   [e] Hag. ii. 6—9.

X

such things." On that occasion, adapting his
answer to their question, he referred them, as
he always afterwards did, when they demanded
a sign, to his resurrection from the dead. "Destroy
ye this temple, and in three days I will raise it up."
But in the latter case, when they merely proposed
the question, "by what authority he did these
things, and who gave him this authority," he then
prepared to reason with them respecting the passage of Malachi, which connected the "sudden
coming of the Lord whom they sought to his
temple," with the "sending of the messenger to
prepare his way before him," by asking of them,
"whether the baptism of John were from heaven
or of men." They knew the message that John
had delivered; if then they allowed the authority
of that messenger, whom he had immediately followed, and who had borne witness to him, his
authority was that of "the messenger of the covenant, and of the Lord, whom they sought;" and he
had suddenly come to his temple, as "one greater
than the temple[a]." And Jesus had also previously
prepared them for considering this question, by his
solemn entry into Jerusalem in the manner described by the prophet Zechariah; by receiving during
his progress to the temple, and in the temple itself,

---

[a] Compare 2 Chron. vi. 16—18, and Isai. ix. 6, 7, with
Haggai ii. 7, and Mal. iii. 1.

the acclamations of the multitude, who saluted him as "the blessed one that cometh in the name of the Lord," and as " the Son of David." He refused to forbid or restrain these acclamations ; nay, he even declared that " if they were silent, the stones would immediately cry out." And when the Pharisees put to him the significant question, "Hearest thou what these say?" He answered, "Yea;" and added, citing the words of the Psalmist, "Have ye never read, Out of the mouths of babes and sucklings thou hast perfected praise[b]?" Thus fully and willingly did Jesus appeal to the prophets, and cite from them such passages as either proved or illustrated his mission. And fain would he have reasoned with the Jews more largely upon the testimony of prophecy to those circumstances, which were already sufficiently before them, and to which such a discussion was already applicable.

When our Lord made the enlarged defence of his conduct before the Sanhedrim, and stated to them the evidences of his authority, he expressly stated, " If ye had believed Moses, ye would have believed me, for *he wrote of me*."—We can readily call to mind the several *promises* made to Adam, Noah, Abraham, Isaac, and Jacob; all of which are recorded by Moses ; as are the *predic-*

---

[b] Psalm viii. 2.

tions of Jacob and Balaam. But that which should have seemed most likely to have had influence with those, who boasted that they were Moses's disciples, was his prediction of the "Prophet like unto himself, who was to be raised up from among their brethren, and to whom they were to hearken." Yet as many of that generation would not hearken to the words, which that Prophet "spake in the name of God, who had put his words in his mouth," God did, as he had predicted by Moses, "require it of them." All the temporal calamities, which God's former dealings with the Jews would lead them to anticipate from such a threatening, "came," as our Lord predicted, "on that generation." For as before for their idolatries, so now for their rejection of him, in order to whose manifestation they had been preserved as a separate nation, their city and temple were destroyed, and themselves led away into captivity. And we have reason to believe it an historical fact, that none but those Jews, who became Christians, escaped from the calamities of the ruined Jerusalem.—Our Lord did not indeed *actually cite* any of these predictions during his *public* ministry. But we shall see, in our next Lecture, that he alluded very intelligibly to the first promise made to Adam; and that he also made a declaration, which shews that he intended us to recognize in himself that Seed, promised to Abraham, and also to Isaac, and to Jacob, "in which all the families of the earth were to be blessed." And we would also remind you of his frequent assertions that the doctrine which he taught was that " which he had heard of God,"— that " *he* did not judge the man who rejected his words," but that there was one " who sought to be glorified, and would judge him,"—that " the word spoken, the same would judge him," because " the Father had given to himself a commandment what he should say, and what he should speak, and, as the Father gave him commandment, so he spoke." Now if these expressions do not, in the first instance, remind us of the prediction given by Moses, they at least receive an important illustration, and claim an increased and serious attention, when we read that prediction. For whosoever that Prophet was, whom God " raised up like unto Moses," and to whom he charged them to " hearken," it was said of him by God himself, " I will put my words in his mouth, and he shall speak all that I shall command him ; and whosoever shall not hearken unto my words, which he shall speak in my name, I will require it of him."

But there was another way in which " the law prophesied" of the blessings of the future dispensation, viz. by type and figure. This subject was fully unfolded by the Apostles after Jesus had actually accomplished all that was thereby shadowed forth. But there are at least three instances in which Jesus has himself touched upon this subject. In allusion to the brazen serpent, which was raised on high amidst the Israelites dying of the plague, that they might look thereon, and be miraculously cured, our Lord said to Nicodemus ; " As Moses lifted up the serpent in the wilderness, even so must the Son of man be *lifted up,* that whosoever *believeth in him,* should not *perish,* but have *everlasting life*[a]." — After our Lord had fed the five thousand, the people, probably from a recollection of the manner in which Moses miraculously fed the Israelites in the wilderness, said, " This is of a truth that Prophet that should come into the world." And, finding Jesus, they spoke of " their fathers having been fed with manna in the desert." Jesus said, " Verily I say unto you, Moses gave you not that bread *from heaven ;* but my Father giveth you the *true* bread *from heaven.* For the bread of God is *he,* which cometh down from heaven, and *giveth life* unto the world[b]." — And when Jesus instituted the feast which is to be kept in remembrance of " his being sacrificed for us as our passover," he noticed the typical nature of the Jewish passover ; " for he said unto the disciples, With desire I have desired to eat this

---

[a] John iii. 14, 15.   Numb. xxi. 6—9.

[b] John vi. 31—63.   Exod. xvi. 14, &c.   Psalm lxxviii. 24, 25.

passover with you before I suffer; for I say unto
you, I will not any more eat thereof, until it be
fulfilled in the kingdom of God[c]."—And, when he
said to the Jews, that "their father Abraham rejoiced to see his day, and saw it, and was glad[d],"
we may justly suppose that he alluded to the typical nature of the sacrifice of Isaac. For it was
doubtless on that occasion that Abraham was enabled to foresee, and, in some measure, also to
understand, the manner in which the promised
Seed would become "a blessing to all nations," by
dying for them. And that sacrifice of Isaac,
when considered in connection with the predictions of that Seed, who was to descend from
Isaac, ' was a key to the sacrifices even of the law
itself.'

Thus did Jesus appeal to the law, of which he
declared, when he repeated on another occasion
some of the words of our text[e]; "It is easier for
heaven and earth to pass, than one tittle of the law
to fail." We have already noticed in some measure
how he appealed to the prophets. But he appealed
to them much more largely than the limits of this
discourse will allow us fully to lay before you.
One other detached example we shall notice, and

---

[c] Luke xxii. 15, 16. ἕως ὅτου πληρωθῇ ἐν τῇ βασιλείᾳ
τοῦ Θεοῦ.—Exod. xii. and xiii.

[d] John viii. 52—56. Gen. xxii.   [e] Luke xvi. 16, 17.

we shall then briefly class the principal remaining instances under two general heads.

Jesus was frequently addressed by the title of "the Son of David," nor did he decline it; although it is evident that they conceived that title as synonymous with the title " Messiah the Prince ;" and indeed the prophets authorized them ₍ₛₒ₎ to do. But they doubtless understood by it the heir of David's earthly throne; and therefore our Lord undertook to shew them, that David had himself spoken of him in such a manner, as to shew that the expected Potentate was not such, either as to his original, his character, or the nature of his dominion, as they fondly supposed. " Jesus asked the Pharisees, What think ye of the Christ? whose Son is he? They say unto him, The Son of David. He saith unto them, How then doth David in Spirit call him Lord, saying, The LORD said unto my Lord, Sit thou on my right hand, until I make thine enemies thy footstool? If David then call him Lord, how is he his Son? And no man was able to answer him a word." This was indeed not the only difficulty which the same hundred and tenth Psalm, which is so often cited in the New Testament, would present to the Pharisees. For it spoke in figurative language of the *sufferings* of the Son of David as *prior* and *introductory* to his exaltation; and described him also as "a priest for ever after the order of Melchizedec, and

as therefore being, as Zechariah also had predicted, "a priest upon his throne[a]."

I. One of the subjects, just alluded to, upon
which our Lord very frequently, though not
always avowedly, cites the prophecies of the Old
Testament, is the *infidelity* of that generation,
and the consequences of it in the *persecution*
of those who *believed*, and in the *vengeance* which
overtook those who disbelieved, because " they
knew not the time of their visitation." " In them,
said our Lord, is fulfilled the prophecy of Esaias,
which saith, By hearing ye shall hear, and shall
not understand ; and seeing ye shall see, and shall
not perceive; for this people's heart is waxed gross,
and their ears are dull of hearing, and their eyes
have they closed; lest at any time they should
see with their eyes, and hear with their ears, and
understand with their heart, and should be converted, and I should heal them[b]." This passage
is also cited by the Evangelist St. John, when
speaking of the unbelief of the Jews, "although
Jesus had done so many miracles before them." ·
And our Lord, when speaking of the same subject, observed, " This cometh to pass, that the
word might be fulfilled that is written in their

---

[a] Ps. cx. Matt. xxii. 41—46. Mark xii. 34—37.   Luke xx.
40—44. Zech. vi. 13.

[b] Matt. xiii. 14, 15. Isai. vi. 9, 10.—See also Jer. v. 20—23.

law, They hated me without a cause[a]." For he " had done among them the works which no other man did."—And again, " Ye hypocrites, well did Esaias prophesy of you, saying, This people honoureth me with their lips, but their heart is far from me[b]." And the next verse of that prophet contains a threatening, to which our Lord seems also to have alluded, when he said; " Father, I thank thee, that thou hast hid these things from the wise and prudent, and hast revealed them unto babes[c]."

When our Lord says, " I am come to set a man at variance against his father, and the daughter against her mother, and a man's foes shall be they of his own household," he adopts the language of the prophet Micah[d]. And it will also be found that he has very largely cited the ancient prophets in many of his statements respecting the destruction of Jerusalem, of which indeed he expressly says, " For these be the days of vengeance, that *all things which are written may be fulfilled*[e]." And it is scarcely needful to re-

---

[a] John xv. 22—25. Ps. xxxv. 19 ; lxix. 4.

[b] Matt. xv. 7. Mark vii. 6. Isai. xxix. 13. Ezek. xxxiii. 31.

[c] Matt. xi. 25. Our Lord had just been speaking of his miracles. See ver. 18. of the same chapter of the Prophet. Compare also Isai. xxxii. 4; xliv. 18; liv. 13.

[d] Matt. x. 35, 36. Micah vii. 6, 7.

[e] Luke xxi. 22. Deut. xviii. 19; xxviii. 15 — 68. Dan. ix. 24—27. Zech. xi. and xii. Mal. iii. and iv.

mind you of the awful words which he subjoined
to the parable of the wicked husbandmen, to whom
one messenger was in vain sent after another to
receive the fruits of the vineyard [f], until the
owner "last of all sent unto them his Son."
" Did ye never read in the Scriptures, 'The
stone which the builders refused, the same is
become the head of the corner?' *Whoso* shall
fall on that stone shall be broken ; but on *whomsoever* it shall fall, it will grind him to powder [g]."
And when he added, on that occasion, that " the
kingdom of God, which was taken from them,
would be given to a nation bringing forth the
fruits thereof," he doubtless alluded to the approaching call of the Gentiles, which in several
other instances he had even more distinctly predicted, in strict conformity to what the prophets
had stated respecting those who would be included
in the Messiah's kingdom [h].

II. But lastly, Jesus also referred, before his
sufferings commenced, to the prophetic testimony

---

[f] See 2 Chron. xxiv. 19—21; xxxvi. 15, 16.   Neh. ix. 26.
Jer. xxvi. 4—6.

[g] Ps. cxviii. 22.   For the sources, whence our Lord borrowed
the *general* warning subjoined to his citation of the Psalmist,
see Isai. viii. 14, 15. lx. 11, 12. Zech. xii. 2, 3. Dan. ii. 34, 35.

[h] Matt. viii. 11, 12. John x. 16. Gen. xxii. 18. Ps. lxxii. 10,
11, 17—19. Isai. xi. 10; xlii. 1—6. Zech. ii. 11 ; viii. 22, 23.
Mal. i. 11.

of the Old Testament respecting them, and the events by which they were to be brought about. At the same time, however, by additional and still more minute statements, he made them the subjects of his own original and more express predictions. " Behold," said he to the twelve, " we go up to Jerusalem, and all things that are *written by the prophets* concerning the Son of man shall be accomplished.—The Son of man goeth, *as it is written of him,* but woe unto that man by whom the Son of man is betrayed.—I speak not of you all, I know whom I have chosen, but *that the Scripture* may be fulfilled, ' He that eateth bread with me hath lifted up his heel against me.'—All ye shall be offended because of me this night, for *it is written,* ' I will smite the Shepherd, and the sheep shall be scattered.' He that hath a purse, let him take it, and he that hath no sword, let him sell his garment, and buy one; for I say unto you, that *this that is written* must yet be accomplished in me, ' And he was numbered among the transgressors;' for the things concerning me have an end[a]."

Such things had he said to his disciples, before there was yet any apparent fulfilment of the things which he had thus predicted. — When

---

[a] Luke xviii. 31.　Matt. xxvi. 24.　John xiii. 18, 19.　Matt. xxvi. 31.　Luke xxii. 36, 37.

those who came to apprehend him in the garden
of Gethsemane were approaching ; he endeavoured to awaken their recollection of these
previous assurances, and to arouse them to a
sense of his and their danger by the declaration,
" He that betrayeth me is at hand." And when
they were astonished and confounded, he reminded
them once more that nothing had occurred, which
had not been prophesied respecting him, nothing,
from which his Father, if it were expedient, could
not deliver him. " Thinkest thou," said he to
Peter, " that I cannot now pray unto my Father,
and he shall presently give me more than twelve
legions of angels ? But how then shall *the Scriptures* be fulfilled, that *thus it must be*[b]?" He
noticed the same to those who came to apprehend
him. " All this has been done, that the Scriptures
of the prophets might be fulfilled.—The Scriptures
must be fulfilled.—This is your hour, and the
power of darkness[c]."

When on his trial, he professed himself to be
the Christ, he cited the prophecy of Daniel, respecting the Son of man, and argued respecting
the nature and object of his kingdom. — But
these things will be considered in a future
Lecture.

---

[b] Matt. xxvi. 53, 54.
[c] Matt. xxvi. 56. Mark xiv. 49. Luke xxii. 53.

When suspended on the cross, "knowing that
ALL THINGS WERE NOW ACCOMPLISHED, *that the
Scripture might be fulfilled*, he said, I thirst[a]."
And "being numbered with the transgressors,
and having made intercession for them," he
vented the feelings of his agonized soul in the
opening verse of that Psalm, which had so distinctly predicted those sufferings which he had now
been enduring, the minute circumstances which
had attended them, and the cruel taunts which his
enemies had unwittingly uttered against him[b]."
And soon, appealing both to the law, and to the
prophets, which had prophesied of all these things,
and which were now accomplished, he declared
with a loud voice, "IT IS FINISHED[c]." He "bowed
his head, and gave up the ghost."

To these words, and to all those which we
have cited, may we not apply the exhortation of
our text? "He that hath ears to hear, let him
hear." We have not even alluded to more than
an extract from the great volume of Prophecy.
We have noticed those predictions only, which
we know that our Lord actually cited, and to
which he appealed, and even these but in an imperfect and cursory manner. But do not even
these shew to us, that "the law and the prophets

---

a John xix. 28. Ps. lxix. 21.   b Ps. xxii. Matt. xxvii. 46.
c John xix. 30.

prophesied" of Him? He, therefore, "that hath ears to hear, let him hear." Let us hear "the voices of the prophets," directing us to Jesus as "the Lamb of God that taketh away the sin of the world." And let us hear also the voice of HIM, who says, "Look unto me and be saved, all the ends of the earth." And "to whom else should we go? for he hath the words of eternal life." Yet, how "slow of heart are we also to believe all that the prophets have spoken!" How careless about that salvation, "of which the prophets enquired and searched diligently, who did but *prophesy* of the grace that *has come* unto us!" To them "it was revealed, that not unto themselves, but unto us, they did minister these things; which are now reported *to us* by them, that have preached the Gospel unto us, with the Holy Ghost sent down from heaven." "Blessed, then, are our eyes, because of the things which we have seen, and our ears, because of the things which we have heard. For many prophets and kings have desired to see those things which we see, and have not seen them; and to hear those things which we hear, and have not heard them."

"He, therefore, that hath ears to hear, let him hear!"

LECTURE XIV.

———◆———

OUR LORD'S *DEBATES* WITH THE JEWS.——THAT RE-
CORDED IN ST. JOHN'S EIGHTH CHAPTER CON-
SIDERED——IN THE COURSE OF WHICH OUR LORD
SPECIFIES THE PERIOD AT WHICH THE EVIDENCE
OF HIS MESSIAHSHIP WOULD BE COMPLETE; AP-
PEALS TO THE PURITY OF HIS LIFE, AND OF HIS
DOCTRINE; HINTS AT THE FULFILMENT IN HIM
OF THE PROMISE TO ABRAHAM; AND ASSERTS
HIS PRE-EXISTENCE.

———◆———

St. John VIII. 28, 29, 45—47.

*Then said Jesus unto them, When ye have lifted up the
Son of man, then shall ye know that I am he, and that
I do nothing of myself; but as my Father hath taught
me, I speak these things. And he that sent me is with
me: the Father hath not left me alone; for I do always
those things that please him.*

*And because I tell you the truth, ye believe me not.
Which of you convinceth me of sin? And if I say the
truth, why do ye not believe me? He that is of God,
heareth God's words; ye therefore hear them not, because ye are not of God.*

THE arguments of our Lord before the Sanhedrim
having been considered in our former Lectures,
and also such other arguments as were immediately referable to the *same* general heads, we
shall proceed, in this and the three following
Lectures, to discuss such as remain unnoticed.

The subject of our next Lecture will be, our Lord's reference to his own prophecies as furnishing an evidence of his character. We shall afterwards notice his sayings at his apprehension, at his trial, and at his crucifixion. And our review of his statements on the subject of evidence will then be completed, by considering the manner in which he proved the reality of his resurrection, and his reasonings upon the prophecies after that event.—Our attention will be directed, in this Lecture, to the *debates* which our Lord held with the Jews at an advanced period of his ministry. They are recorded in the sixth and following chapters of St. John; and we have selected, as a specimen, that which occupies a large portion of the eighth chapter. We find in this debate the same kind of instruction, argument, and expostulation as in the others. And in the words of our text, which are extracted from it, three distinct heads of evidence are noticed, which we have not yet considered in the same point of view, and in the same connection; viz., his death as supplying the complete and convincing demonstration of his character; and the purity of his life, and of his doctrine, as also claiming the confidence of all candid and devout inquirers. Our Lord concluded the debate with a significant intimation, that in him was accomplished the promise made to Abraham.

And as he had, on other occasions, advanced a claim
to divinity, had reasoned upon it, and had given
evidence of it, so he here repeated the same claim,
by the declaration of his existence before Abraham. These various topics must be noticed in
a very brief and cursory manner. But it is observable, that in these debates, as well as in those
set discourses, to which the subject of these
Lectures had led us to advert, our Lord ever
combined with the statement of evidence, declarations respecting the character and design of his
mission, and forcible addresses to the conscience
of his hearers.

It will be expedient, with reference to the
first topic which will offer itself, to renew our
recollection of the state of opinion, which existed
among the Jews at Jerusalem at the time when
this debate took place [a].

For some time after the cure of the impotent
man at the pool of Bethesda, and his arraignment
before the Sanhedrim in consequence of it, "Jesus
walked in Galilee; for he would not walk in Jewry,
because the Jews sought to kill him," offended
by his supposed disregard of the sabbath, and
still more, because "he called God his own proper
Father, making himself equal with God." His
brethren in Galilee were anxious that he should

---

[a] See John, chapters vi. and vii.

go into Judea at the approaching feast of tabernacles, and "shew himself to the world." Jesus
declined for a time; stating that "the world hated
him, because he testified concerning it, that the
works thereof are evil." About the midst of the
feast, however, "Jesus went up into the temple,
and taught." There had previously been "much
murmuring among the people concerning him;
for some said, He is a good man; others said, Nay,
but he deceiveth the people." They were however astonished that, "having never learned," he
was able to deliver such instructions; and were,
therefore, not a little divided in their opinions respecting him. Jesus himself in several instances
adapted his remarks to their own difficulties and
objections; and, more than once, alluded to their
murderous wishes against him. "Then said some
of them of Jerusalem, Is not this he whom they
seek to kill? But, lo, he speaketh boldly, and they
say nothing unto him. Do the rulers know indeed that this is the very Christ? Howbeit we
know this man whence he is; but when Christ
cometh, no man knoweth whence he is." Upon
his repetition of the supposed blasphemy, in
noticing these their doubts, "they sought to
take him." But "many of the people believed on
him, and said, When Christ cometh, will he do
more miracles than this man doeth?" And on the
last day of the feast, after Jesus had spoken, under

the metaphor of water, of the future gifts of the Spirit, "many of the people when they heard that saying, said, Of a truth this is the Prophet. Others said, This is the Christ. But some said, Shall Christ come out of Galilee? Hath not the Scripture said, That Christ cometh of the seed of David, and out of the town of Bethlehem, where David was? So there was a division among the people because of him. And some of them would have taken him; but no man laid hands on him." Even these officers of the chief priests gave this reason for not bringing him, "Never man spake like this man."

Thus deeply had the people been impressed in favour of Jesus by his miracles and doctrine. Nay, so strongly were they disposed even to confess him to be the Christ, that the Pharisees, as we read in the following chapter, at this time deemed it necessary to denounce the penalty of excommunication from the synagogue, against all who made such a confession. Yet even the doubts which they entertained proceeded upon erroneous suppositions. And Jesus, as we shall see, at this season endeavoured to assist their inquiries, and to strengthen and direct their faith, at the same time that he avoided every thing that might encourage the carnal and worldly views of such, as dreamt only of the restoration of a temporal kingdom to Israel.

"*Early in the morning*," on the day after the feast of tabernacles, " he went into the temple, and all the people came unto him[a]." Borrowing an illustration from the rising sun, and thereby also applying to himself several prophetic descriptions of "the Redeemer who should come to Zion, and unto them that turn from transgression in Jacob," he said, "I am the light of the world; he that followeth me shall not walk in darkness, but shall have the light of life[b]."—A discussion arose in consequence of this declaration; in the course of which Jesus stated, in answer to the objection of the Pharisees, that even his record concerning himself was true, " because he knew whence he himself came, and whither he went." And he also reminded them that " the Father had borne witness of him," as well as he himself by his miracles.— But we need not dwell upon this part of the discussion, as we have already had occasion to consider it[c].

" Then said Jesus again unto them, I go my way, and ye shall seek me, and shall die in your sins; whither I go, ye cannot come[d]."—When they cavilled at him, as if he had spoken of an intention to kill himself, he reproved them be-

---

[a] John viii. 12—20.   [b] Isai. lix. 20, 21 ; lx. 1.
[c] See the former part of Lecture VI, and Lecture XI.
[d] John viii. 21, &c.

cause of the earthliness of their minds, which not only made them indulge the hope of a temporal Messiah, but also seemed to incapacitate them for learning better things. "Ye are from beneath, I am from above; ye are of this world, I am not of this world. I said therefore unto you, that ye shall die in your sins; for if ye believe not that I am he, ye shall die in your sins."—Our Lord was evidently now conversing with some of those, who were disposed to side against him; and he was kindly cautioning them against persisting in those interested and deluding prejudices, which now so effectually blinded their understandings. Had they but had a disposition to judge impartially, or even to suspend their judgment, they would, at the period to which he alluded, when he said, "I go my way," have seen fully that he was the Messiah that was to come, though not such as they expected. But he foresaw that they would, unhappily for themselves, cling to the fond hope of a Messiah triumphant upon earth, while they rejected him who was indeed the Messiah, but who had then "ascended where he was before[a]," and "gone whither they could not come." The promised Messiah would have gone his way; they would still seek him; and in the agony of disappointed hope, and amidst the destruction which

---

[a] John vi. 62.

threatened them, would die in their sins. Because
of their inveterate carnal prejudices, would they
die in their sins ; "for if ye believe not that I am
he"—I, who appear in humility, in righteousness,
in the character of a prophet and divine instructor,
not of a warrior and monarch—" if ye believe not
that I am he, ye shall die in your sins." Whether
Jesus were proved to be the Messiah or not, he
had already given them such proofs that "God
was with him," that he had the full sanction of
heaven to demand of them a confidence in such
a declaration as he now made ; and the awful
alternative which he announced to them, might
justly dispose them to inquire, as they immediately
did, "Who art thou?"—Jesus saith unto them,
"Even the same that I said unto you from
the beginning[b]." He had already made many
declarations respecting himself. At Jerusalem at
a preceding passover he had publicly, before the
Sanhedrim, stated to them the authority which as
the Son of man he had received of the Father.
During the feast of tabernacles, which was just
over, he had not been backward in speaking of his
doctrine, of the source from whence he derived it,
and of the blessings which he would be empowered
to bestow on all that believed on him. On that
very morning, in the beginning of this conver-

---

[b] See Note in page 319.

sation with them, he had declared himself to be
"the light of the world." But he proceeded to
inform them that he had not yet fully declared
either his own office, or their responsibility; but
that, at a certain *period,* and after a certain *event,*
they would have the whole matter before them;
and such complete evidence would then be proposed to them, as would make their unbelief no
longer excusable." "'I have many things to say
and to judge of you; but he that sent me is true;
and I speak to the world those things which I
have heard of him.' They understood not that
he spake unto them of the Father. Then said
Jesus unto them; When ye have *lifted up the
Son of man,* then shall ye *know that I am he,* and
that I do nothing of myself; but as my Father
hath taught me, I speak these things. And he
that hath sent me is with me; the Father hath not
left me alone; for I do always those things that
please him."

The Evangelist adds, that " as he spake these
words, many believed on him." They were probably impressed with an admiration of his fearless
declaration of his doctrine in the midst of danger;
they recollected both his former and his recent
instructions, and they could not but confess their
truth and propriety; they felt an assurance, justified by the past wonders which had borne witness
to Jesus, that the future instruction and evidence

of which he spoke would hereafter be afforded
them ; and that " what they knew not now, they
should know hereafter." Perhaps they did not
understand what he meant by " the lifting up of
the Son of man." They might even still understand this as spoken of his exaltation to the temporal throne of David, rather than of his being
" lifted up from the earth" upon the fatal tree.
Probably, however, they had some imperfect notion
of his meaning; for we find them afterwards
observing, upon his use of the same expression,
" We have heard out of the law, that Christ
abideth for ever; and how sayest thou, The Son
of man must be lifted up? Who is this Son of
man[a] ?" Jesus did not, even then, explain it; for
the event, which so speedily followed, could alone
properly explain it. But he then added a caution,
which might also have suited the occasion and
connexion of the words before us, if the question
had been at that time proposed to him, " Yet
a little while the light is with you ; walk while ye
have the light, lest darkness come upon you.—
While ye have light, believe in the light, that ye
may be the children of light."

As far as it respects the full understanding of
this difficulty, of the way in which the Son of man
was lifted up, and of all the glorious consequences

---

[a] John xii. 34.

of that great but awful event,—to this extent, *we* are all " children of light." We know how Jesus died, and rose again; how he thereby fulfilled what was written, and was declared to be the Son of God with power. Hereafter we shall have to consider this more at large; let it suffice for the present to have observed, that Jesus previously specified this event as *completing the evidence of his mission.* Yet during his personal ministry "he that sent him was with him, the Father left him not alone." Even before the Sun of Righteousness arose upon the earth in all the brightness of his meridian splendour, those who waited for his salvation, saw the brightness and felt the genial warmth of those healing beams, which gave full assurance that the light of Israel was come, and which prepared them to expect the glory that should follow. But to us are made known both the wonders of his holy and spotless life, the heavenly doctrine that flowed from his lips, the miracles which he wrought, the witness of heaven and of earth, of Prophets and Apostles, of holy men and holy Angels. And in whom have we therefore believed, but in Jesus, the Mediator of the new Covenant; in Jesus, of whom all these things " were written, that we might know that he is the Christ the Son of God, and that believing we might" not die in our sins, but " have life through his name." To us, therefore, who have

known and received all these things, as well as to
those who " believed on him, as he spake the
words" which we have been considering, Jesus
says ; " If ye continue in my word, then are ye
my disciples indeed, and ye shall know the truth,
and the truth shall make you free."

That in these words he spoke of that slavery
of sin, which is unto death, and of that spiritual
liberty wherewith he maketh his people free, we
learn from his own subsequent explanation of his
words. In us there are probably few prepossessions so likely to frustrate his gracious intentions for our deliverance, as those which result
from the debasing influence of that our slavery,
which makes us in love with our fetters, which
causes us even gladly to remain in the darkness of
our prison-house, and which disposes us to hear with
apathy, if not with regret, the words of him who
" says to the prisoners, Go forth ; to them that
are in darkness, Shew yourselves[a]." But whatever be the nature, and however domineering be
the influence of the unhappy principles, which make
us reluctant to be liberated from that service, of
which "the wages is death," by the Son, "who can
make us free indeed," we shall do well to reflect
how severely Jesus reproved and expostulated
with those Jews, to whom these words appeared

---

[a] Isai. xlii. 7.

to suggest, not, as to a Christian, a salutary and yet encouraging admonition, but an attack on the supposed hereditary and indefeisible prerogatives of the children of Abraham. If *they* were culpable for their ignorance and neglect of this freedom, how much more so are *we!*

Forgetful of the *national* dependence on a foreign power to which they then were, and had been so often before, subject; forgetful, also, that as little could they boast of uninterrupted *religious* liberty, the Jews answered Jesus with the words, " We be Abraham's seed, and were never in bondage to any man; how sayest thou, Ye shall be made free?"—" Verily, verily, answered Jesus, I say unto you, He that committeth sin, is the servant of sin. And the servant abideth not in the house for ever; but the Son abideth ever. If the Son therefore shall make you free, ye shall be free indeed. I know that ye are Abraham's seed; but ye seek to kill me, because my word hath no place in you. I speak that which I have seen with my Father; and ye do that which ye have seen with your father." They were right in supposing that Jesus intended to impute criminality both to themselves and to their father; and they repeated the assertion, that " Abraham was their father," as if to ask, whether he meant to apply such an imputation to him. But if Abraham were pure from guilt, it did not follow that they were his children in that respect, and that they inherited his integrity. Jesus disproved their claim, acquitted Abraham, and advanced his position against them in nearly the same words as before. " If ye were Abraham's children, ye would do the works of Abraham. But now ye seek to kill me, a man that hath told you the truth, which I have heard of God ; this did not Abraham. Ye do the deeds of your father." They had no resemblance to Abraham in that very particular, for which he was especially commended ; for " Abraham believed in the LORD, and he counted it to him for righteousness[a]." But still, what could Jesus mean by " their father," if he meant not Abraham? Did he mean to accuse them of idolatry, termed by the prophets *fornication,* as being a breach of that covenant of God with his people, which was described under the similitude of a marriage[b]? " We be not born of fornication ;" they replied ; " We have one Father, even God." Still had they not been aware of whom Jesus spake. He had to refute another of their unauthorized claims. He had to prove to them, that idolatry was not the only modification of error. He had to reveal to them the humiliating

---

[a] Gen. xv. 6.

[b] 2 Chron. xxi. 11.   Jer. iii. 1—14.   Ezek. xliii. 7—9. Hos. ii. 19, 20 ; iv. 12.

truth, which referred their original, in a spiritual
sense, ₜₒ another and more ancient progenitor
than Abraham; to one, however, who had been
described in their own Scriptures; and their
relation to whom fully accounted for their opposition to himself, if he were what he *claimed*, and
what *he knew* himself to be.

" Jesus said unto them, If God were your
Father, ye would love me; for I proceeded forth,
and came (am come[a]) from God; neither came
I (have I come) of myself, but he sent me. Why
do ye not understand my speech (i. e. my *phraseology*)? even because ye cannot hear my word
(i. e. the *truths* which I declare). Ye are of
your father the devil, and the lusts of your father
ye are willing to do. He was a murderer from
the beginning, and abode not in the truth, because
there is no truth in him. When he speaketh a lie,
he speaketh of his own; for he is a liar, and the
father of it. And because I tell you the truth, ye
believe me not. Which of you convinceth me of
sin? And if I say the truth, why do ye not believe
me? He that is of God heareth God's words; ye
therefore hear them not, because ye are not of
God."

---

[a] ἐκ τοῦ Θεοῦ ἐξῆλθον καὶ ἥκω· οὐδὲ γὰρ ἀπ' ἐμαυτοῦ ἐλήλυθα,
ἀλλ' ἐκεῖνός με ἀπέστειλε. Διατί τὴν ΛΑΛΙΑΝ τὴν ἐμὴν οὐ
γινώσκετε; ὅτι οὐ δύνασθε ἀκούειν τὸν ΛΟΓΟΝ τὸν ἐμόν.
v. 42, 43.

This is a most important passage. That the devil " was a murderer from the beginning, that he abode not in the truth, and that he is the father of lies," the very first pages of Revelation inform us. God had said, that if man eat of the forbidden fruit, "he should surely die." "The old serpent, which is the devil and Satan," said, " Ye shall not surely die." The lie was believed. Man disobeyed, and the sentence of death was pronounced. A declaration was at the same time made by the Almighty, that " he would put enmity between the seed of the serpent, and the seed of the woman." The Jews identified themselves with the seed of the serpent, by seeking to kill him, "who told them the truth which he had heard of God." They proved themselves to be " children of the devil," not only by being thus " willing to do the lusts of their father," but by disbelieving Jesus, " because he told them the truth." For they were " of the world;" and he " testified, that the world's works were evil," and therefore they " hated him, and could not hear his word." " If he told them the truth," and that he did, the conscience of every one who has either heard or read the words of Jesus must testify, why did they not believe him, but " because they were not of God." For " he that is of God will hear his words." And if they were of God, they would not have hated, but on the contrary have loved him, who had by so many proofs evinced that he "proceeded forth, and was sent, and had come from God, and not of himself."

These declarations he fearlessly and confidently advanced respecting himself. He feared not that they should retort the charge; for he feared not to assert that "he did always those things that pleased the Father." Nay, he even anticipated and defied their objections in this matter, by the challenge, "Which of you convinceth me of sin?" Full well, indeed, he knew that they would proceed in co-operation with their father. The time was at hand, which would be "their hour, and the power of darkness;" in which they would accomplish their murderous purpose, and accomplish his death. But it would be "with wicked hands" that they would "crucify and slay him;" and both in his life, and in his death, did both they and their father fail to "convict him of sin." They could never bring any charge against him, excepting as it regarded his supposed violation of the sabbath, and his supposed blasphemy, in calling himself the Son of God[a]. Both these he

---

[a] For the defence which our Saviour made, both by argument and miracle, against these imputations, see Lecture V. and the conclusion of the present Lecture.—The comprehensive character of the debate, which is the subject of this Lecture, has rendered it necessary to consider the appeal of our Lord to the purity of his *life* and *doctrine*, only in immediate connexion with the course of the discussion. A more *general* view of both those topics has, indeed, been before taken in the latter part of Lecture VI.

ever refuted by unanswerable arguments; and at the same time he demonstrated by his miracles, that "the Father did not leave him alone," and, therefore, that always, and in all these things, he did "those things that pleased him." Satan had already been vanquished in his early attacks upon our Lord's faithfulness and integrity; and when "the prince of this world came" unto him at the closing scene, he "found nothing in Jesus," and was himself "cast out." Nay more, their present rivalry and opposition would issue in that decisive conflict, described in the original prediction of the enmity which would subsist between "the Seed of the woman, and the seed of the serpent." This was he, whose "heel was indeed bruised," but who "bruised the head of the serpent;" who thereby "destroyed him that had the power of death," and obtained that victory, by which the forfeited immortality was restored, and eternal life procured for all that obey him. And Jesus *on this very same occasion*, gave that promise of eternal life, which he was so soon to be empowered to perform; thereby predicting the speedy accomplishment of the *original* promise, as he also immediately afterwards asserted the accomplishment of that *given to Abraham.*

His opponents contended, that by these imputations he manifested such hostility to the Jews, that he might justly be considered as siding with

Z

the enemies of their country and religion, and could scarcely be otherwise than infatuated. "They answered and said unto him, Say we not well, that thou art a Samaritan, and hast a devil? Jesus answered, I have not a devil; but I honour my Father, and ye do dishonour me. And I seek not mine own glory; there is one that seeketh and judgeth. Verily, verily, I say unto you, If ι man keep my saying, he shall never see death." Not long before, in his discourse before the Sanbedrim, he had advanced a similar statement in the most confident and solemn manner. " Verily, verily, I say unto you, He that heareth my word, and believeth on him that sent me, hath everlasting life, and shall not come into condemnation, but is passed from death unto life[a]." He now repeated the same declaration in a connexion still more striking, and in one which more particularly explained its meaning. For a comparison of his expressions in the *earlier* part of this debate, and of those *immediately preceding* the declaration in question, will shew, that he claimed, and in the strongest manner asserted his possession of the power to deliver those, who were the bondslaves of sin and Satan, not only from the present dominion, but also from the future condemnation, of sin. But the Jews, staggered still more than ever at such a statement, demanded of him, " Art thou

---

[a] John v. 24.

greater than our father Abraham, which is dead,
and the prophets are dead: whom makest thou thyself?" He concluded a defence, similar to that
which we have just cited [b], with the words, "Your
father Abraham, eagerly desired that he might see
my day, and he saw it, and was glad." Whom
therefore did Jesus profess himself to be, but that
predicted Seed of Abraham, "in whom all nations
of the earth were to be blessed?" For whose
day but his, could Abraham ever have desired to
see? And then, doubtless, did he see it, when the
typical sacrifice of Isaac was offered on mount
Moriah, and when the substitution of the ram in
the place of Abraham's son was followed by
a more particular repetition of the promise. And
all nations have been blessed by the actual sacrifice
of him, whom Isaac typified; who, "after he had
been lifted up, was known to be he," of whom
"the law and the prophets prophesied," and who
thenceforth "drew all men to him [c]," as the Shiloh
whom Jacob had predicted.

---

[b] " Jesus answered, If I honour myself, my honour is nothing:
it is my Father which honoureth me; of whom ye say, that he is
your God. Yet ye have not known him: and if I should say,
I know him not, I should be a liar like unto you; but I know
him, and keep his saying.—Your father Abraham eagerly desired
that he might see my day ($\dot{\eta}\gamma\alpha\lambda\lambda\iota\acute{a}\sigma\alpha\tau o$ $\ddot{\iota}\nu\alpha$ $\ddot{\iota}\delta\eta$ $\tau\dot{\eta}\nu$ $\dot{\eta}\mu\acute{\epsilon}\rho\alpha\nu$ $\tau\dot{\eta}\nu$
$\dot{\epsilon}\mu\dot{\eta}\nu$); and he saw it, and was glad." ver. 54—56.

[c] See Gen. xlix. 10. " To him shall the gathering of the people
be." E. T. 'Ουκ $\dot{\epsilon}\kappa\lambda\epsilon\acute{\iota}\psi\epsilon\iota$ $\ddot{a}\rho\chi\omega\nu$ $\dot{\epsilon}\xi$ 'Ιουδα— $\ddot{\epsilon}\omega\varsigma$ $\dot{\epsilon}\dot{a}\nu$ $\ddot{\epsilon}\lambda\theta\eta$ $\tau\dot{a}$
$\dot{a}\pi o\kappa\epsilon\acute{\iota}\mu\epsilon\nu\alpha$ $\alpha\dot{\upsilon}\tau\hat{\omega}$· $\kappa\alpha\dot{\iota}$ $\alpha\dot{\upsilon}\tau\dot{o}\varsigma$ $\pi\rho o\sigma\delta o\kappa\acute{\iota}\alpha$ $\dot{\epsilon}\theta\nu\hat{\omega}\nu$. Septuagint.

But the Jews misunderstanding or perverting what Jesus had said, asked him, not whether Abraham had really " *seen his day*," but whether " *he*, not being yet fifty years old, *had seen Abraham*.*" Jesus did not shrink even from meeting this new state of the question, which demanded an answer respecting his *pre-existence*. He unequivocally answered " Before Abraham was, I am."

On many other occasions had Jesus virtually affirmed the same position. His divinity, if he did really and justly claim it, certainly implied his pre-existence. And he frequently used language from which the Jews inferred, that he made himself " equal with God," nor did he disavow the claim. When the Pharisees asked, " Who can *forgive sins*, but *God alone?*" he cured the paralytic, for the express purpose of proving that " the Son of man *had power* on earth *to forgive sins*[a]." He spoke of the Son of man " *ascending up* where he was *before*," to prove that he said truly, " *I came down from heaven*[b]." He appealed to prophecy to prove that he, who was David's Son, was also David's Lord[c]. He appealed, on another occasion, both to the *Scriptures* of the Old Testament as *justifying*, and to his

---

a Matt. ix. 6.　Mark ii. 10.　Luke v. 24.
b John vi. 42, 61, 62.　　　c Matt. xxii. 42—45.

own *works* as *proving*, his claim to divinity. " Is it not written in your law, I said, Ye are gods? If he called them gods, to whom the word of God came, and the Scripture cannot be broken; say ye of him, whom the Father hath sanctified, and sent into the world, Thou blasphemest, because I said, I am the Son of God? If I do not the works of my Father, believe me not. But if I do, though ye believe not me, *believe the works*, that ye may *know*, and *believe*, that *the Father is in me, and I in him*[d]." He again appealed to his works in proof of the assertion that he ought to be believed in such declarations, when he said to Philip, " He, that · hath seen me, hath seen the Father; and how sayest thou, Shew us the Father? Believest thou not that I am in the Father, and the Father in me? The words that I speak to you, I speak not of myself, but the Father, that dwelleth in me, he doeth the works. Believe *me*, that *I am in the Father*, and *the Father in me;* or else believe me for the very *works' sake*[e]."

Thus does it appear, that Jesus supported by the most cogent argumentation, and by diversified evidence, every claim which he advanced. This very circumstance itself, that he thus founded his religion *on argument*, the truth also and the purity of his *doctrine*, the unimpeachable purity and

---

[d] John x. 29—39.   [e] Ibid. xiv. 6—11.

disinterestedness of *his own life*, the accomplishment of every *type* and *prophecy* in the events and purposes of his mission, and the many and various attestations of a *miraculous* nature which evinced its divine authority,—all these considerations may justly demand "the obedience of our faith." And having now considered at length this debate of our Lord with the Jews, let me briefly direct your attention to the circumstances under which it was concluded.

Jesus delivered himself by a miracle from the effects of that indignation, which the assertion of his pre-existence had excited. "They took up stones to cast at him; but he was concealed from them, and went out of the temple, going through the midst of them, and so passed by[a]."—But remark also what followed.—"*As Jesus passed by,* he saw a man which was blind from his birth[b]." He restored to him his sight; and the severest scrutiny of the perplexed rulers, only proved the reality of the miracle, and that it had been wrought by Jesus. Shall *we* then consent to the declaration, of the Pharisees, that "we know not whence Jesus is?" Rather let every such thought give way to the force of that rational expostulation of the man, on whom this signal miracle was wrought. "Why herein is a marvellous thing, that ye know

---

[a] John viii. 59. —Ἰησοῦς δὲ ἐκρύβη, καὶ, &c.   [b] Ibid. ix. 1.

not from whence he is, and yet he hath opened my eyes. Now we know that God heareth not sinners; but if any man be a worshipper of God, and doeth his will, him he heareth. Since the world began, was it not heard that any man opened the eyes of one born blind. *If this man were not of God, he could do nothing*[d]." When Jesus declared to this candid, and reflecting man, that he was the Son of God, he answered, "Lord, I believe," and worshipped him[e]. Jesus also declared, at the commencement of the debate which we have been reviewing, that he is "the light of the world." And he avowedly wrought this very miracle to demonstrate the truth of that assertion. For, immediately before he wrought it, he assigned to his disciples his reason for so doing. "I must work the works of him that sent me, while it is day; the night cometh, when no man can work. As long as I am in the world, *I am the light of the world*[f]."—We may know then the blessedness to which we are invited; for Jesus himself declared, "he that followeth me shall not walk in darkness, but shall have the light of life[g]." But hear also the condemnation of those, who persist in unbelief; for this also our Lord declared after the miracle. "For judgment am I come into this world, that

---

[d] John ix. 30—33.   [e] Ibid. 35—38.   [f] Ibid. 4, 5.
[g] Ibid. viii. 12.

they which see not might see, and that they which see might be made blind^a."

Sensible, then, of our necessities, and touched with gratitude to him, who hath visited, enlightened, and redeemed us, let us "walk in the light of the Lord;" let us not shrink and retire from it, even though it discovers to us our sinfulness and guilt, our responsibility and danger. Let us not disbelieve Jesus "because he tells us the truth." When it is demanded of us, " Dost thou believe in the Son of God ?" *we* can now have no plea to offer in excuse for that ignorance, which would lead us to say, as the man who was cured of his blindness said, " Lord, who is he, that I might believe on him ?" Let us then answer with him, " Lord, I believe."—He worshipped Jesus. And we must also "honour the Son even as we honour the Father."—Jesus hath also declared that "whoso keepeth his saying, shall never see death, but shall have the light of life." He has "visited us, as the day-spring from on high, to guide our feet into the way of peace." And oh! that "the things, which belong to our peace, may never be hid from our eyes;" that "the God of this world, who blindeth the minds of them that believe not, may not prevent the light of the glorious Gospel of Christ, who is the image of God, from shining

---

^a John ix., 39.

unto us." Such alas! has been, and is, and may again be the case with many. Many of those, who saw this signal miracle, scrutinized it, perceived its reality, and yet disregarded its force and intention. And even now "the true light, which cometh into the world to enlighten every man, shineth in the world's darkness," and even enters into the dark chambers of our own souls, and yet we see it not, we comprehend it not, we are not guided by it. Yet "our light has come, and the glory of the Lord has risen upon us." Let us then "arise," and, "though we were sometime darkness, let us be light in the Lord;" and "let our light shine before men, to the glory of our heavenly Father, by our good works which they shall behold." For dreadful and hopeless is the state of those, "who say they see, and whose sin therefore remaineth;" "who love darkness rather than light, because their deeds are evil." May, therefore, that "God, which commanded the light to shine out of darkness, shine in our hearts, to give the light of the knowledge of the glory of God in the face of Jesus Christ; so that we may be changed into the same image from glory to glory, even as by the Spirit of the Lord."

LECTURE XV.

OUR LORD'S STATEMENT THAT THE FULFILMENT OF HIS OWN PREDICTIONS WOULD EVINCE HIS MESSIAHSHIP. THE MANNER IN WHICH HE DISPLAYED AND NOTICED HIS UNLIMITED KNOWLEDGE OF MEN AND THINGS.

St. John XIII. 18, 19.

I know whom I have chosen: but that the Scripture may be fulfilled, He that eateth bread with me, hath lifted up his heel against me. Now I tell you before it come, that, when it is come to pass, ye may believe that I am He.

IT was asserted by our Lord of John the Baptist, that "there had not arisen a greater prophet than he;" nay that he was "even more than a prophet." And the reason which he assigned for such an assertion was this, that John was the very "messenger of whom it was written, that he should be sent to prepare the way of the Lord." "He came for a witness" to that dignified Person to whom all the prophets had referred; and his predictions were, in many respects, more minute and particular than those of his predecessors. "He came for a witness," not by his verbal annunciations alone, but by his personal, and therefore more definite testimony to him " whom God had sent."

Now in all these particulars Jesus as far surpassed his forerunner, as the immediate forerunner did the remoter prophets. Jesus was the very personage, to whom all these, " at sundry times and in divers manners," gave their inspired testimony; and in and by whom their predictions were to have their accomplishment. He carried forward the scheme of prophecy still further; describing in more precise and even in *literal* terms the great events which were approaching. He applied the language of preceding prophets to those events, so as to decide *beforehand* the true *interpretation* of their predictions. And he included, at the same time, such a distinct mention of additional particulars, as proved that futurity was much more extensively open to his view. Nay further, the events predicted were such *in themselves*, and *so circumstanced*, and Jesus also manifested such a familiar acquaintance with them, as an original prophet, that his *Messiahship* is as fully proved from hence as his *divine Mission*. And this his extensive prescience is also in another way illustrated and proved, by the knowledge which he ever displayed of past and present things, as well as of futurity; by his knowledge of the characters, surmises, and intentions of all with whom he was

concerned; a knowledge, such as nothing less than
omniscience could have communicated to him.

These considerations are pointed out to us by
our Lord himself in the words of our text, with
which he prefaced and prepared his distinct intimation of the treachery of Judas. He asserted
his acquaintance with the characters of his disciples, although not as yet displayed by their conduct. When he spoke these words he was about
to prove that " he knew whom he had chosen,"
by declaring beforehand not only the treachery of
Judas, but the denial of Peter, and the cowardly
desertion of all of them in that hour of danger,
which, though by them not foreseen, was near at
hand. He cited the Scripture, which declared the
hostile conduct of one " that eat bread with him,"
that he might expressly apply it to one of those
individuals, who then sat with him at the table.
And he explained the design with which he predicted this to them, in a declaration, similar to
which he made many others. " Now I tell you
before it come, that, when it is come to pass, ye
may believe that I am he."—It will be our endeavour to remind you of some of the instances of
this wondrous prescience of Jesus, in order that
we may shew how it bears upon the question of
the divine mission and Messiahship of Jesus; and
that you may thus duly apprehend the force of
those arguments, which our Lord has derived from

the accuracy with which he both spoke of things to come, and discerned the spirits of men.

The predictions of Jesus extend even to the general resurrection, and to the consummation of all things. If we believe that he was what he claimed to be, we may confidently expect that all these predictions will be fulfilled in their season, although the season for the accomplishment of some of them is yet distant, and others are but imperfectly fulfilled. They are all such as it became the promised Messiah to deliver ; they are all such as it appertains to him to accomplish. And our conviction of his power and authority will indeed rest on the most solid basis, if to every other demonstration of it, we can also establish the prescience of Jesus, by shewing the fulfilment of his numerous predictions. We must for this purpose consider those which have received their accomplishment.

I. Let us first consider such as were not accomplished until after the Evangelists published a record of them in their Gospels. Such was the frequently repeated prediction of the calamities which were coming upon the Jews, and of the overthrow of their temple, and city, and nation. Jesus at one time gave only a general intimation of the sad event, or couched it under an illustrative parable[a]. In other instances he concisely noticed

---

[a] Matt. viii. 12. Luke xiii. 6, 35 ; xix. and x.

the fact, and a few of its circumstances; as in his addresses to the Pharisees[a], and in the pathetic lamentation over Jerusalem when he beheld it from the mount of Olives[b]. And when the women who stood round the cross wept for him, who had so lately wept for their country, he repeated some of the alarming intimations with the expressive exhortation, " Daughters of Jerusalem, weep not for me, but weep for yourselves, and for your children[c]." On each of these several occasions he distinctly pointed at the same event, but scarcely ever in the same form, and always with an allusion to some different circumstances. But in the longest of all his predictions, delivered to his disciples in private, he described the circumstances which would precede, attend, and follow that signally calamitous event, with a wonderful but awful precision. Yet "that generation did not pass, till all was fulfilled;" and the fullest confirmation was given to the declaration of Jesus, which he connected with these predictions, " Heaven and earth shall pass away, but my words shall not pass away[d]."

It was also declared by Jesus, that his Gospel should first be extensively preached throughout

---

[a] Luke xvii. 20.   Matt. xxiii.   [b] Luke xix. 43.
[c] Ibid. xxiii. 28—31.
[d] Matt. xxiv. 35.   Mark xiii. 31.   Luke xxi. 33.

the Roman empire; that the "kingdom of God, which should be taken from the Jews, would be given to a nation bringing forth the fruits thereof;" that he must bring together " into one fold, and under one Shepherd," sheep of " other folds;" and that " many would come from the east, and from the west, and sit down with Abraham and Isaac and Jacob in the kingdom of God, while the children of the kingdom were cast out[e]." Hereby he announced the accomplishment, in a manner which the Jews were not prepared to expect, of the divine promise given to Jacob at Bethel. " I am the Lord God of Abraham thy father, and the God of Jacob; the land whereon thou liest, to thee will I give it, and to thy seed; and thy seed shall be as the dust of the earth, and thou shalt spread abroad to the west, and to the east, and to the north, and to the south ; and in thee and in thy seed shall all the families of the earth be blessed[f]."

That the commission given by Jesus to " teach all nations" will one day be effectual, and that " the Gospel will be preached in the whole world," and " the fulness of the Gentiles come in," we retain the assured and consolatory hope. But as

[e] Matt. xxiv. 14; xxi. 41—43. John x. 16. Matt. viii. 11. Luke xiii. 29.

[f] Gen. xxviii. 13, 14.

we see not as yet " obedience to the faith among all nations," so, *in this very circumstance,* do we recognize the prescience of Jesus, reaching to every age of that Church, of which he has declared, that "the gates of hell shall not prevail against it[a]." For he also announced to his disciples, that " the Jews would fall by the edge of the sword, and be led away captive into all nations; and that Jerusalem would be trodden down of the Gentiles, until the times of the Gentiles be fulfilled[b]." This prophecy has continued to receive its accomplishment for nearly two thousand years. The Jews who were then carried captive, have ever since remained, and still do remain, in the same dispersed, despised, and often persecuted condition. Jerusalem is still trodden down of the Gentiles; because the time of the Gentiles is not yet fulfilled. Yet has the Gospel of Jesus, though rejected by the Jews, and though opposed by Gentiles, not been arrested in its progress. Those who first promulgated it, did endure the various sufferings, and met with the unbelief and hatred, of which their Master forewarned them[c]. But, through their labours and writings, the Gospel, like the " leaven hid in three measures of meal," to which Jesus compared it, has ever

---

[a] Matt. xvi. 18.   [b] Luke xxi. 24.

[c] Matt. x. 17, 18; xxiii. 34; xxiv. 9. John xv. 20; xvi. 2.

since continued and extended its beneficent influence in the world, and we doubt not will finally
leaven the whole. Already has the " grain of
mustard-seed" sown in Judea, become a tree, and
many nations have reposed under its shadow, and
nestled among its branches[d].

These prophecies, and their accomplishment,
are of themselves sufficient to establish the prophetic character of Jesus, had he delivered no
other. Their fulfilment had not begun in his
own life-time, and some of the most important
were not fulfilled until after the death of all those
who have ·transmitted them to us[e]. Yet their
correctness is proved both by the history of past
ages, and by the present state of the Christian
Church, of the Jews, and of the world. It is,
however, obvious, that the accomplishment of
these had no share in producing that faith in
Jesus as the Messiah, and that patience and tranquillity in the midst of sufferings, which the *Apostles*
did undoubtedly derive from some prophecies of
their Master ; and the production of *both* which
results he expressly assigned as his motive for the
delivery of them, as we shall hereafter shew. But
the notice of these may have prepared us with

---

[d] Matt. xiii.

[e] St. John, who survived the destruction of Jerusalem, and
probably wrote after it, has not mentioned the prophecy respecting that event, which the earlier writers so carefully recorded.

fuller confidence to proceed to the consideration of others, the accomplishment as well as the delivery of which we learn from the New Testament, and some of which more directly tend to prove the divine mission of Jesus as the Messiah.

II. Some predictions of a *detached* character which Jesus delivered, received an almost immediate accomplishment.—Such was the declaration to his disciples, a few days before the raising of Lazarus. " Our friend Lazarus sleepeth ; but I go that I may awake him out of sleep." Soon after " he said unto them plainly, Lazarus is dead. And I am glad for your sakes that I was not there, to the intent ye may believe." To Martha also Jesus said, when he first met her, " Thy brother shall rise again ;" and again at the grave, when he had ordered the stone to be removed, and she began to expostulate with him, " Said I not unto thee, that, if thou wouldest believe, thou shouldest see the glory of God?" The event itself also was preceded by an address to the Father, with the avowed design that they might see that it was done with his approbation and by his power, and that thus " they might believe that the Father had sent him." And doubtless that conviction would be much strengthened by the circumstance, that he in this manner *foretold* it[a].—A similar effect would

---

[a] John xi.

also be produced, in a more lively and impressive
manner than we can conceive, when the disciples,
who had been directed to go into the adjoining
village, found, as Jesus had told them, " the ass
tied, and the colt with her, and when the owners
upon being told that the Lord had need of them,
straightway sent them to him." " His disciples
understood not at first" the meaning of his entry
into Jerusalem in that manner;" but when Jesus
was glorified, then remembered they that these
things were written of him, and that they had
done these things unto him." Here also the conviction produced by the recollection of Zechariah's
prophecy, would strikingly recal to their minds
how the display of the prophetic character of
Jesus himself preceded the fulfilment of Zechariah's prediction; and that it related, though in
a manner wholly distinct, to a circumstance specified by that prophet[b].—Similar remarks might
be made on the foreknowledge which Jesus again
exercised, when he directed the disciples where to
find a place for the celebration of that passover.
They found as he had said, and made ready for
that last passover, at which he delivered his farewell discourses, and his intercessory prayer, so full
of promise and important prophecy; at which
also he instituted the perpetual memorial of his

[b] Matt. xxi. Mark xi. Luke xix. John xii.

approaching death; and immediately after which, that death, and all the other transactions which he had predicted, were hastened and accomplished [a].— Thus do our Lord's *own predictions*, even in these *detached* instances, shed a lustre to the attestation of his own *miracles* and of *ancient prophecy;* and some of them even strengthen the conviction produced by others.

But it is time to notice his predictions of those important events, by which his own ministry was terminated, by which the great object of his mission and office. was evinced, and which fully opened the way for the display of its full evidence, and for the erection, establishment, and perpetuity of his Church. Some of these things, in a less explicit and precise manner, were foretold to the people in general; but all of them in the most plain and circumstantial manner to those whom he had chosen.

It will suffice briefly to remind you of some of the principal predictions of this nature, which were delivered to the *people in general.*—They are concise and figurative, yet fully explained by the events which correspond to them. The earliest of them was one which referred to his death and resurrection; and the remembrance of it by the disciples of Jesus, had an important influ-

---

[a] Matt. xxvi. 17, &c.   John xiii. 17.

ence in inducing them to " believe, not only in the *Scripture* prophecy, but also in the *word which Jesus had said.*" A sign being demanded from him as the proof of his authority, He answered, " Destroy ye this temple, and in three days I will raise it up; speaking of the temple of his body [b]."— To Nicodemus, and to his hearers on two other occasions, he spoke of the "lifting up of the Son of man ;" of the *fact* and *design* of his death, under the phrase that he would "give his flesh for the life of the world ;" and of the *consequences* of it in " drawing all men to him," and of causing much success to attend his mission [c]. He several times promised that " the sign of Jonah the prophet would be given to that generation ;" and that "as he was three days and three nights in the belly of the whale, so the Son of man would be three days and three nights in the heart of the earth [d]." —In consequence of these, and perhaps of other still more definite predictions, the chief priests came to Pilate, to request that he would " command that the sepulchre be made sure until the *third day ;*" because, said they, "we remember that that deceiver said, while he was yet alive, After three days I will rise again [e]." Yet all these

[b] John ii. 19.

[c] Ibid. iii. 14 ; viii. 28 ; xii. 32 ; vi. 51 ; xii. 24.

[d] Matt. xii. 39, 40 ; xvi. 4. Luke xi. 29, 30.

[e] Matt. xxvii. 62, &c.

things were, notwithstanding, accomplished. It
was even by their own "counsel and deed," that,
Jesus, as he had predicted, was "cast out of the
vineyard, and slain by the wicked husbandmen."
And it was by their endeavour to prevent the
accomplishment of his predicted resurrection, that
the evidence of that event was strengthened by
one of its most convincing proofs. And equally
did it come to pass, that "the Son of man," as he
had also predicted, "was seen to ascend up where
he was before[a]." In the people of that generation also was accomplished the parable of "the
unclean spirit who returned, and made the last
state of that man worse than the first; and Jesus
had declared that so it would be to that wicked
generation[b]." "The stone, which they rejected,
became the head of the corner[c];" "false Christs
and false prophets deceived many[d];" "they sought
the true Messiah in vain, and died in their sins[e];"
and by the subversion of their whole polity was it
brought to pass, that "neither at Gerizim,
nor at Jerusalem alone, was the Father worshipped[f]." For our Lord had hinted to the Jews
at Nazareth, that as it had pleased God, in the
time of their fathers, to send Elijah to relieve
a woman of *Sidon*, and to enable Elisha to heal

---

[a] John vi. 62. [b] Matt. xii. 43—45. [c] Matt. xxi. 42.
[d] Matt. xxiv. 24. [e] John viii. 21. [f] John iv. 21.

Naaman the *Syrian* leper, while the "many
widows and lepers, that were then in *Israel*" were
not benefited, so, in their own age, he would send
the Apostles to "bring many from the east, and
from the west," to partake of the privileges of that
kingdom, of which they thought themselves exclusively the children [g].

These things which Jesus himself predicted
respecting "the Christ crucified," were as unwelcome to *the twelve disciples,* as they were to
their fellow-countrymen. But they were disciplined by their Master, "as they were able to
bear it," so that they were not ultimately " offended in him." And no means did our Lord
more studiously employ to secure an object, so
necessary for evangelizing the world, than by de-
tailing to them, during the time that he remained
with them, all the leading particulars of those
distressing transactions by which he would be
removed from them ; as well as that astonishing
change from death to life, from humiliation to
glory, from apparent weakness to divine power,
which shewed that though he had first suffered
many things, yet hereby "was the Son of man
glorified, and God was glorified in him [h]." And
the series of prophecies which Jesus delivered on
these subjects, is so perspicuous and comprehen-

---

[g] Luke iv. 25—27.   Matt. viii. 11, 12.   [h] John xiii. 31.

sive, that we may well conceive with what complete satisfaction the disciples in due season called to mind the words of our text, and several other similar declarations with which Jesus accompanied these predictions; "Now I tell you before it come, that when it is come to pass, ye may believe that I am he."

No sooner had the disciples avowed to Jesus their joyful and assured confidence that he was "the Christ, the Son of God," than he began to prepare them for the knowledge of these events by the declaration, "Have not I chosen you twelve, and one of you is a devil[a] (a false accuser)?" And "he began from that time to shew unto his disciples that he must go unto Jerusalem, and that the Son of man would be betrayed unto the chief priests and unto the Scribes, and that they would condemn him to death, and deliver him to the Gentiles, to mock, and to scourge, and to crucify him. And that the third day he would rise again[b]." And, repeating these things, he solemnly prefaced his declaration by saying, "Let these sayings sink down into your ears[c]." These particulars are for the most part specified by the ancient prophets. But the circumstance that he should be "*delivered to the Gentiles*," was a prediction wholly original, and upon the completion

---

[a] John vi. 70.　　[b] Matt. xvi. 21; xx. 18, 19.　　[c] Luke ix. 44.

of it depended, both the peculiar indignities which were to precede his crucifixion, and even that mode of execution itself. In one of his earlier predictions of the overthrow of Jerusalem, he noticed the *previous* occurrence of his own sufferings. "But first, said he, must the Son of man suffer many things, and be rejected of this generation d." And "when Jesus knew that the hour was come that he should depart out of this world unto the Father," he rendered his predictions still more demonstrative of his perfect and familiar knowledge of all things that were coming upon him, by specifying the *very day* of crucifixion. "Ye know," said he to his disciples, "that after two days is the feast of the passover, and the Son of man is betrayed to be crucified e." Yet even after this prediction was delivered, the chief priests and Scribes came to a resolution, that it would not be prudent even "to take him by subtilty, and to kill him, on the feast day, lest there should be an uproar of the people." They abandoned the design; and they would not have resumed it, had not the very circumstance which Jesus himself previously mentioned, induced them to do so. "The Son of man was *betrayed* unto them; for they accepted the offer which Judas made "to deliver him unto them in the absence of the multi-

---

d Luke xvii. 25.   e Matt. xxvi. 2.

tude[a]." Thus had Jesus twice predicted the treachery of Judas before he had, as it appears, even conceived the design. And a third time, when, humanly speaking, it seemed incredible, that any steps would be taken in the matter, he declared still more particularly, in the words of our text, his perfect knowledge of the respective characters, of those whom he had chosen. He was aware that one of them was then harbouring the design of betraying him, and that the Scripture would in that very way be fulfilled; because it had described one so circumstanced, as they all then were, one "who eat bread with him," as the faithless one who would "lift up his heel against him." Afterwards, in a very remarkable manner, he pointed out to them the *very individual;* and shewed to *him,* though the others misunderstood his words, that he was well acquainted with his purpose.

Judas, "having received the sop, went immediately out," to "do quickly" that which he had designed and covenanted to do. "It was night;" and he therefore went to repair to "the garden, whither, as he knew, Jesus oft times resorted with his disciples." Jesus knew that the transactions, which he had so often predicted, would now immediately take place. He therefore solemnly

---

[a] Matt. xxvi. 14—16.

declared to the remaining eleven the importance of the crisis at which they had arrived; and during the short time that intervened, he endeavoured to prepare them for the approaching circumstances, and reminded them of some of his public intimations respecting them. " Now is the Son of man glorified, and God is glorified in him. If God be glorified in him, God shall also glorify him in himself, and shall straightway glorify him. Little children, yet a little while I am with you. Ye shall seek me; and, as I said unto the Jews, whither I go ye cannot come [b]." He predicted the fears and desertion of all them that very night, and especially the actual denial of any knowledge of him by St. Peter. These events were not merely contingent upon circumstances which had occurred very suddenly, and which were as yet unknown to them, but they appeared in every respect very improbable at that time. For both Peter, and all of them, made the most solemn protestations of inviolable fidelity, even if any danger occurred. Little, indeed, had they been willing to understand his former intimations to the same effect. And they were quite incapable of so far receiving them, as to *remain* faithful to him, and to acquiesce in this sudden disappointment of their darling hopes. Yet their Master

---

[b] John xiii. 30, &c.

proceeded in such a manner to instruct and to pray for them, and to foretel the things that were approaching, and the glory that should 'follow, as might *afterwards*, at least, from their recollection of his words, lead them to a right view of the design of these transactions, and of his own character, and induce them still more confidently than ever to believe in him, "because of whom they were all offended in that calamitous night." When he foretold, in the earlier part of that evening, the treachery of Judas, he assigned that reason for his forewarning them of it; and he now con-joined with it a present proof of that his unlimited knowledge, which he had often before displayed, and which caused them now to feel, still more strongly than ever, a conviction of his divine mission, and very earnestly to declare it.

He had been interrupted in his discourse by the protestations of Peter and his companions; and, doubtless, his distinct declaration, that they would not act suitably to their late protestations, would perplex and distress them. But he wished to console, to exhort, and to inform, as well as to caution them[a]. " Let not your heart be troubled; ye believe in God, believe also in me. I go to prepare a place for you." He reminded them of the evidence of his miracles in order to assure

---

[a] See John xiv. &c.

them of the truth of these various and mysterious statements. He predicted the "greater works which would be done by those that believed on him; because," said he, "I go unto the Father." But he proceeded to predict the gift of " *another* Comforter to abide with them for ever," after his departure, "even the Spirit of truth;" by whom, after the suspension of their faith, they would be finally convinced that "he was in the Father, and the Father in him;" who would "teach them all things, and bring all things to their remembrance, whatsoever he had said unto them." Having exhorted them to tranquillity, conjured them not to be afraid, and assured them that his return to the Father was a fitter cause for joy than regret, he repeated his declaration, that "he told them these things before they came to pass, that, when they had come to pass, they might believe."

He then exhorted them to persevere in their obedience; and proceeded also to foretel their own sufferings, and, repeating the promise of the Comforter, declared that "he would testify of him; and that they also would testify of him, because they had been with him from the beginning." Fully to state how the Comforter, by miracles, and knowledge, and the gift of tongues,—and the Apostles, by their testimony and miracles, by their conduct and sufferings, by their reasonings and success, testified of Jesus, would be to review the whole history of the Acts of the Apostles.

Lastly, as an immediate assurance of the truth of what he said, Jesus convinced them of his knowledge of their own thoughts, and doubts, and surmises, and availed himself of their conviction of this to repeat his prediction of future things, and also the reason why he thus foretold them. He knew that although he had so repeatedly and plainly predicted his removal from the world, and his glorification with the Father, they did not understand, what he meant by the statement, "A little while, and ye shall not see me; and again a little while, and ye shall see me, because I go to the Father." He knew that they were inquiring among themselves respecting it, that they decided that "they could not tell what he said," and that "they were desirous to ask him." He explained it unasked, telling them that he was aware of the difficulties which they had felt. And they exclaimed, as soon as he had concluded, "now are we sure that thou knowest all *things*, and needest not that any man should ask thee; *by this we believe* that thou camest forth from God.—Jesus answered them, Do ye *now believe?* Behold, the hour cometh, yea, is now come, that ye shall be scattered, every one to his own, and ye shall leave me alone, and yet I am not alone, because the Father is with me. These

things have I spoken to you, that in me ye might
have peace. In the world ye shall have tribulation. But be of good cheer. I have overcome
the world."

Here let us pause. We have reviewed a vast
number of predictions, which were uttered by the
mouth of Jesus, and all of which we know to have
been accurately fulfilled. By that fulfilment it is
clearly proved to us that he was sent of God, and
an original Prophet; and we may therefore justly
believe all his other communications. But we
have somewhat more than this evinced to us. We
see that he possessed such a familiarity with all
the detail of the events which he predicted, as
shews that he was far superior to all preceding
prophets; for they seem to have had but a very
imperfect knowledge of the meaning of what
they were commissioned and inspired to deliver.
" When the Spirit—that was in them testified
beforehand the sufferings of Christ, and the glory
that should follow, they inquired and searched
diligently what or what manner of time was sig-
nified." Now it was " the Spirit *of Christ* that
was in them[a]," and we believe that *Jesus* was the•
Christ; for we have seen that he knew fully both
the time, and the manner, and the object of all these
transactions. He foretold them, and they were

---

[a] 1 Pet. i. 10—12.

accurately accomplished. He foretold them, and *in him* they were accomplished. He foretold them, and they were the very things, which, at the same time that they fulfilled his predictions, fulfilled all those of the ancient prophets respecting the sufferings, and death, and resurrection of *the Christ,* and respecting the nature and establishment of *his kingdom.* He, therefore, who foretold events of such a nature, and having such consequences; who *so* foretold them, as to prove that he was acquainted with the whole scheme of the divine counsels, and that the arrangement of the means and events by which they were accomplished, was known to him in such a manner as cannot be conceived of any other than of him, "between whom and the Father was the counsel of peace," —he, I say, could himself be no other than " the Messiah, who was " to be cut off, but not for himself," and who became " the Author of eternal salvation to all them that obey him." We may therefore ourselves derive from these predictions, a conviction such as the Apostles themselves attained thereby, in conformity to our Lord's own declaration. " Now I tell you before it come, that, when it is come to pass, ye may believe that *I am he.*" When all these things had taken place, Jesus enforced the argument, and to the full establishment of their faith. " These are the words *which I spake unto you, while I was yet*

with you, that all things must be fulfilled, which
were written in the law of Moses, and in the prophets, and in the Psalms, concerning me." They
had then seen, and they believed; and, through
their word, we also may believe in Jesus as the
Christ of God.

Since, then, the foreknowledge and the Messiahship of Jesus are so demonstrable, we may
expect that all his other predictions will be fulfilled
in their season. Those, of which the accomplishment is yet future, may exercise our confidence in
the perpetuity of his Church. We may believe
that "the gates of hell will not prevail against it[a]."
We may in hope expect the day when "the times
of the Gentiles will be fulfilled[b]," when "the
Gospel will be preached to every creature[c],"
when "all men will be drawn" to the standard
of him, who was "lifted up that whosoever believeth in him should not perish, but have everlasting life[d]." We may pray that "his kingdom
may come[e]." And ere long also, "all that are in
the graves shall hear the voice of the Son of
man, and shall come forth, they that have done
good to the resurrection of life, and they that have
done evil to the resurrection of damnation[f]." The
Son of man will then "come in the glory of his

---

[a] Matt. xvi. 18.   [b] Luke xxi. 24.   [c] Mark xvi. 15.
[d] John iii. 14; xii. 32.   [e] Matt. vi. 10.
[f] John v. 28, 29.

Father, with his holy angels[a]." Then shall we indeed know that he is the Christ, the Holy one of God, the Saviour. May we now so believe in him, as not to be confounded before him at that day; that we may not then be " denied by him before the angels of God[b]." But rather let us now so " believe in God, and also believe in him," that we may now partake of the consolation, and hereafter share in the accomplishment of those delightful and animating words: " In my Father's house are many mansions; if it were not so, I would have told you. I go to prepare a place for you. And if I go to prepare a place for you, I will come again and receive you unto myself, that where I am, there ye may be also[c]."

---

[a] Matt. xvi. 27. [b] Luke xii. 9. [c] John xiv. 1—3.

LECTURE XVI.

———

THE REMARKABLE SAYINGS OF OUR LORD AT THE
TIME OF HIS APPREHENSION, ON HIS TRIAL, AND
ON THE CROSS, CONSIDERED. HIS INSTITUTION
OF THE SACRAMENT IN COMMEMORATION OF HIS
DEATH.

———

St. John XVIII. 36, 37.

*Jesus answered, My kingdom is not of this world; if my
kingdom were of this world, then would my servants
fight, that I should not be delivered to the Jews: but
now is my kingdom not from hence. Pilate therefore
said unto him, Art thou a king then? Jesus answered,
Thou sayest that I am a king. To this end was I
born, and for this cause came I into the world, that
I might bear witness unto the truth. Every one that
is of the truth heareth my voice.*

WHEN the Apostle Paul exhorted Timothy to
" fight the good fight of faith, and to lay hold on
eternal life," he gave him charge to keep this
commandment " in the sight of God, who quickeneth all things, and before Christ Jesus, *who
before Pontius Pilate witnessed a good confession* [a]*.*" That confession, in part at least, you

---

[a] 1 Tim. vi. 12—14.

have heard in the words of our text. If, however, we agree with those, who so understand the words of the Apostle, as to suppose that he spoke of " the good confession which Jesus witnessed *in the days of* Pontius Pilate [a]," we shall then conceive that the Apostle also referred to an equivalent confession which he had then just made before *the high priest;* and we shall also be reminded of the short but expressive declarations previously made, at the time of his *apprehension,* and afterwards during his *crucifixion.* We propose, in this Lecture, to take a cursory review of this series of our Lord's sayings; for in various respects they strikingly exhibit to us the character and office of Jesus, and they will also suggest many considerations respecting the evidences of his divine mission and Messiahship, different, perhaps, from any upon which we have yet touched.

In the conclusion of our last Lecture, we noticed the farewell discourses of our Lord to his disciples, which were followed by his intercessory prayer to the Father on their behalf[b]. He then announced to them his approaching sufferings and departure; and we have now to

---

[a] ἐνώπιον—Χριστοῦ Ἰησοῦ τοῦ μαρτυρήσαντος ἐπὶ Ποντίου Πιλάτου τὴν καλὴν ὁμολογίαν. ver. 13.

[b] John xvii.

accompany them and their Master to the garden
of Gethsemane, where his sufferings were to
commence, and where, having prepared them, he
was about to prepare *himself* for the trying scene.

Leaving the other disciples with a charge to
" pray lest they should enter into temptation, and
to tarry while he retired to a little distance from
them to pray also," he took with him Peter, and
James, and John. Having told them of the "exceeding sorrow, even unto death," which had come
upon him, "he withdrew about a stone's cast" from
them also, leaving it in charge to them "to pray
and to watch." The words and the subject of the
prayer, which, " being in an agony," " he poured
out with strong crying and tears unto his Father,"
you cannot but remember[c]. Nor need I remind
you that his full knowledge of " the iniquity of us
all, which was about to be laid on him," and of
" the stripes and chastisement which he was about
to undergo for our peace and healing," put him to
grief, deep and still increasing. Returning from
his more earnest supplication for " the third time,"
and " strengthened by an angel from heaven,"
by the annunciation, perhaps, that he " had been
heard in that he feared," he comes to arouse them
to the full sense of their danger by the alarming assurance, " It is enough, the hour is come; behold

---

[c] Matt. xxvi. 36—44. Isai. liii. Heb. v. 7.

the Son of man is betrayed into the hand of sinners. Rise up, let us go; lo, he that betrayeth me is at hand[a]." " While he yet spake," Judas appeared with his company. And the contrast exhibited between the conduct of the disciples and of their Master was, if possible, more striking than ever. They acted as men; yet as those in whom an affection for their Master was deeply seated; whose hasty zeal in his behalf, and whose almost immediate fear and flight, were equally natural in their circumstances. But Jesus in his words displayed a composure, a courage, and a perseverance in the discharge of his mission, which was uniformly supported in his whole demeanour, from the first moment of danger, even until the last struggle of dissolving nature. Let us then attentively consider all that from this time fell from his lips, and also, as we have occasion to do, the intelligible significancy even of his silence.

Jesus fearlessly advanced to meet the approaching company of armed men[b]. " Knowing all things that should come upon him, he went forth, and said unto them, Whom seek ye?" When he had told them that he was the person they sought, " they went backward, and fell to the ground;" either overpowered by a consciousness of his innocence and prophetic character, or

---

[a] Mark xiv. 41, 42.   [b] John xviii. 4.

because Jesus himself exerted upon them a miraculous power. When they arose, still determined to persevere in their design, Jesus pleaded for the personal safety of his disciples only ; "that the saying which he had just spoken might be fulfilled, Of those that thou gavest me, I have lost none [c]." "I have told you," said he again, "that I am he ; if then ye seek me, let these go their way."

Three other separate addresses he made at the same season.—When *Judas* advanced to give the signal, upon which he had agreed with the officers beforehand, Jesus intimated to him his knowledge of the plan which he had concerted, and of its object. "Friend, wherefore art thou come ? *Betrayest* thou the Son of man with a kiss?" The officers, emboldened by the perseverance of their guide, laid hands on Jesus, and bound him.—And is *he* then bound, and led away as a malefactor, who is surrounded by those who professed their readiness to "go with him even unto prison, and unto death ?" He, who *claimed* the peculiar co-operation and protection of his heavenly Father; who had wrought so many wonders of mercy and of power; who had "spoken as never man spake?" Is *he* now found unaided, and powerless, and silent? He is not indeed delivered. Yet he shewed, once and

---

[c] John xviii. 9. See xvii. 12.

again, that he could even then be rescued, though
by no human arm; that he could escape out of
their hands, in such a manner as he had done
aforetime. And he at this juncture so expressed
himself, as to leave his character as a divine
teacher unimpaired by these apparently humiliating incidents, and to prepare us to expect
consequences from them of the highest importance, and of the deepest interest. He spoke
such things both to *his own disciples,* and to *his
enemies.*

His disciples eagerly inquiring whether they
should smite with the sword, and Peter having
actually done so, Jesus charged him to "put up
again his sword into its place." "For," said he,
"all they that take the sword, shall perish with
the sword. Thinkest thou that I cannot now pray
to my Father, and he shall presently give me more
than twelve legions of angels? But how then shall
the Scriptures be fulfilled, that thus it must be[a]?
The cup which my Father hath given me, shall
I not drink it[b]?"—He had before apprised them
of the approaching fulfilment of prophecy by the
delivery of the Son of man into the hands of sinners. They had also just heard him declare to
his heavenly Father his acquiescence in his will,
and his readiness to drink the cup which was

---

[a] Matt. xxvi. 52—54.   [b] John xviii. 11.

presented to him, since it was not to "pass from him, except he drank it." They might therefore collect from his present observations that nothing had come upon him which he had not foreseen. And if, by such a destiny, Scripture was fulfilled, and the Father's will accomplished; and if he, who had to drink the bitter cup, was himself unmoved and resigned, and exhorted them to be so; they might reasonably, not only so far submit, as to abstain from actual resistance, but they might also contentedly acquiesce in, and await the approaching developement of the purposes of God.

To those, who came to apprehend him, Jesus spoke in a different manner. Their present conduct was prompted by the spirit of malignant unbelief, rather than occasioned by the infirmity of human nature. With them therefore he expostulated, not at all with the design of procuring his liberation, but that he might shew them the injustice and cowardly baseness of their present procedure, and also announce to them that while they followed the suggestions of their own depravity, they would *unwittingly* be the agents for the fulfilment of Scripture. But he prefaced his words by the miraculous cure of the wounded Malchus, thereby once more demonstrating the authority of that doctrine, for which he was "an ambassador in bonds." Having checked the too forward zeal of his disciples, he thus addressed those who had apprehended him. " Are ye come out, as against a thief, with swords and staves for to take me? I sat daily with you teaching in the temple, and ye laid no hold on me. But all this has been done that the Scriptures of the prophets might be fulfilled[a]. This is your hour, and the power of darkness[b]."

Not far dissimilar were his remarks when, brought before the Sanhedrim, assembled in the house of Caiaphas, he stood alone, forsaken of all his disciples, and was questioned by the high priest respecting his disciples, and his doctrine. " I spake openly to the world : I ever taught in the synagogue, and in the temple, whither the Jews always resort, and in secret have I said nothing. Why askest thou *me?* ask them which heard me, what I have said unto them. Behold, *they* know what I said[c]."—The rulers knew that they could bring forward no witnesses who could give evidence upon which he might be capitally convicted. That nothing less than this would satisfy them, or answer their purpose, is evident from their former watching of Jesus, and from their consultations " how they might put him to

---

[a] Τοῦτο δὲ ὅλον γέγονεν, ἵνα πληρωθῶσιν αἱ γραφαὶ τῶν προφητῶν. Matt. xxvi. 55, 56.

[b] Luke xxii. 53.　　　[c] John xviii. 20, 21.

death;" and their whole conduct both in their own court, and before Pilate, proved the same. In default of evidence, Caiaphas was desirous to draw from him some incautious expression, which, being publicly heard, might supply a pretext for his condemnation. He might hope, when he questioned him concerning his disciples, and his doctrine, to be able either to convict him of tumultuous proceedings, or of impugning the law of Moses, or of blasphemy. But this mode of procedure was as unavailing, as it was unjust. Jesus knew that even his condemnation, which was shortly to follow, would be found perfectly consistent with his innocence, and that it would even furnish many unequivocal proofs of it; and he therefore challenged them to bring forward those who had heard him in public. He manfully and calmly maintained his ground, even when angrily smitten, by one of the officers that stood by, because he had " so answered the high priest." " If," said he, " I have spoken evil, bear witness of the evil; but if well, why smitest thou me[d] ?" His answer to the high priest was perfectly just and respectful, unless it could be proved that he had taught some dangerous doctrine. He required of the officer to do so, if he could bring witness of any such. An endeavour was made by the rulers to

---

[d] John xviii. 22, 23.

establish such an accusation, but in vain. " False witnesses were sought," and when at length they found them, their testimony was contradictory, and insufficient[a]. They were obliged to abandon this method of prosecution.—Let it, therefore, be borne in mind, that Jesus could be convicted of no *moral* or *political* crime. He had advanced nothing in his doctrine, which calumniated or opposed the laws and institutions of Moses; he had stated nothing respecting *himself*, which he had not established by argument, and confirmed by miracles. And, in the face of such demonstration, they ventured not at this time to repeat their former imputations of blasphemy, lest, as aforetime, he should baffle their designs.—He was questioned again as to his defence of himself against these varied, though inadmissible accusations. " The high priest stood up in the midst, and asked Jesus, saying, Answerest thou nothing? What is it which these witness against thee?— But he held his peace, and answered nothing."— He left them to their own conviction of the insufficiency of the testimony; and would enter on no defence, when, in fact, there was no crime even apparently proved.

But the trial soon took a different turn. The high priest proposed a definite and leading ques-

---

[a] Matt. xxvi. 59, &c. Mark xiv. 55, &c.

tion, and accompanied it with *an adjuration;* in
order that Jesus, in obedience to a specific precept of Moses, might be compelled to give an
answer[b]. " I adjure thee by the living God, that
thou tell us whether thou be the Christ." And
he said unto them, If I tell you, ye will not
believe; and if I also ask you, ye will not answer
me, nor let me go." He thus stated that he was
fully aware of the manner in which they would
receive his answer; yet he gave it, and said,
" I am." And that they might learn that although
he hitherto appeared in humility, yet he did not
disavow a claim to the glories ascribed to the
Lord's Christ, he assured them that though the
time was not yet come for his exaltation, it would
hereafter be known and recognized. He applied
to himself the prophetic descriptions of the second
and hundred and tenth Psalms, and of a passage
in the book of Daniel. "Nevertheless, I say
unto you, that hereafter ye shall see the Son of
man sitting on the right hand of the power of
God, and coming in the clouds of heaven." They
all exclaimed in consequence of this declaration,
" Art thou then the Son of God?" He said to

---

[b] Ἐξορκίζω σε κατὰ τοῦ Θεοῦ τοῦ ζῶντος ἵνα ἡμῖν εἴπῃς,
κ.τ.λ. Matt. xxvi. 63.—See the precept concerning the φωνὴ
ὁρκισμοῦ in Lev. v. 1. And see also 1 Sam. xiv. 24, 26.
1 Kings ii. 42, 43; viii. 31, 32; xxii. 16. Prov. xxix. 24.—
ἐὰν ὅρκου προτεθέντος ἀκούσαντες μὴ ἀναγγείλωσι. Septuagint.

them, "Ye say that I am." He assented to the justness of their supposition, that he asserted his right to that, as well as to every other dignity of the Messiah; and they all, contending that he had spoken *blasphemy* in their presence, declared that he was worthy of the capital punishment assigned to blasphemers by the law of Moses[a].

If he was not the Christ, he was justly condemned to death. If by that death itself he was not glorified, if he was not redeemed from the power of the grave, then the hopes of all that trusted in him were buried for ever with him. But assuredly he did burst through the bands, in which death for a season detained him; "because it was not possible that he should be holden of it." He died in the character, the avowed character, of the Christ, the Son of God. As the Christ he died. As the Christ he is risen from the dead, and "declared thereby to be the Son of God with power." He has "sat down on the right hand of the Majesty on high." But if he were the Lord's Anointed, he was anointed to inherit *a kingdom.* And the next question to be determined, is, what is the nature and object, and who are the subjects of his kingdom? This we shall find stated in due time by Jesus, when he was accused to Pilate by the high priest of asserting himself to be "Christ, a king[b]."

---

[a] Lev. xxiv. 16.   [b] Luke xxiii. 1—3.

It was not lawful for those, who had decided that a cause of death was found in Jesus, to execute that punishment without the authority of the Roman governour; who required of course to be satisfied that the sentence was just. It was not sufficient that they assured Pilate that " if he were not a malefactor, they would not have delivered Jesus unto him[c]." They were required to " take and judge him according to their law." But that would not content them, because they could not inflict that punishment which alone would satisfy them. They therefore contended that he was guilty of sedition, by assuming the title of the Christ, and therefore " making himself a king, and speaking against Cesar;" adding that he " forbad to give tribute to Cesar;" an assertion which they did not attempt to prove, and which was directly *contrary* to the truth[d]. The question which Pilate had first to decide, was whether *he* really declared himself the king of the Jews; for *they* brought no witnesses to prove it. He asked Jesus whether he was so. Jesus demanded in return, " whether he asked this of himself, or whether others had told it to him?" Pilate implied that the latter was the only source whence he, a Roman, could have

---

[c] John xviii. 29—31.

[d] Luke xxiii. 2.—See Matt. xvii. 27; xxii. 21.

learnt it. "Am I a Jew? Thine own nation
and the chief priests have delivered thee unto me.
What hast thou done?" He answered in the
words of our text; not merely alluding to the absence of any proof that he had done any thing which
could be considered seditious, but even appealing
to fact to shew the contrary; and applying that
circumstance in illustration of the *nature* of the
kingdom to which he advanced a claim. "My
kingdom is not of this world; else would my
servants fight that I should not be delivered to the
Jews. But now is my kingdom not from hence."

There was therefore nothing which brought
his claims under the cognizance of Pilate. He
avowed his right to a kingdom; but not such as
either had occasioned, or would occasion, any
disturbance to the political order and civil govern-
ment of the world. He had taught indeed the
approach of a kingdom, but it was the kingdom
of God; for admittance into which repentance,
and the belief of promises relative to religious
blessings, were requisite[a]. He had taught that
this kingdom "cometh not with observation," but
that it is situated in the hearts of men[b]. He
had avoided every thing that might encourage
tumults and insurrections for his temporal exaltation[c]. He had refused to act as " a judge and

---

[a] Mark i. 15. Luke iv. 21.   [b] Luke xvii. 20.   [c] John vi. 15.

a divider" even among his own followers[d]. He
had checked and endeavoured to eradicate those
anticipations of earthly grandeur, which arose in
the minds, either of the multitude, or of his own
disciples[e]. The topics of his instruction had been
the duties of morality,—the attributes of God,
his promises and his will,—the evidences and
spiritual purposes of his own mission.　Thus had
he ever taught, as they were able to bear it, that
" his kingdom was not of this world ;" and the
same truth he now declared in " his good confession before Pontius Pilate."　In the former part
of this avowal of his character, for we can scarcely
call it a defence, he had declared himself to be
the Christ.　This he declared to *Jews*, who were
qualified to judge of his claim to that title.　But
when arraigned before *Pilate*, he further declared,
that the kingdom which belonged to him as such,
was not in any sense of a political nature, and
that he was not thereby rendered accountable to
a *civil ruler*.

But if such were his kingdom, did he then
profess himself to be a king? Pilate put this question also.　And the answer of Jesus was to the
same *purport* as before ; but he did not now speak
so much of the *nature* of the dispensation which

---

[d] Luke xii. 14.

[e] John vi. 7, 12. Matt. xvi. 17; xx. 17—28; xxii. 41—46.

C c

he was introducing, as of the *employment* and *procedure* by which it has been *his* commission to introduce it. " For this end was I born, and for this cause came I into the world, that I might bear witness unto the truth. Every one that is of the truth, heareth my voice." He declared that those were the subjects of his kingdom, who obeyed his commands as a teacher of moral and religious truth. In such a character he had appeared, and all his statements and labours had been suitable to it. He had been born in order to promote the establishment of a spiritual kingdom of truth and righteousness. He had gone forth into the world to fulfil the end for which he was born. He had borne witness to the truth. Those only he expected to be his followers, who were of the truth, and were, therefore, willing " to receive the truth in the love of it." No others would obey him, for none but they had correct apprehensions respecting the purposes of his mission. His kingdom not being of this world, he required not in his subjects any of the qualifications for the warlike or diplomatic transactions of the kingdoms of the earth. It had not been proved by his accusers that he had given any handle for such an imputation ; nor did they afterwards establish the truth of the statements, which they had so repeatedly advanced.— But Jesus thenceforth made no declaration whatever until the ground of accusation was changed ; and not even then until an occasion was given by a remark from Pilate.

In answer to the observations of Jesus, Pilate exclaimed, "What is truth?" 'Why do you speak of *truth?* What connection can that have with the accusation of the chief priests? They have brought no evidence to *support* their accusation; and it does not appear, from your professions, that you have given them any *ground* for it.' He therefore went out to the accusers, who stood without Pilate's judgment-hall, "lest they should be defiled," and disqualified for the celebration of the passover. He announced to them that "he found in Jesus no fault at all," and would fain have released him, according to the usual custom at the time of the passover. But they requested the release of Barabbas, who, indeed, not only had headed an *insurrection,* but had committed murder. Determined to accomplish their purpose, they changed their plea; and, as they could convict Jesus of no political delinquency, they endeavoured to obtain the sanction of Pilate to their own previous sentence[a]. "By our law," said they, "he ought to die, because he made himself the Son of God.—When Pilate heard that saying, he was the more afraid." Perhaps he was already disposed to think, from what he had now seen, and might

---

[a] John xix. 7, &c.

formerly have heard, that Jesus was a remarkable
personage; or some superstitious fears were awakened in his mind; or finding, not only that " the
Jews had delivered him for envy," but that the
occasion of their enmity was connected with
questions of their own religion and law, he was
alarmed by the indications of an inclination to
rebel, and to accuse him to Cesar, if he refused to
give up Jesus to their will. He therefore asked
Jesus, " Whence art thou?" But no answer was
given to the Gentile ruler. The title of the *Son
of God* was by the prophets ascribed to the
Messiah, but it was one of which Pilate, as a
Gentile, could not judge; and he had already
proved to Pilate that he was clear of every charge
which came under his cognizance. But when
Pilate pleaded for an answer on the ground that
" he had power to crucify him, and had power to
release him," then Jesus made *his final declaration*
to the same purport as those made at the time
of his apprehension. " Jesus answered, Thou
couldest have no power at all against me, except it
were given thee from above; therefore he that
delivered me unto thee hath the greater sin."
The rulers knew, and by their recent proceedings
in their own Council had in fact allowed, that the
Messiah was to be the Son of God. Yet they
had separated the claim to the latter character;
and had condemned Jesus, regardless of his own

declaration that he was the Christ, and forgetful
of all the arguments and evidences by which he
had supported his divine authority. They had
endeavoured upon *false* pretences to procure his
condemnation by Pilate; and when they mentioned the *real* one, upon which they had themselves proceeded, they did in fact still make an
improper and imperfect statement. The declaration, however, which Jesus made to Pilate, was
quite consistent with his former statements to him;
and, if he were the Son of God, it was evidently in
character. It certainly increased the fear of
Pilate, and his reluctance to condemn him; for
" he sought thenceforth to release him," and not
Barabbas. But " the voice of the multitude and
of the chief priests prevailed." " He gave sentence
that it should be as they required, and delivered
Jesus to their will."

Thus did the trial of Jesus proceed in such a
manner, as to produce the most various and incon-
trovertible attestations of his complete innocence
with reference to man. Occasions also arose which
called forth declarations of the character in which
he professed to be sent of God, viz. that he was
the Christ, the Son of God, hereafter to come in
power, as then he appeared in humility; and that
he was born, and sent into the world that he might
testify of the truth, and declare " not the wisdom
of the world, nor of the princes of this world,

which come to nought," but the necessity of repentance for the remission of sins, and of obedience
to his precepts in all such as were willing that he
should reign over them, and who desired to enter
into those mansions which he would prepare for
his faithful soldiers and subjects. He declared also
that the issue of his trial and condemnation not
only was conformable to the predictions of the
prophets, but to the will of God; and that Pilate
was indeed permitted to authorize it, but that,
without that permission, his power would have
been ineffectual.

Connect these declarations with what we have
already heard from the lips of him who made
them; of him, who had appeared, at a former
period of his ministry, before the tribunal of the
Jewish council; and who then fully stated to them
his authority and the proofs of it. And though his
hour was now come, and the day of Jerusalem's
visitation expiring, yet are not the words that we
have this day considered, the words of one sent
of God; of one who was about to " finish the work
which the Father had given him to do?" Such
indeed he was, though, after cruel mockeries and
humiliating indignities, " he went forth bearing his
cross," and touching the tenderness of the female
heart with pity even to tears. He was going forth
to offer himself for the life of the world. But he
foresaw the obstinacy, and unbelief, and ruin of

that generation; and well might he exhort "the daughters of Jerusalem to weep for themselves, and for their children," upon whom the guilt of that innocent blood had so thoughtlessly been imprecated and entailed[a]. Well did he know, and often would he fain have taught them, the things that would have made for their peace. But now he could only pray, as they nailed him to the tree, "Father, forgive them, for they know not what they do[b]." Yet behold again the authority and power, and benevolence of him, who was then made "a spectacle to angels and to men." He could confidently anticipate his Father's acceptance of his sacrifice, and could declare to the penitent thief who attested his innocence, and prayed to be remembered in his kingdom, that "That day he should be with him in Paradise[c]." Soon did he perform the last office of filial affection to his earthly parent; and, declaring in several ways that "all things were accomplished," he commended his Spirit into the hands of his Father, and gave up the ghost[d]. The darkened heavens, and the convulsed earth, the opening graves, and the unveiled sanctuary, rebuked the madness of the agents in that scene; and declared

---

[a] Matt. xxvii. 25.   Luke xxiii. 28—31.   Acts v. 28.
[b] Luke xxiii. 34.   [c] Luke xxiii. 39—43.
[d] Matt. xxvii. 46, 50.   John xix. 30.   Luke xxiii. 46.

to them and to every child of Adam that hears of these transactions, that "truly this was the Son of God," who had then "brought in an everlasting righteousness," and finished the work which the guilt of man required, and which the mercy of God had promised.

And is not Jesus Christ, in the word of God, and by the preaching of his ministers, evidently set forth among you as *Christ crucified?* And is not an institution observed amongst us, which purports to be a *commemorative* ordinance, designed to be celebrated, even unto the end of time, wherever a Christian church exists, that Christians, "eating of that bread, and drinking of that cup, may shew forth the Lord's death till he come?" *We* have derived the custom from our *forefathers*, who believed in Jesus Christ, and him crucified. *They* derived it from those, who first preached to them these great truths. And in what did it *originate*, in what *could* a commemorative ordinance originate, but in the fact which it commemorates? We can account for the first observance of this rite, only by believing that it is an *historical fact* that Jesus *died*. And it was observed in obedience to *his* injunctions, and in consequence of *his* celebration of it *before* he died. And how should any but an innocent person, one who knew that his innocence would be undeniably attested, institute a rite to keep up "a perpetual memory" of his public and ignominious death? Again, why should *he wish* it to be celebrated, and why should any *others* even be *persuaded* to celebrate it, unless they discerned in the Lord's body and blood, somewhat in which they had a great concern? And what does this, and every other argument in support of the Gospel, prove to us, but that he spoke not only with foreknowledge of the fact, but with a full acquaintance with its *design*, and *success*, when he declared, " This is my body which is broken for *you;* This is my blood of the New Testament which is shed for *you* and for *many* for the *remission of sins.* Do this in remembrance of ME[a]."

These benefits, doubtless, will be commemorated, and be received by multitudes, even till the Lord, by whose death they were obtained, shall come again in such manner as he has declared that he will come. Our share in keeping up the remembrance of them is confined within a very brief portion of these latter times; but that portion is to us " the accepted time, and the day of salvation." We must therefore meditate on the design of this event, on the necessity for it, on the purposes accomplished by it, on the consequences of it here and hereafter. And it should be our prayer and endeavour, that " by the merits

---

[a] Matt. xxvi. 26—29.   Mark xiv. 22—26.   Luke xxii. 17—22.

and death of Jesus Christ, and through faith in his blood, we and all his whole church may obtain remission of our sins, and all other benefits of his passion." If we can with heartfelt gratitude and joy " glory in the cross of our Lord Jesus Christ," and if " by it the world is crucified unto us, and we unto the world," then " all things are our's, whether life, or death, or things present, or things to come, all things are our's; for then are we Christ's, and Christ is God's."

Let us remember, however, that the cup, of which Jesus drank even the last bitter dregs, will one day be presented to our lips; and we too must drink of it. And if the draught be not sweetened, by a hope of deliverance from its deadly consequences in eternity; if we have not a well-grounded hope that the sufferings of this present time, and the pains of dissolution, will issue in the attainment of " a far more exceeding and eternal weight of glory;" then has Jesus died in vain for us, and in vain have these things been written, that " through patience, and comfort of the Scriptures, we might have a good hope" of inheriting the promises. How strong and how fatal a delusion must have come upon us, if, when death approaches, and makes us feel his presence and his power, we are in such a moment still insensible to our guilt and danger, still regardless of the judgments and of the mercies of God!

And, on the other hand, how agonizing will be our reflections, if an awakened conscience then utters her voice, and can give no other testimony than this, "Thy sins, which are many, are not forgiven thee!" Yet it is not always thus, even when the summons is most sudden and unexpected. "The righteous hath hope in his death." Death still is clad in the garb of the king of terrors, but he delivers a message of peace. He is still an enemy, but he is "the last enemy" of the Christian, and one day he will "be destroyed." Even his present hostilities have by our Redeemer been converted into blessings. By the anticipation of these we are the more readily induced to "take to ourselves the whole armour of God." "Arming ourselves with the same mind which was in him, who once suffered for us in the flesh, we cease from sin." We are no longer "subjected to bondage through the fear of death." "God giveth us the victory through our Lord Jesus Christ."

We hear from time to time how thickly the shafts of death fly around us; how one fellow-creature is cut off in his sins, another in the midst of his virtuous and useful designs; one because threescore years and ten have worn out his short-lived frame, another in the vigour of youth; one by the disorders of the body, another by some unlooked for accident. These dealings of Providence, while they answer wise ends with respect to the individuals taken away, are also intended to remind us of our own insecurity. And yet we are marvellously forgetful of so important a consideration. The soldier, indeed, in the field of battle, is heedless of the thousands that fall around him, and of the weapons which may the next moment level him with his dying comrades. But this may be accounted for. It is said that, at the first onset, a pale terror sits on every brow, and that those of the stoutest heart feel a momentary conviction of the awful situation in which they are placed. But the instant that they are engaged, this gives way to an earnestness and exertion, which leaves no time, almost no possibility, for fear and reflection. Reflection, and fear, and even the thought of death is then certain destruction. With us the case is different. We have time for reflection, and it is our security. The busiest has more than time so to "number his days, as to apply his heart unto wisdom." Why then are we as heedless as the soldier, though perhaps really in as great peril? Not because we cannot reflect—not because time has been wanting— not because it increases our danger. None of these suppositions are true in point of fact. The reason is that we are unwilling. We dread the thoughts of death, because we "love the world and the things of the world,"—because the things unseen have little hold upon our affections—because we are sinners by nature, by practice, and almost by determination—because we " hate to be reformed "—because with the thought of death is associated the fear of " a judgment to come." We tremble when we realize such things to our minds, and we therefore hate the recollection of them, and scarcely dare to encourage it.

It is true that such subjects are solemn, melancholy, and alarming. But are they unprofitable? Is it better to attend to them, or to dismiss them—to avoid them—to drown the remembrance of them in vanity and indulgence? Such, indeed, is the way in which the worldling acts. " Let us eat and drink, for to-morrow we die," is his law and gospel. " Let us banish care and sorrow," is his resolution. But what says the wisest of men? " The day of death is better than the day of one's birth. It is better to go to the house of mourning, than to go to the house of feasting ; for that is the end of all men, and the living will lay it to heart. Sorrow is better than laughter ; for by the sadness of the countenance the heart is made better. The *heart of the wise* is *in the house of mourning*." This is at all times more satisfactory, and it has a far greater blessedness in reserve. It is more safe, for it presents fewer temptations. It is more profitable, for it shews us the value of those principles and hopes, which in the house of feasting we may undervalue or forget. We come away from thence improved in heart, and strengthened in every holy purpose. It lies most directly in the road to heaven; and it displays to us the operation, and directs us to the acquirement of " that consolation wherewith we ourselves may be comforted of God."

But alas! Solomon did not speak as a prophet when he said, " The living will lay it to heart." He knew that too generally they would do far otherwise. At the same time he also knew, and so do we, that if the living are wise, if they are prudent, if they are not content to inherit " shame and everlasting contempt," " they will lay it to heart." We know that all men must die. But we must apply the truth to our own case. The mercies of God's providence, and the wonders of his grace, the compassion and sufficiency of a crucified Redeemer, will be worse than lost upon us, unless our hearts and consciences whisper to us daily—I too must die—I must then be ready—I must prepare to meet the Son of man—I must make him my friend—I must glory in his cross—I must have faith in his blood—I must rely upon his intercession—I must be sanctified by his Spirit —I must live a life of faith, and devotedness, and holy obedience. Nothing less than this is " to lay it to heart." Nothing less than this is " to be of the truth, and to hear the voice of Jesus."

Have you done this ? are you disposed to do it ?
Go on in this way, and " in due season you shall
reap, if you faint not." But " be ye always ready ;
for in such an hour as ye think not, the Son of
man cometh." " Have your loins girt, and your
lights burning," and then, "through the grave,
and gate of death, you will pass to your joyful
resurrection, for his merits who died, and was
buried, and rose again for us, Jesus Christ our
Lord[a]."

---

[a] It may probably occur to those who read, as it did to some
who heard this Lecture, that some particular circumstance must
have suggested the reflections with which this Lecture concludes. On
the day before it was delivered, the Author had seen removed from
his own house the corpse of a Clergyman, whose useful life had suddenly been terminated in consequence of the injuries which he acci-
dentally received on the preceding Thursday. When the Author
left that which had so unexpectedly become " the house of
mourning," and sat down to finish this Lecture, the preparation of
which had been suspended by that melancholy event, the recollection of the uncertainty of life, and of the blessedness of a state
of preparation for death, mixed itself with all his thoughts. The
contemplation of our Saviour's death also directed his thoughts
into the same channel ; and perhaps it was not surprising that he
should, under such circumstances, endeavour to communicate to
others the lessons which himself had so profitably, and yet so
painfully, been receiving. For he had witnessed the last hours of
one to whom death had given a sudden summons ; yet who
received it with a rare and enviable composure, and submitted to
the stroke in faith, and hope, and resignation. He had " adorned
the doctrine of God our Saviour by his life," and it was sufficient to support him in the hour of death.—Another exemplary
Clergyman,

Clergyman, whom the Author had known from childhood, was in Cambridge when the *next* Lecture was delivered, and with him the Author conversed respecting the recent accident, of which that friend had heard on his way to Cambridge. And little did it then seem likely that he also, within eight days from that time, would be removed to another state of being. The Author cannot refrain from embracing this opportunity of bearing testimony to the steady and beneficent lustre of those truly Christian virtues, which characterised the lives of the Rev. Thomas Wilson, and the Rev. Walter Smith. Their memory will doubtless ever be embalmed in the hearts of their parishioners, and relatives, and friends ; and " though they have been punished in the sight of men, yet was their hope full of immortality."—The former died Oct. 12 ; the latter Oct. 29. A. D. 1821.

LECTURE XVII.

—◆—

—◆— ‥

St. LUKE XXIV. 44—48.

*And he said unto them, These are the words which I
spake unto you, while I was yet with you, that all
things must be fulfilled, which were written in the law
of Moses, and in the Prophets, and in the Psalms concerning me. Then opened he their understandings,
that they might understand the Scriptures, and said
unto them, Thus it is written, and thus it behoved
Christ to suffer, and to rise from the dead the third
day, and that repentance and remission of sins should
be preached in his name among all nations, beginning
at Jerusalem. And ye are witnesses of these things.*

THESE words are ascribed to Jesus of Nazareth;
to him, into whose name we were baptized, and
whose religion we profess. And what are the
things of which he spoke, but those indignities,
and sufferings, which did indeed end in death,
but which were followed by his resurrection from
the dead? He, whose words we have read, had

been apprehended, condemned, and crucified by the Jews. He had died, and he had been buried. But he now visibly appeared, and stood alive before those, who had so lately misunderstood, and denied, and forsaken him; and who, even then, scarcely had recovered from their disappointment and despondency. At this, as well as at all previous seasons, Jesus is found to be his own apologist. . No sooner are the requisite data furnished, and circumstances brought into a posture, which admits an explanation and defence of his pretensions, than he proceeds to obviate the doubts and difficulties of those around him, and to draw, from familiar and acknowledged facts, the most important inferences respecting the evidence, nature, and purposes of his mission.

Whether, or not, the *resurrection* of Jesus be found to rest upon satisfactory evidence, there can at least be no hesitation, in the most sceptical mind, with respect to the reality of his *death*. If, indeed, there could be any doubt of that event, it would be mere trifling to talk of his having *risen* from the dead. But the proofs that Jesus truly died were both public and various. Not to mention the miraculous circumstances which attended the death of Jesus, and which added an awful solemnity to the conviction of its reality; would not the attention of the surrounding multitude be attracted by the loud voice

with which he cried out, "It is finished," and
"commended his Spirit into the hands of the
Father[a]?" Even if the darkness, which until the
ninth hour overspread the land, prevented some
from seeing how "he bowed his head," when
"he gave up the ghost;" would they not draw
near, to behold the paleness of death sitting on his
brow? Would not a decided conviction of the
fact have been universal among "all the people
that came together to that sight," ere they, "be-
holding the things that were done, smote their
breasts and returned[b]?" What was the declaration of the centurion, "who stood over against
Jesus," but a testimony to the character of one,
whom he believed to be dead; occasioned indeed
by his "seeing him so cry out and give up the
Ghost[c]?" Why did they omit to break the legs
of Jesus, as they did those of the malefactors, but
because they saw that he was already dead[d]? The
symptoms of a violent and painful death are not
indeed either imitable or equivocal. But lest we
should have any ground for supposing that they
continued such in the case of Jesus, while he yet
remained on the cross, the spear of the soldier
pierced his side; and that weapon which would
have produced the extinction of life, if any had

---

[a] Matt. xxvii. 50—53. John xix. 30.   [b] Luke xxiii. 44—49.
[c] Matt. xxvii. 54. Mark xv. 39.   [d] John xix. 31—33.

remained, gave the demonstration that life had then already departed, by the out-pouring of blood and water. Of which transaction, St. John, "who saw it, has borne record, and his record is true, and he knew that he said what was true, that we might believe[a]." When Joseph applied for permission to take down the body from the cross, he too must have had the full conviction, that it was in a state fit only for interment. Pilate, who "marvelled if Jesus were already dead," inquired of the centurion himself; and not until he knew it of the centurion did he give the body to Joseph[b]." And assuredly both Joseph and Nicodemus, who wound the body in linen clothes with spices, as the manner of the Jews is to bury; and the women also, who sat over against the sepulchre, and beheld both where, and how the body was laid[c]; all these could have no reason but to be fully satisfied that they had thus committed to the sepulchre a lifeless corpse; and, if it were otherwise, they must have discovered it. And those, who had accomplished the execution of Jesus, could have no doubt that they really had taken away the life of Jesus. For if otherwise, why did they "make the *sepulchre* sure, and seal the stone, and set a watch?" Why this precaution,

---

[a] John xix. 34, 35.   [b] Mark xv. 42—45.

[c] Matt. xxvii. 59—61.   Mark xv. 46, 47.   Luke xxiii. 50 —56.   John xix. 39—42.

lest the disciples should "steal away" his dead body[d]?—We can in no respect suggest a doubt as to the reality of that event, which was a subject of lamentation and despair to the friends of Jesus, and of a malignant complacency and expected triumph to his enemies. It was witnessed, and attested by the leading individuals of either party; and also by Pilate, and the centurion, and the soldiers, who were less interested in the issue.

Well might the Infidel triumph, and the Christian despair, if the *resurrection* of Jesus *from the dead* were not also ascertained by the most satisfactory evidence. Then should we have no reason to hope, as now we do, that "they which are fallen asleep in Christ have not perished;" and "we should be yet in our sins." "Our preaching, and your faith, would alike be vain[e]." Vain also would have been the instructions and the miracles, the promises and the sufferings of Jesus. The religion, of which he had laid the foundations, would either never have been established, or long since would have fallen to decay, had not his resurrection, as the key-stone, completed, and strengthened, and adorned the whole. —But we, as the ministers of Jesus who was crucified, maintain that he "both died and rose again;" and "for this end, that he might be

---

[d] Matt. xxvii. 62—66.   [e] 1 Cor. xv. 14, 17, 18.

Lord both of the dead, and of the living."" And such was the personal character of those who were witnesses of these things to the world—they gave their testimony with such exhibitions of divine approbation—yet under circumstances which would have been so trying to those whose consistency was supported by any other principle that a conviction and a love of truth—that we need little more, to justify a reliance upon their authority, than to be satisfied that they were not, and could not have been, *deceived* into a persuasion, that Jesus "shewed himself alive after his passion by *many infallible proofs*[a]." If we recall the train of events to our recollection, we shall be able to place ourselves in the circumstances of those, to whom the words of our text were addressed, and to ascertain both *how the resurrection of their master was evidenced to them*, and *what he taught them after that event*.

I. The chief priests and rulers of the Jews waited only for the arrival of the third day, in the hope that they should then be able finally to disabuse the people of their opinions respecting Jesus, by demonstrating the failure of the prediction that "after three days he would rise again." His own disciples were already so completely confounded, as to have no disposition to

---

[a] Acts i. 3.

occasion any further jealousy. They had given up all for lost; and the prediction, which had occasioned the precaution of the rulers, had left almost no trace on the minds of those, who were occupied by all the contending emotions of disappointed ambition. As far as Jesus was concerned, they, who had slept when they attended him in the garden, had now sunk into a deep mental lethargy. None of his followers were found in motion, save only a few women, who having, on the eve of the sabbath, " prepared spices and ointments, and rested the sabbath-day according to the commandment," went early on the morning of the first day of the week to pay their last tribute of affection and respect to the remains of their entombed friend [b]. Little did they think that the body, which they were desirous to embalm, would " never see corruption." They had no opportunity to accomplish their purpose. The stone which had closed the sepulchre was rolled away, and " entering in, *they found not the body* of Jesus [c]." Whilst Mary Magdalene ran to

---

[b] Luke xxiii. 54—56; xxiv. 1.

[c] Luke xxiv. 2, 3, &c. Compare also Matt. xxviii. Mark xvi. John xx.—This short notice of the very numerous events of the morning of the resurrection is of course not designed as any thing more than a *general* statement, and does not profess to include all the incidents, or notice all the feelings, and surmises of those concerned.

inform Peter and John, that the Lord had been "taken away from the sepulchre, and laid they knew not where," an angel appeared to her companions, on the spot within the sepulchre where they had before seen Jesus laid. They were doubting concerning the matter, when the angel informed them of the fact, reminded them of the predictions of Jesus, and sent them to communicate to his disciples the intelligence they had received. " Be not afraid; I know that ye seek Jesus who was crucified. Why seek ye *the living* among the dead. He is not here, but *is risen*; come, see the place where they laid him. Remember how he spake unto you while he was yet in Galilee, saying, The Son of man must be delivered into the hands of sinful men, and be crucified, and the third day rise again. And go quickly, and tell his disciples that he is risen from the dead; and behold, he goeth before you into Galilee; there shall ye see him, as he said unto you[a]." "They," says the Evangelist St. Luke, " remembered his words, and returned from the sepulchre, and told all these things unto the eleven, and to all the rest."—Peter and John also came to the sepulchre, and found the intelligence of Mary Magdalene confirmed by their own observation. She, again coming to the sepulchre, beheld two angels

---

[a] Matt. xxviii. 5—7. Mark xvi. 6, 7. Luke xxiv. 5—7.

sitting therein; and her lamentations to them respecting the body, were followed by *the first appearance of Jesus*, who sends her to the disciples with an assurance of his approaching ascension[b]. But her report was disbelieved. Jesus *again appeared* to the other women, and confirmed the direction of the angel to go and tell the disciples that they should "go into Galilee, and there they should see him." To the disciples these things as yet "seemed as idle tales, and they believed them not[c]." Yet Jesus brought them, ere that day closed, to a full conviction of the fact of his resurrection.

Two disciples, in the course of the same day, journeyed towards Emmaus, having left Jerusalem before they had received an accurate report of *all* the incidents which we have just noticed[d]. But they were very deeply impressed by the events of those days. They could think of nothing else, they could talk of nothing else. These things had happened in a manner the very reverse of all that they had wished, and hoped, and expected. They therefore communed together respecting them, in the hope that they might assist each other in reviewing and accounting for them, and in judging of the prudence and

---

[b] Matt. xxviii. 9, 10.   John xx. 14—18.
[c] Luke xxiv. 10, 11.   [d] Luke xxiv. 13—32.

propriety of their past conduct. But they saw
evident difficulties. They had various doubts.
They were perplexed. They were sad.—A stranger
who joined them observed their sadness. He asked
its cause. He concluded that it could be no other
than the subject of their earnest discourse together.
He would fain be made acquainted with it. Their
minds were indeed so full of it, that they scrupled
not for a moment to communicate, even to a
stranger, the subject of their grief, and all its
particulars. But indeed what need had they to
detail the events, by which they were overwhelmed
with such despondency? 'Though a stranger to
us, said they, " Art thou only a stranger in *Jerusalem*, and hast not known the things which
are come to pass there in these days?"' They
entered into a disclosure of their feelings respecting them. They were shocked and distressed by
the proceedings which had taken place respecting
Jesus of Nazareth. They confessed that they
were his disciples, his devoted followers. They
could not even now doubt that he was " *a prophet,*
mighty in deed and word before God and all the
people." And yet how could they still rationally
believe it? For " the chief priests and the rulers
had delivered him to be condemned to death, and
had crucified him." God, whose Messenger they
had conceived him to be, appeared to have disowned and abandoned him. Yet they had here-

tofore even ventured to hope "that it was he, *who should redeem Israel*," and fulfil the promises made of God to Israel by the prophets. Yet he, whose exaltation to a throne they had expected, had been executed as a malefactor, had died, had been buried! Their hopes were at an end! And yet had they not had reason to believe them just and reasonable? And even now the matter was pregnant with fresh and yet unexplained wonders. "Besides," added they, "this is the *third day* since these things were done." 'We remember certainly that he did speak something, which we never could comprehend till the event explained it, about being delivered up, and crucified. And he spoke also of *rising again on the third day*. That day has arrived, and, though we have certainly had no convincing proof that he has fulfilled a promise of such a nature, yet, strange to tell, some women and others have been to the sepulchre, but have found it empty! They have reported also that they had " seen a vision of angels, which said that he was alive. And certain of them that were with us also went to the sepulchre, and found it even so as the women had said; but him they saw not." What are we to think?'— Their companion was not slow to answer, and not incompetent to teach them what they ought to think; what indeed they would have thought before, had not their understanding of the Scriptures been imperfect, had they not been " slow of heart to believe all that the prophets had spoken." They expected one " to redeem Israel." They formerly believed that Jesus was anointed of God for that end ; nor were present circumstances at all inconsistent with that supposition. Had they attended to *all* that the prophets had spoken, they would have seen that " the Christ ought to have suffered those things, which they knew that Jesus had suffered, and to enter into his glory." " Beginning, therefore, at Moses and all the Prophets, he expounded to them in all the Scriptures the things concerning himself." For it was Jesus—whom they had confessed to be the Christ, but of the validity of whose pretensions they were now in doubt—who then addressed them. He shewed them, while he remained *unknown* to them, that their belief of the Messiahship of their Master *ought not to be destroyed by his sufferings and death;* and that they might justly expect *that he would rise from the dead.* Soon he removed their doubts on that subject also by *revealing* himself to them ; thus shewing that he who had died, *had already risen,* and that they had for some time seen and conversed with him. " He took bread, and blessed it, and brake, and gave to them. And their eyes were opened, and they knew him." They saw him administer to them that ordinance, which he had celebrated with them before his death, then explaining its design, and commanding them to continue it "in remembrance of him." But in the joyful moment of recognition, "he vanished out of their sight;" and left them to their own reflections on all that he had taught them from the Scriptures, in connection with the fact that he had risen from the grave, and was alive. They had even before been deeply interested in the conversation of this stranger; and therefore was it that they requested him to "abide with them" on their arrival at "the village whither they went." And, after his miraculous departure, recollecting, in the fulness of their conviction, every circumstance which contributed to communicate and confirm it, they observed to each other, " Did not our heart burn within us, while he talked with us by the way, and while he opened to us the Scriptures?" It was Jesus himself, still speaking " with *authority* and with *power*," as one " who had the words of eternal life."

This conference very fully discovers to us the views and feelings of the disciples at this juncture, when they had heard of the absence of the body of Jesus from the tomb, and that angels had declared that it was not in consequence of the *removal* of the body, but of the resurrection of Jesus from the dead. The same hesitation was manifested by the whole body, when the two

of the reality of his bodily presence, and of his identity, but, also invited their attention to the circumstances which proved it, with an express and pointed reference to those *secret* fears and surmises of their minds, which they had neither time nor inclination to state in words. By thus alluding to "the thoughts which arose in their hearts," and directly answering them, he in another way identified himself. For he thereby shewed that he was the same Jesus who had often, during his ministry, displayed his knowledge of the hearts of all men. Their feelings, therefore, must now have been the same, as when they exclaimed on a similar occasion, "Now are we sure that thou knowest all things, and needest not that any man should ask thee; by this we believe that thou camest forth from God[a]."

The same union of both these proofs is also observable, in the method by which, eight days afterwards, our Lord convinced Thomas, who on this occasion was absent. Jesus did not in the intermediate time continue his intercourse with the disciples; but he entered among them, on the eighth day, in the same miraculous manner as before. Introducing himself with the same benedictory salutation, he shewed that he was perfectly aware of the resolute perseverance of Thomas

---

[a] John xvi. 30.

in disbelieving the report of his brethren. For immediately he said to him, "Reach hither thy finger, and behold my hands; and reach hither thy hand, and thrust it into my side; and be not faithless, but believing." Unable any longer to resist a conviction of the truth, for which he had been prepared by the testimony of others, and of which he himself now had such perceptible and varied demonstration, he answered in faith and with joy, "My Lord and My God."

II. We have reviewed the circumstances, and the declarations of Jesus, which preceded the delivery of the words of our text. They were addressed to those, who by a series of clear and satisfactory proofs, had ascertained the certainty, not only of the death, but also of the resurrection of their Master. His body was not found in the sepulchre. The women who first discovered this, saw a vision of angels, who said that he was alive. The disciples ascertained the absence of the body; Peter and John found the sepulchre in such an orderly state, as indicated the probability that the body had not been surreptitiously removed. Peter saw Jesus. Mary Magdalene, and the other women also saw him. The two disciples going to Emmaus for some time conversed with him. He then appeared to the eleven, and proved to them that he was risen in the body, and in the *same* body in which he had died. This complete identity

E e

was also still further evinced by his celebration of his recently appointed ordinance, by the subject, and comprehensiveness, and impressiveness of his instructions, by his supernatural knowledge of the human heart, and by his miraculous disappearance and re-appearance. And, in the words of the text, spoken at his interview with the eleven, he takes occasion from the full demonstration given of his resurrection, and from the conviction which his disciples had attained of its reality, to re-establish and advance them in the knowledge and belief of his divine mission and Messiahship, as fully and decisively proved by this event. And he also announced to them the purposes which were now accomplished, the blessings which were from that time to be published to the world, and the means through which their publication was to commence, with sufficient evidence to convince mankind. We can do little more than call your attention to the several considerations which Jesus proposed to the disciples at this interesting crisis. But such a brief notice as we can take, will bring to a close our review of the evidences of Christianity, as stated and defended in the discourses of its founder.

The first argument upon which Jesus entered on this occasion was that derived from *his own prophecies;* and though some of them were wholly original; yet they were more generally an ap-

plication of the ancient prophecies to himself,
and to the events in which he would be the
principal agent or sufferer.   He cited and applied those predictions in such a manner, as to
shew that he was previously aware of the true interpretation of them; and described in literal terms
the events, which, at an earlier period, had been
described in figurative language.   He specified
many additional particulars, announced the speedy
fulfilment of them in his own person, and even
limited the precise day for their accomplishment.
His prophetic character was shewn not only by
the exact accomplishment of these numerous
predictions, but by the peculiar nature of those
unexpected incidents, which so rapidly fulfilled
his anticipations.   The *events* themselves had
now become familiar to the minds of his disciples.
The *predictions* had perplexed and distressed them
at the time of delivery ; the *fulfilment* was more
deeply and sensibly afflictive.   But from considering both in connection, from remembering
his words before the events occurred, and from
observing that none of those words had failed,
they might derive consolation and conviction.
We may well, therefore, conceive what entire satisfaction would possess their minds, when Jesus
directing them to these considerations, said unto
them, " *These are the words which I spake unto
you, while I was yet with you,* that all things must

be fulfilled which are written in the law of Moses, and in the prophets, and in the Psalms concerning me."—We have in a former Lecture considered the entire series of our Lord's predictions, and shewn how he stated beforehand the purpose for which he delivered them, in order that "when the things referred to, came to pass, they might remember that he told them of those things; and, thus remembering his words, might believe." And when "all things were brought to their remembrance, whatsoever he had said unto them," every previous fear that they might have been deceived in Jesus, was replaced by the most perfect confidence in him, and the most consolatory belief of his divine mission. Nor do I know any consideration more convincing to ourselves, than that Jesus distinctly foresaw, accurately described, and with the utmost composure and complacency looked forward to those painful transactions, which terminated his ministry, and produced consequences so astonishing, and so permanent.

It obviously appears from the resurrection of Jesus, that God did not disown him, though he did not deliver him from sufferings, and from death. Nay, those very sufferings were almost immediately followed by that event, which confirmed his words as a *prophet*, and established his authority as a *divine teacher*. But in order to the complete discovery

of his character, we must advance still further,
and once more advert to the consideration, that
the things, which had happened to him, were such
as had been described by the *Prophets*. Jesus
was therefore one, whose mission had long before
been designed in the counsels of God. But this
may also be said of Cyrus and of John the Baptist.
A comparison of the sufferings and resurrection of
Jesus, with the predictions respecting them, enables us to ascribe to *him* a more exalted character; no other than that of *the Messiah,* whose
coming had been foretold to the Jews, and who
was by them expected to come.

Jesus himself enlarged upon this subject to
his disciples after his resurrection, then entering
upon the more particular detail of those statements, which, as we have shewn in a preceding
Lecture, he frequently made before his death.
" These are the words which I spake unto you,
while I was yet with you, that *all things must be
fulfilled, which were written in the law of Moses,
and in the Prophets, and in the Psalms, concerning* Me." Even a very general and superficial
view will discover to us that the circumstances of
the birth of Jesus, the character and office of his
forerunner, and his own character, ministrations,
and miracles, were certainly conformable to prophetic description. If, then, his claim to be the
Messiah is established as far as these are con-

cerned, are his sufferings and death sufficient to refute his pretensions? They still more strongly confirm them. For these very things are as distinctly and variously specified " in the law of Moses, and in the Prophets, and in the Psalms," as any of the others [a]. And in order to shew this important truth to his disciples, and thus perfectly to instruct them unto the kingdom of God, Jesus advanced still farther than to announce the mere fulfilment of the prophecies in himself; for he applied the obvious fact to establish them in the belief of his *Messiahship*, and in the right knowledge of the *purposes* of his now finished commission. " Then opened he their understandings that they might understand the Scriptures; and said unto them, Thus it is written, and thus it behoved THE CHRIST to suffer, and to rise from the dead the third day, and that *repentance* and *remission of sins* should be preached in *his name* among *all nations*, beginning at Jerusalem."

He led them to see that one consistent and ever growing testimony to the character, and office, and proceedings of the Messiah, is observable in the prophetic writings; and that all their sublime, and varied, and seemingly contra-

---

[a] As the establishment of this position would occupy more room than the plan of these Lectures will allow, the Author must content himself with referring to Mede, Discourse 13. and to Dr. Hales's Chronology, Vol. II. Part II. p. 929.

dictory descriptions were fulfilled in those things which had happened to himself. They had seen reason, before his "delivery into the hands of wicked men," to acknowledge his Messiahship. But his death had wholly staggered them; for "as yet they knew not the Scripture, that he must rise from the dead." But that death which had overwhelmed them with despair, and that resurrection which they had so little expected, and of which they were with such difficulty convinced, were as necessary as any other particulars, to prove his Messiahship. For "thus it was written, and thus it behoved the Christ to *suffer*, and to *rise again* the third day." Since therefore such things were predicted of the Christ, and since they had been fulfilled in himself, he was by new and *decisive* evidence proved to have a just claim to that title.

He announced to them further, that "it behoved the Christ thus to suffer, and rise from the dead," not in order that he might be exalted to an earthly throne, but that "*repentance* and *remission of sins* might be preached *among all nations*." For thus also "it is *written*" of the Christ. The occasion and the terms of the original promise of the deliverer from evil—the succeeding promises and predictions of the patriarchal ages—the typical observances of the law —the prayers and promises, and predictions,

found in the writings of the later prophets—all
these asserted and explained the spiritual nature
of the blessings which it was his office to procure
and to bestow.—And although the Messiah was
to be born in Judea, and "the word of reconciliation" was to be ministered by Jews, and to
begin at Jerusalem, yet *all nations* have ever been
contemplated as having an interest in this design.
So had it been expressed in *all* the earlier prophecies; nothing had been stated to the contrary
in the later ones; and to all nations would this
grand scheme in due time be made known.

Although only the heads of that discourse, in
which our Lord unfolded and illustrated these
things, are recorded in the Gospels, yet in the
citations of prophecy, and allusions to it, by all
the Evangelists, and by the Apostles, in their
discourses recorded in the Acts, and in their
Epistolary writings, we are furnished with ample
aid for taking a survey of the whole prophetic
scheme, and for ascertaining the fulfilment of the
prophecies, and the accomplishment of the divine
promises, in the character, and office, and work
of Jesus. Enough, probably, is already familiar
to each of us to enable us not only to comprehend
the reasonings of our Saviour in the text, but also
to derive from thence a conviction of the truth of
the Gospel, and an illustration of its nature. And
Jesus having thus instructed his disciples, in the

purposes and previous design of these events, added, " And ye are witnesses of these things. And behold, I send the *promise of my Father* upon you; but tarry ye in the city of Jerusalem, until ye be endued with *power from on high.*" He had before his death given the promise of the Holy Spirit; he now predicted its speedy communication and the design and consequences of it. " John truly baptized with water; but ye shall be baptized with the Holy Ghost, *not many days hence.*" " Ye shall receive power, after that, *the Holy Ghost* is come upon you; and *ye shall be witnesses unto me* both in Jerusalem, and in Judea, and in Samaria, and unto the uttermost part of the earth[a]." As Jesus predicted, so it came to pass; and we have reason to cherish feelings of the most lively gratitude to God for those inspired writings which the Evangelists and Apostles have bequeathed to the world, and for the wisdom, and boldness, and success, with which they were enabled to discharge the ministry committed to them.

The commission which Jesus gave to his Apostles was suitable to the declarations which we have been considering. " Go ye into all the world," said he to them, " and preach the Gospel *to every creature.* He that believeth and is bap-

---

[a] Acts i. 5—8.

tized shall be saved; and he that believeth not
shall be damned[a]." This is an alarming sanction,
a fearful penalty. If these things be so,—if he,
who declared these things, had that dignity and
authority which has been so abundantly evidenced
to us, then a great responsibility rests upon us,
who have been made acquainted with the glad
tidings of salvation through him. We shall hereafter have to consider the danger, as well as the
causes of infidelity. Let us now ask, what does
the *Christian,* who fully comprehends the purport of the title which he bears, *profess to believe?*
—Our text will furnish us with an answer.

" *Thus it is written*—that the Christ should
suffer, and rise again the third day, and that
repentance and remission of sins should be preached in his name among all nations."—Promises of
such things, and predictions of their accomplishment in the fulness of time, had existed for ages
before the Christian era. And the fulfilment of
such previously existing intimations may convince
the Gentile, as well as the Jew, that the communications of God's mercy, and the interpo-
sitions of his providence, have not been made in
vain. Important purposes were thereby to be
answered, or these things would neither in such
a manner, nor even at all, have been foretold and
transacted.

---

[a] Mark xvi. 15, 16.

And not only "thus is it written," but "*thus it behoved* the Christ to *suffer.*" There was a moral necessity for it, the whole *extent* of which we can but imperfectly comprehend ; but the *nature* and *occasion* of which we know. The same God who "created man upright," when man fell from the security of innocence into the peril of guilt, gave to him the promise of restoration and deliverance. That general *intimation* of mercy, and the perfect and explicit *revelation* of it through the Christ, are the only ground of present consolation and future hope, amidst the depravity and sinfulness of our nature. Hence alone the assurance of pardon of sin, the means of sanctification, and the hope of future glory. The origin and prevalence of evil does indeed still perplex us ; but we may justly believe, that all will finally issue in the glory of God, and that, through the Gospel of Jesus Christ, there is " Glory to God in the highest, and on earth peace, good will towards men."—"God was in Christ *reconciling the world to himself ;*" and therefore, "it behoved the Christ to *suffer,*" "the *just* for the *unjust,* that he might bring us to God."—It was necessary that we should have sufficient grounds for faith and hope in him ; and therefore " it behoved the Christ to *rise from the dead.*"— It was necessary, in order that the world might be reformed and regenerated, that these facts and

their design should be *made known* to the sons of
men ;—and, therefore, it behoved that *repentance
and remission of sins* should be *preached among
all nations.*" We have still in our hands those
records, which shew us how the merciful design
was at first formed and promised, how it was
carried on, and how it was completed.

The facts and miracles, the types and prophecies, by which the divine intention respecting
" so great a salvation," is evinced, form the highest
possible moral demonstration. All is harmonious
and consistent; all tends to the great and important end, the salvation of man through a long predicted, divine, incarnate, and crucified Redeemer.
The demonstration is as complete in its kind to
prove the *mercy* of God to his sinful creatures,
as is that, by which, from the wonders and order
and arrangement of the material world, we deduce
the *existence* and *wisdom* and *power* of the Creator.
And so abundant is the evidence, and so satisfactory to all who will seriously consider it, that
it is as little needful that *Jesus* should now *repeat*
his miracles, and that all the other proofs both of
his divine mission, and of the success of it, should
again be exhibited, as that the world should be
created anew, to prove the being and attributes
of the Creator.

What then remains for us but to " believe
in the Lord Jesus Christ that we may be saved?"

His words and his works, his sufferings and his exaltation, are all recorded for our instruction, "written" with the pen of inspiration, "that we may believe that Jesus is *the Christ, the Son of God,* and that believing we may have *life* through his name." Therefore were we "baptized into Christ, that we might put on Christ," "baptized in the name of the Father, and of the Son, and of the Holy Ghost," the authors of our salvation. Therefore are we "taught to observe all things whatsoever Jesus hath commanded us." We also have the sure and encouraging promise, "Lo I am with you alway even unto the end of the world."

One other evidence of the truth of the Gospel, was noticed by our Lord, the *exhibition* of which depends upon *ourselves;* which, through the "special grace of God preventing and following us," we may be *enabled* to illustrate, and than which none will be more effectual for our own consolation, and for the conversion and establishment of others in "the truth as it is in Jesus." Our Lord himself prayed for us and for all men, after he had prayed for the Apostles, who were to be his witnesses to all men of "what they had seen and heard." "Neither pray I for these alone, but for them also which shall believe on me through their word, that they all may be one, as thou, Father, art in me, and I in thee, that they also may be one in us; *that the world may believe that thou hast sent me.* And the glory which thou gavest me I have given them; that they may be one even as we are one; I in them, and thou in me, that they may be made perfect in one; and *that the world may know that thou hast sent me,* and hast loved them as thou hast loved me.—And *I have declared unto them thy name,* and will declare it; that the love wherewith thou hast loved me, may be in them, and I in them[a]."

May therefore "God, the Father of our Lord Jesus Christ, our only Saviour, the prince of peace, give us grace seriously to lay to heart the great dangers we are in by unhappy divisions. May he take away all hatred and prejudice, and whatsoever else may hinder us from godly union and concord; that as there is but one body, and one Spirit, and one hope of our calling; one Lord, one faith, one baptism; one God, and Father of all; so we may henceforth be all of one heart, and of one soul, united in one holy bond of truth and peace, of faith and charity, and may with one mind and one mouth glorify God, through Jesus Christ our Lord[b]."

---

[a] John xvii. 20, &c.

[b] Collect in the Service for the Anniversary of the King's Accession.

HULSEAN LECTURES

FOR 1821.

—————

PART III.

LECTURES XVIII—XX.

—o—

OUR LORD'S NOTICE OF THE REJECTION OF HIS CLAIMS BY THE JEWS;
AND OF THE CAUSES, PROGRESS, AND CONSEQUENCES OF
INFIDELITY.

LECTURE XVIII.

St. John V. 40—46.

Ye will not come to me that ye might have life. I receive not honour from men. But I know you, that you have not the love of God in you. I am come in my Father's name, and ye receive me not ; if another shall come in his own name, him ye will receive. How can ye believe, which receive honour one of another, and seek not the honour that cometh from God only ? Do not think that I will accuse you to the Father : there is one that accuseth you, even Moses, in whom ye trust. For had ye believed Moses, ye would have believed me; for he wrote of me. But if ye believe not his writings, how shall ye believe my words?

WE have cited in our text the whole of the third and concluding division of that discourse of our Lord before the Jewish Sanhedrim, the former portions of which have occupied so much of our attention in the course of these Lectures. We have done this in order that we might at once announce the subject of this day's Lecture.

F F

You cannot, I conceive, have heard these words, without calling to mind the *infidelity of the Jews*. You must already have pictured to yourselves that sullen perverseness and watchful malignity, which exposed our Lord, during his public ministry, to contradiction, calumny, and persecution; that enmity, which continually became more fixed, determined, and extensive, till, through the machinations of the rulers, and with the consenting plaudits of the multitude, they finally rejected and crucified him. Carrying forward your recollections to the days, when the Apostles, "with great power, gave witness of the resurrection of the Lord Jesus," and wrought those " notable miracles[a]," which the rulers could not deny, yet by which they were not persuaded to embrace the Christian faith, you observe them rejecting and persecuting the servants, in like manner as they had before hated their Master. You behold every Jewish prejudice and jealousy rousing them to vehement and desperate opposition to the doctrine of Christ; amidst the excesses of which " deceivableness of unrighteousness," and partly through its instrumentality, their " faith became faction," their polity was subverted, and their name and place as a nation removed.

---

[a] Acts iv. 16.

But we must not even here terminate our survey of the fate and fortunes of this misguided, but remarkable people, as if then they ceased to exist, as if they could no longer be traced amidst the inhabitants of the earth. We may follow them from kingdom to kingdom, and from century to century, till we come to look upon the times in which we ourselves live, and traverse the cities and kingdoms through which our race is distributed. In these, the Pagan, the Mahometan, and the Christian, partake of the general characteristics of their several countries and manners. The conquerors and the conquered become assimilated to each other. All other distinctions change and cease, except those by which the Jew is known, amidst every revolution, and in every age, country, and nation; the same in his religious and civil peculiarities, in his person, and in his sufferings. It is not enough to say, that all this is unprecedented; it is a miracle, which has hitherto been lasting and universal, and which appears destined to continue for ages yet to come; for there is yet little appearance of its cessation. The Jew as yet retains his infidelity, and, therefore, his distinguishing characteristics. His ancestors rejected the lesson taught them by those miracles which were a counteraction and suspension of the laws of *nature,* and therefore the laws of *providence,* which mould and affect the destiny of all other

nations, are still, *since* the Christian era, as well
as *before* it, suspended with respect to them; that
they may be *a standing miracle*, obvious to the
view and apprehension of every people, and
nation, and language. And what does it testify,
but that truly they have been so separated, and so
governed, and so preserved, by a divine council
and design, for important and still progressive
purposes; for purposes which respect every nation
of the earth, since in all are they present, and to
all they may establish the same truths? They
hold in their hands the oracles of ancient revelation, delivered by Moses and the prophets, and
they account them divine. We also hold in our's
the writings of the Evangelists and Apostles, and
them also we account divine. The antiquity and
divinity of *both* is proved by *their unbelief* and
marvellous history, for these are an exact and
abiding fulfilment of what Moses and the prophets,
of what Jesus and his Apostles, have foretold.
Although they deny that Jesus is the Christ,
although they " would not come to him that they
might have life," yet by what they believe and by
what they disbelieve, by what they do and by
what they suffer, they condemn their own infidelity, and they justify our faith. This we believe
to be " eternal life, to know the only true God,
and Jesus Christ whom he has sent." The oracles
of God committed to the Jews, and which they

themselves received as the record and charter of eternal life, did " testify of Jesus." The same testified also of their infidelity, and of its punishment; and their prejudices, their peculiarities, and their fortunes, remain unaltered after the lapse of near two thousand years, and are, therefore, proved to be not transitory, but abiding. This is a fact, which at once bespeaks the interposition of God in the ages that are present, and evidences both his interposition and foreknowledge in the ages that are past, and the more remarkable consequences of which are reserved to be seen in ages yet to come.

Behold, then, the solitary individuals of that nation, who in almost every town offer themselves to your observation. Behold them congregated in your metropolis. Cross the sea, and see them in still greater numbers inhabiting the metropolis of Holland, and the cities of Poland. See them abiding alike under Christian, Mahometan, and Pagan dynasties in every quarter of the globe; sometimes restricted, persecuted, and oppressed, sometimes enjoying a portion of liberty and prosperity, but still unmixed and readily recognized. Ask yourself what, and of what original, is this strange tribe, whose fortunes and peculiarities form one solitary exception in the history of mankind. One people alone is found destitute of those affinities, by which men of like faculties, and opportunities, and pursuits, are ever amalgamated, and united in the same political and social relations? The drama, the fictitious narrative, and the historical annals of our own and other nations, shew the universal belief and experience, that such as they are, such have they long been. If we search the records of classical writers, and those which the sacred and ordinary writers of their own nation have handed down to us, we identify the same people, then subsisting as a nation, and then as remarkable in their theology, and character, and fortunes, as they have since been. The fact admits of no denial; the conclusions drawn from it are certain and satisfactory. The infidel cannot either refute, or weaken the argument. He rather directs his attention to one particular period of the Jewish history, and contends that their rejection of the Gospel is a valid objection to the claims of Jesus, and to the reality of the evidences in favour of Christianity. Now we contend that, in *some* respects, the case is completely the reverse of his representation, and that he cannot, in *any* respect, establish the validity of his inference.

We undoubtedly grant, that the infidelity of the Jews is an astonishing, and, in some respects, a mysterious fact. Of course the entire body of the Jews of the present day are characterized by a rejection of the Gospel. But we cannot say so of those who lived in the reign of Augustus, and who heard the instructions, beheld the miracles, and were witnesses of the crucifixion of Jesus. Great multitudes, in Jerusalem, and in Judea, and in the other countries in which they were dispersed, did embrace the Gospel, and no longer were ranked with their unbelieving fellow-countrymen, but with the Christians. The numerous and increasing society, which received that title first at Antioch importing their convictions that Jesus of Nazareth was the Christ, consisted, for many years, *only of believing Jews ;* who are, therefore, not incompetent, but admissible witnesses of the miraculous works of Jesus and his Apostles. The reality of these miracles was not indeed denied, even by those who remained in unbelief: We know that these unbelieving Jews did not admit that the *prophecies* were fulfilled in Jesus. But we must still bear in mind that a very large proportion of the nation thought otherwise ; and that more of those in power were not of that number, renders the argument which is supplied by the conviction of others, more satisfactory. For the circumstance, that those who had the disposition, had also the power to persecute the early Christians, is a very decisive demonstration of the assurance and sincerity of that belief, which impelled men to join the standard of the cross, when the warfare to which it engaged them was so hazardous, and even when the hottest fire of persecution was

directed against the company of the Apostles and
their followers. If we consider the inhabitants
even of this land, where Christianity is established,
and where it has an influence so extensive, I know
not whether we should find that the number of
converts in Jerusalem fell very far short of the
number of those who, among ourselves, give evidence of their Christian faith, by regularly attending on the worship and sacraments of the Christian
Church, and by a life which adorns the doctrine
of God their Saviour. Surely, then, there is no
view, which can rightly be taken of the infidelity
of the Jews, which can at all impair our conviction of the reality of the Christian miracles, of
the justness of the Christian interpretation of the
prophecies, and of the cogency of the various other
arguments, which persuade us, with " the full assurance of understanding, with the full assurance
of faith, and in the full assurance of hope," to
think that, " both in the Old and New Testament,
we have eternal life offered to us by Jesus Christ,
as the only Mediator between God and man," and
that " to him we must be willing to come that we
may have life."

But we may, and ought to proceed still further
in considering the infidelity of the Jews; we
must fix our attention more exclusively on those
who remained and persevered in unbelief. We
must investigate the causes, and motives, and

operations of this unbelief. This will in two respects be useful to us. It will shew that the Gospel was rejected from no just, defensible, or sufficient motive, and, therefore, that their infidelity need not hinder us from seeking the blessedness of those, " who have not seen, and yet have believed." It will also give to us an impressive and salutary caution, lest we fall after the same example of unbelief.

It must suffice merely to remind you of those erroneous interpretations, or rather of that partial selection of Scripture, which led them to reject a spiritual and suffering Messiah; to believe in the perpetuity and sufficiency of the Mosaic ritual; and to claim an interest in the promises made to Abraham in virtue of their lineal and natural descent from him, and also an unconditional and indefeisible right to the land of Canaan. It was not, however, until the scheme of the Gospel was fully unfolded, and found to be directly opposed to these favourite notions, which they had embraced so firmly, and which so many refused to abandon, that the Jews became " exceedingly jealous of the traditions of the Fathers," and mad against the Christians. Those principles had then their full operation ; and the topics just mentioned became the subjects of open controversy between those who embraced, and those who rejected the Gospel of Christ. Those topics had been slightly touched upon even by the Baptist. They were also occasionally adverted to by our Lord ; and in one or two instances became the subjects of his discourses, parables, and reasonings with the Jews. But, in general, as in the words of our text, we find our Lord unfolding the *moral causes of infidelity* ; causes which, of themselves, if unchecked and predominant, are sufficient to choke the good seed of Evangelical truth, and to render it unfruitful. And when to these moral impediments prejudices and errors were added, such as those just noticed, we may cease to wonder that the Jew remained incapable of conviction, and proof against every argument which might persuade him to embrace the Christian faith.

These moral obstacles, which are the substratum in which all other *accidental* ones inhere, and whence the latter derive their strength and permanency, are not, alas! confined to the Jew. They result from that "fault and corruption of the nature of every man that naturally is engendered of the offspring of Adam, whereby he is of his own nature inclined to evil," and "is not subject to the law of God, neither indeed can be." For so long as "the flesh thus lusteth against the spirit," it will produce, amongst its other deadly fruits, "heresies[a] ;" some, it may be, only slightly

---

[a] Gal. v. 20.

deviating from " the truth as it is in Jesus," but others also those " damnable and destructive ones, by which men even deny the Lord that bought them, and draw back unto perdition[b]." But let us remember the judgments which came upon that generation among whom our Lord preached; and let us also reflect that these things, as well as those that befel their fathers in the wilderness, " happened unto them for ensamples, and are written for our admonition, upon whom the ends of the world are come[c]." Let the judgments, then, with which the Lord visited his once favoured and peculiar people, excite us to " remember how we have received and heard, and to hold fast, and to repent, if peradventure our works have not been found perfect before God, lest our candlestick be removed out of its place[d]." Hereby also let us be individually warned to prepare for the terrors and justice of that day, when " the Son of man shall come in the glory of his Father, with his holy angels ;" when " all the nations shall be gathered before him ;" when " he will take vengeance on them that know not God, and that obey not the Gospel of our Lord Jesus Christ." We have been " grafted" into the body of his Church, and " partake of the root and fatness of the olive[e] :

---

[b] 2 Pet. ii. 1.　　　　　　　　[c] 1 Cor. x. 11.

[d] Rev. ii. 5; iii. 2, 3.　　　　　[e] Rom. xi. 17, &c.

the natural branches being broken off, that we might be grafted in." " Well ;" says the Apostle to each one of us, " because of unbelief they were broken off, and thou standest by faith. Be not high-minded, but fear. For if God spared not the natural branches, take heed lest he also spare not thee. Behold, therefore, the goodness and severity of God; on them which fell severity; but toward thee goodness, if thou continue in his goodness; otherwise thou also shalt be cut off. And they also, if they abide not in unbelief, shall be grafted in ; for God is able to graft them in again."—Here is, indeed, a salutary and awakening caution. And its concluding words forcibly remind us of that glorious season, which is rapidly advancing on the wheels of time, when, " the times of the Gentiles being fulfilled," the " blindness which hath in part happened unto Israel" shall cease.

Let us now more particularly direct our attention to the remaining words of our text, with which our Lord concluded his discourse before the Sanhedrim. In them he upbraided the Jews for their unbelief and hardness of heart ; and in such a manner as will also upbraid us, if we are not " holding fast the form of sounds which we have heard, in faith and love which is in Christ Jesus."

Did Jesus, as he passed on from laying before the Jews the evidences of his divine mission, declare that they " would, not come to him that they might have life?" Had he declared, in the former part of his discourses, that " whoso heareth his word, and believeth on him that sent him, hath everlasting life; and that all judicial authority was committed to the Son, that all men should honour the Son even as they honour the Father?" Was, then, the applause, respect, and adulation of man the object at which he aimed? This he explicitly renounced; this he ever refused.—"I receive not honour from men."—He *claimed* it not, as if he needed any such thing; nor as if that could accomplish his purposes, or increase his joy. He *sought* it not, except so far as it might lead to higher and more holy principles; he *demanded* it not, except upon the motive that " he, who honoureth not the Son, honoureth not the Father which had sent him." If it were not of this character, he rejected, exposed, and repressed it. And little did he find of the honour which was due to him, who left the bosom of the Father that he might be made in the likeness of men. He was " by men despised and rejected; they hid, as it were, their faces from him, and esteemed him not." " He came to his own, and his own received him not."

Do we inquire into the cause of their strange infatuation? We may learn it from the mouth of him, " who knew all men, and who needed not

that any should testify of man, because he knew
what was in man ;" who exhibited throughout his
ministry this intimate knowledge of the thoughts
of the heart, who thereby confounded his enemies,
and drew from Nathanael, and the woman of
Samaria, and his own disciples, an acknowledg-
ment of his divinity and prophetic character.
" *I know you*ᵃ," said he to the Jewish rulers,
" that ye have not the love of God in you." Do
we say, this is a hard saying? Yet can we not
discover evident proofs of it in their principles and
conduct? Though " to love the Lord their God
with all their heart, and soul, and strength," was
" the first and great commandment of their law,"
did they not, " while they made their boast of the
law, through breaking the law dishonour God?"
Did they not " make void his commandment
through their traditions ; and omit the weightier

ᵃ We took some notice, in one or two former Lectures, of this
instance of our Saviour's superhuman knowledge. It is often
expressly stated by the Evangelists, and in many other cases it
supplies a valuable illustration. See Newcome's Observations on
our Lord's Conduct. Chap. ii. Sect. 7, 8. Dr. Gerard observes,
that our Lord " scarce ever urged or appealed to it as an evidence."
(Dissertations, p. 165.) He certainly never noticed it *in the same
form* as he did the other arguments. But it appealed so *directly*
to the heart and conscience that it was not so necessary to do it.
But he did *expressly notice* it, and in a very *varied* manner. See
John i. 50. Matt. ix. 2, 4. Luke vii. 39—50 ; viii. 45—48;
ix. 47. John xiii. 10, 11 ; 18—27 ; xvi. 30, 31. Luke xxii. 61.
Mark xvi. 14. Luke xxiv. 38. John xx. 27.

matters of the law, judgment and mercy, and the love of God?" Did not a scrupulous and spiritless formality and a specious hypocrisy distinguish some, while profaneness and licentiousness characterized others? Undoubtedly so it was; and, therefore, we cease to wonder at those, who, in the face of a public miracle wrought on the sabbath, arraigned, and then would fain have stoned Jesus, because he called God his Father; and who scrupled to enter into the judgment-hall lest they should be defiled, at the very time when, by a foul conspiracy, they employed bribery and subornation to put Jesus to death, in order to satisfy their malignity.—But let us beware how we judge them, lest we condemn ourselves. For how imperfectly do we obey the word of Jesus, and believe in him that sent him! How little are we impressed with the majesty of God! How little do we seek his glory, dread his wrath, or seek his favour! Hereby do we prove that we are not Christians in deed and in truth, and that " the love of God is not in *us;*" and we are not Christians in deed and in truth, if " the love of God is not in us." For he loveth the Father, who loveth the only-begotten Son who hath declared him; whom, " though he has not seen him in the flesh, he loves, and in whom, though he sees him not, yet believing, he rejoices with joy unspeakable and full of glory." If we say that we love

God, where then are the effects of it ?   " He that
loveth not his brother whom he hath seen, how can
he love God whom he hath not seen?"   "This
is the love of God, that we keep his commandments."   " If any man love the world, the love of
the Father is not in him.   For all that is in the
world, the lust of the flesh, and the lust of the
eyes, and the pride of life, is not of the Father,
but of the world."   Now if it be an evident and
notorious truth, that there is much unchecked
disobedience, and little habitual obedience, even
in the Christian world ; does not this prove a pro-
portionate want of the love of God ?   If it be true,
that he who loveth another will desire to possess
a conformity of disposition, it follows that if we
are not " partakers of a *divine nature,* so as to
escape the pollutions that are in the world through
lust," we do not love God, and cannot be his
obedient children ; and, therefore, cannot *rightly*
value, esteem, and believe in him, whom God hath
sent to " call us with a *holy* calling."

But mark another symptom and operation of
unbelief.   " I am come *in my Father's name,* and
ye receive me not; if another shall come *in his
own name,* him ye will receive."—The history of
the Jews, both as it respects their rejection of
Jesus, and also their readiness to follow any
impostor, who, for his own purposes, deluded
them, affords a lamentable illustration of the just-

ness of this declaration. We find them despising, opposing, and calumniating him who called them to holiness, and gave to his followers the promise of eternal life. Yet he alone came with the witness of the law, of the prophets, of the Baptist; with the witness of his miraculous works, and of the Father himself. He alone " sought not his own glory." All his instructions and labours and sufferings tended to the glory of God, and to the benefit of mankind. In what dark and melancholy colours, therefore, does the infatuation of the Jews appear, when we behold that " deceivableness of unrighteousness," which led myriads to follow, and perish with every interested, ambitious, and deluded upstart; who succeeded so far, not because he could offer any evidence of his mission, but because he came in his own name, and encouraged those temporal hopes, to which that unhappy people have ever clung with such unparalleled pertinacity, even amidst the ruins of their city and temple, and in every country through which they have been dispersed.—But they have not been the only people thus deluded. Not Jews only, but Pagans, and even Christians, received and followed the Arabian impostor, treading in the path of lust, murder, and ambition, without a single argument but such as would appeal to men's interests or sensualities.—But here again let us also look at ourselves. Do we not live in times " when men will not

G G

endure sound doctrine?" Does not every novelty, whether in ceremony, manner, or doctrine, however unmeaning, and however dangerous, attract its thousands both from among those who have not been taught better things, and from among those who have? The Christian minister proclaims the truths of the Gospel, and the realities of eternity, to empty seats, to unwilling ears, to reluctant hearts; while the ravings of pretended prophets, the rhapsodies of a Swedenbourg, a Brothers, and a Southcott, and even the venal prognostications of the fortune-telling beggar, can awaken the fears, obtain the confidence, and call forth the self-denial of deluded thousands. Nay, do we not all, because our interest is concerned in it, receive "the witness of men" without suspicion, even after we have repeatedly been deceived, and although we know that they are so powerfully biassed by interest? Yet by how many is " the witness of God, which he hath given us of his Son," neglected and undervalued, if not actually rejected! ―These surely are facts, indicative of human folly, and humiliating to human pride! They show how liable the mass of mankind is to imbibe the most gross delusions, how much *all* are occupied by present interest and gratification, how calamitously they are beguiled even with respect to terrestrial and sensible objects, and how little they are disposed to rise to the contemplation of spiritual things, and to look forward to eternal realities.

But to proceed with our Lord's further remarks on the operation of such a frame of mind. " How *can* ye believe[a], which receive honour *one of another*, and seek not the honour *which cometh from God only ?*" Those there are, in every age, who never even frame a wish for divine appro-bation, or whose conduct, at least, is never in-fluenced by such a motive. Those of our Lord's contemporaries who were of such a description, would of course be negligent of his instructions, and little anxious to inquire into the nature of his claims. Nay, to such persons every system and modification of *religion* would be a subject of little interest, and would excite no attention, except so far as a compliance with custom might be necessary to preserve their reputation with others. But " the fear of man brought a snare " even upon some who were otherwise minded. It led some who *believed* in Jesus, "not to *confess* him, lest they should be put out of the syna-gogue ; because they loved the *praise of men* more than the praise of God." The observance of their own religious ordinances, and the dis-charge of the duties of morality, were in others rendered useless to their own hearts, and worthless in the sight of God, because they " did all their works *to be seen of men.*" " Verily, they had

---

[a] Ηῶς ΔΥΝΑΣΘΕ ὑμεῖς πιστεῦσαι, κ. τ. λ.

their reward," for the praise of men is easily obtained. But "they had no reward from their Father which is in heaven;" for they did not these things "as seeing him who is invisible, nor as having respect unto the recompense of the reward," which he will bestow. But he requires the service of the heart; and will "reward openly," because he has "seen in secret."—Has this fear of human censure, this love of human applause, ceased to affect the external conduct, and to influence the motives of mankind? Does it not still afford an inducement to "obey man rather than God," to suppress the convictions of conscience, to disobey the dictates of the understanding, to sacrifice integrity to interest, and to purchase the friendship of the world by sinful compliances with its irreligious maxims and unholy customs? Yet if our ears are attuned only to the praises uttered by human lips, if our feelings and our fears depend for their quietness upon the smiles and frowns of our fellow-men, we cannot look forward in faith and hope to the time, when "the Lord will make manifest the counsels of the hearts, and when every man shall have praise *of God.*" We can derive no comfort from that prospect, if we are doing "those things which, although highly esteemed among men, yet are abomination in the sight of God,"—if our "hearts are not right in his sight,"—if we "seek

not the honour which cometh from him only,"
by doing his will, and living to his glory. If
this be not our desire and endeavour, " we *cannot*
believe in him, nor in Jesus Christ whom he has
sent." We shall find religion an enemy to our
peace; and our every wish and feeling will have
a fatal tendency to make us shrink from the
consideration of our present duty, and of our final
accountableness. " We *cannot* serve both God
and Mammon." The service of two masters of
opposite interests, and therefore of *contrary commands,* is impracticable. The duties and events
of every day will call upon us to make our choice
between them. We must give a preference to
the one or to the other. Our habitual conduct in
consequence of that preference, will determine
whether we " seek for the honour that cometh
from God only," or whether we are pursuing such
a course, as will one day bring us to that sense of
woful desertion, and to that feeling of unavailing
regret, which once prompted the well known
words, " If I had served my God, as faithfully
as I have served my King, he would not have
forsaken me at my latter end."

" Do not think," said our Lord in conclusion,
" that I will accuse you to the Father: there is
one that accuseth you, even Moses, in whom ye
trust. For *had ye believed Moses,* ye would have
believed me ; for he wrote of me. But if ye

believe not *his writings,* how shall ye believe *my words?*" That an actual disbelief both of Moses and of the Prophets prevailed very extensively among the Jews in our Lord's time, we have the express testimony of Josephus; and it is obviously assigned by our Lord as one leading cause of their rejection of himself. If they had had a firm belief in Moses, and a thorough acquaintance with his predictions and institutions, and with his account of those of the earlier ages, they would have allowed, upon his authority, that they might expect the Messiah to be a Prophet like their original legislator, a spiritual Deliverer from moral evil, "a blessing to all nations." His writings they had it in their power to study, and to compare with later revelations. If they disbelieved them, or if their prejudices and interested views were stronger than their convictions, or if they were ignorant of them,—from whatever cause they *believed not* what Moses taught, it was not likely, that they would receive the doctrine of Jesus; for " Moses wrote of him." It is asserted that a similar infidelity is far from uncommon among the Jews *of this day.* It would of course be of little avail to attempt to convince any such, that Jesus was the Messiah. We must consider them as consenting with *all other Deists* in a denial not only of the fact of Revelation, but also of its importance, and necessity, and probability.

All who profess *Christianity*, thereby imply a confession of the divine authority both of the Old and New Testaments. Why, then, is the efficacy of Christianity so incomplete? Why, but because all the causes and motives which we have already considered do in fact *weaken*, if they do not destroy, the belief of its certain and authoritative truth? If it is really believed, why not also valued, and obeyed? A *firm* conviction of those things, which, if true, involve such an awful responsibility, and lead to such momentous consequences, would at least excite our desires, and arouse us to diligent endeavours. If we really are not disposed to *deny* the truth of the Scriptures, our obedience may be imperfect, and our impression of their importance insufficient and inefficacious, because our *attention* to them has probably been too slight. Yet will not the religion which we profess, and the Scriptures which we believe, convict us of criminality in this unhappy negligence?—If, again, we repose our hopes of salvation on merely outward conformity to the ceremonial of Christianity, or if we hope that our obedience to some commands will compensate for our neglect of others, will not the Scriptures, which command and require *all these*, in this case also condemn us? If we think that the dictates of unassisted reason are sufficient, and if therefore we are not careful to appeal " to the law and to the testimony," will not our own consciences tell us that our imperfect obedience requires that more perfect rule, and that better righteousness, which the Scriptures teach us? And if we place our trust in the *general* belief of the mercy of God, will not the Scriptures again condemn us, because God has not promised mercy except to those, who have " repentance towards him, and faith in our Lord Jesus Christ? If we trust in uncertain riches, and in the sufficiency of our own skill and diligence, will not our own experience of the vanity and uncertainty of all earthly things, and the testimony of the Scripture to the certainty and importance of the things unseen, again condemn us?—Jesus as yet condemns us not. He now is preached to us as a *Saviour*. There is "an appointed day," in which he will be our *Judge*. He needs not to accuse the sons of men. Moses and the prophets will accuse *the Jews*. Their word, and that which Jesus spoke, and the writings of his Apostles, will accuse *us*. " The same will judge us at the last day." And it will then appear, however it may seem to us now, that in whatsoever way we have " departed from the living God," we have evidenced the existence, and been subject to the influence of " an evil heart of unbelief." To all who are in such a state " the Gospel is hid." Its promises do not invite, and its terrors do not impress them. They feel not their need of pardon, and righteousness, and salvation; and the Gospel, therefore, is not to them "the power of God unto salvation," because it is so only "*to him that believeth.*"

"Examine yourselves, therefore, whether ye be in the faith." For if this Gospel was "first spoken to us by the Lord, and confirmed to us by them that heard him, how shall we escape if we neglect so great salvation?" If we abide in unbelief, in error, or in unholiness, we shall have no sufficient plea to be *excused*, but shall be counted *unworthy* to be partakers of that "eternal glory to which we are called by Christ Jesus." Are ye then *meet* for that inheritance? Seriously, I beseech you, consider that question.—Ere another sabbath arrives, most of you, that are present here this day, will have separated from each other for a considerable season[a]. If the last week has announced to us the removal from life of *two of the younger members* of our body, what may be the events of so long a period? *I* may not be permitted to conclude my appointed labours; some of *you* may never return to resume your's. But, even if this should not be the case, are we prepared to meet the trials which may come upon

---

[a] This Lecture was delivered June 3, 1821, two days after the division of the Easter term, and it *completed* the Spring course.

us, should we be continued in life? How are we
fitted to endure the reverses of fortune, the removal of our dearest relatives, and the lengthened
days of sickness? Are we armed with patience?
Are we prepared to receive such visitations " to
our profit, that we may be partakers of God's
holiness?" But religion is requisite not only to support and instruct us in the hour of adversity, but
to keep us from falling in the still more slippery
path of prosperity, to direct us in every duty, to
preserve us in every temptation. It is 'our light
in darkness, and our life in death.' Therefore,
" beloved, building up yourselves on your most
holy faith, praying in the Holy Ghost, keep yourselves in the love of God, looking for the mercy
of our Lord Jesus Christ unto eternal life[a]."

---

[a] Jude 20, 21.

LECTURE XIX.

———◆———

THE INFIDELITY OF THE JEWS IN ITS MORE *ADVANCED* STAGE NOTICED BY OUR LORD WITH ALLUSION TO A PASSAGE OF ISAIAH.——THE OCCASION AND PURPORT OF HIS REMARKS; AND A SIMILAR AP-PLICATION OF THE SAME PASSAGE BY THE EVANGELIST ST. JOHN.——OTHER CAUTIONS AND DIRECTIONS GIVEN BY OUR LORD RESPECTING THE *TEMPER* AND *METHOD* PROPER FOR RELIGIOUS INQUIRY.

———◆———

St. Matt. XIII. 14—16.

And in them is fulfilled the prophecy of Esaias, which saith, By hearing ye shall hear, and shall not under-stand; and seeing ye shall see, and shall not perceive. —For this people's heart is waxed gross, and their ears are dull of hearing, and their eyes they have closed; lest at any time they should see with their eyes, and hear with their ears, and should understand with their heart, and should be converted, and I should heal them.

To bestow on mankind a remedy for the diseases of the soul, and to heal the wounds which sin had inflicted, was the office and merciful purpose of him whose words we have cited. But the 'com-fortable words' in which he offered these benefits, gave the assurance of them only to such as 'truly turned to him;' to those who were converted from the error of their ways, who recognized both their own need of healing, and his power to heal ; who "came unto God by him," who "loved him, and kept his saying." None but persons of such a character could rightly esteem, and desire his interposition on their behalf, or even be fitted to participate in its benefits.

Those who are described in the words of our text, were as yet far from having attained to such a state of mind. They had yet to perceive his divine character, and the commission with which he was charged. They had yet to understand the spiritual nature of Messiah's kingdom, and to discern "the signs of the times" which indicated its approach. They had to purge their hearts from the grossness of their unscriptural opinions and carnal expectations ; to lend a willing ear to statements which combated their favorite prejudices, and which demanded of them conduct and sacrifices little congenial to their wishes. They had to open the eyes, which had hitherto regarded only sensible and temporal good, to contemplate the blessedness and glory of that heavenly kingdom which should dignify them with spiritual and eternal privileges. They had to retrace the steps by which they were now fast advancing towards a determination not to believe, and towards a voluntary insensibility to the force of the most decisive evidence.—When Jesus had noticed the symptoms and fatal operation and increasing influence of unbelief, he passed on to congratulate and encourage the faithful few, who were afterwards to be his witnesses throughout the world, and who, though yet deficient in knowledge, discovered a readiness and desire to obtain an increase of it. "But blessed," said he, "are your eyes, for they see; and your ears, for they hear. For verily I say unto you, That many prophets and righteous men have desired to see those things which ye see, and have not seen them; and to hear those things which ye hear, and have not heard them."

We also, through the labours and writings of these disciples of Jesus, have been made acquainted with those "mysteries of the kingdom of heaven," which were unfolded to them. Yet although these heavenly truths were in old time the subjects of promise and of prophecy, and the objects of earnest expectation to those who had not as yet seen their accomplishment; and although they have exercised the faith and joy and gratitude of thousands, who, since their full revelation, have derived from them consolation, and hope and victory; yet comparatively few, even now, are they, who see and hear and understand them, so as to seek and embrace them, and to hold them fast. Many are they who reject and despise them, and who even endeavour to beguile others of their consolations in time, and of their hopes for eternity, by the revival of objections long since refuted, and often wholly groundless. Many are they also, whose instability, self-indulgence, and depravity make them rejoice in any pretext, by which they may entrench themselves in the short-lived and perilous security of unbelief.—Yet is truth ever the same; and, like its divine Author, hath "no variableness, neither shadow of turning." The hope set before us, the grounds of that hope, and the character of those, to whom alone it belongs, change not. Nay, even error and infidelity, though diversified in form, and modified by circumstances, are in all ages substantially the same as to their sources, and motives, and operations.

We observed in the commencement of our Lectures, that our Lord's discourses very frequently touch upon this important head. He seldom either states to us his pretensions and doctrine, or enlarges upon the evidence of them, without in some way appealing to the conscience, and laying open the depravity and waywardness of the human heart. Almost every passage which has been made the subject of our meditation has furnished some appropriate topic of practical appeal; and our last Lecture was wholly occupied in the consideration of the infidelity of the Jews, and of those moral causes, to which our Lord ascribed its origin in the close of his discourse before the

Sanhedrim. In our two remaining Lectures we purpose to take some further notice of several detached passages on the same subject. In this, such will be noticed as speak of infidelity in a more advanced stage, and those also which may caution us against its approaches, and apprize us of that temper and method, which must be pursued by the impartial and successful inquirer. In our next we shall have to consider infidelity in its last, confirmed, and irremediable stage, and those sanctions and declarations, by which our Lord required us to "believe the Gospel."

The occasion of the words of our text was, the inquiry of the disciples why Jesus adopted the use of Parables. The propriety and meaning of his answer will readily be discovered, if it be remembered, that he spoke to the people without parables, until the time that his miracles were attributed to the co-operation of Beelzebub, and "a sign from heaven" was demanded by those, whom all his former miracles had failed to convince, and yet whose cavils against them had been unanswerably refuted [a]. This obduracy continued to characterize a large proportion of our Lord's hearers, more especially a majority of those in power. Yet had he many truths yet to declare to them, some of which were even still more

---

[a] See Matt. xii. and xiii.

likely to excite their prejudice and opposition; and therefore, because of their unbelief, he veiled them under the figurative language of parables. Frequently they were able to perceive the general design of what he delivered in this manner, and were on such occasions offended and exasperated. Not that such truths were designed to be concealed from them *for ever*. They were only *partially* concealed even for a time. But this method of delivery was sufficient to prove *that Jesus had himself stated* all these unwelcome truths; and not only did he explain all things to his disciples in private, but informed them that they were designed for universal publication, after the objection occasioned by his humble appearance was removed, and the evidence of his character and authority was completed by his entering into glory[a]. Our Lord expressly assigns these reasons for his adoption of the parabolic mode of instruction. The more teachable character of his disciples enabled him to proceed in imparting to them fuller instructions; and the office, which they were afterwards to sustain when the full publication of the Gospel should commence, rendered it necessary thus to inform and discipline them. But in consequence of the non-improvement and rejection

---

[a] See Matt. xiii. 36, 51, 52.   Mark iv. 10—25, 33, 34. Matt. x. 25—27.   Luke viii. 10—18.

of what he had before taught, it was both just and necessary to refrain from communicating to others the same knowledge. It could *as yet* serve no good end, though he "spake to them the word in parables, as they were able to bear it." "It is given unto you," said he to his disciples, "to know *the mysteries* of the kingdom of heaven; but to them it is not given. For whosoever hath, to him shall be given, and he shall have more abundance; but whosoever hath not, from him shall be taken away even that he hath. Therefore speak I to them in parables; because they seeing see not, and hearing they hear not, neither do they understand. And in them is fulfilled the prophecy of Esaias, which saith, By hearing ye shall hear, and shall not understand; and seeing ye shall see, and not perceive. For this people's heart is waxed gross, and their ears are dull of hearing, and their eyes have they closed; lest at any time they should see with their eyes, and hear with their ears, and understand with their heart, and should be converted, and I should heal them."

In the text our Lord distinctly asserts that unbelief was generally prevalent among those, to whom he ministered the words of eternal life; and he so describes it, in the prophetic language of Isaiah, as to shew that he knew that it had already assumed a decided and confirmed cha-

H H

racter. He had previously declared, before the
council, that he was aware that "they were not
willing to come to him that they might have life;"
and he then endeavoured to awaken them to
serious reflection by referring them to several
sinister and unholy principles which were likely to
entangle them in the fetters of unbelief. The fact
was soon found to be such as he had intimated.
The longer he laboured among them, the more
were prejudice, and calumny, and opposition
excited. "Because he told them the truth, they
would not believe him." They closed their ears
against the reception of truths so unwelcome, and,
as they thought, so needless. Hearing with the
outward ear, they understood not with the heart;
like their fathers of old to whom the prophets had
been sent. Every faculty of the soul was armed
and fortified against the supposition that such a
teacher could be their Messiah, or that they had
need of any change in religion, or indeed of any
blessing which the Messiah could bestow, except
deliverance from national subjection, and the
possession of national glory. Seeing therefore
with their eyes the miracles of Jesus, they perceived not the finger of God therein revealing
itself, and, as it were, pointing out Jesus as that
"his beloved servant, on whom he had put his
Spirit." Not that they could disprove, or that
they ever attempted to deny the reality of the

miracles. But they were not disposed to admit their *evidence*, because they had no inclination to admit the *pretensions of him who wrought them*. They could behold the exhibition of the most signal miracles, without any other emotion than a feeling of jealousy and indignation. Some, in consequence of having been eye-witnesses of the raising of Lazarus, immediately went to inform the Pharisees; and they, *avowedly* on the very ground of the reality and notoriety of these "many miracles," coolly deliberated on the safest and surest method of putting him who wrought them to death. Yet, at the same time, they " built the sepulchres of the prophets, and boasted how, if they had lived in the days of their fathers, they would not have been sharers in their blood-guiltiness."—The pure, perspicuous, and heart-searching discourses of Jesus seemed to have as little permanent influence as his miracles. Many even listened with no other feeling or design, than " that they might entangle him in his talk, and have somewhat of which to accuse him." So that *fact* fully justified *the assertion* of Jesus respecting them, in allusion to the words of Isaiah. "Their heart had waxed gross, and their ears were dull of hearing, and their eyes had they closed, in such a manner as if they had determined to secure themselves against any probability that at any time they should see with their eyes, and hear with their ears, and understand with their heart, and be converted, and he should heal them[a]."

Our Lord applies the words of the prophet more especially to their rejection of his *doctrine*. But still, as we have just observed, that rejection had then recently been shewn to be decided and irrecoverable, because the doctrine was rejected *in defiance of those miracles,* by which he established its divine authority, and because they had even ventured to propagate the most malignant *cavils* both against *Jesus* and *his miracles.* But it is worthy of remark, that St. John cites the same, and also another passage of Isaiah, with more immediate reference to the *miracles* of Jesus, after he closed his own narrative of them. He had recorded the caution of Jesus to the people to " walk while they had the light, lest darkness should come upon them." " But," adds the Evangelist, " though he had done so many miracles before them, yet they believed not on him. That the saying of Esaias the prophet might be fulfilled, which he spake, Lord, who hath believed our report, and to whom hath the arm of the Lord been revealed? Therefore they could not believe, because that Esaias said again, He hath blinded their eyes, and hardened their heart, that they should not see with their eyes, nor understand

---

[a] Isai. vi. 9, 10.—Compare Ezek. xii. 2.

with their heart, and be converted, and I should
heal them[b]." To this state of mind the Evangelist
attributes an *incapacity* for believing the report of
the prophets respecting him, " who, when he was
seen, was without form or comeliness, and had no
beauty that men should desire him ; and whom,
therefore, they despised and rejected, and esteemed
not." By all who were affected in this manner
" the arm of the LORD," which upheld, and co-
operated with Jesus, was not discovered ; and
therefore he who was " sent of the Father, and
sealed and sanctified by him," was esteemed
" stricken, smitten of God, and afflicted." No
other than such delusion, and obduracy, could be
the consequence of the state of mind which is
described by the prophet, and which is brought
before our notice, both by our Lord and his
Apostles[c].

But St. John seems to cite the words as if it
were *God* who had thus " blinded their eyes, and
hardened their heart." And St. Mark and St.
Luke also report our Lord's citation of the passage,
as if Jesus adopted the use of parables in order to
give occasion to this blindness and unbelief[d].—We
have already remarked that it is, in a sense, true
that Jesus employed parables to *conceal* some

---

[b] John xii. 37, &c.   [c] See also Acts xxviii. 26. Rom. xi. 8.
[d] Mark iv. 11—13. Luke viii. 10.

obnoxious truths for a time. But it is also equally clear, that St. Matthew teaches us that this very *blindness and unbelief* was itself the *occasion* of his first use of the parabolic method. But if we consult the passage as it stands in the prophet himself, we find that Jesus, in the *latter words* of our text, has rather *interpreted* than cited the *latter part of the prophecy.* For the prophecy itself has the form of expression which is found in the other three Evangelists. " Go and tell this people, Hear ye indeed, but understand not, and see ye indeed, but perceive not. *Make* the heart of this people fat, and *make* their ears heavy, and shut their eyes; lest they see with their eyes, and hear with their ears, and understand with their heart, and convert, and be healed." But it does follow even from hence, that this " shutting up in unbelief" is wholly, and *in the first instance* to be ascribed to divine influence on the mind. This is a phraseology adopted in many other places of the prophetic writings ; and it is designed only to express the lamentable *certainty* with which the event is foretold. And we will illustrate this pecu- liarity of the prophetic style by one citation from the prophet Jeremiah. " The Lord said unto me, Behold, I have put my words in thy mouth. See, I have this day set thee over the nations and over the kingdoms, to *root out, and to pull down, and to destroy, and to throw down, and to build, and to plant."* This passage evidently speaks only of the commission given to the prophet to announce the certainty with which those things could come to pass, of which he is figuratively said to be the instrument. No other interpretation could for a moment be entertained. Upon the very same principle should we interpret the passage under consideration. It predicts the existence, and prevalence, and fatal strength of unbelief among those, who heard the words of God, and had the arm of the Lord revealed before them. But it ascribes not the effect *to God* as the cause. The cause was in themselves, and resulted from the depravity of the human heart. It is not the God of heaven, but " *the god of this world* that blinds the minds of them that believe not[a]." " No man can say when he is tempted, I am tempted of God; for he is but drawn away, and enticed of his own lust[b]." The Spirit of God *strives* with man, to convince, recover, and reform him. But we must add, with all faithfulness and admonition, that he does not *always* strive with man; that he *may* be grieved and resisted, and that his holy influence *may* be quenched. Then, indeed, do we allow that man is given over to *a judicial blindness;* that they, " who like not to *retain God in their knowledge*[c], who believe not the

---

[a] 2 Cor. iv. 3, 4.   [b] James i. 13—17.   [c] Rom. i. 28.

truth, and have *pleasure in unrighteousness,* are at length given over to a reprobate mind." Because they " received not the love of the truth, that they might be saved, God sends upon them strong delusion, that they should believe a lie[a]." And therefore are we called upon to " suffer the word of exhortation" respecting this matter. There-fore are we bound to " teach every man, and to warn every man." Therefore do we beseech every one to inquire respecting himself, whether he has, with the heart, and with a true and lively faith, believed in Jesus Christ ; or whether there be any unsatisfied doubt, any secret reserve, any unmorti-fied lust still abiding within him. For ought he knows, such disorders of the soul, if they receive not a timely check, may generate in the end a deadly and incurable malady. The understanding may be blinded, the will become alienated from the life of God, and the conscience be rendered insensible to every warning and visitation. He who is not recovered from such a state, " will wax worse and worse, deceiving and being deceived," and " not having the spirit of Christ, and therefore being none of his," may finally " make shipwreck of faith, and of a good conscience ;" and " not understand, nor be converted, nor be healed."

" But, beloved, we are persuaded better things

---

[a] 2 Thess. ii. 10—12.

of you, and things that accompany salvation, though we thus speak." Yet our Lord himself exhorted his disciples to " watch and pray, lest they should enter into temptation ;" and assigned for the precept a reason, which our own experience very abundantly confirms, that even when " the spirit of man is willing, the flesh may be weak[b]." Let us not, therefore, shrink from the most minute and awakening view of the dangers which beset us ; that thus we may be excited to seek the peace, and rest, and joy, which Jesus promised and bequeathed to his disciples. If we have already followed him, let us not, " having put our hand to the plough, look back," and thus " unfit ourselves for the kingdom of God[c]." But rather let us " sit down, and count the cost, and consider whether, having begun to build, we shall be able to finish." Let us ascertain our strength for this long and arduous warfare, and see " whether we be able, with ten thousand, to meet him that cometh against us with twenty thousand[d]." If " in the world we have tribulation," let us be cheered by the recollection that " our Master hath overcome the world[e]." And when, " because iniquity abounds, the love of many waxes cold," and when others, who " have endured for a season,

---

[b] Matt. xxvi. 41.   [c] Luke ix. 62.
[d] Luke xiv. 28—30, 31.   [e] John xvi. 33.

in time of temptation fall away[a]," let us remember the words which Jesus repeated on more than one occasion, " He that endureth to the end, the same shall be saved[b]."

We have not alluded to difficulties and temptations which have no existence, or of which Jesus did not forewarn mankind, when stating to them the nature and design of his Religion. There are " fightings without, and fears within." There are trials to be endured, and sacrifices to be made, if need and occasion be, which deter the unbeliever, and try the stedfastness of the believer. It was not without reason that Simeon declared of the holy child Jesus, " Behold this Child is set for the fall and rising again of many in Israel, and for a sign that shall be spoken against, that the thoughts of many hearts may be revealed[c]." It was a declaration which Jesus, himself afterwards confirmed. Both by various general statements, and in his instructions to his disciples, and also in his answers to several who professed a readiness to follow him, he has sufficiently made it known that " if any man come after him, he must deny himself, and take up his cross daily, and follow him[d]." He prepared his Apostles and early followers to expect " scourg-

---

[a] Matt. xxiv. 12.   Mark iv. 17.   Luke viii. 13.

[b] Matt. x. 22; xxiv. 13.   [c] Luke ii. 34, 35.   [d] Luke ix. 23.

ings, and persecutions, and death, and to be hated
of all men, and of all nations, for his name's sake,"
even by all that numerous class in all ages, who
" have not known the Father nor him[e]." He
distinctly told them that though " in him they
should have peace" of mind, yet " he came not
to send external peace on earth, but a sword;" and
that " a man's foes would be those of his own
household[f]." — Yet he made no allowance for
apostacy even in this extreme case: he appealed
to them for the reasonableness of what he spoke,
by the question, " What would a man be profited,
if he should gain the whole world, and lose his
own soul?" For what earthly thing is so precious,
as to be " given in exchange for the soul[g]?"
He therefore distinctly stated the absolute necessity of stedfastness, the danger of swerving
from it, and the reward and true policy of main-
taining it. " He that loveth father or mother
more than me, is not worthy of me; and he that
loveth son or daughter more than me, is not
worthy of me. And he that taketh not his cross,
and followeth after me, is not worthy of me.
He that findeth his life shall lose it, and he that
loseth his life for my sake shall find it[h]." " He

---

[e] Matt. x. 17, 22; xxiv. 9. John xv. 20; xvi. 3.
[f] John xvi. 33. Matt. x. 34—36. [g] Matt. xvi. 26.
[h] Matt. x. 37—39.

that is ashamed of me, and of my words,—he that shall deny me before men,—of him will I be ashamed, and him will I deny before the angels of God[a]. Those that confess me before men, I will confess before the angels of God." He promises to those, that forsake all for his sake, that "they shall receive manifold more in this present time; *with persecutions,* and in the world to come life everlasting[b]." Now it is clear, from the very *nature* of the case, that all this is neither unreasonable nor unnecessary; and although we of this age and country are not called to endure such persecutions, in testimony either of our fidelity to the *Gospel itself,* or to its *essential doctrines,* yet we know not how soon it may come upon us. A generation has scarcely passed away since such a trial came upon all the professing Christians of a neighbouring nation. Though we are not likely to experience the persecuting intolerance of *Paganism,* nor the effects of the " exceeding madness " of a *Jew's* malignity against the Gospel, nor, we trust, the restoration to power of the *most intolerant* professors of the *Christian* faith, who once lighted up the fires of persecution in the cities and Universities of England, and perpetrated the most unheard of massacres;—yet have we not found

---

[a] Mark viii. 38; Matt. x. 32, 33.   [b] Mark x. 28—30.

that Deism itself, which so proudly boasts of its philanthropy, and disclaims all bigotry and into-lerance, can surpass all other systems in the " cruelty of its tender mercies," and in the dead-liness of its hatred to Christianity? The intimations of those things "that are to come hereafter," recorded in the Scriptures of truth, do not permit us to hope that such scenes will never again be exhibited on this earth. Have we, then, that *firm conviction* of the truth of the Gospel, and of the value and certainty of its promises, and that *devotedness* also to the cause of God and of truth, which would enable us to retain our in-tegrity in such a fiery trial? Those who are not *ready* to make such sacrifices, and to practise such self-denial, if any circumstances should arise to require them, cannot be the disciples of Jesus. Yet how many are even unable to endure the contemptuous *look* and the slanderous *word!* How many are *more than ashamed* of Christianity, and even are *proud* of their disregard both of its threats and promises! This fear of man, this unhappy vanity, this love of self and of this world, are fertile sources of infidelity and inconsistency.

Our Lord has also cautioned us against the unhappy influence of *worldly wealth.* " How hardly shall they that have riches—they that trust in riches—enter into the kingdom of God[c]!" We

---

[c] Mark x. 23, 24.

know too well how readily our hearts become attached to the " good things of this life,"—how soon they are " overcharged with the cares of this life,"—how rapidly covetousness is generated, and how firmly it seats itself in the soul,—not to understand how soon " the word of God becometh unfruitful, when choked by the cares of the world, and the deceitfulness of riches[a]."—" Take heed then, and beware of covetousness[b];" and seek first the kingdom of God, and his righteousness[c];" like the merchant in the parable, " even selling all that ye have, to purchase the pearl of great price[d]."

But not only must the love of riches be abandoned, and " poverty of spirit " be cultivated, but *purity of heart* must also be maintained. The love of sin naturally disposes us to " love darkness rather than light, because our deeds are evil[e]." Yet the sin that most easily besets us, though as dear, and seemingly as necessary to our comfort, as " a right hand, or a right eye," must be " cut off and cast from us, that we may enter into life[f]." We must bring into our Christian life, not only the hatred of sin, but also the love of holiness, and a readiness to practise it, if we are rightly to

---

[a] Luke xvi. 25 ; xxi. 34.   Matt. xiii. 22.
[b] Luke xii. 15.   [c] Matt. vi. 33.   [d] Matt. xiii. 46.
[e] John iii. 19.   [f] Matt. xviii. 8, 9.

apprehend either the divinity and excellency of our religion, or to make progress therein, or not to dislike and shrink from it. "If any man be willing to do his will, he shall know of the doctrine whether it be of God, or whether I speak of myself[g]."—And we must make continual advances in every good and holy purpose, improving the graces to which we have already attained, and desiring and seeking after an increase of them. For " whosoever hath, to him shall be given, and he shall have more abundantly ; but whosoever hath not, from him shall be taken away even that he hath[h]." After we have " done all," we are but " unprofitable servants;" but he, who is "an unprofitable servant" because he hath not employed the talent committed to him, " will be cast into outer darkness."—And that the necessity of walking in all purity of heart and life may be more deeply impressed upon our minds, let us hear other declarations of our Lord. " That servant, which knew his Lord's will, and prepared not himself, neither did according to his will, shall be beaten with many stripes. But he that knew not, and did commit things worthy of stripes, shall be beaten with few stripes. For unto whomsoever much is given, of him shall be much required ; and to whom men have committed much, of him

---

[g] John vii. 17.   [h] Matt. xiii. 12.

they will ask the more[a]." "In that day," said our Master and our future Judge, "I will profess unto them, that have not done the will of my Father which is in heaven, *I never knew you, depart from me, all ye that work iniquity*[b]."

Coming to the study of the truth as it is in Jesus, with purity of heart and purposes of obedience, we must also come with *docility* and in *humility*. "For except we be converted and be as little children," and receive the kingdom of God as meek, teachable, guiltless infants, "we shall not enter therein[c]." We shall never either rightly apprehend its nature, or be impressed by its promises. They that are "proud," as well as "they that do wickedly," will inherit not favour, but shame. For said Jesus again, "Whosoever exalteth himself shall be abased, but he that humbleth himself shall be exalted[d]."

And lastly, in carrying on the important inquiry after divine truth, we must ever remember that it must be *learnt from God;* from his written word, from the words and upon the authority of Jesus, who "spoke as the Father gave him commandment,"—and through the enlightening, and sanctifying, and transforming influence of that Holy Spirit, who can 'give us a right judgement

---

[a] Luke xii. 47, 48.   [b] Matt. vii. 21—23.   [c] Matt. xviii. 3.
[d] Mal. iv. 1. Luke xiv. 11. and xviii. 14.

in all things, cleanse the thoughts of our hearts by his holy inspiration, that so we may think those things that be good, and by his merciful guiding perform the same.' This our Lord has distinctly taught in that important, though difficult, discourse respecting the " living bread which came down from heaven, and giveth life unto the world."
—" But I said unto you, That ye also have seen me, and believe not. 'All *that the Father giveth me* shall come to me, and him *that cometh to me* I will in no wise cast out.' 'This is the Father's will which hath sent me, that of all which he hath given me I should lose nothing, but should raise it up again at the last day. And this is the will of him that sent me, that *every one which seeth the Son*, and *believeth on him*, may have ever-lasting life; and I will raise him up at the last day.' 'Murmur not among yourselves. No man can come unto me, except the Father, which hath sent me, *draw him*. It is written in the prophets, And they shall be all TAUGHT OF GOD[e]. Every man, therefore, that hath *heard*, and hath *learned of the Father*, cometh unto me. Not that any man hath seen the Father, save he which is of God, he hath seen the Father[f]."—I need scarcely to repeat to you, what I have already stated, as collected from a careful examination of these

---

[e] Isai. liv. 13.   Jer. xxxi. 33, 34.   [f] John vi. 37—46.

words, that if we are so to believe on the Son
as to obtain at the last day a resurrection to eternal life, we must learn of the Father by the
witness which he has given of his Son. We must
be taught of him through his word, and be drawn
by his Spirit, by that holy Spirit of his promise,
which " he giveth to them that ask him ;" and
which " shall be in us a well of water springing
to everlasting life;" refreshing and fertilizing our
souls, and causing us to " wait for the hope of
righteousness by faith[a]."

We must, therefore, diligently avail ourselves
of those means of grace, by which the knowledge of God may be obtained and increased,—
our affections drawn heaven-wards,—our holy
resolutions strengthened; until we are brought
into that happy state, of which our Saviour speaks
in those mysterious, yet consolatory words: "If
a man love me, he will keep my words; and my
Father will love him, and we will come unto him,
and make our abode with him." But if, on the
other hand, we neglect those ' means of grace'
which are designed to communicate a ' hope of
glory,'—if we neglect to pray for ' God's continual help,'—if we are wilfully ignorant of his
word,—if we are puffed up with a conceit of

---

[a] See 1 John ii. 20—27; iv. 1—6, and 12—16; v. 9—13.
Luke xi. 13. John iv. 14. Gal. v. 5. James i. 5, 17, &c.

our own sufficiency and wisdom,—if we are averse from the holy ways and requirements of God, and prefer the lusts, and riches, and indulgences of the world, to the promised blessings of eternity, — if we are unwilling to practise patience and self-denial, — if the fear of man deters us from duty, and the applause of man is more esteemed than the approbation of God,—if we are suffering any of these propensities to grow and gather strength within us, then are we in imminent danger of apostacy and infidelity.

Let our's, then, be the endeavour and the prayer, that we may ever share in the character and hopes of those, of whom Jesus said, " My sheep hear my voice, and I know them, and they follow me; and I give unto them eternal life, and they shall never perish; neither shall any man pluck them out of my hand. My Father, which gave them me, is greater than all, and no man is able to pluck them out of my Father's hand. I and my Father are one[b]." For, upon hearing such words as these, we may say with the beloved Apostle, " We know that the Son of God is come, and hath given us an understanding, that we may know him that is true ; and we are in him that is true, even in his Son Jesus Christ. This is the true God, and eternal life[c]."

---

[b] John x. 27—30.   [c] 1 John v. 20.

LECTURE XX.

———◆———

OUR LORD'S NOTICE OF INFIDELITY IN ITS
LAST AND CONFIRMED STAGE.——THE BLASPHEMY
AGAINST THE SON OF MAN, AND THAT AGAINST
THE HOLY GHOST.——THE DEMAND OF ADDI-
TIONAL EVIDENCE, WHEN THAT WHICH IS
OFFERED HAS BEEN REJECTED.——SANCTIONS
WITH WHICH THE GOSPEL IS ACCOMPANIED.——
CONCLUSION.

———◆———

St. Luke XII. 8—10.

*Also I say unto you, Whosoever shall confess me before
men, him shall the Son of man also confess before the
angels of God: but he that denieth me before men,
shall be denied before the angels of God. And whosoever shall speak a word against the Son of man, it
shall be forgiven him; but unto him that blasphemeth
against the Holy Ghost, it shall not be forgiven.*

CONFORMABLY to the directions of the pious founder of this Lecture, I now appear before you for
the twentieth time, that I may on this day complete
the task assigned to me. It has been my endeavour to lay before you, in the very words of Jesus
himself, the claims which he advanced, and the
arguments by which he supported them. Adopting
the same method, I have also considered the

infidelity of the Jews, in connexion with those
moral causes in which it originated ; also calling
your attention, to the statements in which our
Lord himself has specified those dispositions of
mind, which alone can lead to an honest, impartial, and successful inquiry. But I should be
leaving unnoticed, an important department of my
subject, did I not proceed to consider infidelity,
in its *last,* and *confirmed,* and *irremediable* stage ;
and also to bespeak your attention to some of
those passages, in which our Lord has declared
the awful responsibility of mankind, with regard
to their reception, or rejection of his message.

Among the circumstances which finally operated to confirm the infidelity of a great body of
the Jewish people, we may reckon the opposition
and ultimate triumph of the rulers,—and the disappointment of those hopes of a temporal kingdom, which the multitude had entertained, and
which had probably been revived by the solemn
entry of Jesus into Jerusalem. None of the
rulers or Pharisees had openly professed their
belief in him ; and those who were disposed so
to do, suppressed their convictions, because the
majority of their brethren had decided upon the
excommunication of all such, and had issued a
proclamation for the apprehension of Jesus. The
same motives, strengthened by the example of
their superiors, operated very powerfully on the

multitude, so that they concurred "with loud voices," in the demand that he should be crucified.— When Jesus had predicted that "the Son of man should be lifted up," they had objected, in answer to his remark, that they conceived "from the law, that Christ abideth for ever."—Again, both the people and their rulers knew, from the prophets, that "the Christ would come from Bethlehem, the city of David." But they took it for granted, that, because Jesus had principally resided in Galilee, he was a Galilean.—But they had also other doubts respecting his Messiahship. They thought that they knew "whence he was," that he was "the Son of Joseph," and that "his brethren were living among them;" whereas they expected that "when Christ should come, no man would know whence he was." Besides, the mean occupation and obscurity of his supposed parents, and the poverty and external lowliness of his own condition, contributed still further to increase their prejudices against his claims to be the Messiah.—As a person obviously professing sanctity of character, and the office of a divine teacher, he also appeared to act inconsistently, and in opposition to the precepts of their laws, and the custom of their own teachers, by adopting an unreserved and familiar intercourse with persons of all ranks and characters. "He came eating and drinking," observing no particular abstinence, as they supposed that a prophet ought to do; and they were therefore disposed to call him "a gluttonous man and a wine-bibber." He was "the friend of publicans and sinners," and went to eat bread with them. He suffered them "to touch him," as if he had not known their real character, as a prophet ought to have done. He did not, either by his actions, or by his remarks in defence of them, appear to pay sufficient respect to the sabbath; and they therefore contended that he was "not of God, because he kept not the sabbath-day," in the manner conformable to their notions.

These objections proceeded from their own ignorance of the law and prophets, of his real history and original, and of the design of his mission;—or from an impatient wish that he should shew himself openly to the world,—or from the fear of the ruling Jews,—or from inattention to the miracles which he wrought before them, to the arguments by which he defended himself, and to the future evidences which he predicted; by which all their objections to his lowly original, and humble demeanour would be answered. Even *at the time*, they saw that there were many circumstances, for which they could not consistently account, except upon principles which would induce them to believe in him. For "how could he know letters, having never learned?" "Whence had he such wisdom, and such mighty works?"

They were "astonished at his doctrine," they allowed that he was "a good man;" and they justly asked each other, "When Christ cometh, will he do more miracles than this man doeth?" So there was "a division among the people concerning him." And though some of them thought that "the words, which he spoke, were not *the words of one possessed,*" yet many scrupled not to assert that to his face, and to propagate the same insinuation among the people.—When he alluded to the murderous designs harboured against him, they answered, "Thou hast a devil; who goeth about to kill thee?" implying that he was under the influence of a *lying* Spirit[a].—When he appeared to attack their supposed privileges as the children of Abraham, they answered, "Say we not well that thou art a Samaritan, and hast a devil?" Imputing to him the *enmity* of a Samaritan against their law and national privileges; and the *erroneous views* of one possessed[b].—And when he further told them, that "if a man kept his saying, he should never see death," they answered, "Now we know that thou hast a devil[c]."—And some of those who thought that he "deceived the people," said to their associates, "He hath a devil and *is mad;* why hear ye him[d]?"

---

[a] John vii. 20.   [b] John viii. 48.   [c] Ver. 52.
[d] Ibid. x. 20, 21.

Such, and so various, were the instances of that which our Lord terms "the *blasphemy against the Son of man;*" which, as it proceeded in a great measure from ignorance, and from prejudices for which there was at that time a plausible excuse, might therefore be repented of, and obtain *forgiveness.* But the same imputation was, upon some other occasions, propagated with a different connexion and application, which may perhaps be found to *approach* at least to criminality of a deeper dye, if not actually to constitute that guilt to which forgiveness is *denied.* The blasphemy or evil speaking, was not merely directed against the *person*, and *conduct*, and *doctrine* of the Son of man, but even against the *evidences* by which the divinity of his mission was supported. The cavils to which we allude were of two kinds, one, which imputed *the miracles already wrought to diabolical agency ;* the other, which complained of *the absence of a particular species of evidence,* which they chose to require, implying, at the same time, that nothing less than a compliance with their demand, would obtain their acquiescence in his pretensions.

The occasion, and intent, and invalidity of the first of these cavils we have formerly considered[e]." " He hath Beelzebub, and by the prince of the

---

[e] Lecture X.

devils he casteth out devils." · We endeavoured to shew the reality of possessions, and the reality of that class of our Lord's miracles. We considered at the same time his refutation of the cavil of the Pharisees, and the meaning and justice of the other and only tenable inference from those miracles, "If I by the finger of God cast out demons, no doubt the kingdom of God is come upon you." That remark was followed by the solemn declaration respecting *the blasphemy against the Holy Spirit*[a], some brief notice of which is required by the subject of our present Lecture.

I. "Wherefore I say unto you, All manner of sin and blasphemy shall be forgiven unto men, but the blasphemy against the Holy Ghost shall not be forgiven unto men. And whosoever speaketh a word against the Son of man, it shall be forgiven him; but whosoever speaketh against the Holy Ghost, it shall not be forgiven him, neither in this world, neither in the world to come;" or as St. Mark records it, "hath never forgiveness, but is in danger of eternal damnation[b]."

I almost fear to enter on a subject at once so awful and difficult as this, more particularly as

---

[a] Matt. xii. 31, &c. Mark iii. 28, &c.　　[b] Mark iii. 30.

I shall be unable to enter on an enlarged discussion respecting it, because several other topics
must be adverted to in this concluding Lecture.
Three questions, however, obviously suggest
themselves; first, Whether those, *whom our Lord
addressed,* were then *guilty* of this irremissible
sin; secondly, What reference his declaration had
to the period *which followed his personal ministry;* and thirdly, Whether *we* are liable to incur
the guilt by him stated to be unpardonable.

1. With respect to the *first* of these questions
it may be observed, that many suppose that the
Pharisees were at the time guilty of this sin, and
also contend that it was almost peculiar to them.
They ground this supposition on the connexion
of this declaration with *the cavil of the Pharisees* [c],—on the words ascribed by St. Matthew
to our Lord himself, that he "cast out demons
by *the Spirit of God* [d];"—and on the remark
immediately subjoined by St. Mark, after he has
repeated the denunciation itself, "*Because they
said,* He hath an unclean Spirit [e]." But this
observation of St. Mark seems more properly
referable to the *whole answer* of our Lord to the
cavil of the Pharisees, than to the *last clause of it
only.* And with regard to the expression, "If
I cast out demons by the Spirit of God," it may

---

[c] Matt. xii. 24—31.   [d] Matt. xii. 28.   [e] Mark iii. 30.

be observed that from the absence of the article
in the original, it cannot with certainty be
understood of the Holy Spirit as *personally* referred to, but that it would with more probability
be rendered, "If I cast out demons *by divine co-
operation;*" a translation which is rendered still
more probable by the parallel expression of
St. Luke, "If I *by the finger of God* cast out
demons[a]." And certainly when our Lord speaks
of his miracles, he seems to ascribe them to the
Father, rather than to the Holy Spirit. "*My
Father which dwelleth in me,* he doeth the
works[b]."

But the question still recurs, whether it does
not follow, from considering the *occasion* on which
these words were spoken, that our Lord meant
to imply that the Pharisees *had incurred* this
extremity of guilt. I must confess, though I do
it with diffidence, that I conceive that he is not so
to be understood. This was *the very first* cavil
which had been advanced against the *evidences*
of his mission; and it was probably on the second
occasion on which it was brought forward, that
our Lord entered upon these statements respecting
it. But it should be remembered that the words
will equally bear to be understood, as if spoken

---

[a] Εἰ δὲ ἐγὼ ἐν πνεύματι Θεοῦ ἐκβάλλω τὰ δαιμόνια,—Matt.
xii. 28.—Εἰ δὲ ἐν δακτύλῳ Θεοῦ, κ. τ. λ.

[b] John xiv. 10.

only by way of *caution*. Such a caution was
needful; because, in consequence of the same
disposition which induced them then to circulate
such an insinuation, they would be likely both to
remain in the same obduracy with regard to the
evidence afforded during his personal ministry,
and also to reject the future and still greater
demonstration of his resurrection, and of the gifts
of the Holy Ghost. We know that in several
forms, and on many occasions, he spoke of the
evidence of his mission as not yet actually completed. He specified the time which followed
"the lifting up of the Son of man," as being that
in which they "should know that he was the
Messiah;" and he told them that *then*, "if they
believed not, they would die in their sins." Hence,
although their cavil was not directed *personally*
against the Son of man, so much as against the
evidences of his authority, yet it seems probable
that it did not amount to the "blasphemy against
the Holy Ghost."

2. Again, our Lord evidently spoke of the
blasphemy as directed *personally* against the Holy
Ghost[c]. Yet the personal operations, and, as it
were, the distinct dispensation of the Holy Ghost,

---

[c] Ἡ δὲ τοῦ πνεύματος βλασφημία—Matt. xii. 31. ὃς δ' ἂν
εἴπη κατὰ τοῦ πνεύματος τοῦ ἁγίου.—ver. 32. τῷ δὲ εἰς τὸ
αγιον πνεῦμα βλασφημήσαντι.—Luke xii. 10.

by his divers *gifts* and *influences* did not commence until after the ascension of our Lord[a]. We must therefore understand our Lord as speaking *by anticipation* of that future dispensation, and of the increased responsibility which it would bring, and of the heinous guilt which they would incur, if, when more abundant proof was offered, their malignant and calumniating propensities should continue to gather strength, and confirm them in infidelity, instead of yielding to the force of that evidence which demanded their assent. The evidences of the Gospel would then be more numerous, more perceptible, and complete. To those which had already been exhibited, would be added many *others*. Of *all these* " the disciples would bear witness ;" and " not they only, but also the Holy Spirit, which God would give to them that should obey Jesus." For as " the Advocate of Jesus," and as " the Spirit of truth," he would " testify of Jesus," and " reprove the world of sin, because they believed not in *him*."—The principal and original causes of disbelief, both at the time at which our Lord spoke, and afterwards, were virtually the same. But some of those, who remained

---

[a] The Holy Spirit was not yet (given), because Jesus was not yet glorified. John vii. 39. The word *given* is supplementary, and somewhat obscures the sense of the passage. Οὔπω γὰρ ἦν πνεῦμα ἅγιον, ὅτι, κ. τ. λ.—Compare Acts xix. 2.

under the unhappy influence of such delusive views during the time of Christ's humiliation, *might* see reason to abandon them, when after Christ's entrance on his glory, the Holy Spirit was poured out. And probably many of them actually *did* repent, and were converted, and believed, and joined the company of primitive believers; even though, perhaps, a still greater number still " mocked, and contradicted, and *blasphemed* [b]."

These considerations seem to render it most probable, that the declaration of our Lord respecting " the blasphemy against the Holy Ghost" was not immediately, much less exclusively, applicable to those whom he then addressed. It seems rather to have been intended as *a timely caution* to those, who had already begun, not only to resist, but to cavil at the evidence which was furnished; intimating to them the danger in which they would be involved at a future period, if they persevered in their malignity.

The words of our text afford a very strong confirmation of this opinion. The same declaration respecting this unpardonable blasphemy is there found in a connexion wholly different. I have adopted this passage as my text in order to give the greater prominence to it; because

---

[b] Acts ii. 13 ; xiii. 45.

I am not aware that it is generally attended to
in inquiries upon this subject. The context
seems distinctly to shew, that this important
statement of our Lord had a *prospective* reference to the time when the Gospel was published
by the Apostles, that is, after the evidences, as
well as the great transactions of the Gospel, had
been completed, and that salvation, "which first
began to be spoken by the Lord, was confirmed
to mankind by them that heard him, God also
bearing them witness, both with signs and
wonders, and divers miracles, and gifts of the
Holy Ghost." The last of these divine attestations, which was a distinct and most convincing
species of evidence, our Saviour specially notices
in the words *which follow our text.* The discourse
in which they occur was certainly delivered subsequently to the occasion, which at first called forth
this denunciation of our Lord. But it was delivered, though in the presence of the multitude,
only to his disciples; and with reference to their
future ministrations and sufferings, in promulgating the Gospel. For he first exhorted his
disciples to "beware of the leaven of the Pharisees, which is hypocrisy," having directed them
"to proclaim upon the house-tops even all that
he had spoken to them in private," he states that
they ought not to "fear man, but God, who could
both kill and cast into hell;" and he also assures

them of the protection of God's providence. He then adds; "Also I say unto you, whosoever shall confess me before men, him shall the Son of man also confess before the angels of God; but he that denieth me before men shall be denied before the angels of God. And whosoever shall speak a word against the Son of man, it shall be forgiven him; but *unto him that blasphemeth against the Holy Ghost, it shall not be forgiven.* And when they bring you unto the synagogues, and unto magistrates, and powers, take ye no thought how or what thing ye shall answer, or what ye shall say; for *the Holy Ghost shall teach you* in the same hour what ye ought to say."— To the Apostles were given "a mouth and wisdom, which all their adversaries were not able to gainsay nor resist[a]." To "one also was given by the Spirit the word of wisdom; to another the word of knowledge by the same Spirit; to another faith by the same Spirit; to another the gifts of healing by the same Spirit; to another the working of miracles; to another prophecy; to another discerning of spirits; to another divers kinds of tongues; to another the interpretation of tongues[b]." In that day the Gospel came unto mankind, "not in word only, but in power, and in the Holy Ghost, and in much assurance[c]."

---

[a] Luke xxi. 15.　　[b] 1 Cor. xii. 8—10.　　[c] 1 Thess. i. 5.

K K

Its designs were accomplished, its offers universal,
and its evidence complete; and it was accompanied with *demonstration of the Spirit, and
of power[a].*" The offence of the cross had not
ceased; but it was no longer that which perplexed
the understanding, but which was contrary to the
prejudices of mankind, and to the pride and depravity of their hearts. To all that heard it,
it brought either the means of salvation, or the
increase of condemnation.

Yet final negligence, and final impenitence,
though undoubtedly they also *end* in condemnation, are not *the same thing* with "the blasphemy
against the Holy Spirit;" the grand characteristic
of which is, that *it shuts out from the hope of forgiveness*. And if *that* be the consequence of this
guilt, and of this guilt *only*, as our Lord expressly
declares, we shall find several other descriptions
of it in the writings of the Apostles, though it is
there considered in a somewhat different point of
view. And perhaps we may state, that nothing
amounts to this most awful, and only irremissible
sin, but a wilful, malignant, open, and determined
opposition to those truths, of which we have *perceived the evidence*, and of the divine origin of
which we have in our consciences been *convinced*.
Yet it should seem that such was the conduct, in the

---

[a] 1 Cor. ii, 5.

Apostolic times, not only of many of those who never embraced the Gospel, but even of some who had received and understood it, and yet apostatized from it; who, by their wilful, deliberate, and malignant renunciation and opposition, committed that "sin which is unto death," and of which St. John declared that "he did not say that they should pray for it;" for, in fact, it involved the impossibility of *repentance*, as well as of *pardon* [b]. "For," says St. Paul to the Hebrews, "it is *impossible* for those who were once enlightened, and have tasted of the heavenly gift, and were made partakers of *the Holy Ghost*, and have tasted the good word of God, and the powers of the world to come, if they shall fall away, *to renew them again to repentance;* seeing they crucify to themselves the Son of God afresh, and put him to an open shame [c]." And again; "If we sin *wilfully*, after that we have *received the knowledge of the truth*, there remaineth no more sacrifice for sins." And he more fully describes the transgression of this voluntary offender, by stating, that he is one "who hath *trodden under foot the Son of God*, and hath *counted the blood of the covenant*, wherewith he was sanctified, *an unholy thing*, and hath *done despite unto the Spirit of grace* [d]."

---

[b] 1 John v. 16, 17.   [c] Heb. vi. 4—6.

[d] Heb. x. 26—39. Ἑκουσίως γὰρ ἁμαρτανόντων ἡμῶν, κ. τ. λ.

3. It is evident from these descriptions, that no one, who retains the *profession* of Christianity, can be supposed to be included in any of *these* denunciations. Indeed they are not applicable to any but those, who, from *malignity* of heart, *reject* or *apostatize from* the Gospel, and who endanger the comfort and stability of *others* by an open, active, acrimonious cavilling against its evidences and doctrines. And as wilful apostacy and opposition, arising from depravity of *heart,* alone produces the full measure of guilt; none but they who have the gift of *" discerning of spirits,"* can be authorized to ascribe this guilt to any of their fellow-sinners. We cannot now incur it by opposition to *sensible* and *present* miracles. Yet what the evidence of the Gospel now wants in that respect, is perhaps abundantly counterbalanced by many circumstances, which, since the Apostolic times, have augmented, and strengthened, and made still more satisfactory, the arguments in behalf of the Gospel. We therefore cannot deny the *possibility* of the crime, even in our own circumstances; but we must rather dread its approaches in *ourselves,* than venture to impute it to *others.* And as it is a crime which is brought into full operation by actually leading, not only to suppressed infidelity, but to open revilings directed against the Gospel, we shall, at least, do well in suffering the caution,

which our Lord *subjoined to this denunciation,*
to work its full effect upon that " unruly member
the *tongue,*" and upon that corrupt fountain the
heart, " out of the abundance of which the tongue
speaks." " Either make the tree good, and his
fruit good; or else make the tree corrupt, and
his fruit corrupt; for the tree is known by his
fruit. O generation of vipers, how can ye, being
evil, speak good things? for out of the abundance
of the heart the mouth speaketh. A good man
out of the good treasure of his heart bringeth
forth good things, and an evil man out of the
evil treasure bringeth forth evil things. But
I say unto you, that every idle word that men
shall speak, they shall give account thereof in the
day of judgment. For by thy words thou shalt be
justified, and by thy words thou shalt be condemned."

II. I observed that a second cavil was also
advanced against the sufficiency of the proofs, by
which the mission of Jesus was supported, in the
demand of a particular species of evidence which
the Jews chose to require. One of the occasions
upon which it was advanced, was after our Lord
had refuted the former one. " Then certain of
the Scribes and Pharisees, answered, saying,
Master, we would see a sign from thee." This
demand was however made on *several* occasions;
and it is more fully expressed by St. Mark, when

he mentions the repetition of it after the feeding of the four thousand. " The Pharisees came forth, and began to question with him, seeking of him *a sign from heaven*, tempting him. And he sighed deeply in his Spirit, and saith, Why doth this generation seek after a sign ? There shall no sign be given to this generation[a]." No sign, such as they required, would be exhibited to them. For alas! they knew as little *what* they asked, as do those who, in playful but thoughtless depravity, invoke ' damnation on their souls.' They referred to the sign of " the Son of man coming in the clouds of heaven," of which Daniel had spoken. But, as our Saviour observed with reference to the same prophecy, " *When the Son of man shall come in his glory*, and all the holy angels with him, then shall he sit upon the throne of his glory, and before him shall be gathered *all nations*, and he shall separate them one from another, as a shepherd divideth his sheep from the goats ; and he shall set the sheep on his right hand, but the goats on his left.—And these shall go away into *everlasting punishment*, but the righteous into *life eternal*[b]." There was a time, however, when Jesus, avowing his Messiahship to the high priest, said with awful significancy,

---

[a] Mark viii. 11, 12.

[b] Matt. xxv. 31—46. Compare this with Dan. vii. 9—14.

" Hereafter shall ye see the Son of man sitting
on the right hand of power, and coming in the
clouds of heaven[c]." Yet, even after that declaration, they continued the same " blasphemy
against the Son of man," the same neglect,
and even contempt of the various evidences which
he had exhibited of his authority, and again specified that particular evidence, which alone would
induce them to abandon their unbelief. " He
saved others, himself he cannot save. Let Christ,
the king of Israel, descend now from the cross,
that we may see and believe[d]." Again, they knew
not what they asked. Jesus came to destroy every
enemy of man's salvation, by " triumphing over
them on his cross." To have complied with their
demand, would have been to have left undone the
work which he was then about to finish. Jesus
made not any answer to them from the cross ;
for he knew that the glory, which would follow
his sufferings, would be made known by his resurrection from the dead, and that the gifts, which he
would receive for men, would soon be poured down
from on high. But on the former occasions, though
unwittingly they had made a demand with which
it was impossible to comply, he answered them

---

[c] Matt. xxvi. 64.

[d] Mark xv. 29—32. It is worthy of notice that this allows
the *miracles* of Jesus, and that he had advanced a claim to be the
Messiah.

according to their intention. For they meant
to require another evidence, in addition to all that
had previously been afforded. And although no
such sign, as that to which they had alluded,
would be given to that generation, another would
be given, which he described under the phrase
" the sign of the Prophet Jonas." " For," added
our Lord in explanation, " as Jonas was three
days and three nights in the whale's belly, so shall
the Son of man be three days and three nights in
the heart of the earth[a]."

　　In what manner that prediction was fulfilled,
it is unnecessary to repeat. But let it be observed
that, in *two* different respects, the spirit of infidelity ignorantly and erroneously objected to the
sufficiency of the proofs that Jesus was what he
claimed to be.—They hastily complained of the
supposed deficiency, when a little patience would
have furnished them with decisive evidence. It was
not indeed of the precise kind which they demanded; but the question which they ought to have considered was, whether it was not sufficient.—And
again, they insisted on the want of such exhibitions
of the power of Jesus as could not have been
given consistently either with the intentions of
God, or the good of mankind. Yet infidelity
still continues to make similar objections and

---

[a] Matt. xii. 39, &c.

demands. We must, however, take the evidence as
we find it. It is such as God has seen fit to furnish,
and it is sufficient to prove that " he has spoken
by his Son." It is obvious even to our own limited
discernment, that many of the demands of the
infidel are unreasonable; they would probably
appear still more so, if we were more fully acquainted with the scheme of the divine counsels.
There are evidences of the truth of the Gospel
still in reserve. And since we can even now give
a sufficient reason of the hope that is in us, why
should we be dissatisfied that the Gospel is yet
incompletely promulgated, and that *all* the prophecies are not completed? These are proofs
reserved for the conviction of those of *the latter
days;* and one day we shall *all* see " the sign
of the Son of man coming in the clouds of
heaven."

Our Lord took occasion from the allusion to
Jonah the Prophet, to shew, by a beautiful and
impressive contrast, the criminality of those who
rejected his words. " The men of Nineveh shall
rise in judgment with this generation, and shall
condemn it; because they repented at the
preaching of Jonah; and behold a greater than
Jonah is here. The queen of the south shall rise
up in the judgment with this generation, and
shall condemn it; for she came from the uttermost
part of the earth to hear the wisdom of Solomon;

and behold a greater than Solomon is here." Has
he not been proved to be all that he claimed to
be, by demonstration at once varied and convincing? And "he that believeth on Jesus, believeth on him that sent him." And that heavenly
Messenger himself has declared, " He that rejecteth me, and receiveth not my words, hath one
that judgeth him; the word that I have spoken,
the same shall judge him in the last day[a]." Nay,
he has even told us, and it ought to be seriously
considered by all that have heard of his name,
that " he that believeth not in him is condemned
already, because he hath not believed in the name
of the only-begotten Son of God," who has been
"lifted up, that whosoever believeth in him should
not perish, but have everlasting life[b]." " If he
had not come and spoken to us, and done the
works which no other man did, we had not had
sin; but now have we no cloke for our sin[c]."
And though we have not seen him in the flesh,
and have not heard him ourselves, we must
not conceive that hereby we can be excused.
For he declared to those, who were to record his
instructions, and to disperse them through the
world; " He that despiseth you, despiseth me;
and he that despiseth me, despiseth him that sent

---

[a] John xii. 44, &c.   [b] John iii. 16—18.
[c] John xv. 22—24.

me[d]." For Jesus was "that stone, which was laid in Zion for a foundation;" and "*whosoever*," said he again, "shall fall upon that stone shall be broken, but on *whomsoever* it shall fall, it will grind him to powder[e]."

We must then believe, and obey. We must " endure unto the end;" for it is even " better, as the Apostle tells us, never to have known the way of righteousness, than, having known it, to turn away from the holy commandment delivered unto us." And not an Apostle only, but Jesus himself has given us the same admonition, in the concluding portion of that discourse, which was occasioned by the two cavils which we have noticed in this Lecture. He borrows from the case of the demoniacs, by his undoubted miracles upon whom they had not been convinced, a striking illustration of the fatal *progress* of infidelity. " When the unclean spirit is gone out of a man, he walketh through dry places, seeking rest, and findeth none. Then he saith, I will return into my house, from whence I came out; and when he is come, he findeth it empty, swept, and garnished. Then goeth he, and taketh with himself seven other spirits more wicked than himself, and they enter in and dwell there; and the last

---

d Luke x. 16.   e Isai. xxviii. 16.   Matt. xxi. 42—44.

state of that man is worse than the first. Even so shall it be also unto this wicked generation [a]."

It concerns us, who, though Gentiles, have become "fellow-heirs, and of the same body, with the chosen people of God, and partakers of his promise in Christ by the Gospel," to take heed lest we also "frustrate the grace of God,"—lest we "draw back unto perdition,—lest we do not believe to the saving of the soul." For shall anything, but our unbelief, "separate us from the love of God, which is in Christ Jesus our Lord?" Remember, then, that the Gospel gives us the offer of pardon, and the promise of sanctification. It is "the new covenant established upon better promises. It comes to us with sanctions of promise and of threatening. It comes recommended and enforced by numerous evidences, which appeal both to the understanding and to the heart, and which have brought conviction to the minds both of *the learned,* and of *the unlearned.*

Do you delight to peruse the histories of past ages? Are you interested and edified by tracing events up to their causes, and by pursuing

---

[a] 2 Pet. ii. 20—22. Matt. xii. 43—45.—These two passages illustrate each other. And we might, from this parabolic description given by our Lord of the *progress* of the infidelity of the Jews, deduce an additional argument in support of the opinion defended in the former part of this Lecture, that our Lord spoke of the unpardonable blasphemy by way of *anticipation.*

the order in which they produced their consequences? — Consider then the existence, the
operation, and the effects of Christianity. As
inquisitive men, as Scholars, as Philosophers, as
Christians, examine this remarkable era in the
history of the human intellect,—this event which
was prepared by all preceding ones,—which has
since so materially influenced the opinions and
the civilization of the world,—which predicts the
future universality of its own propagation. Come
to some decision respecting these things, which are
important with regard to the faith and guidance of
your fellow-men, and still more so as they concern
yourselves.—While you investigate the laws and
phenomena of the material world, forget not that
there is a spiritual world, hereafter to be revealed,
and that we are the destined heirs of an immortality, which will be happy, or miserable, according
to our characters here. And remember, that for
the knowledge which is requisite in this matter,
you can go to none but to Christ Jesus; for
" he alone hath the words of eternal life."

Remember, that while many are doubting, and
investigating, and deriving from human learning almost as much hindrance as assistance,
many a poor and unlettered peasant in our own
land, many an uncivilized heathen in foreign lands,
is laying hold on eternal life; and finds in the
purifying and consolatory tendency of the Gospel

the most satisfactory evidence both of its truth and utility. For he finds it a provision for all the wants which he previously felt. And if it discovers to him more extensive views of his own guilt and danger, and of the perfections and requirements of God, it does but discover that, of which he allows the justice and the propriety. And in proportion as he is thereby more humbled before his God, he also derives more abundant consolation from his word, and exercises a more confirmed confidence in his promises. And thus, being made perfect in love, and growing in grace and holiness, he waits for the hope of righteousness by faith.

The same meetness for heaven is attainable by all, and is *necessary for all*. But we must "give earnest heed to the things which we hear," if we are to "live and grow thereby." The same arguments which have convinced so many of the truth and of the importance of our religion, are still *sufficient* to satisfy us. And we must be content to receive the Gospel as it is offered to us, neither dissatisfied because of the absence of any evidence which we may suppose ought to have been furnished, nor objecting to the doctrines which are revealed by it. Our Lord referred the Jews to the witness of their own Scriptures; but he declared that "if they heard not Moses and the prophets, neither would they be persuaded though one rose from the dead [a]." He declared that, while some cavilled at the character in which the Baptist appeared, and others at his own, "wisdom would be justified of all her children [b]." And assuredly, though "the Jews required *a sign,* and the Greeks sought after *wisdom,*" we can shew that each of those demands was unreasonable, if they were made in any view which disposed them to a rejection of the Gospel. For it is most abundantly demonstrable, that "Christ crucified is both the *power* of God, and the *wisdom* of God [c]."

But if we allow the evidence, and value, and necessity of the Gospel, let us not remain in ignorance of what is thereby revealed. We not unfrequently meet with some, even in a Christian country, who have had such opportunities, and have arrived at such an age, that, "for the time, they ought to be *teachers;* yet who have need to *be taught* again, which be the first principles of the oracles of God [d]." That ignorance is sometimes openly *avowed;* and those who make the avowal sometimes even appear to be *proud* of it. Yet a young Athenian would have been ashamed to be thought so ignorant with respect to the philosophical systems of his age and city. Nay,

---

[a] Luke xvi. 31.   [b] Matt. xi. 19.   [c] 1 Cor. 1. 24.
[d] Heb. v. 12.

would not many among ourselves be ashamed to
be thought ignorant of the laws, and literature,
and science of our own country, who are yet
negligent of the doctrine, and precepts of Jesus?
Yet there is a more important knowledge than
any that relates to terrestrial objects; there is a
teacher more divine, and of more authority than
any that we can "call Master upon earth[a]."
He calls upon us to hear, and to believe in him;
to repent, and follow him. He declares to us the
authority with which he is invested, and the responsibility which rests upon ourselves.—"*All
power is given to me* in heaven and in earth.
Go ye, therefore, and *preach the Gospel to every
creature.—He that believeth and is baptized* shall
be *saved;* and *he that believeth not* shall be *damned.*"

. We have to conjure you, therefore, by the
dignity of him, whom the Father sanctified, and
sent into the world,—by the miracles which he
wrought,—by the prophecies which he fulfilled,—
by the greatness of the salvation which he purchased,—by the promises, and by the terrors of the
Lord,—by the shortness of life, and the approaches
of death,—by the realities of eternity, and the
inestimable value of your immortal souls—that
you "turn not away from him that speaketh from
heaven."—If we have at all increased your ad-

---

[a] Matt. xxiii. 10.

miration of the beauty and comprehensiveness of the word of God, from whence we have drawn, and ever shall draw, our arguments and representations,—if we have disposed you to peruse it more frequently and attentively,—if we have been able to strengthen your conviction of its truth, to impress you with a sense of its importance, and to persuade you to a compliance with its dictates —our labours will not have been in vain. And if those, who are able, will defend the Gospel against its adversaries, and turn to righteousness those that profess it,—and if all ' that profess and call themselves Christians,' will adorn the doctrine of God their Saviour by a sober, righteous, and godly life, " endeavouring to keep the unity of the Spirit in the bond of peace,"—then will our heavenly Father be glorified. Our Saviour will then " see of the travail of his soul, and be satisfied ;"—and we shall one day be " with him, and behold his glory."

Lightning Source UK Ltd.
Milton Keynes UK
UKHW020319280219
338009UK00006B/714/P